(Reserve)

W9-BUT-728

!T
50
.G286
1997

HARMONIC PRACTICE
IN TONAL MUSIC

HARMONIC PRACTICE
IN TONAL MUSIC

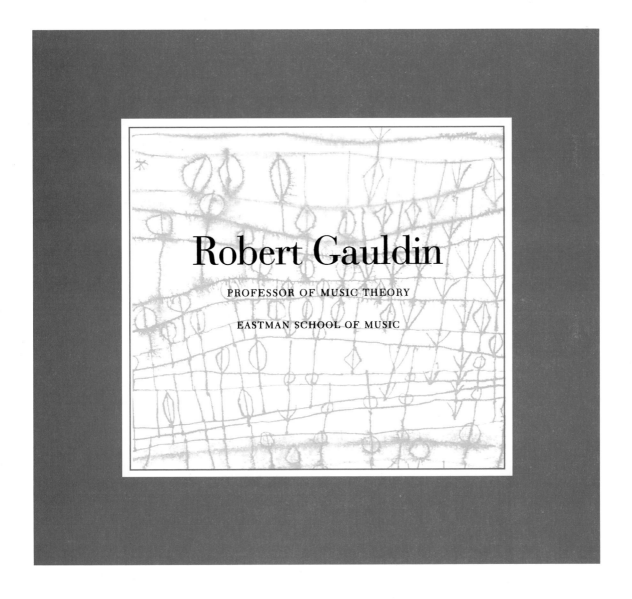

Robert Gauldin

PROFESSOR OF MUSIC THEORY

EASTMAN SCHOOL OF MUSIC

 W · W · NORTON & COMPANY · NEW YORK · LONDON

The text of this book is composed in New Caledonia, with the display set in Bauer Bodoni.
Composition by A-R Editions.
Manufacturing by Courier.
Book design by Jack Meserole.
Cover Illustration: Credit Paul Klee, "Ripe Harvest" © 1996 Artists Rights Society (ARS), New York/VG Bild-Kunst, Bonn.
Cover design by Kevin O'Neill.

Library of Congress Cataloging-in-Publication Data

Gauldin, Robert, 1931–
    Harmonic practice in tonal music / by Robert Gauldin.
      p.   cm.
    Includes bibliographical references (p.   ) and index.
    ISBN 0-393-97074-4
    1. Harmony.   I. Title
MT50.G286   1997
781.2'5—dc20   96-28216

W. .W. Norton & Company, Inc., 500 Fifth Avenue, New York, N.Y. 10110
http://www.wwnorton.com

W. W. Norton & Company Ltd., 10 Coptic Street, London WC1A 1PU

1 2 3 4 5 6 7 8 9 0

FOR

Bear, Stick, Gina, and Dark Angel

CONTENTS

PART ONE   THE BASIC ELEMENTS OF MUSIC

PART TWO   DIATONIC HARMONY

CHAPTER 15 Pre-dominant Chords: IV AND II 192

CHAPTER 16   The $^6_4$ and Other Linear Chords   211

CHAPTER 17   The II^7 and IV^7 Chords   225

CHAPTER 18   The VI, III, and Other Diatonic Chords   239

PART THREE   CHROMATIC HARMONY

EXCURSION 2   More Complex Forms   439

CHAPTER 30   Implication and Realization   460

CHAPTER 31   Ninth, Eleventh, Thirteenth, and Added-Note Chords   477

CHAPTER 32   Embellishing Chromatic Chords   488

P R E F A C E

(T O   T H E   T E A C H E R)

Harmonic Practice in Tonal Music introduces the student to the harmonic and voice-leading principles of tonal music composed during the common-practice period. This body of music has traditionally been approached through a vertically oriented system of harmonic analysis. While this system provides a thorough classification of the various chords and their harmonic tendencies in progressions, it tends to neglect the melodic aspects of the music and the way these linear forces shape the harmony. In this text I have attempted to correct this imbalance by correlating harmony with the inter-action of melodic lines. Therefore, harmonic function itself will be seen as largely deriving from this contrapuntal framework; voice-leading analysis may thus form the basis for insightful performances of the music itself.

The text is divided into four parts. Part One surveys the basic elements of music; Part Two introduces the subject of functional diatonic harmony, modulations, and sequences; Part Three explores the most common proce-dures of chromatic harmony; and Part Four examines more advanced chro-matic techniques.

The chapters are arranged to provide a gradual progression from simple to more sophisticated issues. In Part One, for instance, Chapter 3 (Tonic, Scale, and Melody) places the topics introduced in Chapter 1 (Pitch and Intervals) and Chapter 2 (Rhythm and Meter) within the larger context of tonality and melody. Likewise, Chapter 7 examines the chordal figuration and melodic dissonance arising from interaction between melody (Chapter 3) and chords (Chapters 4–6).

A working knowledge of the fundamental topics found in Part One is pre-requisite to the study of tonal harmony. In addition to recognizing keys (Chapter 3), meter (Chapter 2), part-writing errors (Chapter 6), and nonharmonic tones (Chapter 7), students must develop a facility in spelling and playing intervals (Chapter 1) and chords (Chapter 4), scales (Chapter 3), and simple figured bass (Chapters 4 and 5).

The review of fundamental materials in Part One provides the basis for the largely harmonic topics in Part Two. The chapters of Part Two systematically present the various diatonic chords and their harmonic functions in different musical contexts, from the tonic and the dominant-family chords (Chapters 9, 11, and 13) to the pre-dominant chords (Chapters 15 and 17) and then the remaining diatonic harmonies (Chapters 18 and 21). The other chapters in Part Two mostly treat broader topics: rhythmic dissonance, phrase grouping, suspensions, the $^6_4$ chord, tonicization, and harmonic sequences. As in Part One, the concepts introduced in one chapter provide the necessary foundation for those introduced later. The introduction of suspensions in Chapter 14, for instance, lays the foundation for the cadential $^6_4$ and treatment of seventh-chord dissonance in Chapters 16 and 17.

Part Three is patterned after Part Two. Some of its chapters focus on specific altered harmonies, such as secondary dominants, mixture chords, the Neapolitan and augmented-sixth sonorities, and embellishing chromatic chords; others examine the use of chromaticism in larger contexts, such as chromaticized diatonic sequences and modulations to foreign keys. Separate chapters are devoted to ninth chords, dominant prolongations, and melodic and harmonic implication and realization.

Finally, Part Four extends the study of chromaticism into more advanced techniques, such as purely chromatic sequences, chromatic contrary motion, more unusual means of effecting foreign modulations, and musical organization based on symmetrical divisions of the octave.

The chapters in Parts Two and Three stress the interaction between melodic and harmonic forces in tonal music. Those chapters that focus on the function of specific chords proceed from generalization to practical application. Conventional terminology is employed for the chords and devices, although a few recently coined theoretical terms that have gained wide acceptance have been incorporated. Several innovative approaches to traditional classification or symbolization are utilized. For instance, emphasis is placed on the accentuation of the various types of nonharmonic tones, which is more in keeping with the way we actually tend to perceive them. In modulatory passages, the new tonality is denoted by its relation to the prevailing tonic (designated by roman numeral) rather than by key designation. The more common harmonic progressions first appear as basic harmonic models in C major or C minor, allowing us to see and hear the essential voice leading of the passage. Excerpts from music literature then demonstrate how these models have been fleshed out and elaborated in various meters, rhythms, and textures.

This "model-to-music" format is often reversed by the reduction of music excerpts to their essential harmonic support and voice leading. Thus, quotations from music literature are frequently followed by one or more layers of reductive analysis. The student is carefully guided through each step of this reduction process.[1] Such analyses, when carried out on complete pieces, can give us insight into the role of tonal function within shifting musical contexts and thereby provide the foundation for a more coherent performance strategy.

The music examples in the text are drawn from a wide range of literature extending from the common-practice period into the twentieth century. Representing various vocal and instrumental media, these examples include not only the traditional "classical" genres (such as sonatas, symphonies, concertos, and art songs), but also excerpts from hymns, chorale harmonizations, folk songs, waltzes, marches, rags, and popular songs. The music examples are seldom longer than eight or sixteen measures; however, three in-depth analyses of complete compositions are included, at the ends of Parts Two, Three, and Four. The great majority of examples require only moderate keyboard ability; some of them have been simplified or shown only in voice-leading reduction. With the exception of lieder and solo sonatas, ensemble works are shown in condensed, two-stave scores rather than open scores. The actual music excerpts are recorded on the accompanying CD set. The harmonic models and analytical reductions are not recorded; the student should play through all of them.

The elements of the text are physically laid out so as to facilitate the student's assimilation of the material. Supplementary or more challenging topics are set off with a gray background. Brief discussions of additional or similar pieces that you can assign for study are enclosed in doubled-columned gray boxes. Guidelines for using the analytical symbols within voice-leading reductions are periodically inserted throughout Part Two.

---

1. Although this text provides the student with an introduction to linear reduction, it does not present a systematic exposition of Schenkerian analytical techniques. The most extensive exposition of Heinrich Schenker's theories of tonal music may be found in his *Free Composition*, translated and edited by Ernst Oster (New York: MacMillan, 1979). Other introductions to his ideas include Oswald Jonas, *Introduction to the Theory of Heinrich Schenker*, translated by John Rothgeb (New York: Longman, 1982), and Allen Forte and Steven E. Gilbert, *Introduction to Schenkerian Analysis* (New York: W. W. Norton, 1982).

Most chapters conclude with separate sections that focus on partwriting procedures and melody harmonization. A list of terms and concepts for review is set off at the end of each chapter.

The two "Excursion" chapters deal with formal design in homophonic and contrapuntal music. Although they can be discussed at any time in the course of study, they are placed strategically near chapters that raise issues of formal organization.

The appendixes contain a wealth of supplementary information. Since some teachers prefer to introduce the basic principles of two-voice linear or contrapuntal writing in the first year of music theory, Appendix 3 provides a short introduction to species counterpoint. In this appendix, some minor changes to the Fuxian species approach bring the presentation in line with common tonal practice. The remaining appendixes address such diverse topics as acoustics, modes and other scales, commercial chord symbols, and conducting patterns. A glossary of terms often found in music scores and two indexes complete the volume.

The accompanying Workbook provides drills, analyses, and keyboard exercises for student assignments. Instructors should feel free to supplement or ignore this material as conditions warrant.

The author is indebted to the theory faculty and teaching assistants of the Eastman School of Music for their numerous suggestions. Special thanks go to Leo Kraft, David Beach, Marie Rolf, Leonard Meyer, John Rothgeb, and Richard Hermann for their helpful comments on portions of the text and analyses. I would like to give particular commendation to Suzanne La Plante, my editor at Norton, and also to Mark Stevens, copy editor of the text and workbook, and Maureen Buja, project editor, for their tireless efforts in molding this material into an effective undergraduate text. Finally, I would be remiss if I failed to acknowledge the continued encouragement and patience of my wife during the long task of writing and revising this book.

HARMONIC PRACTICE
IN TONAL MUSIC

INTRODUCTION (TO THE STUDENT)

As children we memorized songs the same way we learned to speak, by repeating the music or words over and over until we could sing or say them perfectly. We call this method *rote learning.* When we learn to play music that is written down, we first study certain basic information about the music notation, such as intervals, scales, keys, and chords, just as we learned to read sentences by first practicing the spelling of words. These are fundamental subjects that all practicing musicians must master. As we hone our skills in the basics of music we start to focus on what might be called the "chemistry" of music— that is, how it is constructed and how it operates. This inquiry forms the basis of the discipline called *music theory.* In the same way that our study of grammar and syntax enables us to express ourselves better in speech and writing, our study of music theory allows us to express ourselves better when performing and interpreting music. Learning about how the essential components of music are organized and influence each other provides us with an understanding of what makes music so pleasing and satisfying to our ear. It also suggests ways of examining how we may best perform and hear these pieces.

We may summarize the relation between language and music as follows:

Language
  1. imitating speech
  2. learning to spell words
  3. studying grammar

Music
1. learning by rote
2. learning notation and music fundamentals
3. studying music's organization (music theory)

This text focuses on music written primarily during the common-practice, or tonal, period. Extending roughly from the early eighteenth century to the beginning of the twentieth century, this period encompasses the music of late-Baroque composers (such as Bach and Handel), the masters of the Classical era (Haydn, Mozart, and Beethoven), and the figures of the Romantic period (including Schubert, Schumann, Wagner, Brahms, and Tchaikovsky). We also provide examples of some popular genres of the twentieth century, which continue to employ the tonal procedures introduced and developed during the common-practice period.

We will begin our study of music theory with a review of the rudimentary elements of music, found in Part One (Chapters 1 to 7). Some of the information in these chapters may already be familiar to you; other material may be new. All of the subject matter in this rudiments survey is prerequisite to the study of harmony. Therefore, it is essential that you thoroughly understand the underlying concepts and master the preliminary skills outlined in Part One before going on to the topics discussed in Part Two (Diatonic Harmony), Part Three (Chromatic Harmony), and Part Four (Advanced Chromatic Techniques).

Within the text you will notice several types of boxed-in material that accompany the regular discussion. Some, such as the gray boxes interspersed throughout Parts Two, Three, and Four, contain more challenging material, which offer a fuller range of inquiry and can be integrated into your course of study. The gray boxes titled "For Further Study" offer suggestions of additional pieces for you and your class to explore; these pieces show traits similar to those within the pieces covered in the regular discussion. In Part Two, to help you read the reductive analyses that follow many of the music examples and create your own analyses, we have inserted several boxed explanations, titled "Guidelines for Using the Analytical Symbols." Special sections titled "Partwriting Procedures" and "Melody Harmonization" offer guidance in writing your own harmonizations of melodies. Finally, each chapter concludes with a list of review terms and concepts.

On a separate compact disc set we have recorded the actual excerpts from music literature (some of the renditions employ ensembles of reduced size). This CD set not only allows you easier access to the music examples but also should help you widen your knowledge of Western music literature. You should try to play through these excerpts on the piano as well wherever possible. You should *always* play through the harmonic models (given in C major or C minor) and analytical reductions, which are not included on the CD set.

The accompanying Workbook is designed to follow the text closely and offers many types of written assignments and keyboard exercises for each chapter of the text. With these exercises you can develop your skills in basic musicianship.

The purpose of all these aids is to help you better assimilate the material in the text in the process of establishing a solid foundation in music theory. Mastering music theory represents a major step toward becoming a complete musician. It provides listeners with the aural vocabulary necessary for discerning the tonal framework of the works they hear. It supplies composers, arrangers, and improvisers with an essential musical language. And it enables singers and instrumentalists to achieve deeper insights into the tonal drama and coherence of the works they perform.

THE BASIC
ELEMENTS
OF MUSIC

Pitch and Intervals

W E WILL BEGIN our survey of the basic elements of music by considering **pitch,** or the relative highness or lowness of musical tones.

PITCH NOTATION AND THE DIATONIC PITCH COLLECTION

Our first concern is the notation of pitch. How do we write down what we perform or hear? The earliest known examples of notation, from Babylonia, go back as far as 1500 B.C. The notation system of the ancient Greeks from about the second century B.C. employed the first seven letters of the alphabet to represent the musical tones. To lengthen the range, the letter names were extended either up or down, repeating themselves after every seven tones, as in our present notational system. We call these seven different tones the **diatonic pitch collection.** Although we will amplify the meaning of the term *diatonic* in Chapter 3, for the time being we may define the diatonic notes simply as a group of pitches in the same pattern as the white keys on the piano keyboard (see Figure 1).

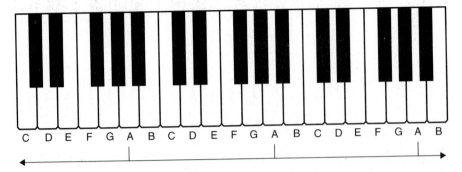

Figure 1

If you start from any white key and play up or down, each new note has a clearly distinct sound until you reach the next key with the same letter name, which sounds very similar to your first note in spite of the difference in pitch. Since this recurrence of pitch sonority occurs on the eighth diatonic note, it is called an **octave** (from the Greek *okta*, "eight"). The similarity in sound is caused by an interesting acoustical phenomenon. The **frequency**—that is, the number of complete to-and-fro motions, or *vibrations*, of an elastic body that occur each second—of the higher octave is exactly double that of the original pitch, while that of the lower octave is exactly half the original. Musical frequencies are generally referred to in terms of *hertz*, after the nineteeth-century German physicist Heinrich Hertz. Our standard tuning pitch, the A above middle C, equals 440 hertz; the frequencies of its higher and lower octaves are 880 and 220 hertz, respectively. The acoustical relationships between pitches are discussed more fully in Appendix 1.

If music had remained only simple melody, such as the ancient Greeks played, letter names would have proved sufficient for pitch notation. However, as multivoiced music began to be written in the Middle Ages, new methods of indicating pitch were developed. One early method showed the relative highness or lowness of pitch in terms of the relative height of symbols placed on the unlined page. This system evolved into staff notation, in which pitches initially were written as notes above and below a single line, then on the lines and spaces of a four-line staff, and later on a five-line staff.

Various clef signs soon appeared at the beginning of the staves to indicate the staff location of pitches with different letter names. The treble and bass clefs are only the most common of those that developed from these early clefs. Certain modern instruments employ other clefs; for instance, the viola uses the alto clef, and the cello sometimes employs the tenor clef; these clefs locate middle C on the third and fourth lines of the staff, respectively. In Example 1, the same notes are written in four different clefs. The notes fit the staff better in some clefs than others; the treble clef, for example, must use several ledger lines to accommodate the pitches.

Example 1

PITCH REGISTER AND PITCH-CLASS

When we talk or write about music, we often need to refer to a note in a specific octave range or register. For instance, the wide range of "The Star-Spangled Banner" requires that we start with the F on the first space of the treble clef rather than the F on the top line. In this text, we will use (when necessary) a system that enables us to specify the exact register of any pitch. We begin with the lowest C on the piano and call it C^1. The white keys immediately above it can be labeled D^1, E^1, F^1, G^1, A^1, and B^1. The next higher C we will call C^2, and the C above that C^3. We continue this same procedure through the succeeding octaves until we have covered the entire keyboard range.

Example 2

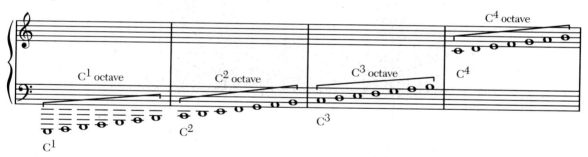

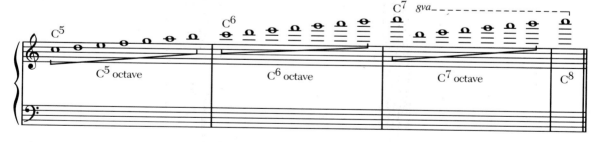

Our familiar middle C is therefore C^4, and our "tuning A" is A^4.[1] Study the various octaves illustrated in Example 2, then locate E^4, E^2, E^5, and E^3 on the piano.

1. This method of octave designation is preferred by acousticians and music theorists today. In the older Helmholtz system, the octaves are CC, C, c, c', c'', c''', where c' is middle C.

Usually, however, we will not need to refer to a note in a particular register. For instance, when we speak of the key of F major, we imply that any F may function as the keynote. We call a note that is identified by its letter name but not by its position in a particular octave or register a **pitch-class.** The pitch-class E, for instance, includes any E, regardless of its registral placement; thus, the pitches E^4, E^2, E^5, and E^3 all represent the same pitch-class.

HALF STEPS AND ACCIDENTALS

If we start with C^4 (middle C) on the keyboard and count all white and black keys up to C^5, we will see that the octave is divided into twelve different notes. The distance between any two adjacent keys is called a **half step** or **semitone,** and is the smallest distance between tones commonly found in Western music. Each of the twelve half steps within the octave is equal in size in our present tuning system, called **equal temperament.**[2]

Two of these half steps occur as natural pitch-classes or white keys on the piano (E–F and B–C). In order to notate the remaining semitones, we must use **accidentals:** a **sharp** (♯), which raises a note by a half step; a **flat** (♭), which lowers a note by a half step; or a **natural** (♮), which cancels out the previous sharp or flat. Thus C–C♯, B♭–A, G–G♯, D–E♭, and F♯–G are all half steps. Accidentals make it possible to "spell" a pitch-class more than one way, depending on its function in a musical context. For instance, D♯ is the same pitch as E♭ on the piano. We say that D♯ and E♭ are **enharmonic spellings** of the same pitch. Example 3 illustrates the twelve different pitch-classes, using naturals, sharps, and flats.

Example 3

The twelve pitch classes constitute the **chromatic pitch collection**—that is, all the pitches normally notated in Western music.

The context of a musical passage may occasionally require the use of the **double sharp** (𝄪) or the **double flat** (♭♭), which respectively raise or lower a pitch by one whole step. The reasons for choosing one musical spelling over another will soon become evident.

2. Each semitone may be mathematically expressed as $12\sqrt{2}$ times the frequency of the tone below.

INTERVALS

Since music is primarily concerned with the relationships between pitches, we need an accurate way of measuring these relationships. Two pitches together represent what we call a **dyad.** The distance between the two pitches of a dyad is called an **interval.** Example 4 illustrates two basic types of intervals.

Example 4

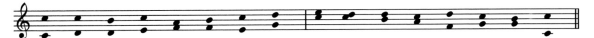

The individual lines form a series of horizontal or **melodic intervals** from one note to the next. When you play both parts together, a series of vertical or **harmonic intervals** results.

We can determine the approximate, or generic, distance between the two pitches of a dyad by simply counting the letter names of the pitches between them, always including those of the dyad itself. For instance, the interval from D up to G is a *4th* (D–E–F–G). Identify all the melodic and harmonic intervals in Example 4, using this method. Do you notice any general difference between the sizes of the melodic intervals, on the one hand, and the harmonic intervals, on the other?

To express the interval sizes more precisely, we must add a modifier before the generic interval number. The octave, 5th, and 4th, as well as the **unison** or **prime** (where two different voice parts intone the same pitch), are called **perfect intervals**, so named for their purity of sound and occurrence as the first three intervallic relations in the harmonic or overtone series.[3]

If you play the 3rds C^4–E^4 and E^4–G^4 and count the number of half steps in each, you will discover that they are of different size: four vs. three semitones. Some other intervals, such as 2nds, 6ths, and 7ths, also occur in two sizes that differ by one half step. In each case we designate the larger interval **major** and the smaller interval **minor;** thus, a minor 2nd contains one half step while a major 2nd contains two half steps. Just as we generically refer to the minor 2nd as a half step or semitone, we call a major 2nd a **whole step** or **whole tone.** Note that a minor 2nd, strictly speaking, is the interval between adjacent pitches with *two* different letter names: for instance, C–D♭, G–F♯, A–B♭, and not C–C♯, G–G♭, A–A♯. The same principle holds for the other intervals; thus F–D♭ is a minor 6th, since it spans notes with six different letter names, but F–C♯ is not.

3. For a discussion of the overtone series, see Appendix 1.

The perfect, major, and minor intervals are called **diatonic intervals,** as they can all be expressed in terms of the natural pitch-classes—that is, pitches using no sharps and flats and corresponding to the white keys of the piano. (Since the diatonic dyad B to F—or F to B—is somewhat different, we will discuss it separately.)

In music theory we refer to most intervals as if they were an octave or less in size, as we will do in this text. However, intervals may exceed the range of the octave; thus, a 3rd plus an octave equals a 10th, a 5th plus an octave equals a 12th, and so forth. A dyad that exceeds the span of an octave is called a **compound interval.** Example 5 illustrates all the types of diatonic intervals (perfect, major, minor) that are up to an octave in size. These intervals are abbreviated in the following way: PU for perfect unison, m2 for minor 2nd, M2 for major 2nd, and so forth.

Example 5

A. MAJOR AND PERFECT INTERVALS

PU   M2   M3   P4   P5   M6   M7   P8

B. MINOR AND PERFECT INTERVALS

PU   m2   m3   P4   P5   m6   m7   P8

Diatonic intervals may be expanded or contracted by one semitone through the use of accidentals. A perfect 5th can be **augmented** by raising the top note (or lowering the bottom note) a half step, or **diminished** by lowering the top note (or raising the bottom note) a half step. The more common augmented and diminished intervals require the use of accidentals. The abbreviations for the augmented 2nd and augmented 4th in Example 6 are A2 and A4, respectively; those for the diminished 5th and diminished 7th, for example, are d5 and d7. In this chapter we use capital letters for major and augmented intervals, and lowercase letters for minor and diminished intervals.

Example 6

A. AUGMENTED INTERVALS

M2   A2   P4   A4   P5   A5   M6   A6

B. DIMINISHED INTERVALS

P4   d4   P5   d5   m7   d7

An interval may also be written enharmonically. For instance, the augmented 2nd A♭–B and the minor 3rd G♯–B both contain three semitones, and it is impossible to distinguish between them by listening to the isolated interval. Their difference lies in how they are notated. One diatonic interval, between the pitches B and F, exists as both an augmented 4th (F–G–A–B) and a diminished 5th (B–C–D–E–F); both contain six half steps. Because the augmented 4th consists of three whole tones (F–G, G–A, and A–B), it is sometimes called a **tritone;** this term is often used generically for the diminished 5th as well. Some common enharmonic intervals appear in Example 7; all employ accidentals.

Example 7

m3   A2   M3   d4   d5   A4   M6   d7   m7   A6

SPELLING INTERVALS

The proper spelling of intervals—that is, assigning each pitch its correct letter name and its correct line or space on the staff—is essential in music theory. The following method will enable you to spell any interval correctly.

1. If the interval you want to spell is the same size as a natural diatonic interval whose notes have the same letter names, then both notes of your interval will carry the same accidental (or no accidental at all). For instance, suppose you are trying to spell a perfect 5th above D♭. Since the white-key pitches of D and A already make a perfect 5th, both pitch-classes in your interval will carry one flat: D♭–A♭. This rule works equally well for building intervals downward and for spelling intervals with any accidentals, including double sharps and double flats (Example 8).

Example 8

P5↑   (P5)   m3↓   (m3)   m7↑   (m7)

2. If the size of the interval you are spelling is not equivalent to a natural diatonic interval whose notes have the same letter name, then one note of your interval requires an accidental. For instance, suppose you are trying to spell a minor 3rd below E. Since the natural pitches E–C represent a *major* 3rd, you must add a sharp to the lower C of your interval to contract it by a semitone: thus, E–C♯. If,

however, the interval you are trying to spell is a minor third below E♭, you need not adjust the C, since E♭ is already one half step lower than the white-key pitch E♮. Examine the three examples in Example 9.

Example 9

3. This procedure also works for augmented and diminished intervals. Let's suppose you are trying to spell an augmented 6th above F. Since F–D is a major 6th, you must raise the D with a sharp: thus, F–D♯. Now let's try to spell a diminished 7th below B♭. Since B–C is a major 7th, B♭–C will be a minor 7th, which must in turn be contracted by an additional semitone: thus, B♭–C♯. See Example 10.

Example 10

INTERVAL INVERSION

In theoretical discussion, intervals that are an octave or less in size are often grouped in pairs that add up to an octave. If we take a perfect 5th (C^4–G^4, for instance) and move the lower tone up an octave or the upper tone down an octave, we retain the same pitch-classes but change the size of the interval from a perfect 5th to a perfect 4th. This process is called **interval inversion.** Thus, a perfect 5th (C^4–G^4) and a perfect 4th (G^4–C^5) are inversions of each other. The sum of inverted intervals will always equal twelve half steps, or an octave.

Example 11 illustrates the seven pairs of inversional intervals, using only white-key notes. (Of course, you can build these intervals and their inversions starting from any note.) You will notice that perfect intervals invert into perfect intervals, major intervals into minor (and vice versa), and augmented intervals into diminished (and vice versa). Remember that the number of half steps in each pair will always equal twelve.

Example 11

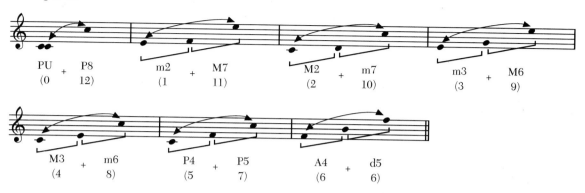

PU + P8
(0 + 12)

m2 + M7
(1 + 11)

M2 + m7
(2 + 10)

m3 + M6
(3 + 9)

M3 + m6
(4 + 8)

P4 + P5
(5 + 7)

A4 + d5
(6 + 6)

Pairs of intervals related by inversion share a similar sound quality. A perfect 5th and a perfect 4th, for instance, sound more alike than a perfect 5th and a minor 7th. In the following section, we will explore why this is so.

CONSONANT AND DISSONANT INTERVALS

An interval can usually be classified as either **consonant** or **dissonant.** The difference between the two is easy to hear but difficult to describe. Consonant intervals sound stable, relaxed, passive, and inert, while dissonant intervals sound unstable, tense, active, and restless.

The grouping of intervals into one category or the other is largely dependent on the stylistic features of music in certain Western historical periods, and may even depend on the context of a given musical passage. Our classification is based on the tonal music of the common-practice era. Unisons, octaves, and perfect 5ths are grouped as **perfect consonances,** while major and minor 3rds and 6ths (which are inversionally related) are grouped as **imperfect consonances.** These intervals (and the perfect 4th) are the intervals that appear between the first eight harmonics of the overtone series, omitting harmonic 7. For a further discussion of this phenomenon, please consult Appendix 1.

Major and minor 2nds and 7ths (which are also inversionally related) are the most dissonant intervals. The perfect 4th and the tritone (augmented 4th or diminished 5th) are considered dissonant when the bottom note of the interval is in the bass. Example 12, which employs the same sets of intervals as Example 4, shows consonance and dissonance operating in a tonal context.

Example 12

The four dissonant harmonic dyads, which are circled, appear within an environment of consonance. While the consonant intervals may occur freely, the dissonant intervals require careful handling in the way they are approached and left. In Example 12 the dissonant notes are approached and left either stepwise or by common tone (i.e., repeated note).

In Chapters 3 and 4 we shall see how intervals operate within the broader contexts of melody and chordal sonorities.

Terms and Concepts for Review

pitch
pitch-class
diatonic pitch collection
octave
frequency
chromatic pitch collection
equal temperament
half step *or* **semitone**
accidentals:
   sharp
   flat
   natural
   double sharp
   double flat
enharmonic spelling
dyad

interval:
   perfect
   major
   minor
   augmented
   diminished
melodic interval
harmonic interval
unison *or* **prime**
whole step *or* **whole tone**
diatonic interval
compound interval
tritone
interval inversion
consonant *vs.* **dissonant intervals**
perfect *vs.* **imperfect consonances**

Rhythm and Meter I

BEAT, METER, AND RHYTHMIC NOTATION

THE PREVIOUS CHAPTER introduced pitch notation and interval relationships. We will now consider rhythm and meter, the temporal elements of music, which are often unduly neglected.

When listening to a piece, we frequently take for granted the regulated rhythmic foundation that underlies its melody. In this chapter, we will first concentrate on how we hear different levels of metrical organization, after which we will discuss rhythmic notation and meter signatures.

THE BEAT

Rhythm deals with the temporal aspect of music, or how time passes in musical compositions. When we listen to a piece, we tend to "keep time" to its rhythm by marking off evenly spaced pulses. This regular pulsation, commonly called the **beat,** becomes the basis for various other rhythmic durations. The speed of the beat, called the **tempo,** is customarily indicated in approximate terms, usually written in Italian:[1] *Adagio* (slow), *Andante*

---

1. Other Italian tempo markings and their English equivalents may be found in the Glossary.

(moderate), *Allegro* (fast), and so on. A metronome provides a more exact measurement of tempo by ticking a precise number of beats per minute; this number, sometimes preceded by "M.M." (for "Maelzel's metronome," named for the inventor of the first practical metronome) or a note value and an equal sign (such as ♩ = 120), appears in a metronome marking. A good measurement of moderate tempo is the normal heart rate, which lies between 70 and 80 beats per minute.

When trying to determine the beat and tempo of a composition by ear, it is important that you match the speed of your beat to the tempo marking indicated in the score. For instance, in Sousa's *Stars and Stripes Forever,* your beat should correspond to *Allegro,* a brisk marching tempo, and therefore equal M.M. 120 rather than M.M. 60, which is exactly half as fast and approximates an *Adagio* tempo. The precise meaning of some tempo indications has changed over the course of the common-practice period. For instance, *Adagio* (literally, "at ease") in the Baroque period meant a relaxed tempo, whereas by 1800 the indication meant extremely slow. As you become acquainted with various musical styles, you will learn to distinguish between these different meanings and apply the most appropriate interpretation to the piece of music you are studying.

Changes in tempo are indicated by terms such as *accelerando* (speed up), *ritardando* (slow down), and *a tempo* (return to original speed). Although more subtle fluctuations in the beat, called *rubato,* are often added by performers, especially in slow movements, they are usually not indicated in the score. Play the Chopin Prelude found on CD1 and tap the beat, noting any variation in its regularity.

METRICAL GROUPING AND METER

Sing or play the melodies "Pop Goes the Weasel" and "America" ("My Country 'Tis of Thee"). You will observe that certain elements in the music tend to group the beats into larger units of equal duration, each of which begins with a stressed pulse. The stronger **downbeat,** preceded by at least one **upbeat,** creates a series of regular units that contain the same number of beats. This pattern of stressed and unstressed beats results in a sense of metrical grouping or **meter.** Each grouping, called a **measure** or **bar,** is indicated in notation by **bar lines.** How many beats are there in each measure of these tunes? Since "Pop Goes the Weasel" has two beats per measure, we say that it is in **duple meter;** since "America" has three beats per measure, we say it is in **triple meter.** The symbol — indicates stressed or stronger beats, and the symbol ˇ indicates unstressed or weaker beats. Thus,

---

In the late nineteenth century, tempo and expression markings began to appear in other languages such as English, German, and French.

duple meter is represented by ‒ ⌣ | ‒ ⌣ | ‒ ⌣ | ‒ ⌣ |, and triple meter by ‒ ⌣ ⌣ | ‒ ⌣ ⌣ | ‒ ⌣ ⌣ |. The melody "America the Beautiful," on the other hand, is in **quadruple meter,** with the primary stress on beat 1 and a secondary stress on beat 3: ‒ ⌣ (‒) ⌣ | ‒ ⌣ (‒) ⌣ |. A measure of quadruple meter may often be heard as two measures of duple meter.

Once a meter is firmly established, we tend to hear this grouping as continuing even in the face of conflicting rhythmic forces.[2]

Figure 1 gives a visual representation of the various types of meters, using the symbols for strong and weak beats.

	Duple meter		Triple meter		Quadruple meter	
Meter level	‒	‒	‒	‒	‒	‒
Beat level	‒ ⌣	‒ ⌣	‒ ⌣ ⌣	‒ ⌣ ⌣	‒ ⌣ (‒) ⌣	‒ ⌣ (‒) ⌣

Figure 1

How does music establish a sense of meter? Sing or play some familiar melodies and identify some characteristics that you believe contribute to your perception of their meter. Consider (1) the repetition of rhythmic patterns, (2) the placement of longer note values, and (3) the rate of chord change and bass notes in an accompaniment.

DIVISION OF THE BEAT

Now sing or play the tunes "Yankee Doodle" and "Pop Goes the Weasel" while marking the beat of each. You will note that the beat is divided into two equal portions in the former and three equal portions in the latter. This procedure is called **beat division.** The beat may undergo **simple** division into two equal parts (‒ ⌣ ‒ ⌣ ‒ ⌣ ‒ ⌣) or **compound** division into three equal parts (‒ ⌣ ⌣ ‒ ⌣ ⌣ ‒ ⌣ ⌣ ‒ ⌣ ⌣). Beats may be further subdivided into even smaller durations of equal length. The meter of a piece is generally identified by the type of beat division followed by the type of meter: "simple triple," "compound duple," and so on.

Now go back to the tunes and identify the metrical organization of each. Play or sing some more tunes you know, analyzing each in the same way. You might want to beat time using the standard conductor's patterns for two-, three-, and four-beat measures; see Appendix 5.

---

2. The question of rhythmical and metrical dissonance is discussed in Chapter 10, p. 117ff.

Our discussion suggests a three-tiered metrical hierarchy of relationships, moving from shorter to longer pulses—(1) beat division, (2) beat, and (3) meter or measure—producing regular recurrences at different pulse or rhythmic levels. The stresses are called **metric accents.** They may occur at the measure level, the beat level, and even the beat-division level. Figure 2 shows one possible representation of this metrical hierarchy.

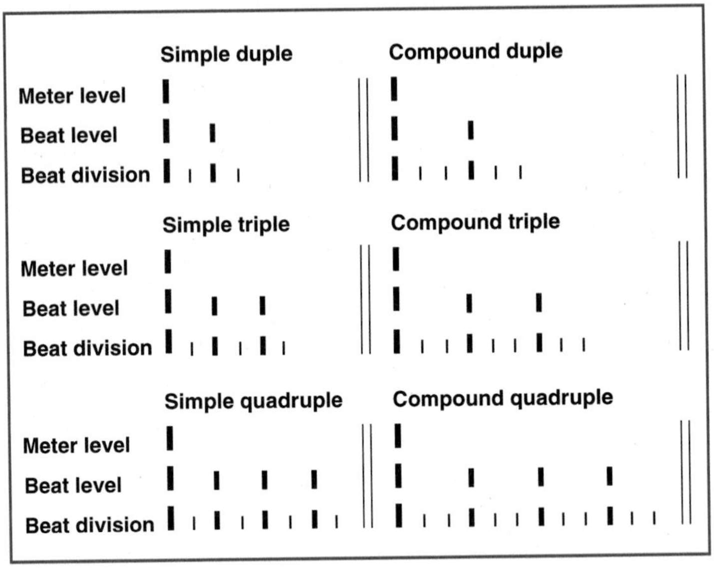

Figure 2

RHYTHMIC NOTATION

The various note values indicate their proportional relations to each other. Undotted notes are successively divisible by twos ($\half = \quarter\quarter$, $\quarter = \eighth\eighth$, and so on); dotted notes may be divided into either two dotted or three undotted notes of equal value ($\dottedhalf. = \dottedquarter.\,\dottedquarter.$ or $\dottedhalf. = \quarter\,\quarter\,\quarter$). Figure 3 displays these relationships using standard music symbols.

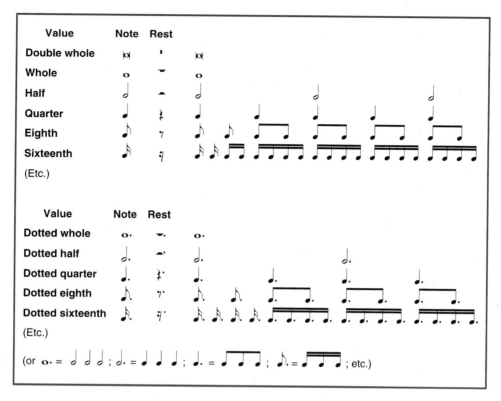

Figure 3

None of these note values represents any fixed duration in real time until it is associated with a specific beat and tempo.

THE BEAT VALUE

We must now choose some note value to represent the beat. This choice is ultimately up to the composer (who may sometimes be you). In judging a piece by our ear alone, we can only guess the **beat value** he or she may have selected. While the beat in "America" (simple triple meter) is normally notated as a ♩, it could just as easily be written as a ♪ or ♪. In simple meter the beat is always an undotted note, while in compound meter it is always a dotted note; thus, in "Pop Goes the Weasel" (compound duple meter), the beat value could be a ♩., ♩., or ♪.

METER SIGNATURES IN MODERATE TEMPO

Since the fourteenth century, certain symbols or numbers have been placed at the beginning of a composition to indicate its metrical organization. Two of these early symbols still survive: **C**, for $\frac{4}{4}$, and **¢** (or *alla breve*), for either $\frac{2}{2}$ or $\frac{2}{1}$. But most **meter signatures** (also called **time signatures**) today consist of two numbers, written one over the other, that are placed on the staff after the key signature. The interpretation of meter signatures is dependent on the speed of the beat—that is, the tempo. For now we will assume a moderate tempo, between M.M. 60 and 120. The two numbers of the signature reveal three things about the metrical organization of a piece: (1) the note value assigned as the beat, (2) the type of beat division (simple or compound), and (3) the number of beats in each measure.

If the top number of the signature is a 2, 3 or 4:

1. The bottom number indicates the undotted note value that receives the beat (4 = ♩, 2 = ♩, and 8 = ♪).
2. The top number denotes the number of those beats in a measure. Thus, you can read the two numbers as a fraction; for example, $\frac{3}{4}$ indicates that there is the equivalent of three quarters in each bar.

If the top number is 6, 9, or 12:

1. Take the bottom number and put a "3" above it, making a fraction. If the resulting fraction is $\frac{3}{8}$, it indicates that the beat value is the sum of ♪♪♪, or ♩.. If it is $\frac{3}{4}$, it indicates a beat value of the sum of ♩♩♩, or ♩.. Since a dotted value receives the beat, the beat division is compound.
2. Divide the top number by 3 to find the number of beats in a measure (6 = 2 beats, 9 = 3 beats, and 12 = 4 beats).

Memorize the charts in Figure 4, which illustrate the various meter signatures in moderate tempo. (Some of the signatures may not be familiar to you.) Then scan through the text or workbook and analyze the meter signatures you find.

It is unfortunate that an easier method of indicating meter has not become standard. In some twentieth-century scores, composers use signatures whose interpretation is more obvious, such as $\frac{3}{♩}$ or $\frac{2}{♩}$, where the bottom number is replaced by the notational symbol of the beat value.

SIMPLE METERS

Beat value

↓	2	3	4	← Number of beats in measure
♪	$\frac{2}{8}$	$\frac{3}{8}$	$\frac{4}{8}$	
♩	$\frac{2}{4}$	$\frac{3}{4}$	$\frac{4}{4}$	
♩	$\frac{2}{2}$	$\frac{3}{2}$	$\frac{4}{2}$	
	Simple Duple	Simple Triple	Simple Quadruple	← Meter type

COMPOUND METERS

Beat value

↓	2	3	4	← Number of beats in measure
♪.	$\frac{6}{16}$	$\frac{9}{16}$	$\frac{12}{16}$	
♩.	$\frac{6}{8}$	$\frac{9}{8}$	$\frac{12}{8}$	
♩.	$\frac{6}{4}$	$\frac{9}{4}$	$\frac{12}{4}$	
	Compound Duple	Compound Triple	Compound Quadruple	← Meter type

Figure 4

METER SIGNATURES IN VERY SLOW OR FAST TEMPO

When the tempo of a composition is either extremely slow or extremely fast, the meter signature must be reinterpreted in a different manner. When the original beat is so slow that it has to be divided into subbeats, we usually employ the next faster level of beat division to mark the beat. For instance, in an *Adagio* ¾ the slow quarter-note beat is divided into eighth notes and forms a 2 + 2 + 2 grouping (♫ ♫ ♫), while in an *Adagio* ⅝ the beat groupings are arranges as 3 + 3 (♪♪♪ ♪♪♪). The result of this procedure is called **a divided beat.** The distinction between these two examples of six "beats" per measure (or sextuple meter) lies in the different way each groups together eighth notes, which is indicated by the beaming. Thus a conductor will mark six eighth-note motions with his baton, but the way in which the motions are grouped will differ between the *Adagio* ⅝ and ¾; consult Figure 6 in Appendix 5 on conducting patterns. Other instances of the divided beat may be found in Example 2 of Chapter 13 (in ²⁄₄, but counted in 4) and Example 4c of Chapter 16 of the Workbook (in ¾ but counted in 6), in both of which the tempo is ♪ = ca. M.M. 100.

When the signatures ⅜ and ¾ are found in very fast tempos, the beat values become the ♩. and the ♩·, respectively, producing a compound beat division with only one beat per measure. This **compound single meter** is frequently found in scherzos and waltzes. When we hear a typical Johann Strauss waltz in ¾, for example, we tend to tap the beat on each ♩· rather than on each ♩. Since we now sense each measure as a single beat, it is only natural that these "beat measures" in turn group themselves into larger metric groupings called **hypermeasures,** each containing two, three, or four "beat measures." One such example occurs in the Scherzo of Beethoven's Ninth Symphony, written in a fast compound single ¾. Here the composer instructs the conductor to "beat in four" (*quattro battute*), indicating that each bar gets one beat and that each group of four bars forms a hypermeasure with four beats (⁴♩·); see Example 1.

Example 1 BEETHOVEN: SYMPHONY NO. 9 ("CHORAL"), II

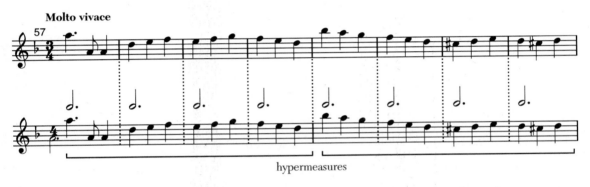

hypermeasures

Now analyze the meter signatures in Figure 5, taking the tempo into consideration. Identify the type of beat division (simple or compound), the note value receiving the beat, and the number of beats in each measure.

	Beat division	Beat value	Beats per measure
1. ¾ Andante			
2. ¹²⁄₄ Moderato			
3. ⁶⁄₈ Largo			
4. ⁹⁄₁₆ Andantino			
5. ¢ Allegretto			
6. ⅜ Presto			

Figure 5

We will return to the topic of rhythm in Chapter 10, where we will discuss some devices that create rhythmic conflicts at the various metrical levels.

Terms and Concepts for Review

rhythm
pulse
beat
tempo
tempo markings:
   Adagio
   Andante
   Allegro, etc.
changes in tempo:
   accelerando
   ritardando
   a tempo, etc.
metrical grouping
downbeat *vs.* upbeat

measure, bar, bar line
duple meter
triple meter
quadruple meter
beat division
simple *vs.* compound meter
metrical hierarchy
metric accent
beat value
meter (time) signature
divided beat in slow tempos
compound single meter
hypermeasure

Tonic, Scale, and Melody

I N THIS CHAPTER we will now see how pitch and rhythm interact to create melody. After a discussion of tonality, major and minor modes, scales, and key signatures, we will examine some basic characteristics of the melodic phrase.

TONIC AND TONALITY

Sing or play the first four measures of "Joy to the World" (Example 1a). This initial phrase exhibits a sense of tonal closure, concluding on the **tonic,** that note of greatest centrality, stability, and finality. The pitches of this passage appear (without rhythm) in Example 1b.

Example 1

A. "JOY TO THE WORLD" (CAROL)

B.

Here, the tune is written with natural (white-key) notes and the tonic pitches are stemmed and beamed together. In Example 2, all the pitches of the melody appear in a stepwise-ascending scale bounded on both ends by the tonic. The notes of this tune constitute a complete diatonic pitch collection, which, as we learned in Chapter 1, is a group of any seven pitch-classes that form the interval pattern of seven adjacent white keys on the piano.[1] If we examine the intervals between each two consecutive pitches in this collection, we see that it contains a total of five whole steps and two half steps. Example 2 illustrates the diatonic pattern, marking these stepwise relations with a ⌣ for whole steps and a ⌢ for half steps.

Example 2

Now locate the tonic notes in "Home on the Range" (melody not given). Into how many sections does the music seem to fall? Compare the endings of each of the sections. Which ones seem more conclusive and why? Can you notate this tune using "white-key" pitches? Where does the tonic lie in relation to the song's range?

Tonality is the broad organization of pitches and harmonies around a central tonic in a passage or piece of music. The diatonic pitches in a composition form a tonal hierarchy in which all the other tones are subordinate to the tonic. We will soon learn the degree of importance of each of the other diatonic pitches, as well as their functions and relation to each other in this hierarchy, which represents the underlying foundation of tonal harmony. For the moment, however, let us focus on the single melodic line and reserve our examination of the role that harmony plays in tonality until Chapter 8.

The use of the diatonic collection does not automatically insure the establishment of a particular tonic. Although melodies employing the white keys of the piano tend to gravitate toward a tonic of C, such melodies may also gravitate toward A or even D.

---

1. Another way to create this diatonic collection is to build upward by perfect 5ths from F to B, and then gather all the notes within one octave: F C G D A E B = C D E F G A B (C).

What exactly are the tonal forces at work that lead us to perceive a specific tonic in a melodic line? Play the tune in Example 3.

Example 3

What is the tonic note? What features of this melody aid in establishing this particular tonic? Which notes seem to pull toward the tonic? How does the metrical positioning of the tonic pitch help in establishing it as the tonic? You may express your observations as general traits and apply them to other diatonic tunes as well. Using this list of traits, improvise or compose a short melody (white keys only) that establishes a tonic of F.

THE MAJOR MODE AND MAJOR SCALE

Two basic systems of pitch organization are employed in tonal music of the common-practice period: the **major mode** and the **minor mode.**[2] We will consider the major mode first. To represent the basic tonal content of the major mode, the white-key diatonic notes can be arranged as in Example 4a. That is, they are placed in ascending order above the tonic C to form a **scale** (from the Italian *scala,* "ladder"); the symbols ⌣ and ⌃ again indicate whole and half steps, respectively. This scale represents the pitch-classes available for composing a wide variety of melodies in the major mode. Sing the first phrase of the carols "Joy to the World" (Example 1a) and "The First Noël" (Example 4b). Both span an octave range upward from the lowest note, which is the tonic, and both are diatonic. Yet the two melodies are completely different. Does "The First Noël" end on the tonic?

---

2. A discussion of the Church modes may be found in Appendix 2.

Example 4

A.

B.   "THE FIRST NOËL" (CAROL)

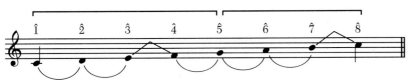

The seven **scale degrees,** or **scale steps,** of the major scale are numbered from the tonic to the note a 7th above. Arabic numbers with small carets denote the various scale degrees: $\hat{1}$ $\hat{2}$ $\hat{3}$ $\hat{4}$ $\hat{5}$ $\hat{6}$ $\hat{7}$. The upper octave is generally called scale degree $\hat{8}$.

The diatonic pitches of a major scale may be *transposed* to another pitch level by raising or lowering all of them by a particular interval. There are twelve possible **transpositions,** one for each note of the chromatic collection. Two transpositions, to E♭ (a minor 3rd higher) and A (a minor 3rd lower), are shown in Example 5. Locate the position of the various whole and half steps in each scale.

Example 5

A.   B.

DIATONIC SCALE DEGREES

In tonal music the individual scale steps have been assigned specific names based on their association either to $\hat{1}$ (the tonic) or $\hat{5}$ (the dominant). The **dominant,** which takes its name from the Latin *dominus* ("lord" or "ruler"), is the next most important note after the tonic, partly because of the acoustical stability of the perfect 5th formed by $\hat{1}$ and $\hat{5}$. The dominant divides the major scale into two unequal segments of five notes (C–D–E–F–G) and four notes (G–A–B–C); refer to Example 4.[3] Scale step

3. The major scale may also be thought of as a pair of *tetrachords,* or four-note spans: C–D–E–F and G–A–B–C.

$\hat{3}$, called the **mediant** because it lies midway between tonic and dominant, determines the mode of the scale: the interval between $\hat{1}$ and $\hat{3}$ is a major 3rd in the major scale. Example 6 charts the remaining scale degrees with their names. Why do you think the **subdominant** and **submediant** are so named?

Example 6

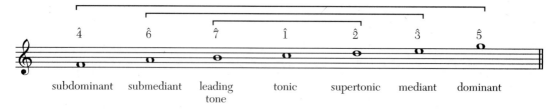

subdominant   submediant   leading tone   tonic   supertonic   mediant   dominant

THE MINOR MODE AND MINOR SCALE

The minor mode is more complex than the major mode. The basic difference between the two modes lies in the minor mode's use of a lowered mediant, or minor 3rd, above $\hat{1}$. Several scales are traditionally used to illustrate different aspects of the minor mode. The **melodic minor scale** in Example 7 shows how the scale degrees tend to operate in actual tonal melodies.

Example 7

As a melodic line rises from $\hat{5}$ to $\hat{8}$, scale steps $\hat{6}$ and $\hat{7}$ are raised by a half step, which increases their inclination toward the upper tonic ($\hat{5}$–$\sharp\hat{6}$–$\sharp\hat{7}$–$\hat{8}$). When a melodic line descends from $\hat{8}$ to $\hat{5}$, scale steps $\hat{7}$ and $\hat{6}$ are lowered, producing a strong half-step pull from $\flat\hat{6}$ to the dominant ($\hat{8}$–$\flat\hat{7}$–$\flat\hat{6}$–$\hat{5}$). The lowered 7th degree is called the **subtonic** rather than the leading tone, since in this form it does not lead to the tonic. You can observe these melodic tendencies in the Beethoven excerpt in Example 8.

Example 8   BEETHOVEN: STRING QUARTET IN F MINOR, OP. 95, I

The **harmonic minor scale** in Example 9 represents those scale degrees that are typically found in the most basic chordal progressions. The harmonic minor scale includes a lowered $\hat{6}$ ($\flat\hat{6}$) and a raised $\hat{7}$ or **leading tone** ($\sharp\hat{7}$).

Example 9

The **natural minor scale** in Example 10 is identical to the scale of the Aeolian church mode; consult Appendix 2. Since the natural minor scale contains both lowered 6th and 7th scale degrees, it is the only version of the minor scale that consists entirely of natural diatonic pitches. Thus it contains the same accidentals found in the signature of the relative major key.

Example 10

If we combine all three forms of the scale into one composite scale, we obtain a better picture of the wealth of musical pitches actually used in minor-mode compositions. Example 11 shows that while the scale degrees from $\hat{1}$ up to $\hat{5}$ are diatonic, the span from $\hat{5}$ up to $\hat{8}$ is completely chromatic, containing both lowered and raised 6th and 7th degrees: $\hat{5}$–$\natural\hat{6}$–$\sharp\hat{6}$–$\natural\hat{7}$–$\sharp\hat{7}$–$\hat{8}$.[4]

Example 11

In this text we will refer to the lower $\hat{6}$ and $\hat{7}$ scale degrees as $\flat\hat{6}$ and $\flat\hat{7}$.

4. A raised third scale degree is sometimes found in the last chord of compositions in the minor mode, especially in Renaissance and Baroque music. This final raised $\hat{3}$ is often called the "Picardy third."

KEYS AND THE CIRCLE OF 5THS

The term **key** is used interchangeably with *tonality* when discussing music of the common-practice period. When we speak of the keys of D major and F♯ minor, for example, we are saying that D and F♯ are the tonics of the respective pieces, and that the given mode identifies the underlying diatonic scale. In this text, major keys are indicated in the music examples with capital letters and a colon (e.g., "D:") and minor keys with small letters (e.g., "f♯:").

In addition to C major, which has no accidentals, there are seven major keys containing sharps and seven containing flats. The fifteen major keys can be arranged along the outer rim in a **circle of 5ths,** as in Figure 1.

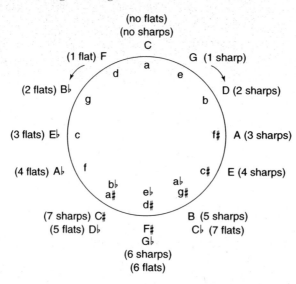

Figure 1

As you move to the right around the circle, each successive key is transposed a perfect 5th higher and therefore requires one more sharp (or one less flat) in its scale. Similarly, moving to the left, each successive key is a perfect 5th lower than the last and has one additional flat (or one less sharp). Notice the three enharmonic keys at the bottom of the circle: C♯/D♭, F♯/G♭, and B/C♭.

RELATIVE AND PARALLEL KEYS

Beginning with A minor, which has no sharps or flats, there are also a total of fifteen minor keys on the circle. They appear on the inner rim of the circle in Figure 1. Since the major and minor keys across from each other on the rim share the same diatonic notes in their scales, they are called **rela-**

tive keys. What is the **relative minor** of A major? What is the **relative major** of C minor?

While relative keys share the same pitch-classes, they have different tonics. **Parallel keys,** in contrast, share the same tonic, but differ in mode and thus in the notes of their scales. Compare the parallel keys C major (no accidentals) and C minor (three flats).

KEY SIGNATURES

Placed at the beginning of each staff in a composition, the **key signature** indicates the accidentals necessary to form the diatonic scale on which the piece is based. This convenient shorthand avoids the tedious task of notating each required sharp or flat throughout the score. For instance, for the key of G major we only need to write one ♯ on the F line in the signature to signal that all the F's on that staff will be raised a semitone. A signature may indicate either the relative major or minor key: for example, one with two sharps may denote either D major or B minor. The various key signatures for relative major and minor keys are given in Example 12. Memorize these signatures, carefully noting the placement of the accidentals on the treble- and bass-clef staves.

Example 12

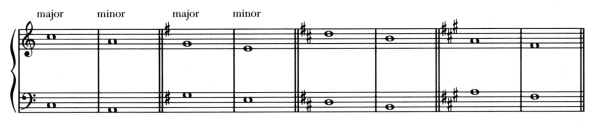

MELODY AND SCALE DEGREES

A melodic line is a succession of rhythmicized pitches that forms a series of melodic intervals.[5] (Other factors, such as dynamics, register, timbre or tone color, and articulation can also become part of what we call melody.) Tonal melodies represent goal-oriented or directed motion that is continually moving toward or away from certain tonal, rhythmic, and formal destinations. The path between these goals may be predictable or ambiguous. As listeners, we become involved in this unfolding drama of tone and time as we trace its course to the music's conclusion.

The scale degrees of a melody convey us on our tonal journey. The various scale steps in the major and minor modes have distinct tonal characteristics that influence their melodic tendencies. Since scale steps $\hat{1}$ and $\hat{3}$ are associated with the tonic, they are the most stable, or inactive, degrees. The dominant ($\hat{5}$) has a strong tendency to return to the tonic, but it assumes a more stable role when it joins $\hat{1}$ and $\hat{3}$ in the tonic triad. The more active scale steps ($\hat{7}$, $\hat{2}$, $\hat{4}$, and $\hat{6}$) tend to move stepwise to the more stable $\hat{1}$ (or $\hat{8}$), $\hat{3}$, or $\hat{5}$. Since the leading tone and submediant exhibit such a strong pull to tonic and dominant respectively ($\hat{7}$–$\hat{8}$ and $\flat\hat{6}$–$\hat{5}$), they are often called **tendency tones.** The following example demonstrates these scale-degree affinities.

---

5. Although some musicians argue that melody arises from harmony, a study of history reveals that single-line melodies—including Greek melody, Gregorian chant, and early secular monophony—evolved first.

Example 13

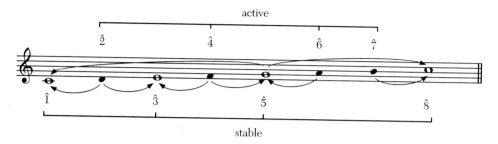

When we take a melodic line and examine it note by note, we may find that the successive scale degrees do not always adhere to the preceding generalizations. But as we begin to look beneath the rhythmic and melodic surface of the music to reveal the underlying tonal framework on which the melody is based, we will discover longer-range stepwise tendencies of that framework that do support these generalizations. The later melodic analyses in this chapter will incorporate some simple methods of illustrating these long-range scale-degree connections; in Part Two more sophisticated techniques will be suggested.

MELODIC PHRASES

When we sing familiar melodies, we will observe that they are usually divided into smaller sections or units. These sections, which may be melodically similar or dissimilar, are usually set off by some kind of rhythmic "punctuation." The way these sections are organized into a whole lends a particular form or design to a melody.

Let us draw on the long association between words and music and employ some grammatical terms to describe these melodic groupings. Consider the sentence: "If you go to the concert tonight, you will hear Beethoven's Ninth Symphony." The end of each phrase is punctuated differently. The opening condition ("If you go . . ."), held in suspension by a comma, is resolved by the consequent action ("you will hear . . ."), concluded with a period. We may thus diagram the sentence as follows:

Condition
    If you go to the
    concert tonight,

Resolution
    you will hear Beethoven's
    Ninth Symphony.

Now sing or play the "Ode to Joy" theme from the last movement of this symphony, given in Example 14, and compare its musical design to the simple diagram above.

Example 14 BEETHOVEN: SYMPHONY NO. 9 ("CHORAL"), IV, "ODE TO JOY" THEME

This simple tune consists of two sections, called **phrases.** Each phrase expresses a well-ordered musical idea that progresses tonally to a point of musical punctuation, or **cadence.** In Example 14 brackets mark off the two phrases. As in this passage, successive phrases in tonal music frequently contain the same number of measures, a trait called **phrase periodicity.** From its first two phrases, we might expect Beethoven's tune to continue its periodicity of four bars per phrase. Examine the complete tune in Example 10 of Chapter 12 and see if this is the case. In Chapter 12 we will consider some factors that contribute to varying phrase lengths.

MELODIC CADENCES

Cadences represent the coming together of melodic, harmonic, and rhythmic factors to create structural punctuation. Every era in music history has devised its own set of standardized melodic or harmonic cadential patterns. We can identify two melodic characteristics typical of cadences from the common-practice period:

1. A momentary cessation of rhythmic motion on the final cadence note. (Is this apparent in Example 14?)
2. The use of certain two-note patterns at the end of the phrase. (What two different scale degrees end each phrase of Example 14?)

The directed tonal motion from the beginning to the end of a phrase can be demonstrated by highlighting its first note and the last two cadence tones with stemmed notes and indicating its interior pitches with unstemmed noteheads, as we have done with the first two phrases of the "Ode to Joy" theme in Example 15.

Example 15

The opening $\hat{3}$ eventually descends to $\hat{2}$ at the end of the first phrase but is stopped before it reaches $\hat{1}$. The second phrase starts again on $\hat{3}$, and this time the phrase descends all the way to the tonic, thereby exhibiting tonal closure. Thus the long-range tonal movement, which can be diagrammed as $\hat{3}$–$\hat{2}$, $\hat{3}$–$\hat{2}$–$\hat{1}$, shows an inclination to descend stepwise from scale step $\hat{3}$ to $\hat{1}$, but at the end of the first phrase is interrupted after the active scale step $\hat{2}$. In Example 15 we denote this interruption by a 𝄽 marking. This break in the tonal motion forms an **inconclusive cadence** ($\hat{3}$–$\hat{2}$) at the end of the first phrase, which is finally resolved by the **conclusive cadence** ($\hat{2}$–$\hat{1}$) at the end of the second phrase.

The short phrases in Example 16 illustrate the most common melodic cadences in tonal music. (These tunes have been transposed to C major and C minor to facilitate comparisons.[6])

Example 16

A. CONCLUSIVE CADENCES

B. LESS CONCLUSIVE CADENCES

C. INCONCLUSIVE CADENCES

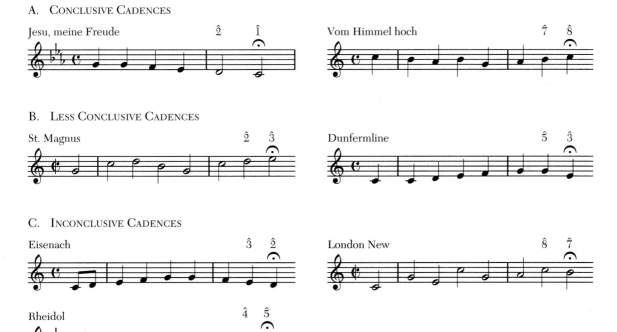

6. The names in Examples 16B and 16C are the titles of the hymn tunes themselves, to which different texts were often set.

The most conclusive cadences exhibit stepwise motion to the tonic: $\hat{2}$–$\hat{1}$ or $\hat{7}$–$\hat{8}$. Less conclusive cadences end on the mediant: $\hat{2}$–$\hat{3}$ or $\hat{5}$–$\hat{3}$. Inconclusive cadences generally employ stepwise motion toward an active scale degree ($\hat{3}$–$\hat{2}$, $\hat{8}$–$\hat{7}$, or $\hat{4}$–$\hat{5}$). Play or sing each of the phrases. What sort of impressions do we receive from the three types of cadences? It is imperative that you memorize these various melodic formulas now; later we will add more melodic cadences to our present list.

LONG-RANGE MELODIC MOTION

Let us examine a complete diatonic melody to see how scale degrees operate within a longer melodic span. The hymn known as the "Old One Hundred" (Example 17a) contains four short phrases, each with a well-defined melodic cadence.

Example 17   LOUIS BOURGEOIS: "OLD ONE HUNDRED" (HYMN)

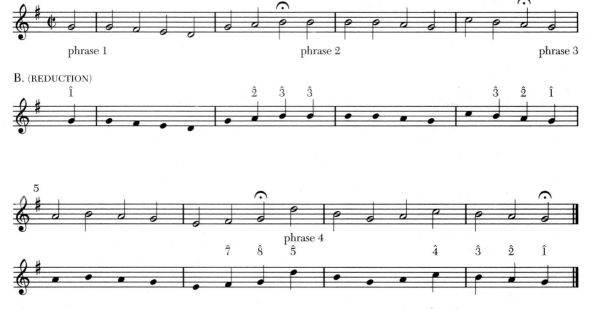

As in the previous "Ode to Joy," we will stem the initial note and last two cadential notes of each phrase, thereby framing their directed tonal motion; see the diagram in Example 17b that accompanies the melody. Phrase 1 represents a rise from tonic to mediant, $\hat{1}$→$\hat{2}$–$\hat{3}$, that is spread out over two measures. Phrase 2 begins on $\hat{3}$ and gradually descends to $\hat{2}$, and phrase 3 begins on the tonic and hovers around it before ending back on $\hat{1}$. The overall tonal motion of these phrases, then, is $\hat{1}{\rightarrow}\hat{2}$–$\hat{3}$, $\hat{3}{\rightarrow}\hat{3}$–$\hat{2}$, $\hat{1}{\rightarrow}\hat{7}$–$\hat{1}$, with the first ending on a less conclusive cadence, the second on an inconclusive cadence, and the third on a conclusive cadence. Notice that this long-range motion proceeds completely by step. Despite the apparent close on $\hat{1}$ at the end of the third phrase,[7] an additional line of text remains to be set. Since we anticipate that the concluding phrase will likewise cadence on the tonic, its sense of closure must be even more emphatic than what has preceded it. Therefore, after the generally stepwise motion in the previous three phrases, the line dramatically leaps to the dominant in the fourth phrase and makes a stepwise descent back to the final tonic: $\hat{5}$–$\hat{4}$–$\hat{3}$–$\hat{2}$–$\hat{1}$.

Example 18

The familiar tune quoted in Example 19a aptly illustrates both short- and long-range tonal goals in melodic writing. In Example 19b we have stemmed the framing pitches of each phrase and notated the interior notes with unstemmed noteheads.

Example 19

A.

B. (REDUCTION 1)

C. (REDUCTION 2)

7. In most harmonizations of this tune, the $\hat{1}$ that ends this phrase is harmonized with some chord other than tonic in order to maintain the tonal tension and motion.

The tune divides into four short phrases of two measures each, the first three of which begin with an upbeat on C⁴ ($\hat5$). The F–E ($\hat8$–$\hat7$) ending of the first phrase is answered by the G–F ($\hat2$–$\hat1$) of the second, which, as we can see by the curved arrow in measures 2 to 4 (Example 19c), resolves the leading tone ($\hat7$) to the tonic $\hat8$ (or $\hat1$). The octave leap to C⁵ ($\hat5$) in measure 5, which disrupts the previous pattern, descends by 3rds to D⁴ ($\hat6$). The B♭⁴ that opens the last phrase eventually moves to the final tonic via scale steps $\hat3$–$\hat2$–$\hat1$. If we examine the tonal summary in Example 19c, we can see that our tune actually consists of two different melodic strands, as indicated by the direction of the stemming. Following the dramatic octave leap to $\hat5$ in measure 5, the melody in measures 6–8 actually descends stepwise to the concluding tonic: $\hat5$–$\hat4$–$\hat3$–$\hat2$–$\hat1$. The latent upbeat $\hat5$ in the first three phrases now pulls up to the $\hat6$ and seems to suggest a stepwise ascent to $\hat8$ through a leading tone that we must imply here, shown in the last example as an E⁴ in parentheses. The only accented dissonance to the harmonic background occurs in measure 6 with the E–D. What occurs in the text at that point?

Our three melodic analyses illustrate characteristics that are similar in several respects. Most of the long-range melodic connections exhibit stepwise motion, thereby demonstrating the tendency of the more active degrees ($\hat7$, $\hat2$, $\hat4$, and $\hat6$) to move to the more stable degrees ($\hat1$, $\hat3$, $\hat5$). In addition, the overall motion of each melody tends to move stepwise from either the dominant or the mediant down to the tonic: $\hat3$–$\hat2$–$\hat1$ or $\hat5$–$\hat4$–$\hat3$–$\hat2$–$\hat1$. Our further melodic analyses will confirm these generalizations.

The diagrams that reduce these last two melodies to their essential melodic tones allow us to see more clearly the functions of the various scale degrees and their longer-range tendencies within the key.

GUIDELINES FOR USING THE ANALYTICAL SYMBOLS

$\hat5$ A caret (̂) placed over an arabic number denotes a scale degree.

♩ Black noteheads with stems represent more important or essential chord tones.

• Black noteheads without stems represent less essential tones.

// An interruption sign denotes a break in the long-range tonal movement toward $\hat1$, usually occurring after scale degree $\hat2$.

Terms and Concepts for Review

tonic
tonality
major mode
minor mode
scale
scale degree *or* scale step:
  tonic
  dominant
  mediant
  subdominant
  submediant
  leading tone
  supertonic
  subtonic

transposition
melodic minor scale
harmonic minor scale
natural minor scale
key
key signature
circle of 5ths
relative major and minor keys
parallel major and minor keys
tendency tone
phrase
phrase periodicity
cadence (inconclusive *vs.* conclusive)

Triads and Seventh Chords

IN THE PREVIOUS CHAPTER we examined some aspects of melody. We will now turn our attention to harmony—that is, the vertically oriented sonorities in music. In this chapter we will focus on chord types, chord spelling and notation, chord inversions, and commercial chord and figured-bass symbols.

ROOT-POSITION MAJOR AND MINOR TRIADS

A **chord** may be produced by playing any combination of three or more pitches simultaneously. Chords may also be implied by playing two or more disjunct intervals in a broken or arpeggiated manner. Tonal music shows a strong preference for **tertian chords,** chords built up of consecutive thirds above the bottom note, or **root.** A tertian chord consisting of three different pitch-classes is called a **triad.** The most common triads consist of consonant intervals above the root. For instance, above C we may build a major 3rd and a perfect 5th (C E G), or a minor 3rd and a perfect 5th (C E♭ G). These consonant sonorities are called **major** and **minor triads,** respectively, and each derives its name from the interval between the root and the note a third above it. When the root of a triad is at the bottom, we say that the triad is in **root position.**

   Commercial chord symbols of the kind used in popular keyboard and guitar arrangements provide us with a quick and handy way of indicating root-position triads. In commercial symbols, a capital letter denotes a major triad (C, E♭, F♯, and so on), while a capital letter followed by a lowercase *m* denotes a minor triad (Cm, E♭m, F♯m, and so on).[1] For the various triads in Example 1, identify the root, 3rd, and 5th of each triad as well as its chord type (major or minor). In some chords, the chord members extend beyond the range of an octave.

Example 1

INVERSIONS OF MAJOR AND MINOR TRIADS

Just as we have inverted harmonic intervals or dyads, we can also invert triads, by placing their bottom note an octave higher or their top note an octave lower. The **triad inversions** that result are illustrated in Example 2.

Example 2

A. MAJOR TRIAD   B. MINOR TRIAD

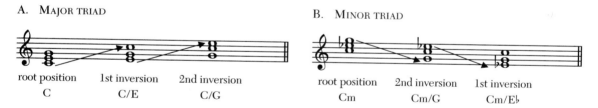

Taking the C-major triad as an example, each pitch may appear in the bass: the chordal root, or C, producing a *root-position triad;* the chordal third, or E, producing a **first-inversion triad;** and the chordal fifth, or G, producing a **second-inversion triad.** In commercial practice the bass note is customarily written after the chord symbol: C (root position), C/E (first inversion), and C/G (second inversion). Because of the strength of the acoustical perfect 5th above the root, the root position is the most stable form of a major or minor triad. The other inversions are less stable, since the root now appears in an upper voice. In first inversion, the intervals above the bass are both consonant with the bass note (a 3rd and a 6th); in

1. See Appendix 4 for a fuller discussion of commercial and jazz chord symbols.

second inversion, one is a dissonant 4th. In this chapter and those that follow, we will cover many aspects of root-position and first-inversion triads, reserving discussion of second-inversion chords until Chapter 16.

DIMINISHED AND AUGMENTED TRIADS

Example 3 illustrates two other types of tertian triads.

Example 3

A. DIMINISHED TRIAD

m3 m3   F♯° F♯°/A F♯°/C

B. AUGMENTED TRIAD

M3 M3   G⁺ G⁺/B G⁺/D♯

The **diminished triad** contains a minor 3rd and a diminished 5th above the root; it takes its name from the diminished 5th, which replaces the perfect 5th of major and minor chords. The diminished triad is traditionally found in first inversion, since in other chord positions a dissonant tritone occurs between the bass and one of the upper notes. Why do you think the sense of triadic root is weaker in diminished triads?

The **augmented triad** contains a major 3rd and an augmented 5th above the root. Like the diminished triad, it is often found in first inversion. The augmented triad conveys little or no sense of root. Since the two major 3rds of the augmented triad divide the octave into three equal parts, its inversions sound identical to each other (except for their pitch level) and any of its tones could therefore seem to be functioning as its "root." Because this sonority occurs so rarely in diatonic tonal music, we will reserve its discussion until Chapter 32, when we take up the topic of embellishing chromatic chords.

In commercial chord symbols, a diminished triad is represented by a capital letter followed by a superscript circle (B° = B D F); an augmented triad is represented by a capital letter followed by a small plus sign (C⁺ = C E G♯).

TRIAD SPELLING AND NOTATION

Musicians use the following method to spell root-position triads. The resultant chord tones can then be "rotated" to obtain the various inversions.

1. To spell a major triad, construct a major 3rd and a perfect 5th above a given root. (Thus, E♭ G B♭ is an E♭-major (E♭) triad).
2. To spell a minor triad, construct a minor 3rd and a perfect 5th above a given root. (Thus, B D F♯ is a B-minor (Bm) triad.)
3. To spell a diminished triad, construct a minor 3rd and a diminished 5th above a given root. (Thus, A C E♭ is an A-diminished (A°) triad.)
4. To spell an augmented triad, construct a major 3rd and an augmented 5th above a given root. (Thus, G B D♯ is a G-augmented (G⁺) triad.)

In Example 4, identify the root, chord type, and inversion of each triad.

Example 4

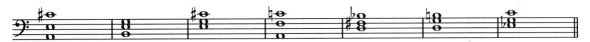

Now practice spelling the four types of triads above each note of the white-key pitch-classes.

FIGURED BASS

By around 1600, composers had devised an efficient method of abbreviating chords by using numbers to represent specific intervals above the written bass note. This practice of **figured bass,** or **thoroughbass,** was a hallmark of the Baroque period, the era of Bach and Handel. Example 5 shows a typical keyboard part from that period; the small notes in the treble staff illustrate what the performer would add to the given figured bass.

Example 5

The player was expected to play, or *realize,* the harmonies when given only the bass line and numerical symbols, in much the same way that a jazz pianist realizes the chords when given the commercial chord symbols on a leadsheet. In harmony manuals written after the Baroque period, these intervallic symbols indicate both chords and melodic motion over the lowest part.

When learning the various figured-bass numerals, remember:

1. The numbers always refer to intervals above the bass. They must not be confused with chord members. The ^{3} of the figured-bass symbol $^6_3$ represents the note a 3rd above the bass; if the bass note is E, this turns out to be the chordal 5th (G), not the 3rd of the C chord (E).
2. Intervals larger than an octave are assumed. Thus, a ^{3} can stand for a 10th (that is, an octave and a 3rd), and a ^{5} can stand for a 12th (that is, an octave and a 5th).
3. The spelling of the intervals is always affected by the key signature. Thus, in the key of G major it is not necessary to include a sharp before any numeral that indicates that scale degree.

The complete figuration for triads is $^5_3$ (root position), $^6_3$ (first inversion), and $^6_4$ (second inversion). Root-position chords traditionally do not require any figures at all, however, and first-inversion chords are usually denoted by simply the digit ^{6}. The figured-bass symbols in Example 6 show typical ways of indicating altered 3rds and 5ths in $^5_3$, or root-position, triads. An altered 3rd above the bass requires only an accidental. A lowered 5th requires both the digit ^{5} and an accidental: $^{\flat5}$; a raised 5th may alternatively be indicated with a slash through the ^{5}: $^{\cancel{5}}$.

Example 6

Some first-inversion triads appear in Example 7. A slash through a ^{6} ($^{\cancel{6}}$) indicates that the 6th has been raised a half step. Since these numbers refer only to the intervals *above* the bass, any accidental that affects the bass does not occur in the figures.

Example 7

Using the figured-bass passages in Example 8, spell each chord to yourself and then indicate the root, chord type, and bass note with commercial chord symbols; the first chord is done for you.

Example 8

A.

B.

SEVENTH CHORDS

There are only six triads in which exclusively consonant intervals are formed with the bass: the root-position and first-inversion major and minor triads, and the first-inversion diminished and augmented triads. In Western music composed from about 1400 to 1650, these consonant triads formed the harmonic basis for compositions. During the later Baroque period, however, the tertian structure of a triad was extended beyond the 5th to the 7th above the root. Such chords were called **seventh chords.** The 7th often originated from a dissonant melodic tone. Example 9 shows how F, passing melodically from G to E, was absorbed into the G chord, producing a new sonority of four different pitch-classes: G B D F. Since the chordal 7th of a seventh chord is a dissonant harmonic interval above the root, we must approach it and leave—or resolve—it with special care.

Example 9

The five basic types of seventh chords found in the music of the common-practice period are illustrated in Example 10.

Example 10

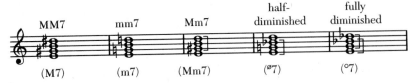

In labeling seventh chords, we must know the type of triad and the size of intervallic 7th above the root. We use two prefixes before the 7 to describe these features, the first indicating the type of triad, the second the size of the 7th. One capital *M* means a major triad, a second one a major 7th. Thus, MM7 stands for a major triad with a major 7th above the root, commonly called a **major seventh chord**. One lowercase *m* means a minor triad, a second one a minor 7th. Thus, mm7 stands for a minor triad with a minor 7th above the root, commonly called a **minor seventh chord.** These two seventh chords are customarily abbreviated as M7 and m7, respectively. The **major-minor seventh chord** (Mm7), a major triad with a minor 7th, uses both capital and lowercase letters, and thus cannot be abbreviated in the same way.

The last two seventh chords in Example 10 are built on diminished triads and therefore use different symbols to denote their chord type. The **half-diminished seventh chord,** abbreviated as ⌀7, contains a minor 7th over the diminished triad. The **fully diminished seventh chord,** abbreviated as °7, contains a diminished 7th. Since the absence or presence of one or more tritones in the various seventh chords is crucial to their identity, we have bracketed the chordal tritones in Example 10.

When the members of seventh chords are rotated, they produce not two but three different inversions. In Example 11, notice that the **third inversion** puts the 7th in the bass.

Example 11

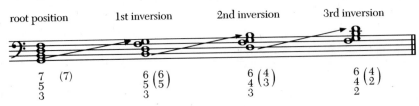

Figured-bass numbers for seventh chords, like those for triads, denote the intervals above the bass voice, and employ appropriate symbols for altered intervals. The standard abbreviations are: ^{7} (root position), $^6_5$ (first inversion), $^4_3$ (second inversion), and $^4_2$ (third inversion). The stability of these chords weakens as we move up through the higher inversions. Analyze the chords resulting from the figured bass in Example 12. (Remember that a slash through a digit raises the pitch a half step, and a solitary accidental alters the third above the bass.)

Example 12

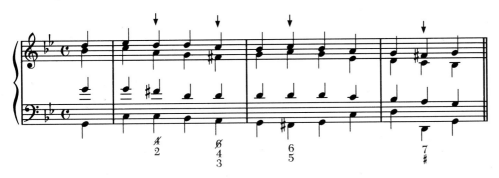

Terms and Concepts for Review

chord	diminished and augmented triads
tertian chord	figured bass *or* thoroughbass
triad	seventh chords:
major and minor triads	major seventh chord (MM7)
root	minor seventh chord (mm7)
root position	major-minor seventh chord (Mm7)
commercial chord symbols	half-diminished seventh chord (ø7)
triad inversions	fully diminished seventh chord (°7)
first and second inversion	third inversion

Musical Texture and Chordal Spacing

I F WE LISTEN CAREFULLY to an orchestral composition, we will notice relationships between a variety of musical elements. Such elements include not only particular combinations of pitches and rhythmic patterns but also density, register, range, timbre, dynamics, and doublings. These relationships, which combine to produce what we call musical **texture,** may be compared to a woven fabric: its thread, color, tactile properties, density of weave, and interplay of patterns. In this chapter, we will address the similarities and differences between individual voice parts in a musical passage and the spatial arrangement of pitches in chords, including doubling of chord members and chord structure.

BASIC CATEGORIES OF TEXTURE

The interactions between separate voice parts produce three basic types of texture: monophonic, homophonic, and contrapuntal. **Monophonic texture**—that is, single-line melody with no accompanying parts—is rather rare in the music of the common-practice period except in brief passages. Most examples of monophonic texture tend to occur either at the opening of a composition, as in Example 1, or at a later climactic point. Observe the use of octave doubling in the Borodin symphony.

Example 1

A. SIBELIUS: SYMPHONY NO. 1, I

B. BORODIN: SYMPHONY NO. 2, I

In music with more than one voice or part, we tend to direct our attention to a single prominent melodic line and relegate the other parts to secondary status. This foreground/background relationship produces **homophonic texture.** There are two types of homophonic texture. In **chordal** or **homorhythmic texture,** all the voices proceed in the same rhythm. We normally focus on the uppermost part, or soprano, as the melody; see the Bizet excerpt in Example 2. Next, examine the two passages from Handel's *Messiah;* how must we reorient our hearing between these two passages?

Example 2

A. BIZET: FARANDOLE FROM *L'ARLÉSIENNE* SUITE NO. 2

B. HANDEL: 4. "AND THE GLORY OF THE LORD" FROM *MESSIAH*

C. HANDEL: "AND THE GLORY OF THE LORD"

In Example 3 Bach has taken a series of block chords and arpeggiated the harmonies with a consistent figuration, producing a kind of figured chordal texture. In fact, in the autograph manuscript of this prelude, Bach wrote out the figuration for only the first few measures and then simply provided the block harmonies for the remainder of the piece. Although the sense of a melody is weakened by the arpeggiation, we probably hear the upper notes of the broken chords as the principal melodic line.

Example 3   BACH: PRELUDE IN C MAJOR FROM *WELL-TEMPERED CLAVIER*, BOOK I

In the second type of homophonic texture, **melody and accompaniment,** the primary line, or melody, is set apart rhythmically and spatially from the background, or accompaniment. A simple tune above a succession of chords, often using a different rhythmic pattern, as in Example 4a, is typical of this texture. In Example 4b, the melody Gounod has added to Bach's Prelude relegates the original arpeggiated texture to an accompanimental role.

Example 4

A.   BIZET: FARANDOLE

B. Bach-Gounod: "Ave Maria"

Contrapuntal texture consists of the simultaneous combination of melodic lines.[1] Here, each voice retains its own melodic contour and rhythmic identity, producing a web of interweaving parts. Rather than concentrating on a single line, the listener tends to switch back and forth between those parts of greater melodic or rhythmic interest. Example 5a illustrates a contrapuntal combination of the two tunes from Examples 2a and 4; Example 5b presents the theme from Example 2 in strict **imitation,** where the theme in one voice part is immediately restated in a different voice part, usually at the octave or 5th.[2]

Example 5

A. Bizet: Farandole

1. Although the term *polyphonic* is often used synonymously with *contrapuntal*, it literally describes any music that features "many voices."
2. Since counterpoint is the most sophisticated form of musical texture, it is often treated as a separate topic from harmony. Appendix 3 provides a brief introduction to the study of species counterpoint, although it cannot hope to do justice to this complex topic. For additional information, the student should consult a current counterpoint text.

B. BIZET: FARANDOLE

The Farandole from Bizet's *L'Arlésienne* Suite No. 2 provides an excellent review of texture. Listen to the entire movement and identify the various types of texture that appear in the music.

STRICT VS. FREE TEXTURE

Some compositions retain a specific number of separate voice parts throughout, in what is known as **strict texture.** The notation of such pieces allows us to keep track of each voice by its individual rests and stemming. (See, for instance, Example 14 of Chapter 26.) Thus, we speak of a two-part invention, a three-part fugue, or a four-part chorale setting.

Other compositions display a **free-voiced texture,** where the number of parts varies. We can find such textures in much of the instrumental music of the Classical period. In a typical Mozart piano sonata, for instance, a phrase may begin in two-voice texture but conclude with a cadence in four voices. (See, for instance, Example 9 of Excursion 1.) In both strict and free texture we must always determine the number of real or actual parts in a passage. What may seem to be a six-voice texture, for example, could consist of only three individual lines, each doubled at the octave.

Let us now turn our attention to **chord voicing**—that is, how chord members are distributed among a specified number of voices. After first concentrating on the spacing and doubling of chord members in four-voice texture, we will examine how complete triads may be implied or suggested through the use of only two voices. All the examples that follow are chordal, note-against-note settings.

FOUR-VOICE TEXTURE

Since the eighteenth century, music theorists have preferred chordal four-voice examples for illustrating basic harmonic progressions. This preference is supported by a great amount of four-voice music literature. Some familiar media for four-voice texture are the choir (soprano, alto, tenor, bass) and the string quartet or string section of the orchestra (violins 1 and 2, viola, and cello/bass).

When writing choral music, we must consider the appropriate range of each vocal part. The normal range, or **tessitura,** of the different voices is shown between the white noteheads in Example 6; the outer fringes of the ranges are indicated by black noteheads.

Example 6

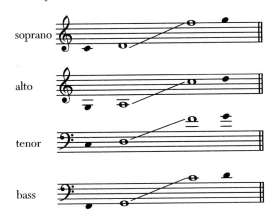

In an *open* or *full score,* with one voice on each staff, the tenor part normally employs the 𝄞 clef, which indicates that the notes sound an octave lower than in the standard treble clef. However, most of the choral four-voice examples in this text employ a condensed score: the soprano and alto parts are written on the treble-clef staff and the tenor and bass parts on the bass-clef staff, each voice having its own individual stemming.

Instrumental ranges are usually wider than vocal ranges. In four-voice keyboard style, the three upper voices are usually written in the treble-clef staff with a common stem for all three notes.

CHORDAL SPACING IN FOUR-VOICE TEXTURE

There are two standard methods of distributing the members of a four-voice chord, which are distinguished by the intervallic distance between the soprano and tenor parts. **Close structure** (C) permits less than an octave between soprano and tenor; consecutive chord members are simply arpeggiated downward from the soprano. In **open structure** (O), there is more than an octave between soprano and tenor, and at least one chord member is usually missing between consecutive voices. First-inversion triads often exhibit exactly an octave between soprano and tenor; we designate this as **open/octave** (O/O) or **neutral structure.** While the interval between consecutive upper parts (soprano–alto and alto–tenor) should not exceed an octave, no restriction is placed on the distance between the tenor and bass. Example 7 shows illustrations of various chord structures.

Example 7

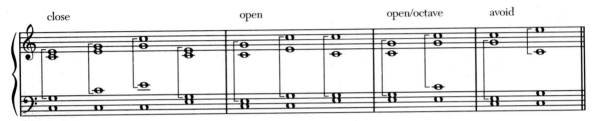

DOUBLING IN FOUR-VOICE CHORDS

Triads in four-voice texture always present questions of doubling, since there are four parts but only three chord members. One chord member must therefore be doubled, either at the unison or at some octave. The following rules reflect the most frequent doublings found in music of the common-practice period; however, other choices may be called for in certain harmonic contexts. The doubled notes are bracketed in Example 8.

Example 8

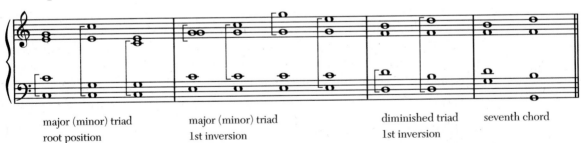

major (minor) triad   major (minor) triad   diminished triad   seventh chord
root position   1st inversion   1st inversion

1. In root-position major and minor triads, double the pitch-class that appears in the bass voice—that is, the root of the chord.
2. In first-inversion major and minor triads, double the pitch-class that appears in the soprano voice, regardless of which chord member it represents.
3. In first-inversion diminished triads (their most common form), double the pitch-class in the bass—that is, the chordal third.

4. In seventh chords, assign each of the four pitch-classes a separate voice part.

During our study of harmony in Part Two, we may modify some of these suggestions for doubling, depending on the progression and chordal context.

VOICE MOVEMENT WITHIN THE SAME TRIAD

Example 9 demonstrates various ways in which voices may move within the same triad.

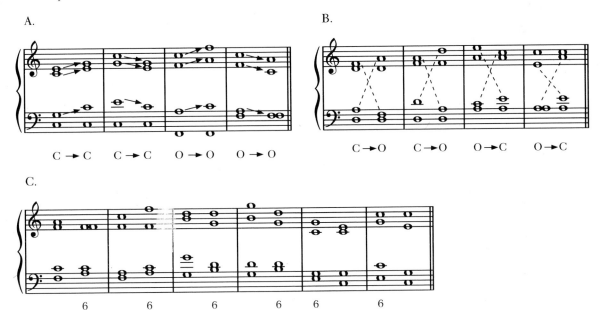

In different positions of a root-position triad, we can either retain or change the chord structure. When the close or open structure is retained (Example 9a), the upper three voices move in the same direction and the same number of chordal members—in other words, if the soprano moves up one chord member, then the alto and tenor do, too. When the structure changes from close to open or from open to close (Example 9b), two of the three upper voices will exchange tones, as indicated by the dotted lines, while the third retains a common tone. When moving from root-position to first-inversion triads or vice versa (Example 9c), the first-inversion chords may exhibit open/octave structure as well. Remember that the soprano is normally doubled at the unison or octave in first-inversion triads. In some of the examples in 9c above, the soprano retains a common tone, while in others the two outer parts move to different chord tones.

Identify each triad in Example 10, noting its root and chord type, inversion, structure, and doubling.

Example 10

CHORDAL IMPLICATION IN TWO-VOICE TEXTURE

Extended passages of two-part texture are frequently encountered in music of the common-practice period. Can you think of some types of pieces that normally employ only two voices? Triads and seventh chords can only be implied in two-voice texture, since the harmonic dyads contain only two potential chord members. A summary of these chordal implications is supplied in Example 11, where the black noteheads complete the implied chord. You may wish to use this example as a reference when dealing with two-part texture.

Example 11

The unison or octave usually occurs at the opening of a phrase or at its cadence, where it suggests the root of a triad. This is likewise true of the perfect 5th; the missing 3rd must be supplied by the tonal context. The most common intervals in the middle of the phrase are the imperfect consonances of 3rds and 6ths. Thirds normally imply root-position triads $(\frac{5}{3})$, although on occasion they may suggest first inversions ($\frac{6}{3}$). Sixths suggest first inversions ($\frac{6}{3}$), although a 6th made up of scale degrees $\hat{5}$ and $\hat{3}$ can also imply a second inversion sonority ($\frac{6}{4}$). When seventh chords are implied by two-voice textures, they are usually inversions of the Mm7th chord: a diminished 5th suggests first inversion ($\frac{6}{5}$), while an augmented 4th suggests third inversion ($\frac{4}{2}$).

Now study the two-part passage in Example 12, identifying the implied chord, root, type, and inversion of each harmonic interval. You can check your answers in the four-voice realization that follows.

Example 12

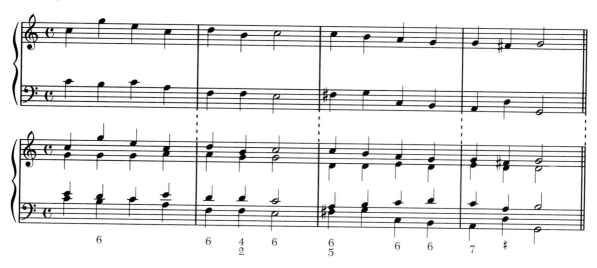

Terms and Concepts for Review

texture
monophonic texture
homophonic texture
   chordal *or* homorhythmic
   melody and accompaniment
contrapuntal texture
imitation

strict *vs.* free-voiced texture
chord voicing
tessitura
close *vs.* open structure
open/octave *or* neutral structure
chordal implication in two-voice texture

Partwriting in Four-Voice Texture

I N CHAPTER 3 we examined some melodies and their long-range tonal connections. In this chapter we will focus on single-line melodic writing and then on the interaction between the melodic or linear features of all the parts in four-voice texture.

CRITERIA FOR MELODIC WRITING

Although it is impossible to formulate a set of rules that will guarantee the composition of a "good melody," we can list some stylistic characteristics of accepted melodic writing in the common-practice period. These include:

1. A predilection toward stepwise motion, with occasional use of melodic leaps: mainly 3rds and 4ths, and less often 5ths, 6ths, and octaves. The larger the interval, the greater the tendency to follow it with motion in the opposite direction.
2. A preference for diatonic intervals, and restricted use of diminished and augmented intervals.
3. The establishing of stable tonal goals at the beginning and the closing cadence of a phrase and a pronounced sense of tonal direction—in

other words, the sensation that the music is moving away from or toward these goals. This results in a well-defined melodic shape or contour.

4. A tendency to reiterate certain rhythmic patterns, which are often associated with reiterated melodic patterns.

Analyze the two melodies in Example 1 using these criteria; do you observe any exceptions to them? (The underlying basis of both tunes is a descending major scale.)

Example 1

A. PUCCINI: "CHE GELIDA MANINA" FROM *LA BOHÈME*

B. HAROLD ARLEN: "OVER THE RAINBOW" FROM *THE WIZARD OF OZ*

MELODIC MOTION BETWEEN VOICES

In multivoiced music we must consider the relative motion produced between two voice parts. There are three basic types of relative motion: (1) **similar motion,** where the voices move in the same melodic direction; (2) **oblique motion,** where one voice remains on the same note while the other moves; and (3) **contrary motion,** where the voices move in opposite directions. **Parallel motion,** a type of similar motion, consists of voices moving in the same direction by the same interval. Contrary motion tends to accentuate the melodic independence of two voices; similar motion—especially in excess—will negate their individuality. Trace the different melodic relations that exist between the soprano and bass voices in Example 2.

Example 2   "Jesu, meine Freude" (Bach chorale harmonization)

A mixture of these motions between two voices is helpful in delineating the separate lines in contrapuntal texture.[1]

VOICE LEADING

When we look at a harmonic setting of a hymn or chorale tune, such as that shown in Example 2, we can see that each of the four voices has its own individual melodic profile. In addition, all the parts combine to produce a musical totality. We call this interaction of the separate voices the **voice leading** of a composition. Just as we previously demonstrated how to un-cover long-range tonal connections in melodies, we will later introduce ana-lytical techniques that will reveal the underlying voice leading of passages of complex music.

In four-voice texture, each voice ideally should exhibit its own distinctive melodic profile. In actual practice, however, the soprano (or "melody") has the greatest degree of melodic freedom or latitude. Since the bass voice must also provide the harmonic foundation, it is sometimes more melodi-cally limited, especially at cadences. The melodic scope of the inner voices (alto and tenor) is further restricted, as they must not only complete the harmonies but also adhere to the rules of chord doubling and structure that we covered in the previous chapter.

Further information on the melodic and harmonic relations between two or more voices may be found in Appendix 3 on Species Counterpoint and in those sections on melody harmonization found in Chapter 11 and following.

1. Refer to Appendix 3 for a fuller discussion of contrapuntal texture.

PARTWRITING

In our presentation of four-voice texture in Chapter 5, we discussed some principles of chord doubling and structure. In the remainder of this chapter we will concentrate on **partwriting,** or how the individual voices move from chord to chord. Music theorists have examined the partwriting techniques of composers of the common-practice period and formulated guidelines or rules that represent their standard procedures, providing us with a workable stylistic foundation for partwriting. These recommendations and restrictions are by no means written in stone, however, and exceptions can and do occur; in such cases we should bear in mind that a particular passage may require its own individual solution, one that may involve unusual procedures.

Partwriting presents a number of potential pitfalls. Four general areas where errors can occur are discussed in this chapter: (1) melodic writing, (2) the melodic motion between perfect intervals, (3) chordal spacing, and (4) chordal doubling. You should consult this discussion frequently as you begin to gain partwriting skills.

ERRORS IN MELODIC WRITING

The linear characteristics of the individual melodic parts are our first concern. As we have stated, stepwise motion prevails. In general, melodic leaps larger than a perfect 5th should be avoided unless they occur within the same harmony (for example, leaping from the root of a seventh chord to its chordal 7th). While octave leaps are possible in the bass, leaps of a 6th are infrequent, and leaps of a 7th should be avoided altogether.

Motion by diminished and augmented intervals requires particular treatment, depending on what the particular interval is. Melodic augmented 2nds and augmented 4ths between different harmonies are discouraged.

Example 3

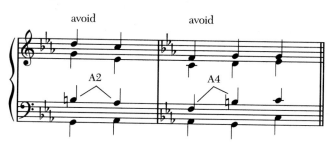

However, a descending diminished 5th or diminished 7th is often found in the bass when the harmonies change, and even an occasional diminished 4th is possible.

Example 4

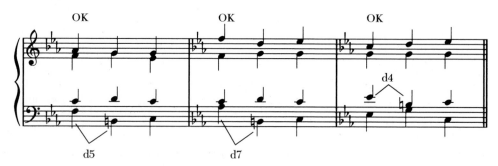

Notice that the melodic intervals shown in Example 4 usually leap to the leading tone ($\hat{7}$), which then resolves to the tonic.

Point out any melodic errors in the following example.

Example 5

PARALLEL, SIMILAR, AND DIRECT PERFECT INTERVALS

Imperfect consonances (3rds and 6ths) may be freely approached and left by contrary, similar, or parallel motion. Melodic motion that involves the perfect consonances (unisons, octaves, and perfect 5ths), on the other hand, is more restricted in the ways in which these intervals are approached and left. Parallel motion between these perfect harmonic intervals generally is avoided in the music of the common-practice period, although it occurs often in folk music and Impressionist compositions.

Example 6

avoid

// 8ves

Parallel unisons and **octaves** are forbidden in four-voice writing, since writing two voices in parallel unisons or octaves reduces the number of voices to only three parts.

Parallel intervals obviously require motion in both voices; thus, octaves that remain stationary are not parallel (Example 7).

Example 7

In orchestral or piano scores, you may encounter melodic lines that have been doubled in octaves, a technique that a composer may use to emphasize or play that part louder. These **octave doublings** are easily distinguishable from parallel octaves because they generally continue for a period of time, as in Example 8, whereas parallel octaves are only incidental partwriting errors, as shown in Example 6.

Example 8

Mark any instances of improper parallel octaves or unisons that you find in the following example.

Example 9

Parallel perfect 5ths, which involves the strongest acoustical interval after the octave, is likewise avoided.

Example 10

Contrary octaves or **5ths** occur when any two voices in the texture produce an octave or 5th and then move in opposite directions to another octave or 5th (Example 11). They should be regarded as parallels and thus avoided.

Example 11

A.   B.

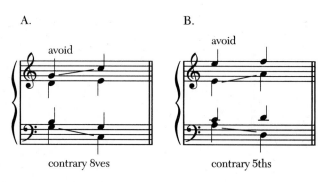

contrary 8ves   contrary 5ths

Similar 5ths occur when one of the 5ths is diminished; they are generally avoided between the soprano and bass on a change of harmony, but they may occur between upper voices (Example 12).

Example 12

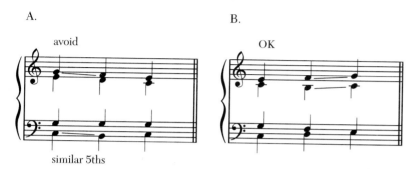

No restriction is placed on parallel 4ths between upper parts; they frequently occur in progressions of successive first-inversions triads (Example 13).

Example 13

Study the passage in Example 14 and point out any errors involving parallels or similar 5ths.

Example 14

Similar motion between the outer parts to an octave or perfect 5th creates what is called a **direct octave** or **direct 5th.** This is normally confined to the cadence (Example 15); its occurrence within the phrase is less common. However, direct octaves and 5ths that involve an inner voice are quite frequent.

Example 15

A.

B.

Use Example 16 as a review, noting all instances of parallel, contrary, similar, or direct octaves and 5ths.

Example 16

CHORDAL SPACING OR STRUCTURE

Examples 17–19 illustrate some potential problems in spacing the voices in a chord. The restricted distance between the soprano and bass will sometimes necessitate close spacing. In choral writing, intervals larger than an octave should not occur between adjacent upper voice parts (soprano–alto and alto–tenor), but are appropriate between tenor and bass.

Example 17

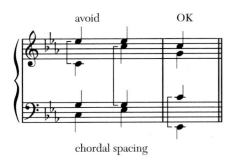

chordal spacing

       Composers generally avoid **voice crossing,** where one part crosses above or below an adjacent voice.

Example 18

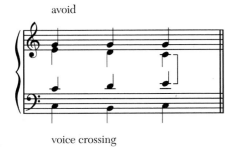

voice crossing

       However, a composer may allow a momentary crossing between the alto and tenor in order to achieve a better melodic line in one of the parts; this can be seen in Bach's alto and tenor parts in Example 19.

Example 19   "Jesu, meine Freude" (Bach chorale harmonization)

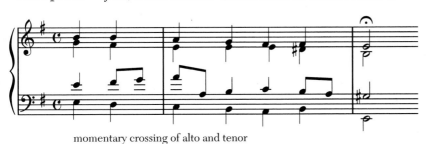

momentary crossing of alto and tenor

       Examples of **voice overlap**—where a note in one part moves higher than the preceding note of the next-higher voice, or lower than the preceding note in the next-lower voice—occasionally appear between the tenor and bass.

Example 20

voice overlap

CHORDAL DOUBLING

The rules for chordal doubling presented in Chapter 5 can be applied to the discussion in this chapter; indeed, we will continually refine these rules throughout this text. Examples 21–23 illustrate some common doubling errors in triads and seventh chords.

Refrain from doubling the more active scale degrees of a key and the tendency tones of a chord. Tones often improperly doubled include the $\hat{7}$ in major and the raised $\hat{6}$ and $\hat{7}$ in minor. Since the leading tone tends to resolve to the tonic, the potential for parallel octaves exists if that scale degree is doubled (Example 21).

Example 21

The final chord of a cadence is occasionally a triad with a **tripled root** and with its 5th omitted; a chord with a tripled root should not be written within the phrase, however (Example 22).

Example 22

While inverted seventh chords almost always include all four chord members, root-position seventh chords must sometimes double the root and omit the 5th in order to avoid parallel 5ths (Example 23).

Example 23

A.   B.

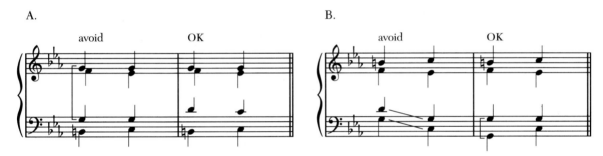

Other common errors include misspelled chords and incorrect figured-bass realizations.

Assuming the figured-bass symbols in Example 24 are correct, point out any partwriting errors—melodic awkwardness, parallels, excessive spacing between voices, improper doublings, misspellings, or other mistakes.

Example 24

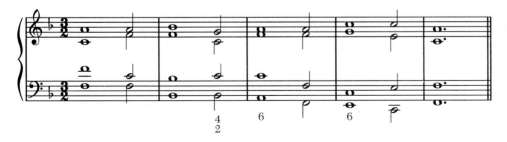

The more frequent partwriting mistakes are summarized below. Take special care to avoid the following, and your partwriting examples will sound expertly crafted!

1. Melodic leaps of diatonic sevenths, as well as most diminished and augmented intervals, especially the augmented 2nd and augmented 4th between different chords.
2. Parallel or contrary unisons, octaves, and perfect 5ths, as well as similar 5ths in the outer voices between different chords; also, when possible, direct octaves between the soprano and bass except at cadences.
3. Intervals larger than an octave between the adjacent upper voices of a chord.
4. Voice crossings.
5. The doubling of tendency tones and altered scale degrees.
6. Incorrect chord spelling and figured-bass realization.

Terms and Concepts for Review

voice leading
partwriting
similar motion
oblique motion
contrary motion
parallel motion
parallel perfect intervals (unisons,
    octaves, perfect 5ths)

contrary octaves and 5ths
similar 5ths
direct octaves and 5ths
voice crossing
voice overlap
octave doubling
tripled root (at cadences)

Melodic Figuration and Dissonance I

NONHARMONIC TONES

I̲N THIS CHAPTER we will explore the role of consonant and dissonant intervals in the interaction between melody and harmony.

When we write a melody over a harmonic background, most of the melodic tones will correspond to the consonant pitch-classes in the supporting chords. Other melodic tones may form dissonant intervals—primarily 2nds, 4ths, 7ths, 9ths, and the tritone—with the prevailing harmony. These are known as **melodic dissonances,** or **nonharmonic** (**nonchord**) **tones.**

Examine the melody in Example 1 and circle the pitch-classes in each measure that are not present in the supporting chord. You will see that the

Example 1

(G   C   G   D/F♯   G   D   G)

melody varies between melodic leaps to consonant tones and stepwise melodic motion with dissonant nonharmonic tones.

The surface characteristics of melodic lines are derived from either **chordal figuration,** which uses only consonant tones of the supporting harmony, or **nonharmonic figuration,** which uses tones dissonant to the supporting harmony. Special notation is necessary to distinguish between these consonant and dissonant tones; we will incorporate two different methods in this chapter. In the music examples, nonharmonic tones will be circled while the chord tones remain in normal notation; refer to Example 7a. In the accompanying reductive analyses, a different procedure will be employed: consonant chord members will be denoted with stemmed black noteheads (♩) and dissonant nonharmonic tones by unstemmed black noteheads (•). Where appropriate, slurs will indicate the melodic connection of the nonchord tone to its adjacent stepwise consonant tone(s). In all cases the melodic notes will be aligned with the underlying harmonies to show the rhythmic placement of the dissonance (on the beat vs. on the offbeat). In this way we can easily ascertain the melodic contours and rhythmic positioning of the different nonharmonic tones. To see how these symbols work, carefully study Example 2 and relate it to Example 1.

Example 2

Now flip back to Example 19 in Chapter 3 (p. 39). In the reductive analysis, can you explain the relationship between the unstemmed and stemmed noteheads?

CHORDAL FIGURATION AND COMPOUND MELODY

Since chordal figuration involves no dissonance, a wide variety of melodic patterns is possible. The passages in Example 3 illustrate both chordal arpeggiation and melodic leaps from chord to chord.

Example 3

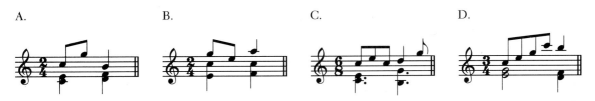

A.   B.   C.   D.

Now play Example 4 and examine its successive reductive analyses.

Example 4   DOMENICO SCARLATTI: SONATA IN F MAJOR, K. 367

A.

B.   (REDUCTION 1)   C.   (REDUCTION 2)

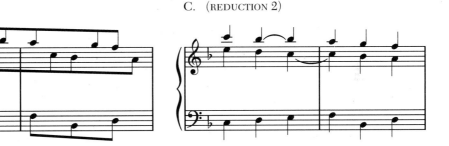

The distribution of pitches in the upper part implies two distinct lines within a single melody; this is an example of what we call **compound melody.** Compound melodies often occur in unaccompanied violin or cello music. Left-hand "Alberti bass" figurations in Classical piano sonatas suggest several different melodic lines using a similar technique.

In Example 5, study the three passages and their analyses; in each case the individual voices of the compound melody exhibit good melodic characteristics and voice leading.

Example 5

A.   BACH: BOURRÉE I FROM CELLO SUITE No. 4   B.   (REDUCTION)

C. BACH: COURANTE FROM CELLO SUITE NO. 3   D. (REDUCTION)

E. HAYDN: PIANO SONATA IN A♭ MAJOR, HOB. XVI:43, I

F. (REDUCTION)

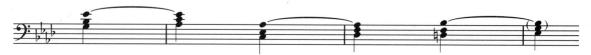

MELODIC DISSONANCE

We traditionally categorize nonharmonic tones according to two criteria: (1) their melodic profile, or how they are approached and left, and (2) their degree of rhythmic accentuation, which results from their metrical placement. Combining these two aspects, we can classify nonharmonic tones into four basic categories:

1. Unaccented-stepwise (US)
2. Unaccented-leaping (UL)
3. Accented-stepwise (AS)
4. Accented-leaping (AL)

Each category in turn contains several specific types of nonchord tones, which will be discussed below. (The accompanying abbreviations will be useful when analyzing actual music.)

UNACCENTED-STEPWISE NONHARMONIC TONES

This first category of nonharmonic tones encompasses three different types of unaccented-stepwise melodic dissonance: passing tones, neighboring tones, and anticipations. All three are approached and resolved by stepwise motion, and all are metrically unaccented.

1. The **unaccented passing tone** (P) bridges the melodic interval of a 3rd, or rarely a 4th. It may move either up or down. Example 6 illustrates passing tones, sometimes in two voices, embellishing a C major triad. The reductive notation includes slurs between the chord tones:

Example 6

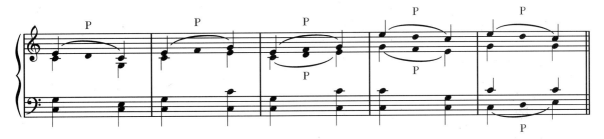

The excerpt from Bach's "St. Anne" Fugue in Example 7 makes frequent use of double passing tones in both similar and contrary motion.

Example 7   BACH: "ST. ANNE" FUGUE FROM *CLAVIERÜBUNG*, BOOK III, BWV 552,2

A.

B.

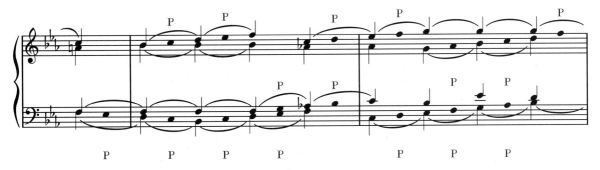

2. The **unaccented neighboring tone** (N) decorates a chord tone by stepwise motion, either above (upper neighbor) or below (lower neighbor): or . Illustrations of single and double neighbors appear in Example 8. Neighboring tones are more static than passing tones, since they return to the same note rather than lead to a new one.

Example 8

The opening melody of the Beethoven sonata movement in Example 9 is based exclusively on upper neighbors.

Example 9   BEETHOVEN: PIANO SONATA IN G MAJOR, OP. 79, III

3. The **anticipation** (A) is aptly named, since it anticipates the next chord tone. It is approached by step from either above or below and falls on an unaccented beat: or . A series of consecutive anticipations is possible, as in Example 10.

Example 10   MOZART: STRING QUARTET IN C MAJOR ("DISSONANT"), K.465, III, MINUET

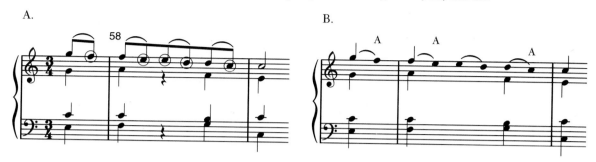

However, this nonchord tone most frequently occurs at cadences, where it precedes the final soprano note (see Example 11).

Example 11   COUPERIN: "LA LUGUBRE," SARABANDE

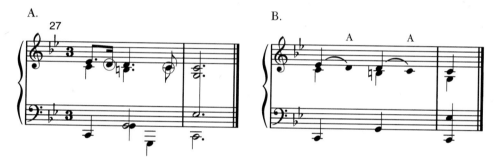

UNACCENTED LEAPING NONHARMONIC TONES

The approach to and resolution of certain unaccented nonchord tones can include a melodic leap to or from the dissonant note. These are less common than the nonharmonic tones that are approached or resolved stepwise. We call leaping unaccented nonharmonic tones **incomplete neighbors** (IN). Two basic melodic contours are possible: the nonharmonic tone maybe approached by step and resolved by leap (IN or IN), or it may be approached by leap and resolved by step (IN or IN). Both contours may combine to produce a **double neighbor** (DN), or **changing tone:** The various incomplete neighbors are illustrated in Example 12.

Example 12

A.

B.

What types of incomplete neighbors are employed in the Handel and Tchaikovsky passages in Example 13?

Example 13

A. HANDEL: ARIA FROM SUITE IN G MAJOR

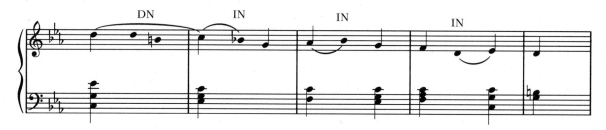

B. TCHAIKOVSKY: WALTZ FROM *SWAN LAKE*, ACT I

ACCENTED-STEPWISE NONHARMONIC TONES

Unlike the nonharmonic tones discussed above, accented-stepwise melodic dissonance immediately attracts our attention. This is not only because of its placement on the beat but also because it delays the resolution to a consonance, which then comes on the offbeat. There are three basic types of accented-stepwise dissonance: passing tones, neighboring tones, and suspensions.

In the Classical period, accented passing tones were often notated with smaller noteheads, indicating their secondary status. See the Mozart excerpt and its realization in Example 14.

Example 14 MOZART: PIANO SONATA IN C MAJOR, K.309, III

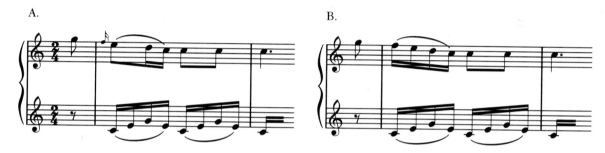

1. **Accented passing tones** (AP) tend to resolve downward.
2. **Accented neighbors** (AN) are less common. Distinguish between the accented passing and neighboring motion in the Minuet passage of Example 15. In the reductive diagram that follows, each dissonant tone is marked with an accent mark (>) to indicate its stressed nature.

Example 15 BACH(?): MINUET FROM ANNA MAGDALENA BACH'S NOTEBOOK, BWV ANH. 114

3. A **suspension** (S or susp.) is an accented dissonance that is held over from the previous beat and resolved downward by step: Because the previous chord tone is held over, the suspension rhythmically delays the following consonance. In Example 16 the tied C^5 forms a 7th and a 4th with the lower voices, resolving with the B^4 to a 6th and 3rd respectively.

Example 16

A.

B.

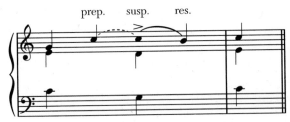

The suspension figure consists of three components: (1) a consonant **preparation** (usually of the same length as the suspended note), (2) the **suspension dissonance** itself (on the beat or on a stressed beat), and (3) its stepwise downward **resolution** to a consonance (on the offbeat or on an unstressed beat).

While suspensions are distinguished by their dissonant relation with the bass voice, they may form dissonances with other voice parts as well. Identify the preparation, suspension, and resolution of each circled suspension in Example 17. What intervals above the bass occur at the point of suspension and its resolution?

Example 17

A.

1. The upward resolution of suspensions will be discussed in Chapter 14, p. 181.

B.

We will return to the topic of suspensions in a more detailed discussion in Chapter 14.

ACCENTED LEAPING NONHARMONIC TONES

In **accented incomplete neighbors** (AIN), the dissonant note is preceded by a leap and resolves stepwise: or . This type of nonchord tone is the least common form of melodic dissonance, partly because of the freedom in the way it is approached. Some typical models are given in Example 18.

Example 18

A.

B.

Circle the accented incomplete neighboring tones in the Weber and Schumann excerpts of Example 19, noting the way they are approached and resolved. The latter passage makes use of some altered scale degrees.

Example 19

A. WEBER: OVERTURE TO *OBERON*

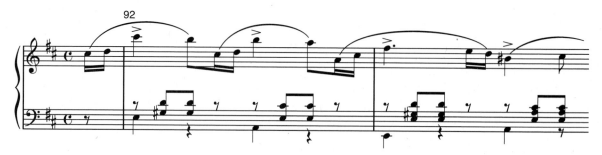

B. SCHUMANN: SYMPHONY NO. 2, III

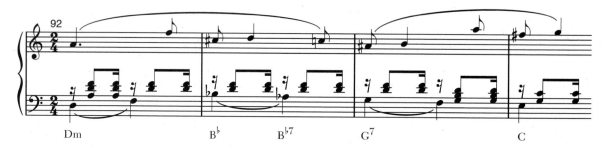

Dm   B♭   B♭⁷   G⁷   C

Historically, the term **appoggiatura** refers to any accented nonharmonic tone that resolves by step. This includes accented passing tones, accented neighboring tones, and accented incomplete neighbors.

FREE TONES

Accented dissonances that resolve by leap are extremely rare. Example 20a shows two accented incomplete neighbors that are approached by step and resolve by leap. A nonharmonic tone that is both approached and resolved by leap is called **free tone.** One occurs in the cello and bass lines at the very end of the third movement of Brahms's Symphony No. 1, where the final cadence moves from an E♭ to an A♭ chord in A♭. The C^3 in the bass is clearly not a part of the $E♭^7$ cadence but rather is a nonharmonic tone approached and resolved by leap.

Example 20

A.

B.   BRAHMS: SYMPHONY NO. 1, OP. 68, III

THE PEDAL POINT

A **pedal point** (often shortened to simply *pedal*) is a bass note that is sustained for a number of measures. (An **inverted pedal** is a long-sustained note in one of the upper voices.) Its name refers to the bass notes played with the pedals of the organ. Since dissonances may result between the pedal note and the chords above it, the pedal point often becomes a nonharmonic tone. Brahms's First Symphony opens with a pedal on the tonic, produced by steady repetition of the same note rather than holding a single note.

Example 21 BRAHMS: SYMPHONY NO. 1, OP. 68, I

THE PERCEPTION OF MELODIC DISSONANCE

The above categories of melodic dissonance are based on the way that we tend to perceive nonharmonic tones in musical passages. Unaccented-stepwise dissonances (passing tones, neighboring tones, and anticipations) are basically decorative in nature. Their rhythmic presence is usually more obvious than their dissonant quality, which often passes almost unnoticed. The melodic leap in unaccented-leaping dissonances (incomplete neighbors) gives the latter more prominence.

Placing these nonharmonic tones on the beat emphasizes their presence by delaying their resolution to consonance. Accented passing tones, accented neighboring tones, and suspensions observe the normal stepwise treatment of dissonance; accented incomplete neighbors are especially conspicuous because of their leaping melodic motion.

Using the same chord progression in the left hand (indicated with commercial symbols), play the four short melodies given in Example 22. Identify the different category of nonharmonic tones in each phrase and compare the musical effect of the various passages.

Example 22

We will return to the topic of melodic dissonance in Chapter 14, where we will examine various successive and simultaneous combinations of nonharmonic tones.

Terms and Concepts for Review

melodic dissonance (nonharmonic *or* nonchord tone)
chordal *and* nonharmonic figuration
compound melody
unaccented passing tone
unaccented neighboring tone
anticipation
incomplete neighbor

double neighbor *or* changing tone
accented passing tone
accented neighbor
suspension
accented incomplete neighbor
appoggiatura
free tone
pedal point

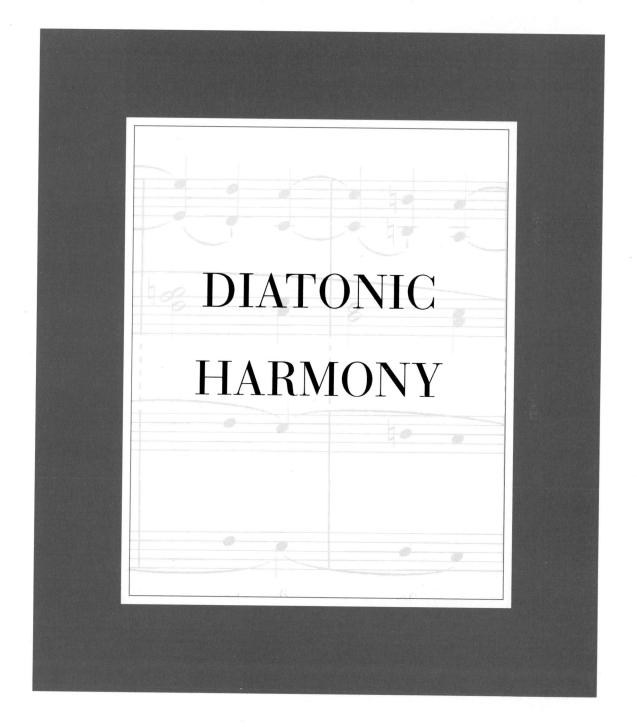

DIATONIC

HARMONY

CHAPTER 8

Introduction
to Diatonic Harmony

WITH THIS CHAPTER we initiate our study of diatonic harmony in the common-practice period. Some chapters in Part Two will focus on the use of specific chords; others will concentrate on more linear issues. In addition, separate chapters will be devoted to rhythm, phrase groupings, modulation, and diatonic sequences.

ASPECTS OF HARMONY

Our examination of diatonic chord progressions grows out of the materials that we reviewed in Part One and embraces a number of different aspects of harmony. The most important of these are the following:

1. The various chord types used in tonal harmony: the four forms of triads (major, minor, diminished, and augmented) and the five forms of seventh chords, as presented in Chapter 4.
2. The use of roman numerals to designate the different scale degrees on which chords are constructed.
3. Root movement, or intervallic distance between the roots of consecutive chords.

4. Melodic figuration, using consonant chord tones and dissonant non-harmonic tones.
5. Partwriting of successive chords in harmonic progressions—that is, the connection between the various voices of chords in succession.
6. Voice leading, or the way in which melodic lines and vertical chords interact within the larger harmonic context.
7. Harmonic tendency, or the tendency of certain chords to progress to certain other chords.
8. Harmonic function, or the way in which chords relate to each other.

We will introduce some of these topics in this chapter; others will be delayed for a fuller discussion in later chapters.

ROMAN NUMERALS

We have previously used commercial chord symbols to identify chord roots, types, and inversions in a harmonic progression. However, these symbols do not provide a way of relating these chords to the tonic of the key. Since the nineteenth century musicians have instead employed **roman numerals** for this purpose. The following two rules dictate how roman numerals are applied to specific harmonies:

1. A roman numeral denotes the scale degree that forms the root of a chord. In the major mode, I designates the triad built on $\hat{1}$, V^7 designates the seventh chord built on $\hat{5}$, and so on. Any chordal inversion is denoted by adding its figured-bass symbol.
2. Capital and lowercase roman numerals are used to indicate the chord type of a harmony. Using the major mode as an example:

capital = major triad (I, IV, V)
lowercase = minor (ii, iii, vi)
lowercase with a superscript ° = diminished (vii°)

Example 1 illustrates the diatonic triads and their roman-numeral designations in both C major and C minor. In the minor mode, note the two forms of subdominant, dominant, and subtonic triads, which make use of both the lowered and raised 6th and 7th scale degrees.

Example 1

A.

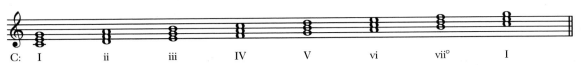

C: I   ii   iii   IV   V   vi   vii°   I

B.

c: i   ii°   III   iv   IV   v   V   VI   VII   vii°   i

In first-inversion triads, the digit ^{6} is appended to the roman numeral; the roman numeral by itself indicates a root-position triad. (Seventh-chord terminology will be presented in Chapters 11 and 13.) Identify the root, chord type, and inversion of each chord in Example 2, and supply the appropriate roman-numeral label below each harmony.

Example 2

A.   B.

F: f:

In themselves, roman numerals tell us little about harmonic function (though they are more descriptive than commercial symbols). To determine how a chord functions, we must understand how it operates in a particular context. In the chapters that follow, we will learn to distinguish between *essential* and *embellishing* chords in harmonic progressions.

CATEGORIES OF HARMONIC TENDENCY

In tonal music, certain chords have a decided inclination to progress to certain other chords. We call this propensity **harmonic tendency.** According to this principle, we may divide the diatonic chords into three basic groups:

tonic, here abbreviated as T (the I chord); **dominant,** here abbreviated as D (including V, vii°, and their seventh chords); and **pre-dominant,** here abbreviated as PD (including IV, ii, and their seventh chords). Those chords in the pre-dominant family (IV and ii) tend to progress to those in the dominant family (V or vii°), which in turn normally progress to the tonic (I). The tendencies of the remaining iii and vi chords are less focused; however, they often precede pre-dominant chords in harmonic progressions. These harmonic tendencies are illustrated in Figure 1; the roman numerals are those of triads in the major mode.

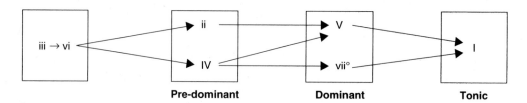

Figure 1   **Pre-dominant**   **Dominant**   **Tonic**

The continual recurrence of certain chord progressions in tonal music has conditioned our sense of harmonic tendency. However, there is also an underlying basis for it. We will focus on two aspects of harmonic tendency: (1) the tendency of an active scale step ($\hat{2}$, $\hat{4}$, $\hat{6}$, or $\hat{7}$) to move to a more stable scale step ($\hat{1}$, $\hat{3}$, or $\hat{5}$), and (2) the frequent occurrence of the movement of chordal roots by descending perfect 5ths. The chords in the dominant family (V, vii°, and their seventh chords) contain the leading tone ($\hat{7}$), which tends to move to the tonic ($\hat{8}$) by stepwise motion. What other common scale step do they share, and where does it tend to move? In addition, the V and V^7 resolve to I by a **root movement** that descends a perfect 5th. In Example 3, play the first two chords (up to the brackets) of each progression and try to imagine how the second chord will resolve to I; then play the third chord to confirm this resolution. All the progressions are in C major.

Example 3

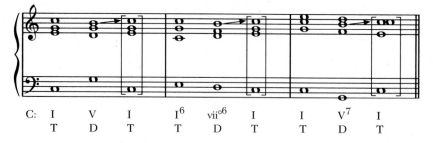

The most active scale degree in the pre-dominant family (IV, ii, and their seventh chords) is $\hat{6}$, which tends to move stepwise downward to $\hat{5}$. Why do you think this inclination is especially strong in the minor mode? The other scale step these harmonies have in common, $\hat{4}$, likewise tends to move to $\hat{5}$. Play through Example 4 exactly as you did in Example 3.

Example 4

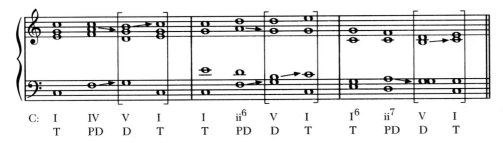

The submediant (vi) and mediant (iii) triads often precede pre-dominant chords and may take part in an extended progression by descending 5ths, as shown in Example 5.

Example 5

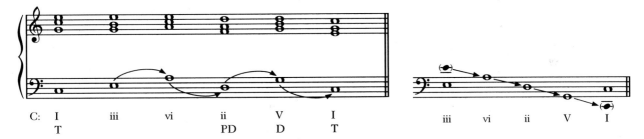

THE INFLUENCE OF MELODIC SEQUENCES
ON HARMONIC TENDENCY

Other forces may influence the harmonic tendency of chords, as shown in Example 6.

Example 6

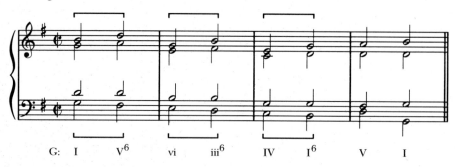

G: I   V⁶   vi   iii⁶   IV   I⁶   V   I

Here some of the pre-dominant chords do not move directly to the dominant (in m. 3, IV moves to I⁶, for example), nor do all the dominant chords move directly to the tonic (in mm. 1 and 2, V⁶ moves to vi). The melodic motion of the outer voices (soprano and bass) often plays an important role in determining the function of a chord within a given context. The progression in Example 6 employs a **sequence**—that is, a short melodic-harmonic pattern (shown here in brackets) that is restated on different scale degrees in succession. The strong linear or contrapuntal direction of the melodic sequence dictates the chordal succession and therefore overrides the chords' normal tendencies.

Although roman numerals provide us with a useful means of expressing harmonic tendency, we should not be misled into thinking that all I chords operate as tonic harmony or all IV chords operate as pre-dominant harmony. It is the musical context that ultimately determines the **harmonic function** of the chords that are used. The preceding discussion presents a very general overview; we will explore this topic in much greater depth in the succeeding chapters. In our study of harmony, we will begin with the tonic and dominant family and then proceed to the pre-dominant chords before concluding with the remaining triads.

HARMONIC MODELS

In order to establish a stylistic standard for how harmonies normally operate in the common-practice period, we will concentrate throughout the text on the common harmonic idioms of tonal music. These idioms will be presented as abstract four-voice harmonic-melodic models, which can be applied to a wide range of compositions. They will use the familiar keys of C major and C minor for easier comprehension and comparison. Less common procedures will be discussed in relation to the norms that we will establish. Those chapters in Part Two that deal with diatonic chords conclude with a summary of partwriting rules and some recommendations for melody harmonization.

The succeeding chapters will also discuss the function of scale degrees and chords in melodic lines and harmonic progressions, as well as provide some analytical methods to express those functions.

While the analyses that we will be producing in the following chapters could be viewed as an end in themselves, in a larger sense they represent the means to an even more important goal—the proper performance of the music. The understanding of how a passage operates provides valuable clues for playing or singing it.

Terms and Concepts for Review

root movement
part-writing *vs.* voice leading
roman numerals
harmonic tendency

tonic, dominant, pre-dominant chords
sequence
harmonic function

Tonic and Dominant Harmony

W<small>E WILL NOW BEGIN</small> to examine the various diatonic chords. In this chapter we will concentrate on root-position tonic and dominant triads and discuss the ways in which they typically function in musical phrases, the partwriting procedures that connect them, and their use in the harmonization of melody.

TONALITY AS THE UNFOLDING OF TONIC HARMONY

Pieces or movements written during the common-practice period tend to exhibit tonal closure: that is, they begin and end with tonic harmony in the same key. In this respect, we may think of **tonality** as the melodic and harmonic extension of the opening tonic triad within the total span of the composition. Each individual composition represents a different way of extending this tonic in musical space and time. Since the process involves both melody (that is, contrapuntal lines) and harmony, we must not consider one to the exclusion of the other.

THE PROLONGATION OF TONIC HARMONY

Pieces based on a single tonic chord are rare, since additional harmonies are usually involved in extending or **prolonging** this harmony. The two excerpts cited in Example 1 are among the few examples from Western literature. Each serves as a prelude to the opening scene of an opera.

Example 1

A. MONTEVERDI: TOCCATA FROM *ORFEO*

B. WAGNER: PRELUDE TO *DAS RHEINGOLD*

The Toccata from Monteverdi's *Orfeo* resembles a festive fanfare. How does the composer manage to sustain this C-major triad? The lengthier Prelude to *Das Rheingold* is a depiction of the Rhine River as a symbol of the primal, unchanging forces of nature. The three brief citations of its main melodic idea illustrate a gradual increase in rhythmic motion and melodic dissonance, although the fundamental Eb-major triad remains constant (for over 200 measures!).

These examples demonstrate three basic ways that a single harmony may be prolonged: by chordal **arpeggiation,** by **passing motion,** or by **neighboring motion.** Example 2 summarizes these techniques in the prolongation of a C-major triad.

Example 2

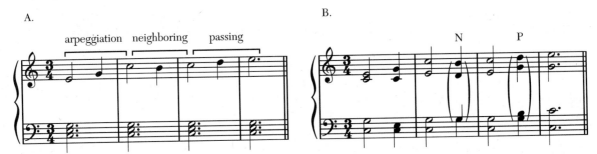

In Example 2a the neighboring B^4 and passing D^5 are dissonant to the underlying tonic harmony. In Example 2b, a variant of this phrase shows that harmonic prolongation may involve other chords as well, chords that are produced by or that support passing and neighboring sonorities.

TONIC AND DOMINANT CHORDS

The two most fundamental chords in tonal music are the tonic and dominant triads. While the **tonic triad** will vary with the mode of a given piece (I in major, i in minor), the **dominant triad** remains a major chord (V) in both modes and always contains a raised leading tone as its middle chord member.[1] As we have seen, this leading tone has a strong tendency to progress to the tonic scale degree.

We will first investigate the tonal opposition or polarity between V and I, and the tendency of the former to resolve to the latter. In musical phrases

---

1. The minor v triad in the minor mode does not normally move directly to tonic: this triad is discussed in Chapter 18, p. 250.

there are two basic types of harmonic motion: I→V–I and I→V. The music proceeds through melodic/harmonic motion (represented by the horizontal arrow) to its final punctuation or cadence. The cadence presents the tonal goal of the phrase: a *closed* cadence ends on I; an *open* cadence ends on V. The initial tonic may be preceded by a dominant upbeat: V͜ I. In Example 3, observe the two types of harmonic motion in the two phrases from "Home on the Range."

Example 3   "HOME ON THE RANGE" (AMERICAN FOLK SONG)

The cadence usually consists essentially of two chords, either V–I or I–V, and certain standard melodic motion in the soprano and bass (see Example 5, below). The most stable triadic form, a root-position triad, is normally used at the cadence. As we introduce additional chords in our study of harmony and focus on how they are used at cadences, we will continue to increase our list of cadential types.

In analytical reductions throughout the rest of this text, we will see that the opening tonic triad and the concluding cadential harmonies of a phrase are of primary importance. Their soprano and bass notes will be stemmed to indicate their significance.

AUTHENTIC CADENCES

The last two notes of the hymn phrases in Example 16 of Chapter 3 represent some of the more common melodic cadences found in tonal music. In Examples 4 and 5 below these notes, as well as the first note of each phrase, are supplied with harmonic settings.

The **perfect authentic** or **closed cadence,** seen in each of the first two excerpts in Example 4, gives us the greatest sense of tonal conclusiveness. Such a cadence displays stepwise soprano motion to the tonic (2̂–1̂ or 7̂–8̂) over the harmonic progression V–I supported by a root movement that leaps from 5̂ to 1̂. The presence of the leading tone in the dominant harmony contributes to our expectation that the V will resolve to I. Notice that the concluding tonic occurs on a relatively strong beat.

Example 4

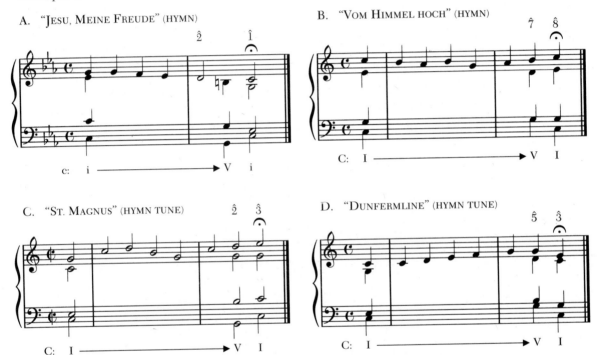

A. "JESU, MEINE FREUDE" (HYMN)

B. "VOM HIMMEL HOCH" (HYMN)

C. "ST. MAGNUS" (HYMN TUNE)

D. "DUNFERMLINE" (HYMN TUNE)

Each of the last two excerpts of Example 4 ends with an **imperfect authentic cadence**—that is, a V–I cadence in which the soprano line does not end on 1̂ (or 8̂). In these cadences the soprano often ends on 3̂, progressing from 2̂ to 3̂ or from 5̂ to 3̂.

HALF CADENCES

In the **half** or **open cadence,** the harmonic motion is reversed: I–V. The soprano generally moves stepwise to the active supertonic or leading-tone degrees—for example, 3̂–2̂ or 8̂–7̂.

Example 5

A. "EISENACH" (HYMN TUNE)

C: I ——————————————————→ I V

B. "LONDON NEW" (HYMN TUNE)

C: I ——————————————————→ I V

The musical effect of a nonconclusive cadence, with its open-ended punctuation, is similar to a grammatical question. In half cadences the metric positioning of tonic and dominant is reversed, with the latter now occurring on a strong beat. Remember that even in the minor mode the dominant chord is still a major triad.

VOICE-LEADING REDUCTIONS

We will find that voice-leading reductions are a convenient way to illustrate the essential tonal anatomy of a phrase or passage. Such reductions strip away the surface melodic and harmonic elaboration in the various voices to reveal the passage's underlying tonal skeleton or framework.

In the overall voice leading of a tonal composition, the initial scale degree of the tonic chord in the soprano, whether it be $\hat{8}$, $\hat{5}$, or $\hat{3}$, tends to descend stepwise through the penultimate $\hat{2}$ to the final $\hat{1}$, as shown in Example 6. These scale degrees are marked with beams.

Example 6

C: I   I   I V I

The bass normally arpeggiates upward from $\hat{1}$ through $\hat{5}$ to the final $\hat{1}$, resulting in an overall progression of I–V–I.[2] Many of the music examples in the text, are based on this same stepwise descent to the tonic (such as $\hat{3}$–$\hat{2}$–$\hat{1}$) in the upper voice; in these instances we will beam together the notes involved in this descent.

Reductive analysis allows us to determine the passage's essential musical features and suggests strategies for its performance. The essential chord tones in the soprano and bass voices form a contrapuntal duet that represents the basic voice leading of the passage. Its fundamental harmonies, indicated with roman numerals, will underlie these voices. Consequently, we will be able to see at a glance the prominent harmonic and melodic features and their interaction.

Observe the following five guidelines when constructing a voice-leading analysis of a musical passage. We will use these procedures to extract the essential voice leading of the music examples in this and later chapters.

1. Label the harmonies with roman numerals, paying special attention to the first chord and the two cadential chords.
2. Circle all nonharmonic tones to expose the chordal notes in the various voices.
3. Now, make a grand piano staff on a sheet of music paper and notate the main chordal tones of the bass voice on the lower staff, eliminating any nonharmonic tones. Use downward stems for all essential bass notes. Add your roman-numeral analysis to this reduction.
4. Repeat step 3's procedure for the soprano voice, notating it on the upper staff. Use upward stems for all essential soprano notes. Since several different chord tones may occur in the soprano over the same harmony, you will have to choose the one tone that produces the best melodic line; in most cases, try to preserve stepwise motion.
5. Use slurs or beams to denote various connections between the pitches in the outer parts. We will explain this procedure throughout the rest of the chapter.

ARPEGGIATED TONIC PROLONGATION WITHIN THE PHRASE

The tonic harmony may be prolonged in a phrase by an arpeggiation of its chordal members. Examine the two passages in Example 7. All nonharmonic tones are circled. In each phrase the tonic chord is extended through to the authentic or half cadence, respectively, as shown by the roman-numeral analysis.

---

2. In works that open with an introduction, the first essential tonic chord in the movement may be delayed until the primary theme is stated.

Example 7

A. HAYDN: PIANO SONATA IN F MAJOR, HOB. XVI:9, III (C. F. PETERS EDITION, 1937)

B. ROSSINI: OVERTURE TO *WILLIAM TELL*

Voice-leading reductions of these passages appear in Example 8. In Example 8a the soprano, following the C^5, moves through $\hat{1}$–$\hat{3}$–$\hat{5}$–$\hat{3}$ within tonic harmony. The framing (that is, first and last) notes of tonic arpeggiations (in this case $\hat{1}$ and $\hat{3}$) should be stemmed and connected by slurs. Why do you think the opening C^5 is unstemmed? The $\hat{3}$ in measure 2 makes a stepwise descent to $\hat{1}$ via $\hat{2}$ at the cadence; this overall $\hat{3}$–$\hat{2}$–$\hat{1}$ is beamed in the example. In arpeggiations of essential dominant harmony, stem only the first note, as in measure 3.

In Example 8b, the arpeggiation of the prolonged tonic chord is handled in a different way. Two $\hat{5}$–$\hat{1}$–$\hat{3}$ arpeggiations, indicated by slurs, are followed by a descent to $\hat{2}$ at the half cadence.

Example 8

A.

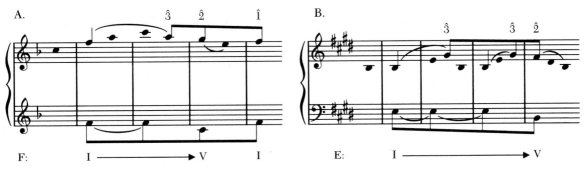

GUIDELINES FOR USING THE ANALYTICAL SYMBOLS

Stem all structural tones of the tonic chord and the cadence; use upward stems for the soprano and downward stems for the bass.

Stem the first and last notes of tonic arpeggiations in the soprano and connect them with slurs.

Stem the first note of dominant arpeggiations and connect the arpeggiation with slurs.

Do not stem pickup or upbeat notes in the dominant chord.

Beam the stemmed notes of the essential voice leading in the outer voices, such as $\hat{3}-\hat{2}-\hat{1}$ (in the soprano) or $\hat{1}-\hat{5}-\hat{1}$ (in the bass).

Using this reductive process as a model, make a voice-leading reduction of the short phrase in Example 9. You can start by sketching in the roman numerals below the staff and then jotting down the opening and cadential tones in the staff that is provided. In your reduction, be sure to include the essential soprano and bass tones—that is, those from all the tonic chords within the phrase as well as from the cadential harmonies at the end of the phrase. How is the cadence approached in the soprano? (The "answer" is given in Example 21 at the end of the chapter.)

Example 9 "DOWN BY THE STATION" (TRADITIONAL)

ESSENTIAL AND EMBELLISHING DOMINANTS WITHIN THE PHRASE

Thus far we have concentrated on the prolongation of the opening tonic harmony and the following cadence. We will now focus on the interior of the phrase, trying to determine which chords there have an **essential** or *primary* function and which chords have an **embellishing** or *secondary* function. Although such judgments are dependent on the context of individual passages, we can establish several general guidelines. For the time being, we will assume that root-position tonic chords are essential harmonies, whether they occur at the cadence or within the phrase; therefore, their bass notes will be stemmed.

Study the model in Example 10.

Example 10

The final V represents the harmonic goal of the phrase. However, the two dominant triads that precede it do not function in the same way; instead, they are embellishing or *linear chords* that result from the neighboring and passing motion in the soprano. We can refer to them as "consonant" passing or neighboring chords, whose role is to prolong the tonic harmony within the phrase. Therefore, our previous indicated harmonic motion of I→V is now expanded to I–(V)–I–(V)–I–V, with the embellishing dominants (in parentheses) extending the original tonic chord.

In our reductive analysis of this phrase (Example 11), the soprano and bass notes of embellishing harmonies are indicated with unstemmed noteheads. As before, the essential tones of the outer parts are stemmed.

Example 11

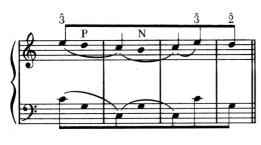

Contrast the unstemmed embellishing dominants with the stemmed cadential V. The overall motion in the upper voice is $\hat{3}–\hat{2}$, shown with beaming.

Now study the pair of phrase models and their accompanying reductions
in Example 12. (All nonharmonic tones are again circled.)

Example 12

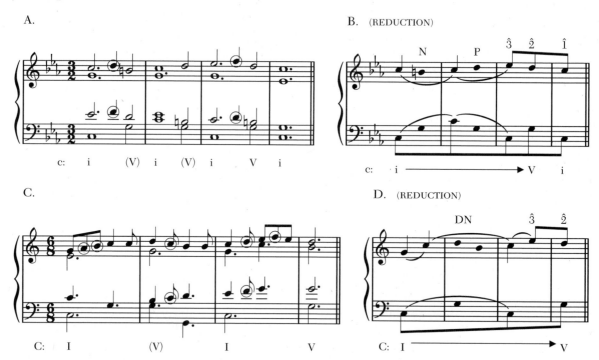

The first model employs two harmonies per measure. Its accompanying
reduction reveals that only the cadential V is essential and that the other V
chords support neighboring ($\hat{8}–\hat{7}–\hat{8}$) and passing ($\hat{1}–\hat{2}–\hat{3}$) motion in the soprano and therefore serve only an embellishing function. We therefore put
the roman-numeral designations of these embellishing harmonies in parentheses. In the second model (Example 12c), the rate of harmonic change is

---

GUIDELINES FOR USING THE ANALYTICAL SYMBOLS

 With embellishing chords, use unstemmed notes in the soprano
and bass and slurs to show voice-leading connections of the
essential harmonies that frame these chords.

one chord per measure. The soprano traces a double neighbor around $\hat{1}$ in measure 2. Since the dominant chords in this measure act to prolong the initial tonic harmony, their noteheads are left unstemmed. The upper voice makes an overall arpeggiation of $\hat{5}-\hat{1}-\hat{3}$) over a prolonged I before descending to $\hat{2}$ in the half cadence. Note that the tonic arpeggiation is not consecutive but is interrupted by an embellishing V; the C^5 in the first and third measures is therefore stemmed, since it acts as the last note of the first arpeggiation and then the first note of the second.

Study the excerpts and their accompanying voice-leading reductions in Example 13, noting the distinction between the essential (stemmed) and embellishing (unstemmed) dominants.

Example 13

A. "PLAINFIELD" (AMERICAN HYMN TUNE)

B. (REDUCTION)

C. BEETHOVEN: "FÜR ELISE," WoO 59

(extended upbeat)

D. (REDUCTION)

E. PALESTRINA: SANCTUS FROM *MISSA PAPAE MARCELLI*

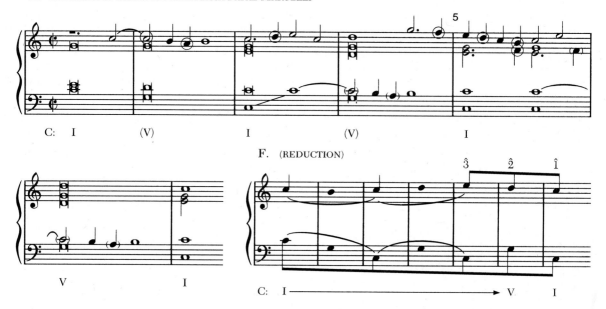

F. (REDUCTION)

In all three reductions, $\hat{3}$ makes a stepwise voice-leading connection to $\hat{2}$, resulting in an overall $\hat{3}$–$\hat{2}$–$\hat{1}$ motion in the soprano. When playing these passages, you should attempt to create a sense of musical flow through the prolonged tonic harmony to the final cadence.

Study the passage in Example 14 and point out any errors in its accompanying voice-leading reduction. Explain any incorrect stemming, slurs, or parentheses around the roman numerals.

Example 14

A.

B. (REDUCTION)

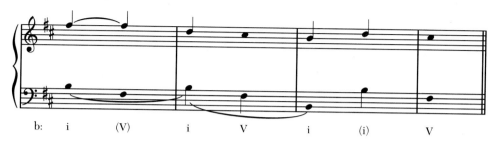

b: i   (V)   i   V   i   (i)   V

Summary of Partwriting Procedures

Our chordal vocabulary so far consists of two root-position triads with their roots a fifth apart: I and V. We will now examine some partwriting procedures involving the melodic connections between these chords. We can apply these principles not only to tonic–dominant progressions but also to any pair of root-position triads whose roots are a perfect 4th or perfect 5th apart. Assuming a doubling of the bass or root in both triads, there are two possible ways of connecting such chords. The first is shown in Examples 15a and 15b, in which the two chords share a common tone (G) and the other upper voices move stepwise in similar motion. The second is shown in Examples 15c and 15d, in which all of the upper parts move in the same direction, two by skip and one by step. The simplest way to write these four progressions is to retain either open (O) or close (C) structure in both chords, as in Examples 15a–15d. If we change the structure between the chords, parallel octaves or 5ths may result, as the two progressions in Example 15e show.

Example 15

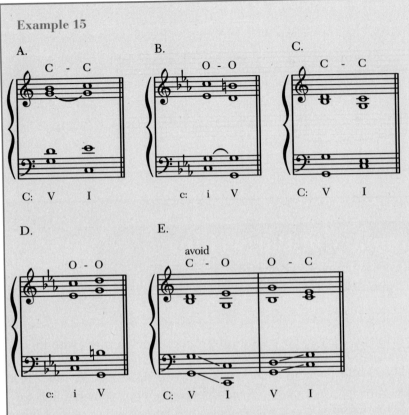

Two exceptions to our rule of "structure retention" are illustrated in Example 16.

Example 16

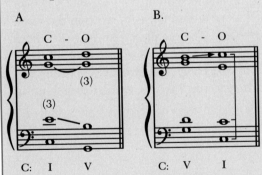

In Example 16a the chordal third of the first triad leaps to the chordal third of the second triad; the change of structure still results in a common tone. In Example 16b the root of the final tonic chord is tripled and its chordal 5th is omitted, allowing the leading tone to resolve directly to the tonic ($\hat{7}$–$\hat{8}$); this tripling of the root normally occurs only in authentic cadences.

Analyze the partwriting in Example 17, following these guidelines. You might also wish to examine the partwriting procedures in Examples 12 and 13.

Example 17

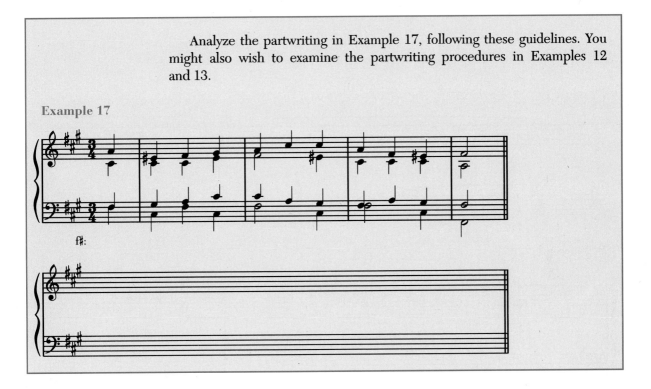

f♯:

Melody Harmonization

Harmonizing melodies allows us to begin to use our knowledge of harmony and voice leading in a creative way, permitting us latitude in choosing harmonies, a bass line, and melodic figuration in the inner voices, and thereby challenging our imagination.

Melodies that can be harmonized with only root-position I and V chords are admittedly rare. Our first step in supplying a harmonic setting for a melody is to scan the tune in order to ascertain which notes are possible chord tones and which notes are nonharmonic. Next we must examine the opening and cadence of each phrase to determine what supporting chords are implied by the melody. Let us start with Stephen Foster's "Oh! Susanna," the first two phrases of which are quoted in Example 18.

The nonharmonic tones in this tune are circled in Example 19. The first phrase opens with tonic harmony, which is prolonged until the half cadence ($\hat{3}$–$\hat{2}$: I→V). The second phrase begins like the first, but the cadence closes on I ($\hat{2}$–$\hat{1}$: I→V–I). The entire tune suggests a tonal scheme that is interrupted and then repeated to its conclusion: $\hat{3}$–$\hat{2}$ // $\hat{3}$–$\hat{2}$–$\hat{1}$.

Example 18 STEPHEN FOSTER: "OH! SUSANNA"

Example 19

If our goal is to create a four-voice harmonization, we can now begin to add the inner parts, using the partwriting procedures we have studied (Example 20). A few passing and neighboring tones can be added in the tenor voice (these are also circled) to create a more elegant line.

Example 20

After examining our finished harmonization in Example 20, play through Examples 18, 19, and 20 as many times as you need to become well acquainted with these partwriting steps.

Example 21 is a reduction of the opening of "Down by the Station" (Example 9), which should be compared with your own reduction.

Example 21

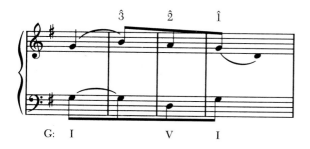

Terms and Concepts for Review

tonality (as expansion of the tonic triad)
harmonic prolongation:
   by arpeggiation
   by passing motion
   by neighboring motion
tonic and dominant chords

authentic or closed cadence (perfect *vs.*
  imperfect)
half *or* open cadence
tonic prolongation
essential *vs.* embellishing chords

Rhythm and Meter II

RHYTHMIC DEVIATIONS
AND METRICAL DISSONANCE

I N THIS CHAPTER we will continue our exploration of rhythm and meter. We will begin by examining some meters and meter signatures that display asymmetrical beat or beat-division groupings. These metrical organizations are only rarely used in common-practice period compositions; they occur more frequently in music composed after 1900. We will then introduce some common rhythmic devices that conflict with the established metrical hierarchy.

ASYMMETRICAL METER

The meters we considered in Chapter 2 display beat groupings or beat divisions by *either* 2 or 3. **Asymmetrical meters** are those that disrupt this regularity by incorporating groupings of *both* 2 and 3. The most common instance is **quintuple meter,** such as $\frac{5}{4}$, where the beats are grouped either 3 + 2 or 2 + 3. Although one particular grouping is usually maintained throughout a passage, we may find alternations or mixing of the two. The Tchaikovsky excerpt in Example 1, which shows a 2 + 3 grouping, suggests a kind of asymmetrical waltz, and was called the "Pegleg Waltz" by contemporary critics.

Example 1 TCHAIKOVSKY: SYMPHONY NO. 6 ("PATHÉTIQUE"), II

What instrument do you think is playing this melody and why?

Examples of compound quintuple meter are practically nonexistent. The Debussy excerpt in Example 2 uses a dotted quarter note as the beat, resulting in a signature of $\frac{15}{8}$.

Example 2 DEBUSSY: "FÊTES" FROM *NOCTURNES*

Asymmetry can also affect the grouping of beat divisions. In a faster $\frac{5}{8}$, the grouping of ♪'s into three and two (♫♫♪ or ♪♫♫) produces a **complex beat division.** This in turn creates "long" and "short" beats of ♩. and ♩; since there are two of these notes in each measure (either ♩.♩ or ♩♩.), we call this meter **complex duple.** In Example 3, the asymmetrical grouping of ♪s effectively pictures the constant ebb and flow of the waves on the beaches of the Isle of the Dead.

Example 3 RACHMANINOFF: *THE ISLE OF THE DEAD*, OP. 29

How many ways can you group the ♪'s of a fast $\frac{7}{8}$, using units of two and three? How many beats are in each measure?

RHYTHMIC DEVIATIONS

In Chapter 2 we established three levels within the metrical hierarchy: beat division, beat, and meter. The meter tends to remain constant throughout a section or piece. This extended regularity establishes a basis of **rhythmic consonance,** to borrow a term from the pitch realm. However, composers may intentionally introduce deviant rhythmic devices that disrupt this prevailing regularity or consonance. These devices can occur at any of the three metrical levels given above.

We call those elements that conflict with the normal beat division **rhythmic dissonance.** In some cases this dissonance may produce only momentary disruptions, while in other cases it may influence long passages. Like dissonant intervals, this momentary dissonance usually "resolves" back to the established rhythmic consonance. The possible range of rhythmic dissonance is considerable, extending from being barely perceptible to destabilizing the entire metrical foundation.

We will introduce various devices that can create rhythmic dissonance, in approximate order of their increasing conflict with the existing meter.

Substituted beat division involves the exchange of simple and compound beat division. This substitution is notated as *triplets* in simple meter (♪♪♪ for ♪♪ in ²⁄₄), as in Example 4, or as *duplets* in compound meter (♪♪ for ♪♪♪ in ⁶⁄₈):[1]

Example 4   WAGNER: "LIEBESTOD" FROM *TRISTAN UND ISOLDE*, ACT III

Since this device occurs within the beat division, it often goes unnoticed by the listener. But on occasion a composer may call our attention to the substitution. In Example 5a the meter is ³⁄₄, but at such a fast tempo that it becomes compound single meter; the ♩. represents the beat, and the ♩ represents the beat division. Although Beethoven actually changes the time signature so as to notate his duplets in terms of ²⁄₂, he could have written them in ³⁄₄ just as well. As Examples 5b and 5c illustrate, substitution may also occur within the subdivision of the beat.

Example 5

A. BEETHOVEN: SYMPHONY NO. 3 ("EROICA"), III

---

1. Duplet division of the dotted-quarter beat in ⁶⁄₈ is written either as ♪♪ or ♩ ♩.

B. RIMSKY-KORSAKOV: *SCHEHERAZADE*, I

C. CHOPIN: NOCTURNE IN F♯ MAJOR, OP. 15, NO. 2

In **superimposed beat division,** both simple and compound division occur simultaneously, producing a literal two-against-three ( ). In the introduction to the Schubert song in Example 6, this superimposition contributes to the depiction of the tempestuous torrent and wind described in the lyric. Chopin incorporates a more difficult figuration of four-against-three sixteenth notes throughout the first section of his *Fantaisie-Impromptu* (Example 6b). In each passage, however, our sense of duple meter remains essentially undisturbed.

Example 6

A. SCHUBERT: "AUFENTHALT" FROM *SCHWANENGESANG*

B. CHOPIN: *FANTAISIE-IMPROMPTU*, OP. 66

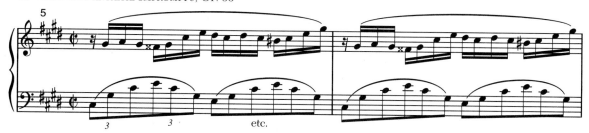

Syncopation shifts longer note durations, which normally occur on metric accents, to unstressed (or weaker) beats or divisions of beats (Example 7). For instance, in a typical ♩ ♫ , the quarter note is displaced and falls on the offbeat: ♪♩ ♪. Syncopation can take place across the bar line or within the measure, and at the level of either the beat or the beat division.

Example 7

The use of accent or *sforzandi* markings (abbreviated *sf* or *sfz*) on weak beats or beat divisions, called **displaced accent,** also creates a conflict with the normal metric accent. In the excerpt in Example 8, Haydn seems intent on calling our attention to the upbeat of each measure by *sforzandi.*

Example 8   HAYDN: SYMPHONY NO. 104 ("LONDON"), III

In performance, avoid making dynamic accents on syncopated notes unless they are specifically called for by the composer (as in the Beethoven passage in Example 5).

METRICAL DISSONANCE

While the devices described above create rhythmic conflicts, they usually do not disturb our overall sense of either the number of beats in a measure or the strong-weak positioning of those beats. However, we will now examine some instances of **metrical dissonance,** where the beat grouping and accentuation are more seriously disrupted. Like their counterparts at the beat and subbeat levels, this "dissonance" is eventually resolved.

Since a measure of $\frac{3}{4}$ and a measure of $\frac{6}{8}$ both contain the equivalent of six eighth notes, it is possible to switch the ♫ ♫ ♫ triple grouping with the ♩♪ ♩♪ duple grouping. This interplay of duple and triple at the metrical level is called **hemiola.** Leonard Bernstein's catchy song "America" (from *West Side Story*) alternates the patterns of 2 and 3: $\frac{6}{8}$ ♩♪ ♫ | ♩♪ ♩♪ | ♩♩♩. In many $\frac{3}{4}$ pieces, the hemiola occurs over the bar line, implying three $\frac{2}{4}$ measures in place of two $\frac{3}{4}$ measures. Tchaikovsky resorts to this device time and time again in his waltz movements.

Example 9   TCHAIKOVSKY: 6. WALTZ FROM *SLEEPING BEAUTY*, ACT II

Some theorists insist that, in order to qualify as a true hemiola, all the voices in the texture must take part in the new apparent meter. In light of this view, which of the two excerpts in Example 10 represents a genuine hemiola?

Example 10

A.   GOUNOD: WALTZ FROM *FAUST*, ACT II

B.   BEETHOVEN: SYMPHONY NO. 4, III

Whereas substituted beat division occurs within the beat, **substituted meter** occurs at the beat or multiple-beat level, resulting in a decided metrical conflict. For instance, in $\frac{2}{4}$ quarter-note triplets can be substituted for the normal pair of quarter-note beats: $\frac{2}{4}$ for . Strauss's "Science" theme in Example 11 employs two different types of triplets, suggesting a $\frac{6}{4}$ grouping in measure 205 and a $\frac{3}{2}$ grouping in measure 206. (From beat 3 of measure 203 through the end of measure 206, how many different pitch-classes appear in this melody? Can you suggest a reason why?)

Example 11   RICHARD STRAUSS: *ALSO SPRACH ZARATHUSTRA*

In Example 12a Brahms divides his ¾ measure into four equal parts (♩. ♩. ♩. ♩.), suggesting a quadruple **superimposed meter,** or four beats in the space of three. He could have also notated it as ♩ ♩ ♩ ♩ (Example 12b).

Example 12   BRAHMS: CLARINET SONATA IN F MINOR, OP. 120, NO. 1, I

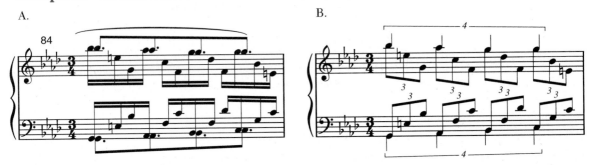

A.

B.

A similar case occurs in Gershwin's song "I've Got Rhythm." The opening measure of the chorus is written as 4/4 ♩. ♩. ♩. ♩. (or 4/4 ♩ ♩ ♩ ♩), although it is usually incorrectly performed as a syncopation: ♩ ♪ ♩ ♩ .

The two excerpts in Example 13 set up more complex **polyrhythmic** relations between the separate voices: 7 against 2 in Example 13a, and 7 against 3 in Example 13b. What other device is implied in the lower part of the Stravinsky excerpt?

Example 13

A.   SCHUMANN: "EUSEBIUS" FROM *CARNAVAL*

B.   STRAVINSKY: *PETROUSHKA*, 1ST TABLEAU (REVISED VERSION)

The simultaneous interaction of two different metric groupings may even produce a feeling of **polymeter.** In Gershwin's "Fascinating Rhythm," successive $\frac{7}{8}$ groupings in the melody (♫ ♫ ♪♩) clash with the continuing $\frac{4}{4}$ accompaniment (♩ ♩ ♩ ♩). Although the song is written in $\frac{4}{4}$, the polymetric conflict suggests that the two meters could be barred separately.

Example 14 GERSHWIN: "FASCINATING RHYTHM," IMPLIED STAGGERED METERS

Metric shift displaces our sense of metric accent forward or backward by one or more beats. Once we have grown accustomed to this displacement of stressed and unstressed beats, a sudden return to the original accentuation can be surprising and even dramatic, as illustrated by the excerpt in Example 15. The notation of Schumann's pompous little march seems at odds with the music's natural feeling of upbeat and downbeat. Although the initial ♩♫ of each phrase occurs on the downbeat, it actually sounds more like an upbeat. At the conclusion of the piece, an "additional" beat, denoted by the arrow, shifts our sense of accentuation and allows the last chord to occur on the downbeat of the final measure. In this passage the implied stressed and unstressed beats are denoted with — and ⌣, respectively.

Example 15 SCHUMANN: "SOLDIER'S MARCH" FROM *ALBUM FOR THE YOUNG*, OP. 68, NO. 2

Changes of meter and meter signature within a passage are rare in the common-practice period. Example 1 in Chapter 5 of the Workbook alternates between $\frac{5}{4}$ and $\frac{6}{4}$; the former implies a grouping of 3 + 2. Such changes

are generally camouflaged by the retention of the same meter signature. In the introduction to his First Symphony (Example 16), Brahms not only employs an elaborate series of implied meter changes but also shifts the metric accent to the second eighth note.

Example 16   BRAHMS: SYMPHONY NO. 1, I

The opening horn solo in Richard Strauss's *Till Eulenspiegel* is an interesting case. The composer takes a simple tune and distorts its rhythm to imply various metric changes, although he continues to employ ⁶⁄₈ as the signature. This musical portrait of the prankster was a kind of self-portrait of Strauss thumbing his nose at the reactionary critics of the time. In Example 17, study Strauss's original ⁶⁄₈ notation and the meter changes it suggests. The eighth-note beat division remains constant throughout.

Example 17   RICHARD STRAUSS: *TILL EULENSPIEGEL'S MERRY PRANKS*, OP. 28

A.   ORIGINAL NOTATION

B.   IMPLIED METER CHANGES

The preceding catalogue of disruptive rhythmic devices only begins to explore this topic. The employment of deviant gestures in one or more aspects of music—rhythm, pitch, texture, and dynamics—may signal the beginning of a process that can stretch over extended passages. In great masterworks their use is never arbitrary, but is instead carefully calculated to play an important role in the musical interplay.

Terms and Concepts for Review

asymmetrical meter
quintuple meter
complex beat division
complex duple meter
rhythmic consonance
rhythmic dissonance
substituted and superimposed beat
   division

syncopation
displaced accent
metrical dissonance
hemiola
substituted and superimposed meter
polyrhythm and polymeter
metric shift
change of meter

The V⁷ and I⁶ Chords

WE WILL CONTINUE to expand our harmonic vocabulary in this chapter by introducing the **dominant seventh chord** (V⁷) and the first-inversion tonic triad (I⁶ or i⁶), and including some suggestions for partwriting and melody harmonization using these new chords.

THE DOMINANT SEVENTH IN ROOT POSITION

The seventh chord built on the dominant (V⁷) is a frequent substitute for V; it intensifies the tendency of the harmony to progress to I. The V⁷ is a major-minor seventh chord (Mm7th) in both modes. For the moment we

Example 1

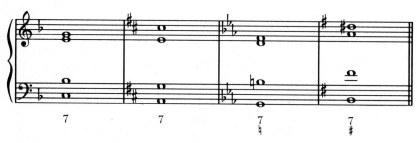

will consider the chord only in its root position. In the major mode its fig-ured-bass notation consists of simply ^{7}, while in the minor mode it is either $^7_{\sharp}$ or $^7_{\natural}$. In what keys do the V⁷'s in Example 1 occur?

PREPARATION AND RESOLUTION OF THE V⁷

Two features of the V⁷ chord merit our special attention. First, its 7th (scale degree $\hat{4}$), which is a legitimate chord tone, nevertheless forms a dissonant interval with its root and requires careful treatment. Therefore, we will leave this particular chord tone unstemmed in our reductions. The approach to and resolution of the chordal 7th are usually accomplished by passing or neighboring motion through scale degrees $\hat{5}-\hat{4}-\hat{3}$ or $\hat{3}-\hat{4}-\hat{3}$. An occasional ascending leap of a 3rd to the chordal 7th is also possible, pro-vided that the first two notes within the incomplete neighboring motion ($\hat{2}-\hat{4}-\hat{3}$) occur within the dominant harmony. Regardless of its preparation, the chordal 7th always resolves downward by step to the 3rd of the tonic triad: $\hat{4}-\hat{3}$. Example 2 illustrates these progressions.

Example 2

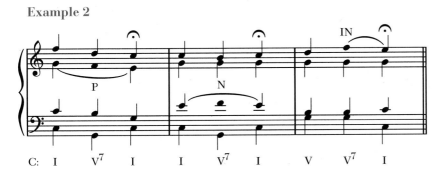

C: I   V⁷   I   I   V⁷   I   V   V⁷   I

Second, the interval between the chordal 3rd and 7th of the V⁷ (scale degrees $\hat{7}$ and $\hat{4}$, respectively) is the unstable tritone. Depending on which voices have the various chord tones, this tritone will appear as either a diminished 5th or an augmented 4th. The former tends to resolve "inward" to a 3rd (Example 3a), while the latter tends to resolve "outward" to a 6th

Example 3

A.

B.

C.

$\hat{7}$ - $\hat{5}$ $\hat{7}$ - $\hat{5}$

C: V⁷   I   C: V⁷   I   C: V⁷   I   V⁷   I

(Example 3b). If, however, both the V⁷ and I are complete chords, we cannot resolve the tritone in this manner. Instead, when the leading tone occurs in the alto or tenor voice, it must skip downward to the dominant ($\hat{7}$–$\hat{5}$) to complete the tonic triad, as in Example 3c.

If $\hat{7}$ occurs in an inner voice and does not move down to $\hat{5}$, one of the chords must be incomplete: either the V⁷, which omits its chordal 5th and doubles its root, or the I, which triples its root; see Example 4. (Remember that the latter occurs only at cadences.)

Example 4

A. INCOMPLETE V⁷

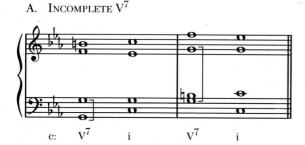

c: V⁷   i   V⁷   i

B. ROOT TRIPLED IN CADENTIAL I

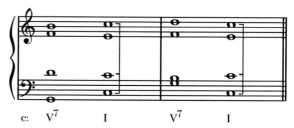

c: V⁷   I   V⁷   I

CADENTIAL AND EMBELLISHING DOMINANT SEVENTHS

We observed in Chapter 9 that the dominant triad may function either as an embellishing chord to prolong the tonic within the phrase, or as an essential chord at the cadence. Although the V⁷ operates in basically the same manner, it rarely appears as the final harmony of a half cadence.

The Schubert excerpt in Example 5 contains some typical uses of the V⁷. Its accompanying voice-leading reduction conforms to the guidelines introduced in Chapter 9 but adds a little twist.

> ### GUIDELINES FOR USING THE ANALYTICAL SYMBOLS
>
> When the soprano (or bass) suggests two distinct voice parts, use different stem directions for each part. In this case only, the stem direction for structural tones does not have to conform with the rule of stemming upward in the soprano and downward in the bass.

Example 5 SCHUBERT: WALTZ IN B MINOR, OP. 18, NO. 6

A.

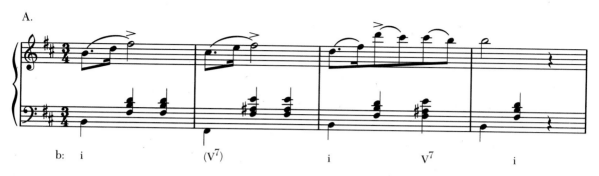

B. (REDUCTION)

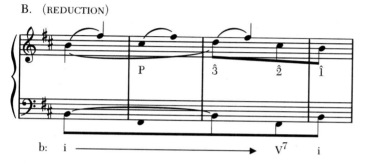

The unstemmed embellishing V^7 in measure 2 supports the passing $\hat{1}$–$\hat{2}$–$\hat{3}$ motion in the soprano, while the last, stemmed V^7 provides the cadential harmony. Near the end of the reduction, the upper voice has been displaced an octave lower to clarify the voice-leading connections. The soprano actually implies two separate layers: the recurring F#⁵ (which resembles an inverted pedal) and a lower line, which links up with a higher one and turns out to be the "real" melody. In this and similar examples, the compound melody is therefore indicated with both upward and downward stems to distinguish the two parts.[1]

Extended alternations of I and V^7 sometimes tend to blur the sense of phrasing. In evoking a gentle lullaby in his dreamy *Berceuse*, Chopin bases his entire composition on a harmonic oscillation between these two harmonies. In Example 6 (next page), the last Ab³ of each measure is the real bass of the V^7. All nonharmonic tones are circled.

The excerpt from the Haydn Scherzo in Example 7 poses two problems for analysis: the wide range of the upper melodic line and a phrase grouping that can be interpreted in two ways. To address the first problem, we can employ in our reductive analysis octave displacements of certain notes in the upper part to facilitate reading the basic voice leading.

1. For examples of other melodies that outline two distinct voices, see Examples 4 and 5 in Chapter 7.

Example 6 CHOPIN: *BERCEUSE,* OP. 57

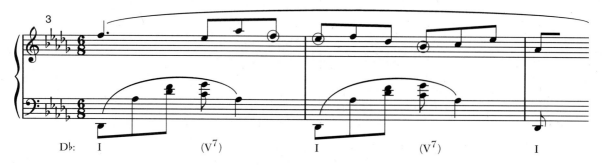

D♭:   I   (V^7)   I   (V^7)   I

Example 7 HAYDN: STRING QUARTET IN E♭ MAJOR ("JOKE"), OP. 33, NO. 2, II

The second problem merits a consideration of two different phrase structures in order to ascertain which is the more appropriate one. At first glance we might divide this passage into two phrases of four measures each. Here, the first four bars outline a movement from I to V^7, with the opening $\hat{3}$ moving eventually to $\hat{4}$ in the first violin. (As before, the framing notes of the tonic arpeggiation in measures 35 and 36 are indicated with stems in the reduction.) This $A\flat^6$ ($\hat{4}$) is then picked up in the second phrase an octave lower (mm. 39–40), where its resolution to G^5 ($\hat{3}$) prepares the $\hat{3}$–$\hat{2}$–$\hat{1}$ cadence over I–V–I in the last two bars.

There are two potential difficulties with this analysis. First, the cadence of our "first phrase" ends with a V^7, whose chordal seventh ($\hat{4}$) is in the soprano; both of these aspects are unusual in half cadences. Second, the tempo of the passage is fast and would produce very short four-bar phrases.

The diagram in Example 7 represents a reduction of the surface musical events of the Haydn passage, with all melodic embellishments and nonharmonic tones removed to reveal the essential notes of the voice leading. We call such surface reductions the **foreground** of the music. The great majority of the voice-leading sketches in this text will consist of such foreground reductions.

If we consider the excerpt instead as a single eight-measure phrase, then the soprano $\hat{4}$ in the middle of the phrase now produces a large-scale neighboring motion ($\hat{3}$–$\hat{4}$–$\hat{3}$) in which the $\hat{4}$ is supported by an embellishing V^7. This preferred interpretation, suggesting a motion of $\hat{3}$–($\hat{4}$)–$\hat{3}$–$\hat{2}$–$\hat{1}$, is shown in Example 8.

Example 8

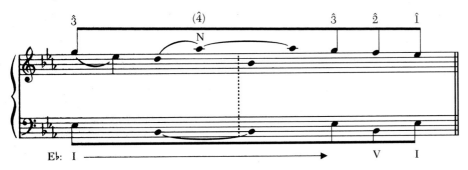

The $\hat{3}$–$\hat{4}$–$\hat{3}$ neighboring motion is a very common long-range embellishment that we will encounter more and more in our analyses.

Notice that our octave displacement now suggests two separate voices in the soprano: G^5–$A\flat^5$ in the upper line and $E\flat^5$–D^5 in the lower; we therefore give the $E\flat$ a downward stem.

Example 8 simplifies even further the surface voice leading shown in Example 7. This additional level of simplification also occurs in Example 15 and throughout subsequent chapters. We call this level of voice-leading reduction the **middleground** of the music. The merits of using two levels of voice-leading reduction will become apparent in Chapter 23, where we will examine the overall voice leading of an entire movement.[2]

THE USE OF THE I⁶ CHORD

Since the soprano and bass parts are the most important structural voices in a musical texture, they should exhibit good melodic characteristics. Up until now we have limited the bass lines in our examples to only the tonic and dominant scale degrees, $\hat{1}$ and $\hat{5}$. Our first step toward composing a more melodically interesting bass line, then, will be to introduce the first-inversion tonic triad, or **I⁶ chord.** Using the mediant ($\hat{3}$) in the bass between $\hat{1}$ and $\hat{5}$ to support the tonic harmony makes it easier to insert passing or neighboring tones, as in Example 9.

Example 9

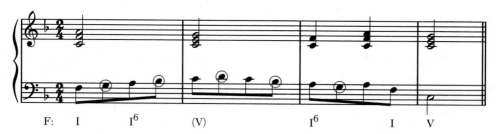

The I⁶ occurs in two basic contexts. First, it may extend the tonic harmony by an arpeggiation, $\hat{1}-\hat{3}-\hat{1}$ or $\hat{3}-\hat{1}-\hat{3}$ in the bass, producing I–I⁶–I or I⁶–I–I⁶. When it serves this function, we do not stem the interior bass note. Second, it may serve as a convenient way to approach or leave V; here we stem the bass note (Examples 10a and 10b). In the third measure of Example 10a, scale degrees $\hat{1}$ and $\hat{3}$ are switched in the outer voices, which creates a **voice exchange** (Example 10b). A voice exchange occurs when the pitch-classes in the outer voices are switched between chords: for instance, when E in the soprano is transferred to E in the bass, and C in the bass is transferred to C in the soprano. This may take place between two consecutive chords, or there may be an intervening embellishing V between the harmonies: I (V) I. We indicate voice exchanges with crossed

---

2. Heinrich Schenker (1868–1935) first used the terms foreground, middleground, and background (the last introduced in this text in Chapter 23) to denote three different structural layers within a tonal composition; see especially his *Free Composition,* 2 vols., trans. Ernst Oster (New York: Longman, 1979). The basis for the analytical method used in this text comes from Schenker's work.

lines. The passage is simplified even further in Example 10c, revealing a longer-range voice exchange that is bridged by an embellishing dominant in measure 2.

Example 10

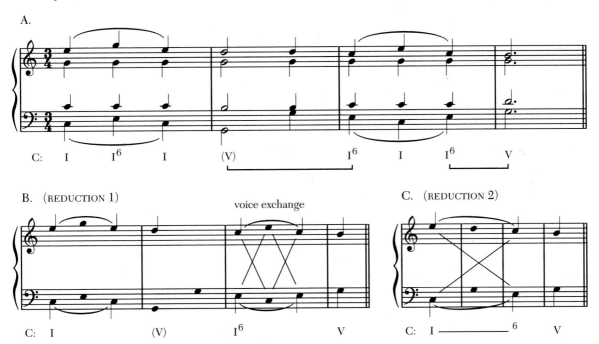

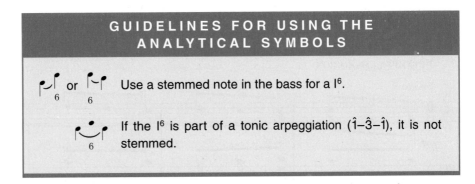

Just as we can reduce a musical excerpt to its essential voice leading, we can elaborate that reduction with various melodic figurations into a passage of interesting music. Example 11 provides two such models as well as possible elaborations of them. Identify the different nonharmonic tones that embellish each model. A further "composing-out" of the second model produces a scherzo-like passage that could be scored effectively for string quartet (Example 11e).

GUIDELINES FOR USING THE ANALYTICAL SYMBOLS

Use a stemmed note in the bass for a I⁶.

If the I⁶ is part of a tonic arpeggiation (1̂–3̂–1̂), it is not stemmed.

Example 11

A. PHRASE MODEL 1

c: i   (V)   i⁶   (V)   i⁶   i   V

B. ELABORATION

C. FURTHER ELABORATION

D. PHRASE MODEL 2

E. ELABORATION

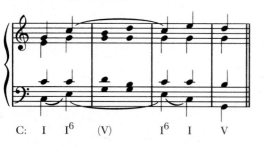

C: I   I⁶   (V)   I⁶   I   V

F. FURTHER ELABORATION

PROLONGATION OF THE DOMINANT BY AN EMBELLISHING I OR I⁶

We have observed how the V and V^7 can prolong the tonic harmony through embellishing motion within the phrase. On occasion, the melodic motion between two dominant chords creates consonant passing or neighboring harmonies that in turn embellish the V. In some cases this embellishing chord may even be a I or I^6. Since the V embellishes the tonic and the secondary I in turn embellishes that V, none of the notes are stemmed. Study the illustration of this technique in Example 12. In the first measure the essential harmony is tonic, I–(V)–I^6; in the third measure it is dominant, V–(I^6)–V.[3] Explain the use of slurs and of stemmed and unstemmed notes, drawing on the explanations of the various reductive symbols in this chapter and in Chapter 9.

Example 12

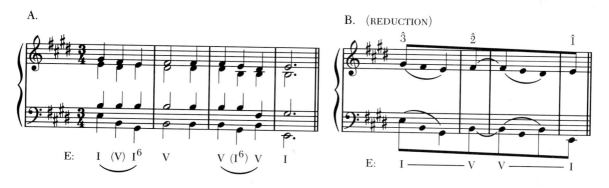

A BRIEF VOICE-LEADING ANALYSIS

The excerpt in Example 13 contains some excellent examples of embellishing dominants and the I^6. In order to understand its underlying voice leading, we will begin by circling the nonharmonic tones and labeling the

Example 13   PURCELL: TRUMPET TUNE IN D MAJOR

3. For a similar illustration of dominant prolongation, see measures 3–4 in Example 2 of Chapter 13.

supporting harmonies with roman numerals. (Since this phrase employs mostly two-voice texture, you may wish to review the topic of implied harmonies found on pp. 58–59 of Chapter 5.) We will assume that the octave A's in measures 1, 2, and 4 imply V chords.

The passage opens with an extensive prolongation of tonic harmony, including no less than four embellishing dominants, leading to the cadential V. We can now sketch in the outer voices in our reduction, using stemmed notes for tonic chord members and the final dominant, and unstemmed notes for the embellishing V harmonies. How are the connective slurs used in Example 14?

Example 14

When the embellishing dominants are eliminated, as in Example 15, we can see that the overall voice leading outlines a $(\hat{5})$–$\hat{3}$–$\hat{2}$ motion in the soprano; the F♯⁴ in measure 3 of Example 14 is displaced an octave in Example 15 to show its obvious connection to the F♯⁵ in the previous and subsequent measures. Since at this level of reduction the I⁶ chords in measures 3 and 4 represent arpeggiations of the tonic, they are not stemmed.

Example 15

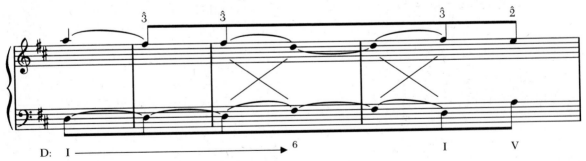

Summary of Partwriting Procedures

As we have seen, the addition of V^7 and I^6 broadens our range of partwriting possibilities. The new procedures that we must follow when using these chords are listed below.

1. The soprano is normally doubled at the octave or unison in the I^6. If $\hat{3}$ appears in both the soprano and bass, the inner voices fill out the remainder of the triad.

Example 16

2. In approaching or leaving V, the I^6 in open/octave structure often acts as a link between close and open structure. (Review the pertinent section in Chapter 5 on retaining or changing structure within the same harmony, such as $I–I^6$ or $I^6–I$.)

Example 17

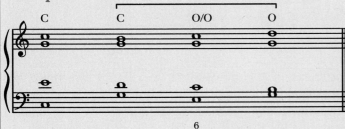

3. The root-position V^7 usually consists of all four chordal members. (For an exception, see item 4 below.) The chordal 7th always resolves downward by step: $\hat{4}–\hat{3}$. It may be prepared by passing, neighboring, or incomplete neighboring motion (see Example 2, p. 127). Never move the root of the V^7 to the 3rd of the tonic triad ($\hat{5}–\hat{3}$), since the simultaneous resolution of the seventh ($\hat{4}–\hat{3}$) will produce undesirable direct octaves.

Example 18

7   6

4. Although the V⁷ and I are usually complete chords, if the soprano moves from $\hat{7}$ to $\hat{8}$ we must use either an incomplete V⁷ (with the 5th omitted and the root doubled) or an incomplete I (with the root tripled), lest parallel 5ths occur.

Example 19

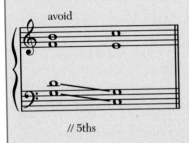

// 5ths

Melody Harmonization

Since our chordal vocabulary is still quite limited, we will start by composing four-voice settings for melodies whose rate of chord change is relatively slow. Always begin by writing in appropriate roman numerals for the opening chord and the final cadence, thereby establishing the tonal framework of the phrase (Example 20).

Example 20   "BRETHREN, WE HAVE MET TO WORSHIP" (HYMN)

A♭:   I   V⁷   I

Then label the remaining harmonies that are implied by the melody while sketching in the bass line, keeping in mind the possibility of using a I⁶ (Example 21).

Example 21

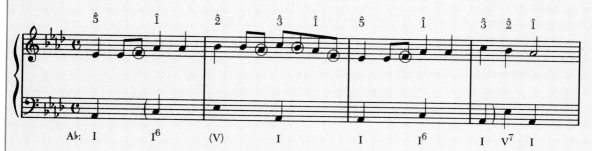

The partwriting of the inner voices completes the harmonization (Example 22).

Example 22

A voice-leading reduction appears in Example 23. Notice the extensive arpeggiation of tonic harmony, using a I⁶, in measures 1–3.

Example 23

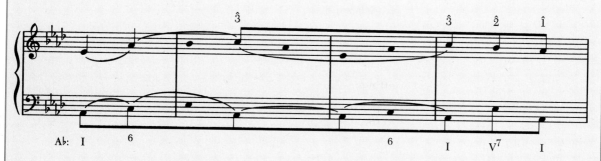

In your own harmonizations, follow this step-by-step procedure as it has been applied to the colonial hymn in Example 20.

Terms and Concepts for Review

dominant seventh chord (V⁷)
preparation and resolution of the V⁷:
   by passing motion
   by neighboring motion
   by incomplete neighboring motion

foreground
middleground
I⁶ chord
voice exchange

Phrase Structure and Grouping

IN CHAPTER 3 we discussed several aspects of melodic phrases and cadences. In this chapter we will explore additional characteristics of musical phrases, ranging from grouping phrases into larger formal units to constructing phrases out of internal motives.[1]

PHRASE LENGTH

Phrases tend to be two, four, or eight bars in length. In the Classical era of Haydn and Mozart, the four-measure phrase was the unquestioned norm; in the earlier Baroque period of Bach and Handel, however, a more fluid sense of phrasing prevailed.

When determining where a given phrase ends, we must consider two factors: the tempo of the phrase and the strength of its cadence. Most phrases range in duration from about six to twelve seconds. An eight-measure grouping in a fast tempo and a two-measure grouping in a slow tempo may both last the same length of time. Phrases normally conclude

---

1. For information on the formal designs and tonal structures of longer compositions, consult the two "Excursion" sections in this text (pp. 269–88 and 439–59).

with a well-defined cadence; therefore, when a cadence is absent or very weak we should suspect that the phrase continues beyond it. As we observed in Example 7 of Chapter 11, the weak "cadence" in measure 38 of the Haydn Scherzo actually represents a continuation of the phrase; the real cadence occurs in measures 41 and 42. The Scherzo's fast tempo likewise suggests a single eight-measure phrase.

THE PERIOD, DOUBLE PERIOD, AND PHRASE GROUP

In homophonic compositions, phrases tend to group themselves into larger units. Two phrases are often linked to create a **period.** The two phrases in a period are interdependent; the first or **antecedent phrase** often finds its completion, or tonal fulfillment, in the second or **consequent phrase.**

We classify periods according to their harmonic scheme, or **tonal structure,** and their thematic relationships, or **melodic design.** Beethoven's "Ode to Joy" theme appears as Example 1, with roman numerals denoting the framing harmonies of the phrases.

Example 1   BEETHOVEN: SYMPHONY NO. 9 ("CHORAL"), IV, "ODE TO JOY" THEME

The half cadence at the end of the antecedent phrase, with $\hat{2}$ in the melody, creates the expectation that the following consequent phrase will close on an authentic cadence with $\hat{1}$. This "question–answer" pairing normally employs one of two basic schemes. In the case of the Beethoven theme, the harmonic motion is I→V, I→V–I. The second design, illustrated by the Mozart excerpt in Example 2, outlines I→V, V→I.

Example 2   MOZART: STRING QUARTET IN C MAJOR ("DISSONANT"), K.465, III, TRIO

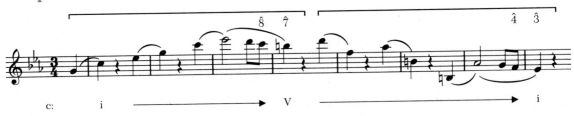

In the Mozart excerpt the dominant is maintained across the phrases. In the first cadence, the soprano moves from $\hat{8}$ to $\hat{7}$; in the second, it moves from $\hat{4}$ to $\hat{3}$. This melodic pairing is a favorite idiom of the Classical period.

In instances where both phrases conclude with an authentic cadence, the first phrase is usually less dependent on the second for its tonal completion. Nevertheless, in Example 3 the concluding $\hat{1}$ in the melody gives a sense of finality that is missing in the $\hat{3}$ of the first cadence.

Example 3   "THE CARNIVAL OF VENICE" (TRADITIONAL)

These complementary relationships between two phrases may also occur at higher formal levels. For instance, if a period ends on V rather than I, the need for its eventual resolution to the tonic frequently requires an additional period; this results in a **double period.** In Example 4 the half cadence on $\hat{2}$ at the end of the antecedent period is resolved by the authentic cadence on $\hat{1}$ at the end of the consequent period.

Example 4   SAINT-SAËNS: PIANO CONCERTO NO. 4, II

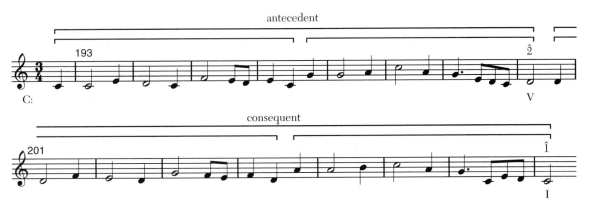

This relationship of phrase to period in the above passage creates a formal hierarchy—that is, an ordered system in which units combine to create progressively more important units (Figure 1). Similar hierarchical designs are common in short homophonic pieces.

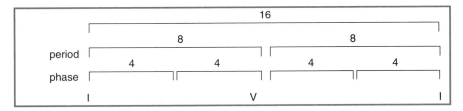

Figure 1

We can also classify periods according to thematic design—that is, the similarity or difference of their melodic content. When the two phrases of a period open with an identical or similar melodic idea, we refer to it as a **parallel period**; see Example 5. Do the passages in Examples 1 and 2 constitute parallel periods?

Example 5   BIZET: HABANERA FROM *CARMEN*, ACT I

Nonparallel periods as in Example 6, are also common.

Example 6   GLUCK: 29. BALLET FROM *ORFEO ED EURIDICE*, ACT II

We use capital letters to denote similarities and differences of successive phrases within periods, and the prime sign (') to indicate a modified repetition. Thus, phrase A' is a modified version of phrase A, whereas phrase B is substantially different from either A or A'. Examine the passages in the previous examples and mark their phrases with the appropriate capital letters. Does Example 4 qualify as a parallel double period?

We may also find phrases grouped together into units of three; these units are called **phrase groups.** The tune in Example 7 is a typical example.

Example 7   FRANZ GRÜBER: "SILENT NIGHT"

In shorter vocal genres, such as folk songs or hymns, each stanza or strophe of text is usually set to the same music, resulting in what is called **strophic form.** Each stanza may consist of similar and contrasting phrases (or periods). Example 8 illustrates a common stanzaic form: the four phrases of this tune produce an A A' B A' form, in which B is open and A' is closed tonally.

Example 8   "AMSTERDAM" (HYMN TUNE)

Compositions that are not more than four phrases in length may also exhibit a two-part or **binary form:** A B, or A A' B B'. Binary pieces are not especially common, probably because the original thematic idea does not return at the end. Both sections (A and B) will usually close in the tonic (Example 9).

Example 9   BRAHMS: "WIEGENLIED," OP. 49, NO. 4

PHRASE PERIODICITY

Music has been associated with word and dance throughout its long history. The repetitive nature of metrical poetry and dance patterns is often reflected in the periodic phrasing of their musical settings. The repetition of musical phrases of equal length results in **periodicity**—that is, the regular recurrence of events or periods (refer to Figure 1, page 143). The complete "Ode to Joy" theme (Example 10) aptly illustrates a periodicity of four-measure phrases.

Example 10 BEETHOVEN: SYMPHONY NO. 9 ("CHORAL"), IV, "ODE TO JOY" THEME

What is the form of this tune?

PHRASE EXTENSION, CONTRACTION, AND ELISION

Although composers may construct an entire piece from a succession of four-measure phrases, they more often provide the listener with some needed relief from the predictability of the established periodicity. Several means are at their disposal. A phrase may be lengthened by a **cadential extension** at its end or by an **internal extension** in the middle. In either procedure, the elongation may result from the addition or repetition of material or from some type of rhythmic augmentation. A phrase may also be **contracted,** by compressing earlier material, or **truncated,** by deleting material. **Phrase elision** occurs when the cadence of one phrase overlaps the beginning of the next. This dovetailing effect (denoted by overlapping brackets in the examples) often produces a seamless rhythmic flow.

Examine the four passages in Example 11 and determine which of these devices has been used in each.

Example 11

A. BACH(?): MARCH IN D MAJOR FROM *ANNA MAGDALENA BACH'S NOTEBOOK*

B. LISZT: *LES PRÉLUDES*

C. BARTÓK: *MIKROKOSMOS*, VOL. 1, NO. 7

D. HAYDN: SYMPHONY NO. 101 ("CLOCK"), IV

VARIED PHRASE LENGTHS

Extended periodicity may be relieved simply by varying the lengths of the phrases—for instance, making some phrases four measures long and others only three measures long. In choosing the "St. Anthony Chorale" as the basis for a set of variations, Brahms was doubtless fascinated by the different phrase lengths in the tune (Example 12a).

Example 12 BRAHMS: *VARIATIONS ON A THEME OF HAYDN*, OP. 56A

A.

B. (REDUCTION)

The tune's composer inserted an extra measure (denoted in the music by brackets) in each of the two phrases of the first repeated section, establishing a five-bar periodicity. The middle section that begins in measure 11 switches to a more regular four-bar grouping. The original grouping returns with the restatement of the original theme in the tonic (m. 19), although this grouping is cut short by an elision of the end of this phrase with the beginning of the "codetta." A cadential extension beginning in measure 27 lengthens the codetta to seven bars. A sketch of this piece's basic tonal scheme (Example 12b) shows that the more important half cadence occurs at the end of the second period in measure 18 (see the downward arrow), just prior to the return of the original theme back in the tonic.

THE INTERNAL ANATOMY OF PHRASES: SUB-PHRASES AND MOTIVES

Some melodic phrases represent a single unified musical idea that resists division. In Example 13, the tonal and rhythmic motion of the phrase continues to its cadence. Play this tune and stop anywhere in the middle; do you feel a sense of closure?

Example 13   WAGNER: "HYMN TO VENUS" FROM *TANNHÄUSER*, ACT II

On the other hand, some phrases divide easily into smaller units. The pair of four-measure phrases in Example 14 divide into a similar pair of distinct two-measure **sub-phrases.**

Example 14   VERDI: "LA DONNA È MOBILE" FROM *RIGOLETTO*, ACT IV

Whereas the Verdi aria given above features a 2 + 2–measure sub-grouping within each phrase, the melody in the following Mozart sonata (Example 15) displays a 1 + 1 + 2–measure partitioning.

Example 15   MOZART: PIANO SONATA IN A MAJOR, K.331, I

The relationship of melodic parts in the Mozart excerpt illustrates what is called **sentence form:** the altered repetition of the original idea—here, a step lower (m. 2)—followed by a motion toward the cadence (m. 3–4). This produces an overall design of A A' → cadence. Sentence design, which is extremely common in the Classical era, may also be found at the level of the phrase or period, as in Example 16.

Example 16   MOZART: CLARINET CONCERTO, K.622, II

In some phrases we may observe repetitions or modifications of a single short melodic fragment. This melodic fragment, which is usually not longer than one measure in length, is identifiable by its distinctive pitch profile and rhythmic characteristics. We call such a short idea a **motive.** Motives are always subjected to some kind of developmental treatment to "fill out" the remainder of the phrase; the most common of these treatments are listed below:

1. **Repetition:** an exact or modified restatement of the motive on the same pitch level.

Example 17

2. **Sequence:** a repetition of a motive on a different scale degree. This device is usually limited to two repetitions following the original motive.

Example 18

3. **Melodic inversion:** a statement of the melody in which it is literally turned upside down interval for interval. This device is also called *melodic mirroring.*

Example 19

4. **Rhythmic modification:** an alteration of the melody's rhythm, often according to some strict proportion. Two standard types are **augmentation,** in which each note value is multiplied by a given figure (usually two), and **diminution,** in which each note value is reduced by a given proportion (usually one-half).

Example 20

5. **Alteration of the harmonic setting:** a resetting that imparts a different character to the original motive.

Example 21

The passages in Example 22 illustrate some ways in which phrases may be constructed out of motives.

Example 22

A. HANDEL: ALLEGRO FROM *WATER MUSIC* SUITE NO. 1 IN F MAJOR

B. CHOPIN: *GRANDE VALSE BRILLANTE,* OP. 18

C. TCHAIKOVSKY: SYMPHONY NO. 6 ("PATHÉTIQUE"), I

D. BEETHOVEN: SYMPHONY NO. 6 ("PASTORAL"), I

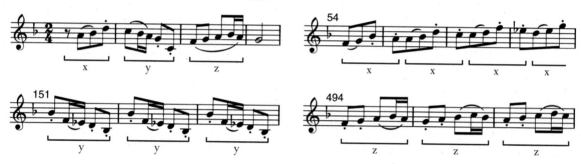

The Handel tune (Example 22a) is based on a single motive (denoted with an *x*) and its descending stepwise sequences. The sequential three-note motive of the initial phrase of the Chopin waltz is freely inverted in the consequent phrase (Example 22b). The Tchaikovsky excerpt exhibits a gradual rhythmic compression of the original four-note motive (Example 22c); what interval pattern is formed by its ascent? The three separate motives that make up the opening theme of Beethoven's *Pastoral Symphony* (*x, y, z*) are later subjected to their own individual motivic treatment (Example 22d).

We tend to recognize a motive in its subsequent recurrences by its distinctive melodic shape and rhythm. However, a composer may choose to retain only its pitches or its rhythm when developing it. A **pitch motive** consists of a short series of distinctive melodic intervals, which may be restated or transposed in a variety of rhythms. This technique, called **thematic transformation,** is a favorite procedure of Liszt and Richard Strauss. In Example 23, observe the magical metamorphosis of the six-note pitch motive (Example 23a) from the plucky little theme that opens *Don Quixote* (Example 23b) to the peaceful resignation of the theme for the final death scene, where the old knight regains his senses (Example 23c).

Example 23 RICHARD STRAUSS: *DON QUIXOTE*

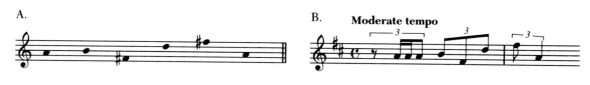

A composer may instead employ a **rhythmic motive,** whose melodic contour may continually change while its characteristic rhythm is strictly retained. Examine the themes from Beethoven's Fifth Symphony in Example 24; what do they all have in common?

Example 24 BEETHOVEN: SYMPHONY NO. 5, I–IV

A. 1ST MOVEMENT

B. 2ND MOVEMENT

C. 3RD MOVEMENT

D. 4TH MOVEMENT

Terms and Concepts for Review

phrase length

period

antecedent *vs.* consequent phrase

tonal structure *vs.* melodic design

double period

parallel *vs.* nonparallel period

phrase group

strophic form

binary form

phrase periodicity

phrase extension, contraction (truncation), elision

varied phrase lengths

sub-phrase

sentence form

motive

development of motives:
    repetition
    sequence
    inversion
    rhythmic modification (augmentation *or* diminution)
    alteration of the harmonic setting

pitch motive

thematic transformation

rhythmic motive

Linear Dominant Chords

V^6, VII$^{\circ 6}$, AND INVERSIONS OF V^7

IN THE PRECEDING CHAPTERS on harmony we have highlighted the important role that the outer voices play in a musical texture. The soprano usually carries the principal melodic line, and the bass, which also should exhibit good melodic characteristics, provides the foundation for the harmony. Until now we have limited the use of functional scale degrees in the bass voice to $\hat{1}$, $\hat{3}$, and $\hat{5}$. In this chapter we will introduce other dominant-function chords that will allow us to compose more melodically interesting bass lines. They will also permit richer contrapuntal relationships and a more varied set of harmonic intervals between the outer parts.

These new chords are the first inversions of the dominant and leading-tone triads (V^6 and vii$^{\circ 6}$) and the various inversions of the dominant seventh: V$^6_5$ (first inversion), V$^4_3$ (second inversion), and V$^4_2$ (third inversion).[1] They are shown in Example 1, grouped by common bass note. (Other positions, such as the V$^6_4$ and the vii$^\circ$, will be discussed in later chapters.) All these dominant-family harmonies, like our previous V and V^7, contain the active scale degrees $\hat{7}$ and $\hat{2}$, which tend to move stepwise to $\hat{1}$ and $\hat{3}$ in the tonic triad. The $\hat{4}$ in the bass of the V$^4_2$ tends to move to $\hat{3}$. But unlike the V and

---

1. You may wish to review the figured-bass symbols for seventh chords in Chapter 4.

V^7, the dominant-family chords that we will introduce in this chapter are all embellishing chords that function as contrapuntal or linear passing or neighboring harmonies.

Example 1

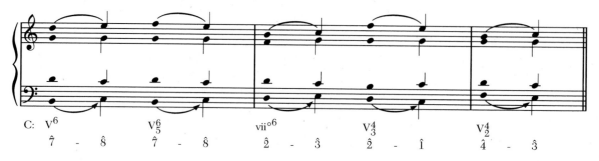

THE INFLUENCE OF CONTEXT ON CHORD FUNCTION

Before examining the nature of these chords, we will consider the effect of the voice leading in a passage on the function of its harmonies. Example 2 gives the opening of the slow movement from a Beethoven piano sonata.

Example 2   BEETHOVEN: PIANO SONATA IN C MINOR, OP. 10, NO. 1, II

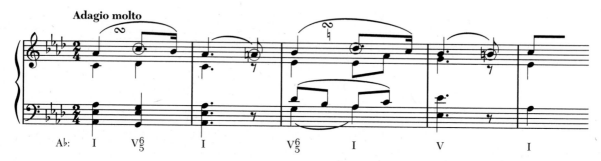

We could explain the musical content of these four measures simply by labeling the chords with roman numerals and circling the nonharmonic tones, as we have done here. But this type of analysis implies that those chords labeled with the same roman numeral are of equal harmonic importance. This exclusively "vertical" approach, by disregarding the melodic influence of the outer voices, gives us a misleading idea of the true function of the chords, in relation both to each other and to the entire passage.

Now study the voice-leading reduction in Example 3.

Example 3

A.

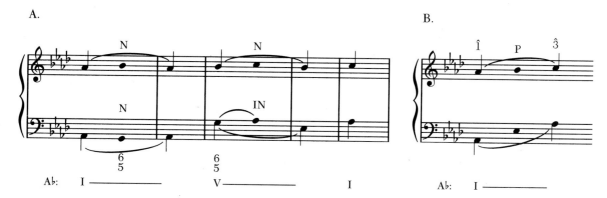

B.

The soprano neighboring motion in the first two measures ($\hat{1}$–$\hat{2}$–$\hat{1}$) is restated a step higher in measures 3–4 ($\hat{2}$–$\hat{3}$–$\hat{2}$). The first setting of this motive embellishes the primary tonic harmony with a neighboring dominant chord, while the second setting embellishes the primary dominant harmony with a I chord. Therefore, the two "tonic" chords in measures 1 and 3 are not functionally equivalent. The first (stemmed) is an essential, or structural, chord; the latter (unstemmed) is not. When we reduce this passage even further (Example 3b), we reveal a larger-scale prolongation of the tonic, in which $\hat{1}$ moves up to $\hat{3}$ via the passing $\hat{2}$. At this level of reduction, the passing V is an embellishing or linear harmony, and is left unstemmed.

This type of reductive analysis reveals the anatomy of a musical passage by highlighting the interaction of melodic and harmonic forces. These analyses can also provide a blueprint or strategy for performance: once we know how a musical passage operates, we have established a basis for how to play or sing it. Always try to perform the music excerpts in this book *and their accompanying reductions,* listening for how the latter reveal the underlying structures of the former. Even though many of the examples are little more than a phrase in length, they can provide a foundation for interpreting more extended passages.

EMBELLISHING DOMINANT CHORDS

Reductive analysis will play an important role in our current discussion of the remaining **embellishing dominant** chords, which embellish the tonic chord by their passing, neighboring, or incomplete neighboring motion in the bass. These chords often occur in the interior of a phrase but only rarely in the cadence, which normally includes the more stable I (or I⁶) and V in root position. Their function derives from both the scale degree in the bass on which they are built ($\hat{7}$, $\hat{2}$, or $\hat{4}$) and their melodic motion, which acts as passing or neighboring motion around $\hat{1}$ and $\hat{3}$ of the tonic harmony.

We will use a series of chordal phrases to demonstrate the function of the individual dominant-family chords. Each phrase in Examples 4–8 moves from I (or i) to V and exhibits the overall soprano motion $\hat{3} \rightarrow \hat{3} - \hat{2}$.

Dominant-family inversions embellish the tonic harmony in various ways. Some of the more frequent uses of these chords are illustrated in Example 4.

Example 4

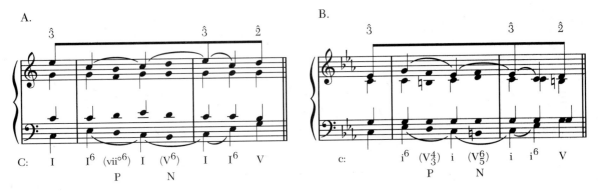

The two phrases employ essentially the same bass line (E♭ replaces E in the second phrase). The C-major phrase uses the triads vii°6 and V6, while the C-minor phrase uses inversions of the dominant seventh, V4/3 and V6/5. The second chord in measure 1 of each phrase features scale step $\hat{2}$ in the bass, a passing tone between $\hat{3}$ and $\hat{1}$. While the line descends here, it could also ascend ($\hat{1}-\hat{2}-\hat{3}$). The last chord of measure 1 in each example includes the leading tone as a lower neighbor to the tonic.

Example 5 demonstrates the usual treatment of the V4/2, in which the chordal 7th is in the bass.

Example 5

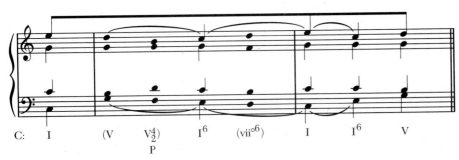

This model shows the typical passing role of the V4/2 ($\hat{5}-\hat{4}-\hat{3}$). Why must the $\hat{4}$ in this chord always resolve downward to $\hat{3}$? What is the function of the last harmony of the first full measure?

The three models in Examples 4 and 5 summarize the normal function of these chords. The models in Examples 6, 7, and 8 illustrate some less common uses. Take a few moments to supply roman numerals for each chord in these examples and to pick out these chords or bass notes that function differently from those in Examples 4 and 5, before reading the comments that follow.

Example 6

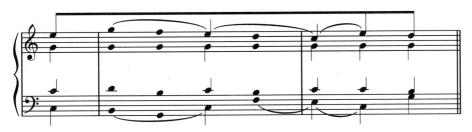

In Example 6 the leading tone in the bass (first chord of measure 1) is momentarily delayed in its resolution to the tonic ($\hat{8}-\hat{7}-\hat{5}-\hat{8}$); the dominant harmony is briefly extended by the skip to the root in the lowest voice against the chordal 7th in the highest voice. At the end of this measure, the $\hat{1}$ in the bass leaps to $\hat{4}$, supporting a V_2^4 chord, which resolves to $\hat{3}$, supporting a I^6. Though such a leap may seem strange because of $\hat{4}$'s dissonance, it is actually quite commonly employed in both the soprano and bass parts.

Example 7

In Example 7, the similar 5ths in the outer parts of the first two chords of measure 1 are allowed because they occur within the same harmony. Here we have yet another example of a dominant extension. The upward resolution of the soprano $\hat{4}$ in the V_3^4 at the end of the measure contradicts the normal downward resolution of the chordal 7th. The voice leading is acceptable here because the strong melodic motion of the similar 10ths between the soprano and bass makes the ear disregard the 7th's unusual resolution.

GUIDELINES FOR USING THE ANALYTICAL SYMBOLS

 Use different stem directions and slurs for an embedded progression to denote separate voice parts.

In arpeggiations of embellishing chords, do not stem any of the notes.

Example 8

Finally, in Example 8 the bass voice's leap from $\hat{3}$ to $\hat{7}$ at the end of the first measure is inconsistent with the usual behavior of a lower neighbor ($\hat{8}-\hat{7}-\hat{8}$). In this case the initial I–(V$_3^4$)–I^6 represents an **embedded** motion within the overall neighboring connection in the bass: C–(D–E)–B–C. Observe the upper slur and stems on the pitches C^3 and E^3, which denote the embedded progression; the lower slur in this voice indicates the neighboring motion. Something similar occurs in the soprano, where the neighboring motion is instead embedded in the rising line: C–(B–C)–D–E. Thus the larger neighboring motion in the bass ($\hat{8}-\hat{7}-\hat{8}$) is complemented by the larger ascent in the soprano ($\hat{1}-\hat{2}-\hat{3}$), as indicated by the outermost slur marks in each part.

ARPEGGIATED EXTENSIONS OF DOMINANT HARMONY

We have seen how tonic harmony (I and I^6) can be prolonged by embellishing dominant chords. In a similar manner, the V^7 may be extended through the use of its various inversions in an ascending or descending bass arpeggiation. In Example 9, I and I^6 serve as embellishing chords whose bass notes bridge the dominant chord members with passing motion. The contrary motion of the two voices generates implied inversions of the V^7.

Example 9 SOUSA: "THE THUNDERER"

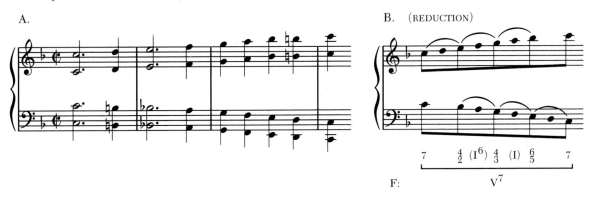

A.

B. (REDUCTION)

In the Beethoven excerpt in Example 10, the dominant is extended near the end of the phrase, where the bass arpeggiates through the dominant seventh, producing V_3^4, V^6, and V^7 in succession before resolving to the tonic. What happens in the soprano during these measures?

Example 10 BEETHOVEN: PIANO SONATA IN E♭ MAJOR, OP. 31, NO. 3, III

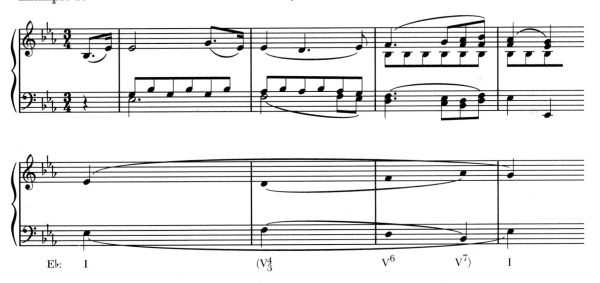

EXCEPTIONAL TREATMENTS OF THE CHORDAL 7TH

The chordal 7th is occasionally treated in less conventional ways. For instance, in a **delayed resolution** the chordal 7th of the V^7 does not move immediately to $\hat{3}$ but is momentarily diverted. This occurs in the Mozart Fantasia in Example 11, where the soprano G^5 in measure 14 takes the form of a **dangling 7th** within the V^6_5 harmony. This chordal 7th does not resolve to F^5 until the second half of measure 15, as the accompanying voice-leading reduction demonstrates. Why isn't the F^5 in measure 14 the tone of resolution?

Example 11   MOZART: PIANO FANTASIA IN D MINOR, K.397

The chordal 7th is sometimes switched, or **displaced,** to a different voice part before resolving. In Example 12a, what happens to the C^5 in the piano (m. 3)? If the $F\sharp^3$ (m. 3, first beat) were allowed to resolve to G^3 on the first beat of measure 4, undesirable similar 5ths would result between the vocal part and bass (Example 12b). Therefore, the C momentarily becomes part of the bass line, as does its resolution tone.

Example 12   SCHUBERT: "HEIDENRÖSLEIN," OP. 3, NO. 3 ·

A.

Sah ein Knab' ein   Rös - lein ⏜ stehn,   Rös - lein auf der Hei - den,

B.

(similar 5ths)

Instances of **transferred resolution,** where the chordal 7th resolves in another voice, are rare. In the Beethoven passage in Example 13, the resolution of $A\flat^5$ in measures 7–8 is transferred to G^4 in a different voice in measure 5.

Example 13   BEETHOVEN: PIANO SONATA IN E♭ MAJOR, OP. 7, I

(7th)

5

EMBELLISHING DOMINANTS IN MUSIC LITERATURE

Opening phrases afford some of the clearest examples of the common uses of linear dominants. As in Chapters 9 and 11, we will go step by step through the various stages of our analyses.

We will begin with the three-measure excerpt in Example 14.

1. First, we circle all nonharmonic tones (in this case there are none). Then we sketch in the roman numerals of the harmonies, identifying the structural chords (usually I, I⁶, or a cadential V) and embellishing chords (usually inversions of the dominant family). We place parentheses around the roman numerals of the embellishing harmonies (Example 14a). We may need to fine-tune the harmonic analysis later, depending on the voice leading of the outer parts.
2. We extract and write out the underlying bass line, stemming all essential notes and leaving embellishing notes such as passing, neighboring, or incomplete neighboring tones unstemmed. We supply the appropriate voice-leading slurs to express these motions (Example 14b).
3. Now we do the same for the soprano line, which may be a bit trickier. We compare the voice leading in the outer parts to our roman-numeral analysis to make sure that everything is consistent. We note

Example 14   BEETHOVEN: PIANO SONATA IN A♭ MAJOR, OP. 110, I

any voice exchanges (Example 14c). What happens between the outer parts in the first two measures?

4. Finally, we see if we can make a further reduction of the passage's voice leading (Example 14d). Here, the overall voice leading shows similar motion in 10ths from I to I^6 through a passing V$^4_3$.

In each of the excerpts in Examples 15–18, play or listen to the music first, then follow the successive stages of the reductive procedure.

In Example 15 we can transfer the soprano and bass pitches of the Bach chorale setting directly into the reduction and simply add the appropriate stemming and slurs to distinguish the essential from the embellishing chords. A large voice exchange (denoted by the crossed lines) spans the middle five harmonies of the phrase. Compare the first six pitches of the soprano with the last six pitches of the bass; what do you notice?

Example 15   "Jesu, Jesu, du bist mein" (Bach chorale harmonization)

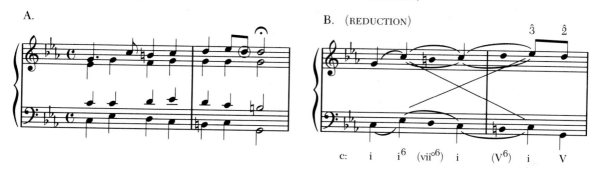

Our sketch of the essential bass notes of the little Haydn phrase (Example 16a) shows a motion from I to I^6 via the incomplete neighbor $\hat{4}$ (V$^4_2$) in measures 1–2, as shown by our sketch of the essential bass notes (Example 16b). When we add the essential notes of the soprano in these two bars, we highlight a voice exchange between the outer voices (Example 16c). But how are we to reduce the eighth-note motion in the third measure? If we look at the essential three-note soprano line of the first two bars ($\hat{3}$–$\hat{2}$–$\hat{1}$), we can see that it is simply restated a step higher in the last two bars with a different embellishment ($\hat{4}$–$\hat{3}$–$\hat{2}$); this is shown in Example 16d. While tonic harmony controls the first two measures, dominant harmony controls the last two; the I in measure 3 functions as an embellishing incomplete neighbor. Do you notice something about the bass that further supports this analysis? Short melodic patterns that lie hidden just beneath the surface of the music, as in the soprano line given in Example 16d, are called **voice-leading motives.** These motives and their reappearances are often not readily apparent until we make a voice-leading reduction.

Example 16 HAYDN: PIANO SONATA IN C MAJOR, HOB. XVI:35, III

C: I (V$^4_2$) I^6 V$^6_{(5)}$ I V

C: I (V$^4_2$) I^6 V$^6_{(5)}$ I V

C: I ——— I^6 V$^6_5$ ——— V

FURTHER EXAMPLES OF EMBELLISHING DOMINANTS

The opening phrase of this theme of a variation set by Beethoven (Example 17) may appear more complicated than the Haydn excerpt in the previous example, but it is actually easier to reduce. To begin with, the initial E♭'s are merely upbeats to the structural A♭'s in the outer parts. Ignoring for the moment the last V of the half cadence, what do you observe about the overall voice leading of the soprano and bass? (If in doubt, refer to Example 8 and its discussion.)

Example 17 BEETHOVEN: PIANO SONATA IN A♭ MAJOR, OP. 26, I

A.

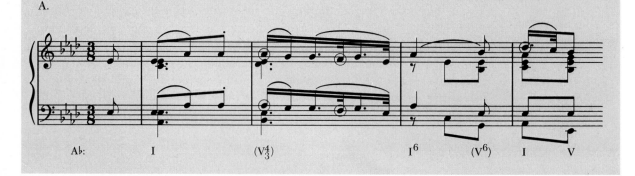

A♭: I (V$^4_3$) I^6 (V^6) I V

B.

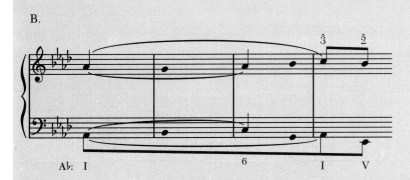

Ab: I   6   I   V

The soprano of the Chopin waltz in Example 18 is trickier to reduce. Clearly, measures 1 and 3 begin with an $F\sharp^5$ (Example 18a). But how do these $F\sharp$'s connect to the $A\sharp$ and B in measures 2 and 4? The upper voice actually implies two different lines; observe the upward and downward stems in Example 18c. The B^4 (m. 1) connects to the $A\sharp^4$, while the $C\sharp^5$ (m. 3) continues the same pattern to B^4. If we now supply a couple of $F\sharp$'s in parentheses to indicate the implied retention of the first note, the two-voice implication in the soprano becomes clear (Example 18d). We could even fill out the harmony by using the upper voice of the left-hand chords in the original music (see the "tenor line" in Example 18d). Compare this reduction to the one in Example 11; what do you notice?

Example 18   CHOPIN: WALTZ IN B MINOR, OP. 69, NO. 2

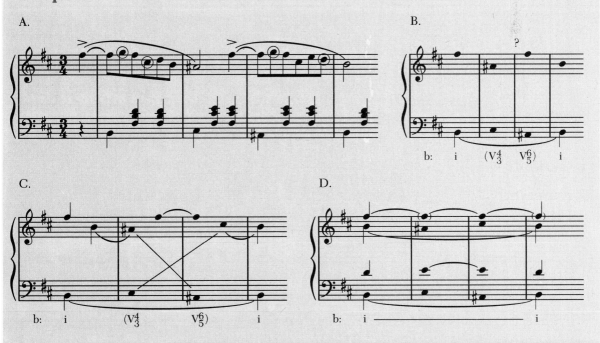

Summary of Partwriting Procedures

The following list summarizes the procedures you should follow to make musically satisfying partwriting connections using the chords discussed in this chapter.

1. *Triads:* Double the root or 5th in the V^6 and the 3rd or 5th in the vii^{o6}. Never double the leading tone in either chord. You may occasionally find it necessary to double the 3rd or 5th of a root-position I.

Example 19

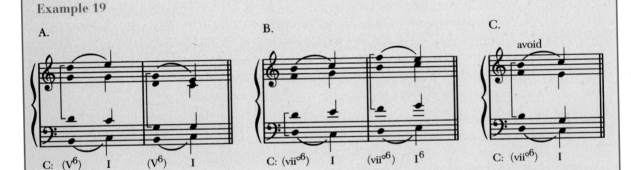

A.   B.   C.

C: (V^6) I (V^6) I   C: (vii^{o6}) I (vii^{o6}) I^6 C: (vii^{o6}) I

2. *Perfect Intervals:* Parallel unisons, octaves, or 5ths must not occur between any two consecutive parts. Similar 5ths in the outer voices may occur within the same harmony but never on a change of chord. However, similar 5ths frequently occur between upper voices in progressions involving the passing vii^{o6} or V^4_3.

Example 20

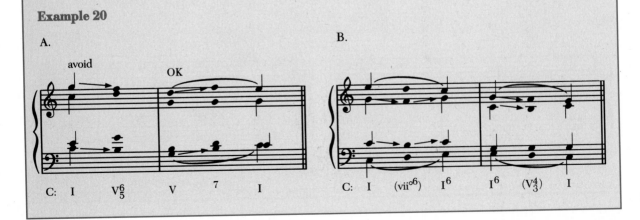

A.   B.

C: I V^6_5 V   7   I   C: I (vii^{o6}) I^6 I^6 (V^4_3) I

3. *Seventh Chords:* All four chordal members should be present in inversions of the V^7. The 5th of the root-position V^7 must sometimes be omitted to avoid parallels. The dissonant chordal 7th of the V^7 is approached by passing, neighboring, or incomplete neighboring motion and resolved downward by step. One exception occurs in a passing V^4_3 when the outer voices ($\hat{2}$ and $\hat{4}$) move upward in similar 10ths. Avoid letting both the root and chordal 7th of the V^7 move to $\hat{3}$, as direct octaves will result. You should also avoid delayed or transferred chordal 7th resolutions wherever possible.

Example 21

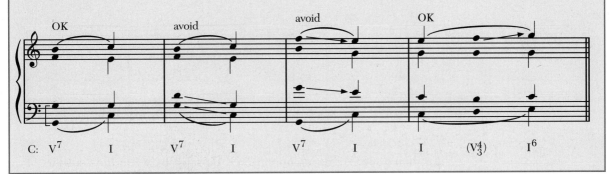

Melody Harmonization

Although we can support all the scale degrees of a melody except $\hat{6}$ with various tonic and dominant chords, we should attempt to harmonize only melodies that actually imply these chords. For example, we could harmonize the opening phrase of "America" with only tonic and dominant-family chords, but we probably wouldn't be satisfied with the result; try it and see.

In Chapter 9 we laid the foundation for subsequent melody harmonizations. We will continue to use the same method here. In chorale- or hymnlike melodies, therefore, you should begin by scanning the tune for the scale degrees that open and close each phrase and choosing appropriately stable chords and bass notes to support them. For the interior of the phrase, we now have a greater variety of embellishing dominant chords available. Thus, we can now focus more fruitfully on the melodic characteristics of the bass and the contrapuntal and intervallic relations between soprano and bass. We must consider all these aspects simultaneously while composing the harmonies for the middle of the phrase.

We should strive to compose as melodically interesting a bass line as possible, an easier task now because of the increased number of scale steps available for that part. The chorale harmonizations of J. S. Bach are excellent models to study in this respect. His bass lines, which often contain numerous nonharmonic tones, are sometimes even better melodies than the original hymn tunes; see Example 22.

Example 22 "LIEBSTER JESU, WIR SIND HIER" (BACH CHORALE HARMONIZATION)

A. B. (REDUCTION)

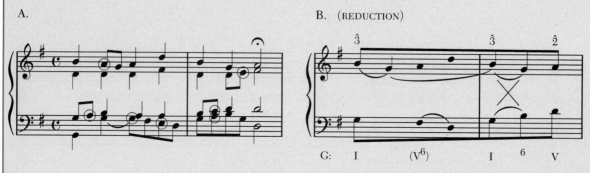

We should also strive for maximum difference between the contours of the outer voices in order to produce two distinctive melodic strands. We can insure this independence through the liberal use of contrary motion, or oblique motion (see Chapter 6). Avoid an excess of similar motion, as it will jeopardize the independence of the parts and could lead to parallel unisons, 5ths, or octaves.

Finally, we should strive for a preponderance of imperfect consonant intervals (3rds and 6ths) between the outer parts in the interior of the phrase. Occasional perfect 5ths and tritones (the result of V⁷ inversions) are possible, but the octave should be avoided unless it occurs as a weak passing sonority in a voice exchange. The beginning and end of the phrase will continue to employ the more stable octaves and 5ths, and at the end of the phrase the bass will tend to leap more, due to the greater use of root-position chords.

Now examine the passages shown in Example 23 and analyze the melodic characteristics of their bass lines and the melodic/intervallic relations between the outer voices. Between the staves, mark the various types of melodic motion, using the abbreviations *C* for "contrary," *O* for "oblique," and *S* for "similar," and indicate the resulting harmonic intervals.

Example 23

A.

B.

In Example 24 you will find a hymnlike tune with three harmonizations, indicated by the different bass lines and figured bass. Critique each setting in terms of the previous discussion and point out any errors or questionable procedures. Which one do you think is best?

Example 24

In folk-song settings the rate of chord change (or harmonic rhythm) is usually slower than in hymns, often only one chord per measure. However, the soprano (that is, the tune) will tend to be more rhythmically active than the typical hymn tune. Play the tune in Example 25; note the primary or stressed note at the beginning of each measure, and examine how the bass and harmonies support these pitches. Where is the only structural dominant in the phrase?

Example 25

A.

B.

Terms and Concepts for Review

embellishing dominants (V^6, $vii^{\circ 6}$, V^6_5, V^4_3, V^4_2)

embedded voice leading

extension of V^7

unusual treatment of the V^7:

    dangling 7th

    displaced 7th

    delayed resolution

    transferred resolution

    voice-leading motive

Melodic Figuration and Dissonance II

SUSPENSIONS AND SIMULTANEOUS DISSONANCES

In CHAPTER 7 we introduced the suspension. We will now examine the various ways in which suspensions are used in both two-voice and four-voice texture. We will then focus on the broader subject of melodic dissonance and how it creates specific musical effects.

The suspension is a particularly expressive device. Because this dissonance occurs on the beat, our expectation of consonance is momentarily thwarted, the resolution being delayed until the next offbeat or weak beat. Play the excerpt in Example 1a and listen to the succession of dissonances on the consecutive beats. We have circled this series of suspensions in the upper voice.

Example 1 BEETHOVEN: PIANO SONATA IN D MINOR ("TEMPEST"), OP. 31, No. 2, I

A.

B.

Now play the reworked version of the same passage in Example 1b. Although the phrase retains the original harmonic progression, its former "tempestuous" character has dissipated. The dissonances have been replaced by consonant chord tones that occur on the beat; these are followed by unaccented anticipations (circled) on the offbeat. The overall effect of the two passages is completely different.

We will begin by illustrating the use of suspensions in two-voice texture, and only subsequently employ the more customary four-voice texture.

SUSPENSIONS IN TWO-VOICE TEXTURE

In the reductions of this chapter, we will continue to use the symbols introduced in Chapter 7. We will stem the consonant preparation and resolution of the suspension and leave the dissonant note unstemmed but mark it with an accent (>); we will use ties and slurs to indicate the melodic direction. We will use a dotted tie to indicate that the suspension note may be either tied over from the preparation note or reiterated. We have omitted the accent mark wherever the accentuation is implied by the rhythmic alignment.

Suspensions are classified according to their intervallic relation with the bass voice. The suspensions in Example 2a, labeled as 7–6, 2–3, 4–3, and 9–8, refer to a 7th moving to a 6th, a 2nd moving to a 3rd, and so forth. Do not confuse a 4–3 (the intervallic motion within a suspension) with $\hat{4}$–$\hat{3}$ (scale degree $\hat{4}$ moving to scale degree $\hat{3}$).

Example 2

A.

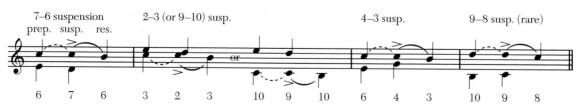

B.

In two-voice texture, three basic forms of suspensions occur: the 7–6, the 2–3 (inversion of the 7–6), and the 4–3. Intervals larger than an octave are assumed; that is, a 2–3 may be expanded by an octave to a 9–10. However, we will generally label all suspensions with resolutions to intervals larger than an octave as if they were in close position. The 7–6 and 4–3 suspensions occur in the upper voice, while the 2–3 occurs in the bass voice. As you can see in Example 2, these suspensions delay the expected consonance of a 6th or 3rd. (The 9–8 is rarely encountered in two voices, since it resolves to an empty octave.) Why are the two suspensions in Example 2b incorrect?

When the suspended note resolves, the other voice may leap to a different consonant interval, resulting in a **change of bass** or **change of part.** In Example 3, the 7–6 becomes a 7–3, the 4–3 becomes a 4–6, and the 2–3 becomes a 2–6.

Example 3

The rhythmic durations of the suspension's three components (preparation, suspension dissonance, and resolution) are dependent on the rate of harmonic change in a passage. For instance, in $\frac{4}{4}$ or $\frac{3}{4}$, they may appear as either eighth notes or quarter notes, as shown in Example 4. The preparation is usually at least as long as the suspension dissonance; exceptions do occur, however, as in the Schumann excerpt in Example 4e.

Example 4

A.   B.

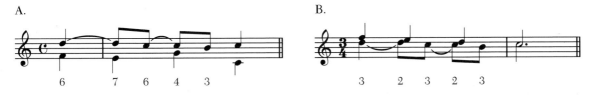

C.

3 6   7 6 4 3

D.

3   2   3

E. SCHUMANN: "CHIARINA" FROM *CARNAVAL*, OP. 9

7   6

Example 5 illustrates several instances of two-voice suspensions in music literature. The soprano (7–6) and bass (2–3) suspensions alternate in the Tchaikovsky symphony. What happens during the resolution of the suspensions in the 16th-century Galilei duet?

Example 5

A. TCHAIKOVSKY: SYMPHONY NO. 6 ("PATHÉTIQUE"), IV

7   6   2   3   7   6   2   3

B. VINCENZO GALILEI: DUET FROM *FRONIMO* (1568)

2   6   4   6   7   3   2   6   7   3

SUSPENSIONS IN FOUR-VOICE TEXTURE

In four-voice texture, normal triadic doubling procedures prevail, but the resolution of the suspension must be handled with special care. As a general rule, never double the resolution note unless it occurs in the bass voice. The more common doublings in chords with suspensions are shown in Example 6; the dash in the third example indicates that the previous 6 continues to hold through.

Example 6

Although the suspension preparation is usually consonant, it may occasionally occur as a dissonant passing tone or as the 7th of a seventh chord (Example 7). However, the dissonant note of a suspension figure occurs less often on a seventh chord.

Example 7

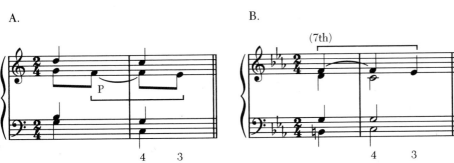

Example 8 illustrates three idiomatic uses of the 4–3 suspension. This suspension sounds most effective in four-voice texture, where its 4th is dissonant with both the bass and another part. Recall that the resolution note should not be doubled. The 4–3 delays the sounding of the dominant chord's leading tone in both authentic and half cadences. A passing 7th often occurs in conjunction with the suspension resolution.

Example 8

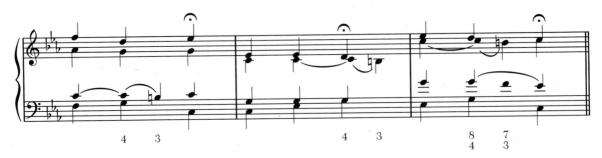

The 9–8 always occurs over a complete root-position triad; since the octave is the interval of resolution, its resolution note is always doubled (Example 9a). The transfer of the 9–8 to the tenor voice may result in the less common 2–1 suspension (Example 7b). The "displaced" 9–8, in which the suspension occurs in the bass voice itself, is even rarer (Example 9c).

Example 9

A. 9–8 SUSPENSION   B. 2–1 SUSPENSION   C. "DISPLACED" 9–8 SUSPENSION

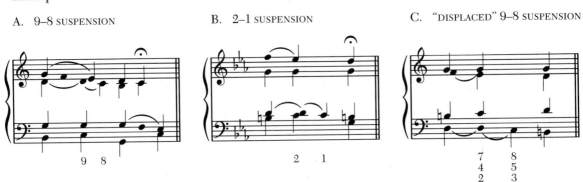

The two passages in Example 10 illustrate how the 9–8, like other suspensions, may incorporate a change of bass upon its resolution.

Example 10

A.   B.

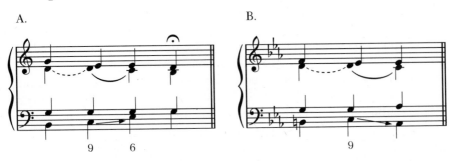

The interlocking **suspension chain** in the Monteverdi excerpt in Example 11 consists of a sequence of alternating 9–8's and 4–3's, in which the resolution of one suspension becomes the preparation for the next. In the example, the implied bass notes are enclosed within parentheses.

Example 11 Monteverdi: "Si ch'io vorrei morire" (text omitted)

The motion from a 6th to a 5th (6–5) above the bass may occasionally suggest a suspension, although no dissonance is present between the held note and the bass (Example 12a). Play the Liszt excerpt (Example 12b) and study its accompanying reduction (Example 12c). What is peculiar about the preparation of the second "suspension" (indicated with an arrow)?

Example 12

A.

B. Liszt: Piano Concerto No. 1 in E♭ major, II (simplified)

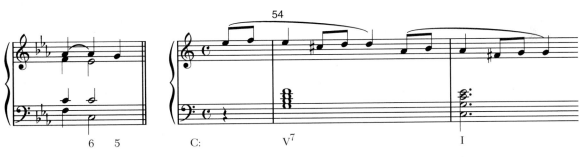

C. (reduction)

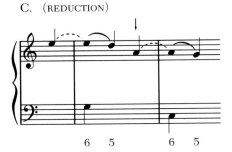

The 7–6 and 2–3 suspensions resolve to first-inversion ($\frac{6}{3}$) chords, as in Example 13.

Example 13

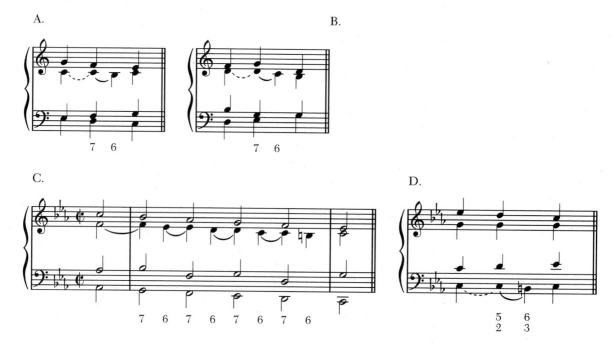

In the 7–6 suspension, we double the 5th of the chord and never the resolution note (Examples 13a and 13b). We can link several 7–6 suspensions together in a chainlike succession, as in Example 13c. In this model, the underlying progression consists of a succession of first-inversion triads. Since the stepwise chordal movement would produce parallel 5ths between the upper voices, we have inserted 7–6 suspensions to disguise or stagger the 5ths. In Example 13d, the 2–3 (or 9–10) bass suspension likewise resolves to a $\frac{6}{3}$ chord. This suspension frequently occurs on a V^6, as here, momentarily delaying the leading tone.

MULTIPLE SUSPENSIONS

We have previously seen instances of multiple dissonances in Chapter 7, including double passing and neighboring tones. **Double suspensions**—in which two tones are prepared, suspended, and resolved together—represent a third type of multiple dissonance.

Two types of double suspensions are possible: the $\frac{9-8}{7-6}$ and the $\frac{9-8}{4-3}$. Locate each in the passages of Example 14 (they are indicated by arrows in the reductions) and determine the inversion of the chord to which they resolve.

Example 14

A.   CHOPIN: *GRANDE VALSE BRILLANTE*, OP. 34, NO. 2

B.   (REDUCTION)

C.   RICHARD STRAUSS: *ALSO SPRACH ZARATHUSTRA*

D.   (REDUCTION)

As the two excerpts in Example 15 demonstrate, the upper members of a cadential V^7 are sometimes suspended over the final tonic chord, a frequent practice in slow movements of the Classical period. Even an upward step-wise resolution, given the curious title of a **retardation,** is possible.

Example 15

A.   BEETHOVEN: PIANO SONATA IN D MAJOR, OP. 10, NO. 3, III

B.   MOZART: PIANO SONATA IN G MAJOR, K. 283, II

ORNAMENTAL RESOLUTIONS

Example 16 illustrates various embellishing melodic figures that are often incorporated into a suspension. In each case, the resolution note of the suspension is indicated by an arrow.

Example 16

Such an embellishment is usually called an **ornamental resolution.** However, this term is a misnomer, since it is actually the suspension dissonance that is ornamented, not its resolution. The ornamentation can encompass a wide variety of melodic figurations and can span one or more beats. In Example 17, the extension of an embellished 4–3 suspension over dominant harmony in the climactic passage from the *Meistersinger* overture effectively heightens our anticipation of its eventual resolution.

Example 17   WAGNER: OVERTURE TO *DIE MEISTERSINGER* (SIMPLIFIED)

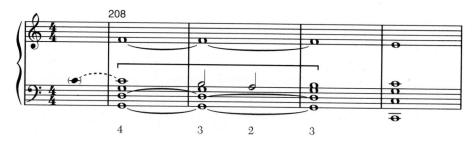

The brief chorale excerpt in Example 18 contains at least one instance of each of the common suspensions mentioned above. Identify each suspension; do you find any instances of embellished figuration or change of bass?

Example 18   "Danket dem Herren" (Bach chorale harmonization)

Suspensions as a Compositional Device in Variation Sets

In sets of variations on a particular theme, composers tend to highlight a particular motive or device in each separate variation.[1] Bach exploits suspension technique throughout the twenty-second variation of his "Goldberg" Variations. In order to appreciate how he does this, we will reverse our usual analytical procedure and start with a voice-leading reduction.

Example 19   Bach: *Goldberg Variations*, No. 22, BWV 988, mm. 1–8.

A.

B.

1. For a fuller discussion of theme and variations, see Excursion I: Simple Forms, pp. 269–88.

C.

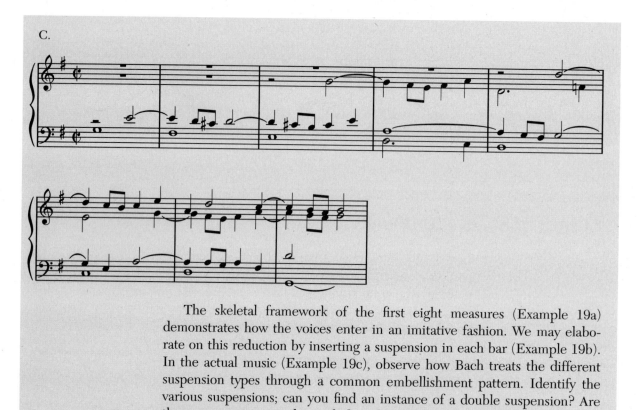

The skeletal framework of the first eight measures (Example 19a) demonstrates how the voices enter in an imitative fashion. We may elaborate on this reduction by inserting a suspension in each bar (Example 19b). In the actual music (Example 19c), observe how Bach treats the different suspension types through a common embellishment pattern. Identify the various suspensions; can you find an instance of a double suspension? Are there any suspensions that include a change of bass or part?

SUSPENSION FIGURES IN SEVENTH CHORDS

We have previously observed that the chordal 7th of the V^7 may be approached and resolved as a neighbor tone ($\hat{3}-\hat{4}-\hat{3}$), passing tone ($\hat{5}-\hat{4}-\hat{3}$), or incomplete neighbor ($\hat{2}-\hat{4}-\hat{3}$) within the dominant chord.

Example 20

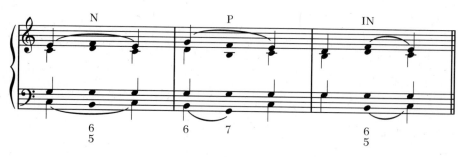

The chordal 7th may also be treated like a suspension—that is, prepared by a common tone and resolved downward by step (Example 21). Since the chordal 7th of the V^7 is scale degree $\hat{4}$, its preparation must be harmonized by a chord that contains this degree, such as IV or II.

Example 21

Identify instances of this procedure in the various inversions of the V^7 in the Bach variation in Example 22.

Example 22 BACH: *GOLDBERG VARIATIONS*, NO. 22, BWV 988, MM. 24–27, REDUCTION ONLY

G:

Melody Harmonization

Since we cannot change a given tune that is to be harmonized, any soprano suspensions must already be present in the melody. (If you compose a new melody, then you can build possible suspensions into it.) Therefore, any suspensions employed in the harmonization of a melody must occur in other voices.

Particular suspensions are associated with particular chords: the 4–3 works best in I, V, or III, and the 9–8 is most appropriate in I, IV, or VI.[2] Since the 7–6 and 2–3 appear in more varied harmonic contexts, you must determine where they will be most appropriate.

2. For a discussion of the III and VI chords, refer to Chapter 18. For the IV chord, refer to Chapter 15.

THE INTERACTION OF NONHARMONIC TONES

In the remainder of this chapter, we will look at some additional characteristics of the melodic dissonances that we introduced in Chapter 7.

Different types of nonharmonic tones may occur in combination, either consecutively or simultaneously. Certain idiomatic uses of these dissonances are especially common at cadences. In Example 23, we quote some typical examples from Bach's chorale harmonizations; identify the circled nonharmonic tones in each cadence. Why do you think the parallel 5ths marked in the third passage are permissible?

Example 23

A. "KOMM, JESU, KOMM"
   (BACH CHORALE HARMONIZATION)

B. "ICH DANK' DIR, LIEBER HERRE"
   (BACH CHORALE HARMONIZATION)

C. "WERDE MUNTER, MEIN GEMÜTE"
   (BACH CHORALE HARMONIZATION)

We may err in identifying dissonant tones in single-line melodies as nonharmonic if we don't take into account the harmonies that accompany or are implied by them. Looking at the Brahms violin tune in Example 24a by itself, we might be tempted to consider the longer notes on the first beat of each bar to be consonant tones. However, when we look at the chordal background (Example 24b), we see that our initial perception is really the reverse of what actually occurs: the first notes are all dissonant appoggiaturas!

Example 24   BRAHMS: VIOLIN SONATA IN A MAJOR, OP. 100, I

A.

consonance?

B.

C.

E: I   I⁶   ii⁶   V   I

Confusion may also arise from difficulty in distinguishing between two different "levels" of melodic dissonance that occur simultaneously. Examine the two passages in Example 25.

Example 25

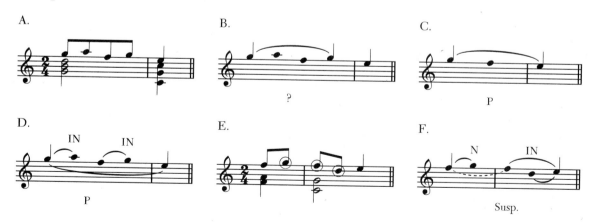

On first glance, the initial figure (Example 25a) resembles a changing tone or double neighbor around G; this is indicated by the slurred notes above the question mark in Example 25b. However, when we play it we hear the

tendency of the F, not the last G, to resolve to E, which produces a passing motion (Example 25c). This passing motion is simply embellished with incomplete neighbors (Example 25d). In Example 25e no less than three consecutive nonharmonic tones occur. A 4–3 suspension (F^5–F^5–E^5) provides the basic dissonant framework; how is this suspension further decorated?

THE AFFECTIVE NATURE OF MELODIC DISSONANCE

Although our discussion of melodic dissonance in Chapter 7 established definitions and an analytical method, we did not address the question of its affective or emotional nature and its aesthetic impact on the listener. Composers do not use nonharmonic tones haphazardly, but rather carefully select particular dissonant notes for specific musical effect. A brief review of the way we grouped nonharmonic tones into four categories (page 76 in Chapter 7) will help us focus on melodic dissonance's affective characteristics.

Unaccented nonchord tones perform a decorative or embellishing function. Their occurrence in the "cracks" between chords softens their dissonant effect. This is particularly true of passing tones, neighbors, and anticipations, since their stepwise motion minimizes clashes with the chordal background. Unaccented leaps or incomplete neighbors draw more attention to their dissonance, since the melodic leap tends to isolate the nonharmonic tone.

However, the affective nature of accented nonchord tones, including suspensions and appoggiaturas approached by either step or leap, is very different. Their placement on the beat highlights the dissonance. More important, their delayed resolution heightens our expectation for consonance: the longer the accented nonharmonic tone, the greater our wish to hear it resolve. As a result, accented dissonance affects the character of a passage more profoundly. In Example 1 we observed that removing the suspensions radically changes the nature of Beethoven's original passage. In the climactic measures of Richard Strauss's *Death and Transfiguration* (Example 26), accented nonchord tones transform a relatively banal passage into one with great emotional impact.

Example 26 RICHARD STRAUSS: *DEATH AND TRANSFIGURATION*

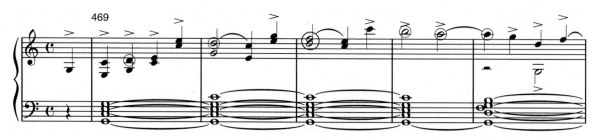

There is no particular beauty in this passage's harmonic background, which consists only of I and V^7 over a dominant pedal. Nor is the passage's basic melodic cell (E–D–C) particularly original or inspiring. The genius of this passage lies in the "bridging" motion of the initial D^4, which generates a series of accented passing tones and suspensions (circled in the example). These accented dissonances are held for at least one beat, and often two. The consistent and cumulative delay in resolving these melodic dissonances within this final transfiguration section creates its strongly affective nature.

The categories of melodic dissonance listed above thus represent a kind of affective continuum, ranging from the simple decoration of unaccented-stepwise notes, through unaccented-leaping notes, to the more striking accented-stepwise and accented-leaping tones. Composers often tend to exploit one category at a time in a passage or piece; several such excerpts are included in Exercise 1 of Chapter 7 of the accompanying Workbook.

Melodic Dissonance in Partwriting and Melody Harmonization

In partwriting exercises or melody harmonizations, you may be asked to supply appropriate nonchord tones to the individual voices. Try to observe the following recommendations.

1. Do not cram the passage full of extraneous nonharmonic tones. Instead, either try to develop a single active part, such as a "running bass" with passing and neighboring tones (Example 27), or simply use less dissonance, selecting what you use for maximum effect. Exercise restraint with incomplete neighbors and accented-leaping dissonances.

Example 27

2. Avoid excessive use of neighboring tones, as in Example 28, since they tend to produce a static effect.

Example 28

3. In a cadence, do not insert a passing tone between scale degrees $\hat{7}$ and $\hat{5}$ in any part, as in Example 29a, which would call attention to the leading tone's lack of resolution to the tonic.

Example 29

A.   B.

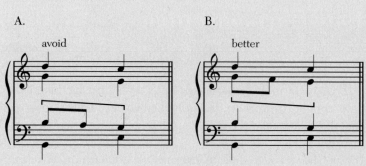

4. Avoid producing parallel 5ths by the addition of nonharmonic tones, as in Example 30.

Example 30

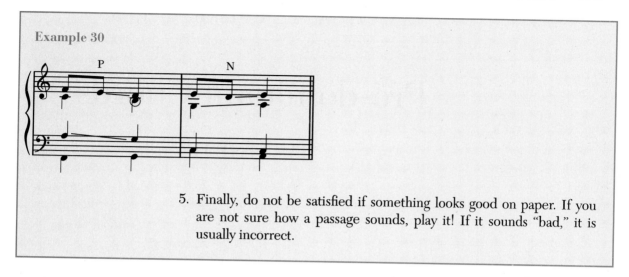

5. Finally, do not be satisfied if something looks good on paper. If you are not sure how a passage sounds, play it! If it sounds "bad," it is usually incorrect.

Terms and Concepts for Review

two-voice suspensions (7–6, 4–3, 2–3)
change of bass *or* part
rhythmic durations within suspensions
four-voice suspensions (including the 9–8)

suspension chain
double suspensions
retardation
ornamental resolution
suspension figures in seventh chords

CHAPTER 15

Pre-dominant Chords

IV AND II

THE SUBDOMINANT (IV) and supertonic (II) chords, which we will introduce in this chapter, are the most common diatonic chords that immediately precede dominant harmony.[1] Both of these chords may function as essential pre-dominant harmonies at the cadence or as embellishing

Example 1 WILLIAM BOYCE: "SHARON" (HYMN TUNE)

A. B. (REDUCTION)

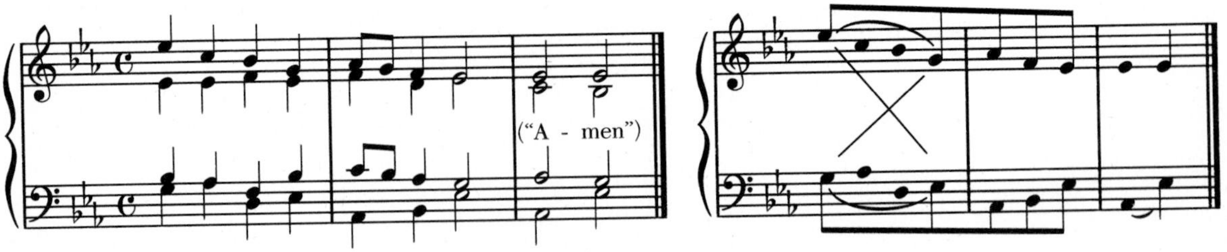

E♭: I^6 (IV V^6) I ii^6 V^7 I (IV) I

E♭: I^6 ____ I ii^6 V^7 I (IV) I

1. When the text refers to these chords in a general sense, they will be indicated with capital roman numerals.

harmonies within the phrase. The subdominant triad may also form part of a IV–I cadence or occur as a neighboring chord to the tonic. Can you point out some of these procedures in the hymn setting in Example 1? You may wish to look at the reduction for help.

THE IV AND II CHORDS

These two triads share scale degrees $\hat{4}$ and $\hat{6}$. In the major mode, the subdominant is a major triad and the supertonic is a minor triad. In the minor mode, the subdominant may be either a minor or major, depending on whether $\hat{6}$ is raised; minor is more usual. The supertonic chord in minor is a diminished triad, and thus is normally found in first inversion. The most common forms of IV and II are illustrated in Example 2.

Example 2

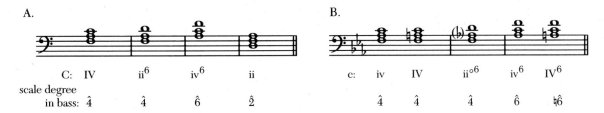

The addition of IV and II to our growing repertory of harmonies greatly increases the possibility of creating smooth voice-leading progressions. We will examine only the more frequent and idiomatic uses of these chords and their inversions, always stating the scale degree that occurs in the bass voice of each; these are given below the staff in Example 2. Learning these chords by scale degree in the bass voice will help you determine which one to choose in order to create a more melodic bass line.

PRE-DOMINANT FUNCTION IN AUTHENTIC CADENCES

Most authentic cadences employ a pre-dominant IV or II to precede the usual V or V[7]–I (in future instances, we will use the symbol V([7]) to refer to V or V[7] collectively). Since such a three-chord progression contains all seven degrees of the scale, it is especially useful in establishing a sense of tonal stability. The cadential pre-dominant is usually supported by scale degree $\hat{4}$, so the typical cadential bass line is $\hat{4}$–$\hat{5}$–$\hat{1}$. The presence of either a 5th or a 6th above scale degree $\hat{4}$ distinguishes a IV from a II[6].

Example 3

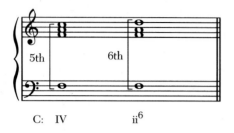

C: IV   ii⁶

In the following models, the pre-dominant harmony at cadences is stemmed.

In a ii⁶–V–I cadence, the most typical soprano line is $\hat{2}$–$\hat{2}$–$\hat{1}$, as shown in Example 4.

Example 4

$\hat{3}$ $\hat{2}$ $\hat{2}$ $\hat{1}$

C: I⁶   ii⁶   V   I

The soprano may also descend from $\hat{2}$ to $\hat{7}$ via a passing $\hat{8}$ ($\hat{2}$–($\hat{8}$)–$\hat{7}$–$\hat{8}$); the descent to the $\hat{7}$ may suggest another voice part, which we indicate by downward stemming. See Example 5. The basic voice leading here still implies the $\hat{2}$–$\hat{2}$–$\hat{1}$ soprano motion, as beamed in the example.

Example 5

A.   B.

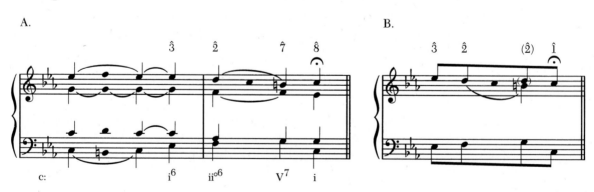

$\hat{3}$ $\hat{2}$ $\hat{7}$ $\hat{8}$ $\hat{3}$ $\hat{2}$ ($\hat{2}$) $\hat{1}$

c: i⁶   ii°⁶   V⁷   i

Some common uses of the root-position subdominant in cadences are illustrated in Example 6.

Example 6

A.   B.

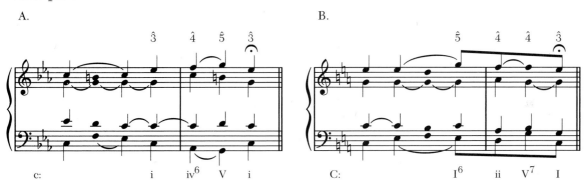

When scale degree $\hat{4}$ is present in an upper voice within a pre-dominant chord, the 7th of the V^7 that follows can be prepared and resolved like a suspension (Examples 5 and 6a).

Scale degrees $\hat{6}$ or $\hat{2}$ may also occur in the bass line at cadences, as in Example 7.

Example 7

A.   B.

The $\hat{6}$ supports the weaker IV^6 or iv^6, and functions as a neighbor to the $\hat{5}$ (Example 7a). Scale degree $\hat{2}$ supports a root-position ii (Example 7b), which usually occurs in a major key. The beamed 10ths in the second progression highlight the stepwise voice leading of the outer parts.

PRE-DOMINANT FUNCTION IN HALF CADENCES

Pre-dominant chords can also precede the dominant in half cadences. The so-called **Phrygian cadence** in the minor mode, iv^6–V, usually exhibits a contrary stepwise approach to an octave (on $\hat{5}$) in the outer parts (Example 8a).[2]

2. This cadence takes its name from compositions written in the Phrygian mode, whose final cadence employs the same voice leading—namely, a half-step motion, usually in the bass voice. For a discussion of the Phrygian and other diatonic modes, see Appendix 2.

Frequently a 7–6 suspension appears over the iv⁶ (Example 8b). What chord precedes the final dominant in Example 8c?

Example 8

A.

B.

c: i iv⁶ V
         (Phrygian)

              7   6

C.

c:

The four excerpts in Example 9 incorporate pre-dominant chords in their cadences. When the rate of harmonic change is relatively slow, as in the Chopin and Strauss quotations, the cadential progression may extend over the entire phrase: tonic–pre-dominant–dominant–tonic.

Example 9

A. CHOPIN: *GRANDE VALSE BRILLANTE,* OP. 34, NO. 1   B. (REDUCTION)

A♭: I   IV V⁷ I

C. BEETHOVEN: PIANO SONATA IN G MAJOR, OP. 14, NO. 2, II   D. (REDUCTION)

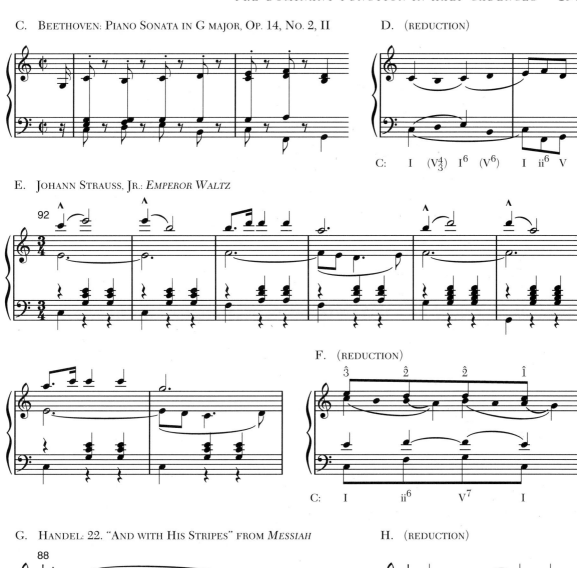

C: I   (V$^4_3$) I^6 (V^6)   I   ii^6 V

E. JOHANN STRAUSS, JR.: *EMPEROR WALTZ*

F. (REDUCTION)

$\hat{3}$ $\hat{2}$ $\hat{2}$ $\hat{1}$

C: I   ii^6 V^7 I

G. HANDEL: 22. "AND WITH HIS STRIPES" FROM *MESSIAH*   H. (REDUCTION)

f: i   iv^6 V

Identify the nonharmonic tones in the melody of the Chopin waltz. What kind of voice-leading procedure occurs in the bass of the first measure of the Beethoven phrase? The soprano of the Strauss passage is actually a compound melody, which is accompanied by a secondary middle voice; study the reduction of this passage carefully. What type of suspension intensifies the Phrygian cadence in the *Messiah* excerpt?

EMBELLISHING PRE-DOMINANT CHORDS WITHIN THE PHRASE

In Chapter 13 we learned that inversions of dominant harmony serve to embellish or prolong the tonic within the phrase, as the soprano and bass voices trace passing or neighboring figures contrapuntally around tonic harmony. These outer voices can assume their most active and varied melodic roles in the interior of phrases, where they are freed from the requirements of the cadence.

The IV and II chords may extend any embellishing dominant progression that prolongs tonic harmony within the phrase. These embellishing progressions are denoted with unstemmed noteheads and slurs in the voice-leading reductions that follow, and parentheses are placed around their roman numerals: I–(IV–vii°⁶)–I, I–(ii⁶–V₂⁴)–I⁶, and so on. Since such a large number of possible progressions exist, we will call attention to only some of the more common.

The pre-dominant cadential models that we have given above can also appear as embellishing progressions. In order to avoid a sense of melodic and harmonic closure, an embellishing ii (or IV)–V usually moves to a weaker form of the tonic, either a I⁶ or a I with $\hat{3}$ or $\hat{5}$ in the soprano. Embellishing dominant chords in inversion are also commonly employed in these progressions. Example 10 illustrates some typical uses of embellishing pre-dominant chords.

Example 10

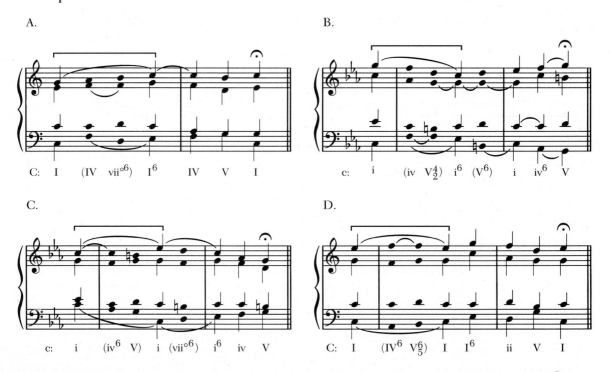

A.

C: I   (IV   vii°⁶)   I⁶   IV   V   I

B.

c: i   (iv   V₂⁴)   i⁶   (V⁶)   i   iv⁶   V

C.

c: i   (iv⁶   V)   i   (vii°⁶)   i⁶   iv   V

D.

C: I   (IV⁶   V₅⁶)   I   I⁶   ii   V   I

E.   F.

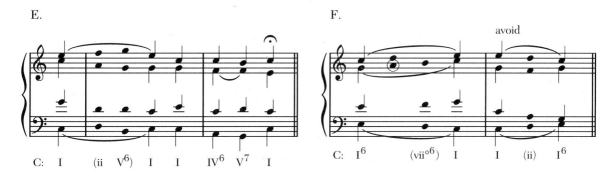

C: I   (ii V^6)   I   I   IV^6 V^7 I   C: I^6 (vii$^{\circ 6}$)   I   I   (ii)   I^6

In Example 10f, the alto $\hat{6}$–$\hat{7}$–$\hat{8}$ motion changes the ii chord into vii$^{\circ 6}$; the ii–I progression rarely occurs, perhaps because it may too easily result in parallel motion between the voices.

The "regressive" V–IV–I is somewhat curious. We may wish to consider the IV as a chord interpolated into the more basic dominant–tonic motion. (Although this succession occurs infrequently in most tonal music, it is a hallmark of the typical blues progression: I–IV–I–V–IV–I.) In the Mozart excerpt in Example 11, notice how the progression I–(V^6–IV)–I^6 outlines a sequence, shown in the voice-leading reduction by brackets.

Example 11   MOZART: PIANO SONATA IN F MAJOR, K.332, II

A.

B.

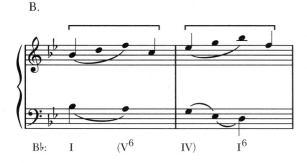

B♭:   I   (V^6 IV)   I^6

THE PLAGAL CADENCE

Example 1a of this chapter concludes with an "Amen." This word is frequently sung at the end of hymn settings, and almost always as part of a **plagal cadence,** IV–I, which usually immediately follows an authentic cadence.[3] Another example is shown in Example 12. This cadential figure closes many of Handel's choral movements.

Example 12 "ST. ANNE" (HYMN TUNE)

The use of plagal motion in the final cadences of phrases is infrequent. Its excessively passive effect, the result of retaining the tonic note as a common tone in an upper voice and a root movement by ascending 5th or descending 4th, contrasts with the more active authentic cadence, which features a leading tone ($\hat{7}$) in one of the upper voices and a root movement by descending 5th (or ascending 4th). The first two phrases of the chorale harmonization in Example 13 conclude with $\hat{6}$–$\hat{6}$–$\hat{5}$ in the soprano; explain how Bach has varied the cadential settings of these phrases.

Example 13 "WIE SCHÖN LEUCHTET DER MORGENSTERN" (BACH CHORALE HARMONIZATION)

THE SUBDOMINANT AS A NEIGHBOR TO TONIC HARMONY

Play the Tchaikovsky excerpt in Example 14, observing the pair of iv chords.

3. The term *plagal* is traditionally used when referring to harmonic progressions that strongly emphasize the motion of IV to I or I to IV.

Example 14 TCHAIKOVSKY: SYMPHONY NO. 5, I

A.

B.

e: i (iv) i   i (iv) i

Here the subdominant harmony does not act as a pre-dominant to V but instead functions as an embellishing chordal neighbor to the tonic.

In most cases the actual neighboring motion occurs in the upper voices ($\hat{3}$–$\hat{4}$–$\hat{3}$ and $\hat{5}$–$\hat{6}$–$\hat{5}$); the IV occurs in root position, and the bass $\hat{4}$ sometimes acts as a neighbor itself (Example 15). The supertonic chord does not normally function as an embellishing harmony to the tonic, either as a neighboring or passing chord. Therefore, instead of a I–ii–I^6 progression, use either a I–vii$^{\circ 6}$–I^6 or a I–V$^4_3$–I^6.

Example 15

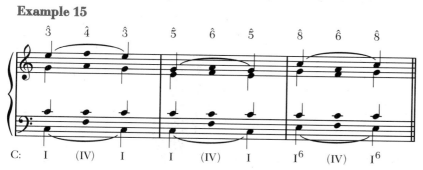

C: I   (IV)   I   I   (IV)   I   I^6 (IV)   I^6

PRE-DOMINANT CHORDS IN MUSIC LITERATURE

The two excerpts in Example 16 contain varied uses of the IV and II triads. Each passage is accompanied by a voice-leading reduction.

Example 16

A. NUN PREISET ALLE GOTTES BARMHERZIGKEIT
    (BACH CHORALE HARMONIZATION)

B. (REDUCTION)

G:

C. PURCELL: "FEAR NO DANGER TO ENSUE"
   FROM *DIDO AND AENEAS*, ACT I

D. (REDUCTION)

C: (V)

Supply a harmonic analysis for the Bach and Purcell phrases. In both passages, an interior embellishing progression is followed by a cadence. Observe that these embellishing progressions avoid closure on the tonic by employing either a I⁶ or a I with $\hat{3}$ or $\hat{5}$ in the soprano.

In your reduction assignments from the Workbook, you should proceed as we have in our reductions throughout. Begin by providing a roman-numeral analysis. Then determine whether each chord is essential or embellishing; if the latter, enclose the roman numerals within parentheses. Next, indicate the structural soprano and bass movement at the opening and at the cadence with stemmed notes. The remainder of your work should focus on the correct reduction of the soprano line; this presents the greatest challenge. Strive to make logical stepwise connections whenever possible, since they are more characteristic of contrapuntal motion in general.

MORE SOPHISTICATED USES OF PRE-DOMINANT CHORDS

In the Loeillet sonata, the pre-dominant chords move down to inverted dominants. You might begin an analysis of this piece by filling in the harmonies suggested by the figured bass, writing them in keyboard style directly below the soprano. Then you could supply the roman numerals for each chord, as we have done here. How many embellishing progressions do you find? Sketching the outer voices, as in Example 17b, is fairly straightforward. When we further reduce the passage to its essential notes only, as in Example 17c, we uncover an interesting voice exchange; can you mark it in the reduction?

In the Beethoven phrase (Example 17d) we initially might consider the IV in measure 16 as a neighboring chord between the two tonic harmonies. However, the soprano's three-note motive in measures 14–15 (C⁵–B♭⁴–A⁴) is followed in measures 15–16 by its sequence a step lower (B♭⁴–A⁴–G⁴),

Example 17

A. J. B. LOEILLET: SONATA NO. 4 IN F MAJOR

$$\begin{array}{cccccc} & {}^6_5 & & 7 & 6 & {}^4_2 & 6 \end{array}$$

B. (REDUCTION 1)   C. (REDUCTION 2)

F: (ii   V$^6_5$)   I   (ii^6 V$^4_2$)   I^6 IV   V   I   F: I   I^6 IV   V   I

D. BEETHOVEN: SYMPHONY NO. 6 ("PASTORAL"), I   E. (REDUCTION)

cover tones

F: I   I^6 (V$^4_3$)   I   IV   (I)   V

which is embedded in the middle voice: $\hat{5}$–($\hat{4}$)–$\hat{3}$, $\hat{4}$–($\hat{3}$)–$\hat{2}$. This is a rare instance where the main soprano part is momentarily covered by higher notes; we notate these **cover tones** without stems in our analyses. (See Example 17e). Since the motive's middle note is supported in both places with passing chords, the I in measure 3 is not essential but rather functions as an embellishing passing harmony. Thus, the intended direction of the IV is to the V at the half cadence: IV–(I)–V.

Summary of Partwriting Procedures

The more common partwriting procedures using the subdominant and supertonic triads are listed below.

1. Since the progression ii–V represents a root movement by a falling 5th (or a rising 4th), we simply retain the same structure for each chord (Example 18a), as we have seen in Chapter 9 (p. 112). It is best to double the soprano in most first inversions of pre-dominant chords (Example 18b); however, a given context may make it necessary to double some other chord member. In a minor key, writing a soprano line that descends $\hat{2}$–($\hat{8}$)–$\hat{7}$ in the progression ii°⁶–V will avoid the potential hazard of producing an augmented 2nd (Example 18c). The progression I(or I⁶)–ii⁶ should always be scanned for possible parallel 5ths or octaves (Example 18d).

Example 18

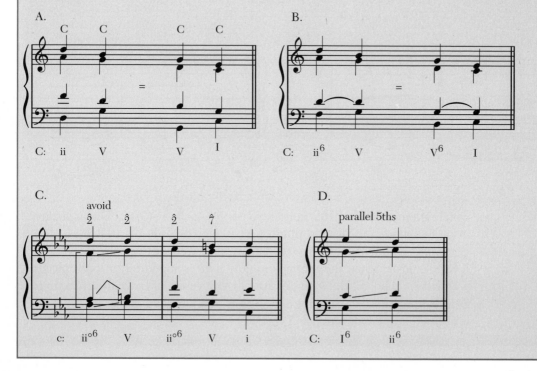

2. Since the progressions IV–V and I–ii involve root movement by ascending 2nd, no common tones are possible. To avoid parallels, move the upper voices in contrary motion to the bass (Example 19a). If the soprano proceeds in similar 6ths or 10ths with the bass, let the inner voices move in the opposite direction (Example 19b). Inserting passing tones can also generate parallels (Example 19c). In the Phrygian cadence, double the chordal 5th of the iv^6 (Example 19d) to avoid parallels or a 7–6 suspension that incorrectly doubles the resolution tone. The progression IV^6–V^6–I is fraught with danger; it is easy to produce parallel 5ths and octaves or double an active scale degree such as $\hat{7}$. Study the correctly realized version of this progression in Example 19e.

Example 19

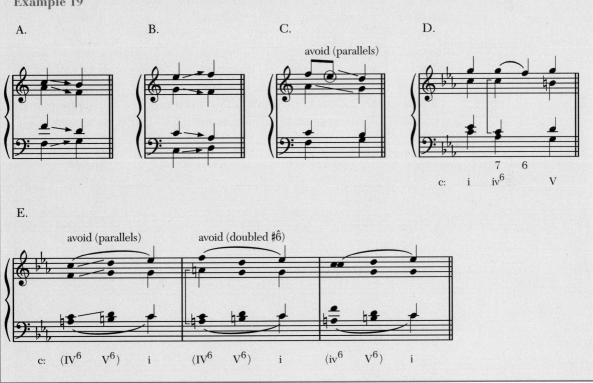

Melody Harmonization

The addition of the subdominant and supertonic to our harmonic resources allows us to make more effective settings of a great many tunes. The following recommendations for setting a melody pertain to the two basic categories of melodies: (1) tunes that imply relatively fast harmonic change, such as chorales or hymns, and (2) tunes that imply a slower harmonic change, such as folk songs. We will consider the former group first.

For any melody, you should begin by sketching in the initial chord and the cadence of the phrase as they are suggested by the melodic scale degrees. Since cadences establish harmonic stability, be sure to emphasize root-position chords there. (Some half cadences, such as I⁶–V and iv⁶–V, represent notable exceptions.) We should usually reserve the more stable 5ths and octaves for the phrase's beginning and cadence. In authentic cadences, determine whether the dominant can be preceded by some form of pre-dominant chord. In longer melodies, try for a variety of different cadential progressions. As an example, we have supplied the soprano notes in Example 20 with suggested harmonies and a bass line at the cadences.

Example 20

Now we are ready to concentrate on the interior of the phrase. You should sketch in a bass line as well as the roman numerals of the chords that your bass line would support. Always strive to use chords and inversions that will produce a smooth voice leading.

We have stressed the importance of the note-against-note contrapuntal framework of the soprano and bass within the phrase. Your bass line not only should be more melodic but also should form mainly consonant 3rds and 6ths with the melody. You must properly approach and resolve a dissonant 7th of a V^7 harmony if one occurs in the soprano or bass.

Example 21 shows a melody with five different bass lines. Roman numerals indicate the chords for each. Study and then critique each outer-voice duet, identifying any questionable harmonic intervals, awkward melodic contours, parallel 5ths or octaves, or unusual progressions. Which setting do you think is the best? Check your answers against the comments that follow.

Example 21

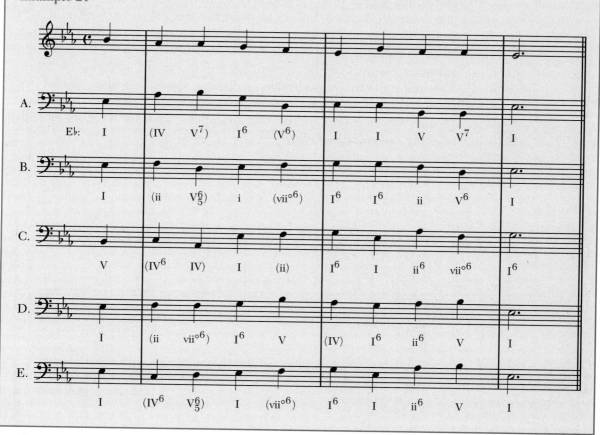

a. Direct octaves on the resolution of V[7] (m. 1, beats 2–3); uneven rate of harmonic rhythm; rather disjunct bass line; excessive use of perfect 5ths and octaves.

b. Weak succession of I[6] chords (m. 2, beats 1–2); parallel octaves (m. 2, beats 2–3); weak final cadence; rather static bass line.

c. Awkward chord progression (m. 1 through m. 2, beat 2); weak final cadence.

d. Weak repetition of A♭ and F (m. 1, beats 1–2); parallel 5ths (mm. 1–2).

e. Free of errors; this particular setting not only features a good bass line that emphasizes contrary motion with the soprano but also a logical harmonic progression.

Now that you've composed a good bass line and ascertained the harmonic implications of the passage, fill in the inner voices to complete the four-part setting. If your bass line and chord progressions are sound, your partwriting should proceed smoothly. You may wish to add some melodic dissonance to the bass, but try to avoid the temptation to overload it with nonharmonic tones. A finished version of the tune from Example 20 is given in Example 22. Examine the relation between the outer parts, the harmonic progression, the partwriting, and the use of nonharmonic tones. The accompanying voice-leading reduction shows a gradual descending stepwise motion in the soprano ($\hat{5}$ to $\hat{1}$), which gives the melody an overall sense of direction. Can you find an instance where a "I" chord embellishes pre-dominant harmony?

Example 22

A.

B.

a: i   (iv   vii°⁶)   i   iv⁶   V   i⁶   iv   (i)   iv⁶   V   i   (V)

i⁶   (vii°⁶)   i   i⁶   V   i   (V₃⁴)   i⁶   ii°⁶   V   I

With melodies that employ a slower harmonic rhythm, first determine where harmonic changes are implied by singing or playing the tune several times. This step is necessary to avoid the common tendency to harmonize every melodic note with a different chord. The German folk song in Example 23, for instance, suggests a harmonic change every measure. Two settings are given: the first employs a conventional four-voice choral texture (Example 23a), the second a simple piano accompaniment (Example 23b).

Example 23   "Erlaube mir" (German folk song)

A.

Terms and Concepts for Review

the IV and II chords as pre-dominant in
   function
Phrygian cadence
essential *vs.* embellishing pre-dominant
   chords

plagal cadence
IV as neighboring chord to tonic
cover tone

The $^6_4$ and Other Linear Chords

ROOT-POSITION and first-inversion triads contain only consonant intervals above the lowest voice part. The $^6_4$ or second-inversion triad, on the other hand, contains a dissonant 4th above the bass. The $^6_4$, arising from contrapuntal motion, functions as an unstable **linear chord.** There are four standard uses of the $^6_4$ chord in music of the common-practice period: (1) as an accented or cadential chord, (2) as a passing chord, (3) as a neighboring chord, and (4) as an arpeggiated chord. Each of these uses outlines a specific manner in which the dissonant 4th is prepared and resolved.

To acquaint yourself with the $^6_4$ triad, locate all occurrences of it in the hymn in Example 1. We will return to this example later in the chapter.

Example 1 "HOLINESS" (AMERICAN GOSPEL HYMN TUNE)

The Accented or Cadential $\frac{6}{4}$ Chord

Play the models in Example 2 and direct your attention to the authentic cadence of each phrase. Each notehead in this and similar examples in this chapter represents a quarter note.

Example 2

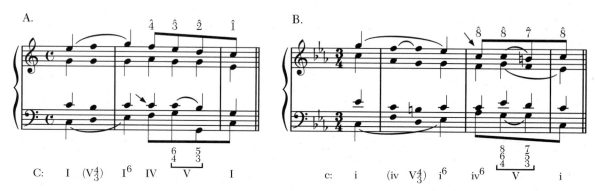

In both progressions, the last four chords represent a pre-dominant–dominant–tonic progression. We could label the second chord in each group as a second-inversion tonic triad, or I_4^6. When we hear this chord in context, however, we find it lacking the stability we normally associate with tonic harmony. In fact, its bass note, G, sounds more like the root of the chord than its 5th, and the C seems curiously suspended in an upper voice. At the cadence, this chord is immediately followed by a root-position dominant chord; the two chords together can be heard as an expansion of dominant harmony. The tone a 4th above the bass is treated like a suspension; it is prepared by the 5th of the preceding IV or IV⁶ (as indicated by the arrows) and resolves on the V. Notice how this suspended dominant harmony is indicated in the roman-numeral analyses of Example 2.

In cadences, this "suspended" $\frac{6}{4}$ chord always falls on a relatively strong beat: beat 1 or 3 in quadruple meter, and beat 1 or 2 in triple meter. For this reason, we call it an **accented** or **cadential** $\frac{6}{4}$. A descending $\hat{4}-\hat{3}-\hat{2}-\hat{1}$ is the most common soprano line; the succession $\hat{8}-\hat{8}-\hat{7}-\hat{8}$ is also possible.

Now contrast the phrases in Example 3 with the models given in Example 2.

Example 3

A.

B.

When the $\frac{6}{4}$ chord is preceded by a ii or ii⁶ instead of a IV or IV⁶, the treatment of the 4th above the bass in the $\frac{6}{4}$ chord resembles an accented passing tone: $\hat{2}-(\hat{8})-\hat{7}$. Compare the alto line in Example 3a and the soprano line in Example 3b with the tenor line in Example 2a and the soprano line in Example 2b.

In all the examples we have presented so far, the actual bass of the $\frac{6}{4}$ chord is doubled. The doubling note may remain on $\hat{5}$ or descend to $\hat{4}$, the chordal 7th of V⁷. Can you find an example of the latter in any of the previous phrases? The 6th and 4th over the bass will descend stepwise to the 5th and 3rd, respectively. When a $\hat{4}-\hat{3}-\hat{2}-\hat{1}$ descent occurs in the soprano, we stem the consonant 6th above the bass (or $\hat{3}$) as a structural note in our reductions (Examples 2a and 3a). However, when the soprano line is $\hat{8}-\hat{8}-\hat{7}$ or $\hat{2}-\hat{8}-\hat{7}$, we do not stem the dissonant 4th ($\hat{8}$) above the bass (Examples 2b and 3b).

Two exceptions are shown in Example 4. Can you give a reason for Mozart's unusual partwriting? Can you explain the soprano motion in the final bars of Beethoven's well-known song? (In this free keyboard style, the octave doublings enhance the sonority but do not represent parallel octaves.)

Example 4

A.   MOZART: STRING QUARTET IN D MINOR, K.421, II

B.   BEETHOVEN: "THE GLORY OF GOD IN NATURE," OP. 48, NO. 4

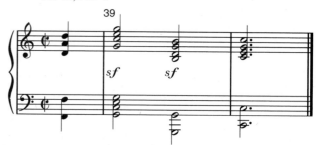

Some further uses of the cadential $^6_4$ appear in Example 5.

Example 5

A.   MUZIO CLEMENTI: PIANO SONATINE IN F MAJOR, OP. 36, NO. 4, II

B.   (REDUCTION)

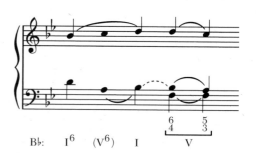

C.   D. SCARLATTI: SONATA IN D MAJOR, K. 492

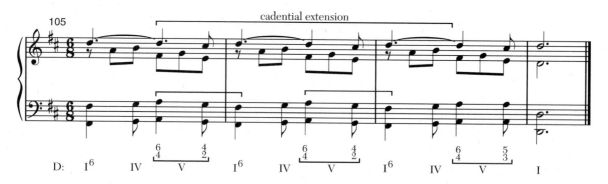

D. JOHANN HASSLER: SONATINA FOR PIANO IN C MAJOR

An accented $^6_4$ in half cadences is frequently used in Classical-period slow movements. What harmony precedes the $^6_4$ in the Clementi phrase? In the Scarlatti excerpt the bass line twice produces $^6_4$–$^4_2$–I^6 progressions, delaying the anticipated close on a root-position tonic and causing an extension of the cadence. We may even encounter accented $^6_4$'s within the interior of a phrase, as in the Hassler example.

The cadential $^6_4$ progression may be extended over several measures. In Example 26 of Chapter 14, for instance, the oscillation of $^6_4$'s and $^5_3$'s over a dominant pedal builds up a harmonic tension that is finally released in the tonic resolution in measure 478. In Classical concertos the last section of some movements may include a solo **cadenza** (Italian for "cadence"). These cadenzas were originally improvisations by the soloist based on thematic material from the movement; some were later written out by the composer. They typically feature virtuosic flourishes that allow the soloist to demonstrate his or her technical abilities. The cadenza is framed by a $^6_4$ chord at its beginning and a dominant resolution at its conclusion. A lengthy trill on $\hat{2}$ leads to the closing orchestral tutti on the tonic, which comes in the next measure; both the $^6_4$ and its $^5_3$ (or $^7_3$) resolution are set off by fermatas. The framing sonorities of the cadenza for the first movement of Mozart's C-major Piano Concerto, K.503, are shown in Example 6. The improvised cadenza, not written out by Mozart, would be inserted between the two fermatas.

Example 6 MOZART: PIANO CONCERTO IN C MAJOR, K.503, I

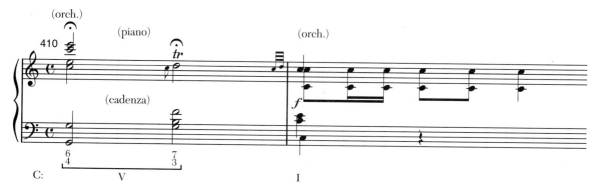

The excerpts in Example 7 illustrate some elaborated cadential ⁶₄'s. Sketch out voice-leading reductions of the first two passages. What nonharmonic tones decorate the cadence of the Bach chorale harmonization? Explain the "suspension chain" in the Schubert song.

Example 7

A. "DA DER HERR CHRIST ZU TISCHE SASS"
   (BACH CHORALE HARMONIZATION)

B.

C. SCHUBERT: "WHO IS SYLVIA?"

D.

E. MOZART: PIANO SONATA IN C MAJOR, K.309, I

F. (REDUCTION)

C: ii⁶

G. VERDI: "CELESTE AIDA" FROM *AIDA*, ACT I   H. (REDUCTION)

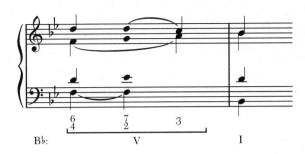

In the Mozart sonata, the florid extension of the cadential harmony with scales and trills is typical of important cadential points in Classical sonatas. The *Aida* passage is embellished with chromatic and other dissonant notes.

THE PASSING $^6_4$ CHORD

The $^6_4$ may also serve as a passing chord between two chords of similar function, linking two pre-dominant, dominant, or tonic harmonies. **Passing $^6_4$'s** invariably occur on an unstressed beat, like other passing chords. Since in this role the $^6_4$ is a nonessential linear chord, we will denote it in our reductions simply with its figured-bass symbol rather than the customary roman numeral, and leave its noteheads unstemmed.

In Example 8a, the $^6_4$ occurs within a prolongation of dominant harmony; thus, the $\hat{5}$ in the bass is sustained while the upper voices move. The passing motion may also involve the $\hat{5}$ itself, which forms a passing 4th with the prolonged tonic note in an upper voice (Example 8c). The resulting $\hat{6}$–$\hat{5}$–$\hat{4}$ in the bass now prolongs pre-dominant harmony: IV⁶–($^6_4$)–ii⁶. The setting by Malotte prolongs the subdominant; note the double voice exchange (Example 8f). Although a $^6_4$ may occasionally provide a bridge between I⁶ and I (Example 8g), the contrapuntal vii°⁶ or V$^4_3$ is preferred by composers in the common-practice period.

Example 8

A. "LYONS" (HYMN TUNE)   B. (REDUCTION)

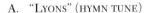

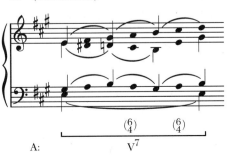

C. HAYDN: SYMPHONY NO. 104 ("LONDON"), III

D. (REDUCTION)

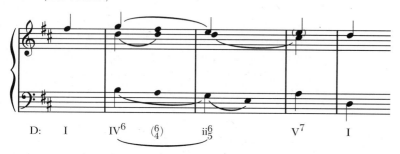

D: I   IV⁶   (⁶₄)   ii⁶₅   V⁷   I

E. ALBERT MALOTTE: "THE LORD'S PRAYER"

F. (REDUCTION)

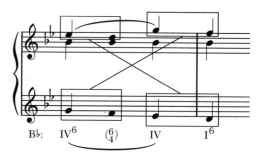

B♭:   IV⁶   (⁶₄)   IV   I⁶

G. MUSORGSKY: "THE GREAT GATE OF KIEV"
     FROM *PICTURES AT AN EXHIBITION*

H. (REDUCTION)

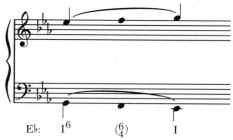

E♭:   I⁶   (⁶₄)   I

THE NEIGHBORING $^6_4$ CHORD

The $^6_4$ may outline an upper neighboring figure over a root-position triad. This **neighboring** (or **pedal**) $^6_4$, like the passing $^6_4$, is designated with only a figured-bass symbol. In Example 9, the reduction of the Schumann excerpt illustrates this embellishment of both tonic and dominant chords. The opening of the "St. Anthony Chorale" (Example 9c) includes a pair of "harmonic" neighbors, the first being a $^6_4$ chord and the second an embellishing IV chord.

Example 9

A. SCHUMANN: "THE WILD HORSEMAN"
   FROM *ALBUM FOR THE YOUNG*

B. (REDUCTION)

C. HAYDN(?): DIVERTIMENTO NO. 1
   ("CHORALE ST. ANTONI"), II

D. (REDUCTION)

Be careful when identifying the note that functions as the actual bass in accompanimental parts. In most cases, the first note of the measure or figuration acts as the real bass. In Example 10, the chords on beats 2 and 3 in the bass staff are not $^6_4$s, since the recurring C^3 on beat 1 is heard as the sustained bass and root. On the other hand, the harmony in measure 3 is a legitimate neighboring $^6_4$. How would you explain the curious clash of $F\natural^4$ and $F\sharp^5$ near the end of this measure?

Example 10   SCHUBERT: *VALSES SENTIMENTALES,* OP. 50

A.

B. (REDUCTION)

C: ⁵₃   ⁵₃   ⁶₄(!)   ⁵₃   C: I   (⁶₄)   I

THE ARPEGGIATED ⁶₄ CHORD

The three uses of the ⁶₄ discussed above are based on treating the dissonant 4th as some form of nonharmonic tone. However, this chord may also occur as an **arpeggiated ⁶₄**, a byproduct of bass arpeggiation, as in Example 11.

Example 11

A.   BRUCKNER: SYMPHONY NO. 7, I

B.   BACH: MINUET FROM PARTITA NO. 1 IN B♭ MAJOR, BWV 825

C. (REDUCTION)

B♭:   I   (V⁶)   I

The B's in the excerpt from the Bruckner symphony produce momentary second inversions; nevertheless, the entire passage should be viewed as an extended E-major root-position harmony. Likewise, in the Bach excerpt the B♭'s and A's (1̂ and 7̂) on the first beats of each measure in the bottom clef act as the bass support, despite the incidental $^6_4$'s (indicated with arrows) created by arpeggiations. The reduction reveals a large-scale neighboring motion: I–(V⁶)–I.

Now return to Example 1 and indicate the function of each of its $^6_4$ chords. Are all four categories represented?

Partwriting Procedures and Melody Harmonization

Partwriting using the $^6_4$ poses no major problems provided that you handle the dissonant 4th above the bass in the manner described in this chapter and remember to double the bass note. In the cadential $^6_4$, this bass doubling allows the "suspended" 6th and 4th to resolve stepwise to their respective 5th and 3rd; the doubling $\hat{5}$ may descend to the 7th of the following V⁷ chord in another voice.

In order to make effective use of $^6_4$ chords in harmonization, you must become familiar with the melodic lines it usually supports. Some of the more common are the following:

1. Cadential $^6_4$: $\hat{4}$–$\hat{3}$–$\hat{2}$–$\hat{1}$, $\hat{8}$–$\hat{8}$–$\hat{7}$–$\hat{8}$, or $\hat{2}$–$\hat{8}$–$\hat{7}$–$\hat{8}$
2. Passing $^6_4$: $\hat{7}$–$(\hat{8})$–$\hat{2}$ (prolonging the dominant), or $\hat{4}$–$(\hat{3})$–$\hat{2}$ and $\hat{6}$–$(\hat{5})$–$\hat{4}$ (prolonging the pre-dominant)
3. Neighboring $^6_4$: $\hat{3}$–$(\hat{4})$–$\hat{3}$ or $\hat{5}$–$(\hat{6})$–$\hat{5}$ over I

Identify the different types of $^6_4$ chords used in the harmonization in Example 12.

Example 12

DIATONIC LINEAR CHORDS

Passing or neighboring triads and seventh chords function contrapuntally or linearly to connect or prolong a harmony. We customarily indicate these embellishing chords by means of unstemmed noteheads and parentheses around their roman numerals. It might actually be more appropriate to dispense with roman numerals altogether and simply write in a "P" or "N" to denote the chord's true harmonic function. Two instances of contrapuntal chords that we discussed in previous chapters are illustrated in Example 13. Identify each chord and indicate its function.

Example 13

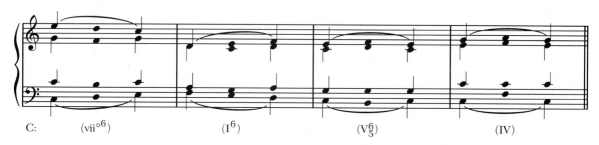

The following excerpts from music literature illustrate some examples of seventh chords used as linear harmonies. We might be tempted to analyze the second measure in the Chopin passage (Example 14a) and the third chord in the following passage (Example 14c) as some form of the supertonic seventh chord, either ii$^4_2$ or ii$^6_5$.

Example 14

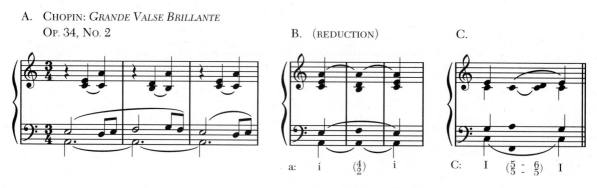

A. CHOPIN: *GRANDE VALSE BRILLANTE*
   OP. 34, NO. 2

B. (REDUCTION)   C.

However, closer inspection reveals that in neither of these apparent seventh chords does the chordal 7th resolve properly ($\hat{8}$–$\hat{7}$). Which do you think is a "P" chord and which an "N" chord? For such chords, we supply the figured bass in parentheses and use unstemmed noteheads, as we did for the passing and neighboring $\frac{6}{4}$'s above.

Confusion can arise from misunderstanding the interplay of harmony and melodic dissonance. Chord reiterations in accompaniment patterns or syllabic vocal settings may produce transient sonorities in which nonharmonic tones occur simultaneously with chordal members. Resist the temptation to analyze such sonorities as freestanding chords with a specific roman-numeral function. Examples of this interplay occur in the short passages in Example 15; carefully examine them and indicate in the reductions whether those sonorities marked with an arrow result from passing or neighboring motion. The first excerpt shows a prolongation of $V^{(7)}$; the second and third illustrate a tonic pedal.

Example 15

A. SCHUMANN: "AN DEN SONNENSCHEIN,"
OP. 36, NO. 4

B. (REDUCTION)

C. "THE MINSTREL BOY" (IRISH FOLK SONG)

D. (REDUCTION)

E. SCHUBERT: "IM ABENDROT," OP. 173, NO. 6   F. (REDUCTION)

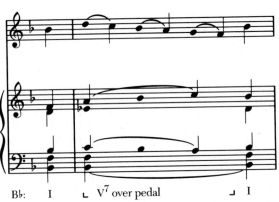

dei - nen Him-mel schon ‿ all - hier.

B♭:   I   ⌐ V^7 over pedal ⌐   I

Terms and Concepts for Review

linear chords   passing $^6_4$
accented *or* cadential $^6_4$ neighboring (pedal) $^6_4$
cadenza   arpeggiated $^6_4$

CHAPTER 17

The II⁷ and IV⁷ Chords

JUST AS WE HAVE CONSTRUCTED a seventh chord on the dominant scale degree, we can also construct seventh chords on the supertonic and subdominant degrees. The **II⁷ chord** and **IV⁷ chord** function much like their triadic counterparts, and may occur either as essential harmonies at cadences or as embellishing harmonies within the phrase. However, the addition of the chordal 7th to the two pre-dominant triads intensifies their tendency to progress to V or V⁷.

The seventh chord built on the supertonic is a minor seventh chord (ii⁷) in the major mode and a half-diminished seventh (ii⁰⁷) in the minor mode. The seventh chord built on the subdominant occurs in three forms: as a major seventh chord (IV⁷) in major and a minor seventh chord (iv⁷) or major-minor seventh (IV⁷) in minor. Note that the subdominant major seventh chord (in major) and the major-minor seventh chord (in minor) employ the same label, IV⁷; the context will indicate what the label stands for. These various forms are illustrated in Example 1.

Example 1

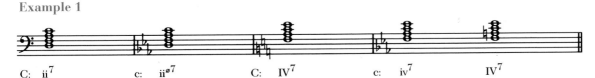

C: ii⁷   c: ii⁰⁷   C: IV⁷   c: iv⁷   IV⁷

TREATMENT OF THE CHORDAL 7TH

Examples 2a and 2b demonstrate that the preparation and resolution of the chordal 7th in these two chords usually occurs as a suspension over a moving bass. However, it may occasionally occur as a passing motion within the same harmony (Example 2c).

Example 2

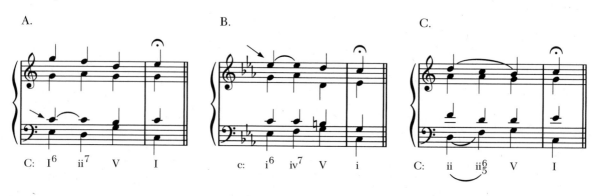

A.

B.

C.

C: I[6] ii[7] V I

c: i[6] iv[7] V i

C: ii ii$_5^6$ V I

THE CADENTIAL SUPERTONIC AND SUBDOMINANT SEVENTH CHORDS

As in Chapter 15, we will introduce each of these chords and their inversions in terms of the scale degree that appears in the bass voice. The ii$_5^6$ or ii$^{\emptyset 6}_5$ (over $\hat{4}$ in the bass) is one of the most common ways to approach the V–I in authentic cadences. In the three typical models given in Example 3, the chordal 7th tone and its resolution are bracketed. How is each dissonance prepared and resolved? What further delays its resolution in Example 3c?

Example 3

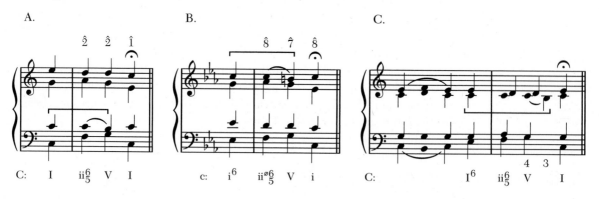

A.

B.

C.

$\hat{2}$ $\hat{2}$ $\hat{1}$

$\hat{8}$ $\hat{7}$ $\hat{8}$

C: I ii$_5^6$ V I

c: i[6] ii$^{\emptyset 6}_5$ V i

C: I[6] ii$_5^6$ V I

4 3

As you might expect, the function of these pre-dominant seventh chords in cadences requires that they be stemmed in voice-leading reductions. We leave the dissonant chordal 7th unstemmed, however, to denote its nonharmonic derivation.

The ii^7 (with $\hat{2}$ in the bass) and ii$^{\varnothing4}_3$ (with $\hat{6}$ in the bass) also occur in cadential formulas; see Example 4.

Example 4

A.   B.   C.

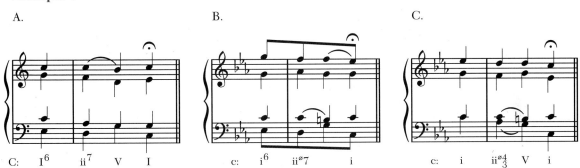

C: I^6 ii^7 V   I   c: i^6 ii$^{\varnothing}$7   i   c: i   ii$^{\varnothing4}_3$ V   i

The ii^7 (or ii$^{\varnothing7}$) normally progresses to V or an incomplete V^7, but never to a V^6. Why not? Observe the beaming of the similar 10ths in the outer voices of Example 4b. In Example 4c, note that the ii$^{\varnothing4}_3$ moves to the root-position V, the bass line producing an incomplete neighbor; this progression is more common in the minor mode.

Scale degree $\hat{4}$ in the bass may also support a IV^7 or iv^7 in authentic cadences. The soprano lines that typically accompany such progressions are shown in the two models in Example 5.

Example 5

A.   B.

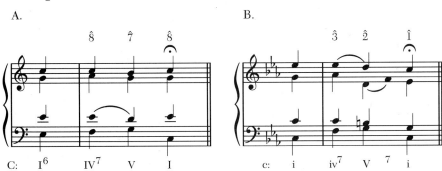

C: I^6 IV^7 V   I   c: i   iv^7 V ^{7} i

In Example 5b the chordal 5th of the V is doubled. What partwriting problem does this doubling avoid?

PRE-DOMINANT SEVENTH CHORDS IN MUSIC LITERATURE

Some typical uses of cadential pre-dominant seventh chords are shown in Example 6.

Example 6

A. PURCELL: "WHEN I AM LAID IN EARTH" FROM *DIDO AND AENEAS* ACT III

B. (REDUCTION)

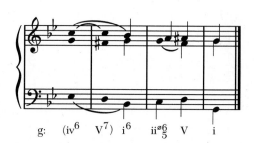

g: (iv[6] V[7]) i[6] ii[ø6/5] V i

C. COLE PORTER: "I GET A KICK OUT OF YOU"

D. (REDUCTION)

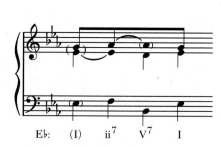

Eb: (I) ii[7] V[7] I

E. MOZART: PIANO SONATA IN Bb MAJOR, K.333, I

F. (REDUCTION)

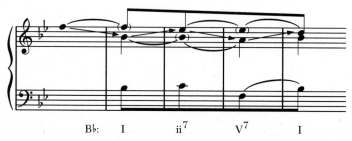

Bb: I ii[7] V[7] I

G. Schubert: "Ständchen" from *Schwanengesang*

Lei - se flie - hen mei - ne Lie - der durch die Nacht _zu dir;

H. (REDUCTION)

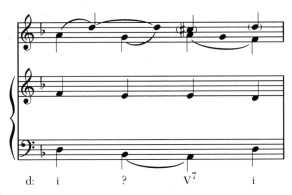

d: i   ?   V⁷   i

I. Chopin: Scherzo in D♭ major, Op. 31

J. (REDUCTION)

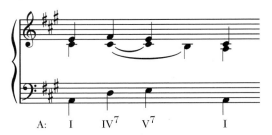

A: I   IV⁷   V⁷   I

What is unusual about the resolution of the V⁷ in measure 62 of the Purcell aria? The first sixteen measures of the chorus to Cole Porter's "I Get a Kick Out of You" are based on the recurring progression ii⁷–V⁷–I. The last four measures of this section are quoted in Example 6c; note the implied voice leading in the reduction. The Mozart excerpt is especially interesting since the soprano part suggests two distinct melodic strands, the lower of which outlines a ii⁷ in the second measure (even though the chordal 7th is only implied). The arrows in the reduction indicate the flow of the original melody. The reduction demonstrates the preparation and resolution of the 7ths in both the ii⁷ and the following V⁷ chord. The vocal part of the Schubert song likewise implies two melodic lines, as shown in the reduction. Which pre-dominant seventh chord is used here, and what is its inversion? In the Chopin scherzo, what happens to the resolution of the 7th of the IV⁷?

EMBELLISHING PRE-DOMINANT SEVENTH CHORDS

The various forms of cadential pre-dominant seventh chords discussed above may also occur in embellishing progressions within a phrase. In such cases, the progression to a weaker form of tonic, such as I⁶ or a root-position I with $\hat{3}$ or $\hat{5}$ in the soprano, avoids the sense of cadential close. We will

Example 7

leave these embellishing progressions unstemmed and enclose their roman numerals in parentheses. In the models given in Example 7, compare these chords with the cadential pre-dominant seventh chords, which move to V in the half cadence of each model.

The ii^4_2 or $ii^{\varnothing 4}_2$ usually occurs during a phrase's opening embellishing progression (Example 8).

Example 8

A.   HANDEL: 20. "HE WAS DESPISED" FROM *MESSIAH*

B.   (REDUCTION)   C.

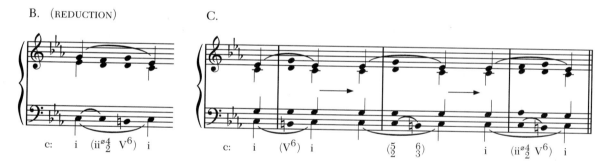

Its voice leading originates from a neighboring figure, I–(V[6])–I, as illustrated in the models in Example 8c. The suspension in the bass resolves to either a V[6] (as here) or a V[6][5]. The dissonant nature of this progression is particularly appropriate for the agitated middle section of the Handel aria, which depicts the scourging of the "Suffering Servant."

Inversions of the subdominant seventh chord also occur in embellishing contexts (Example 9).

Example 9

A.   Mozart: Variations on "Ah, vous dirai-je, Maman," K.265, Var. 4

C:

B.   "Christus, der ist mein Leben"
      (Bach chorale harmonization)

C.   (reduction)

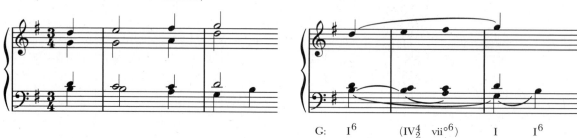

The Mozart excerpt contains the embellishing progression IV_5^6–V_5^6–I. How does the soprano prepare the 7th of the V_5^6? What other nonharmonic tone is emphasized in this passage? (From these few measures, do you recognize the melody for Mozart's variations under another name?) In Bach's chorale harmonization, how is the IV_2^4 prepared and resolved?

PROLONGATIONS OF THE PRE-DOMINANT FUNCTION

We have previously discussed the brief prolongation of both tonic and dominant harmonies. We may also briefly extend both the triadic and seventh-chord forms of pre-dominant harmony in similar ways (Example 10).

Example 10

A. HAYDN: PIANO SONATA IN A♭ MAJOR, HOB. XVI:43, III

B. (REDUCTION)

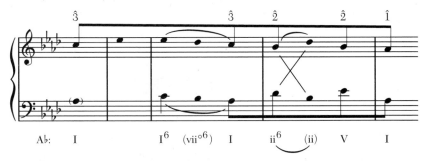

A♭:   I   I⁶ (vii°⁶) I   ii⁶ (ii)   V   I

C. SCHUMANN: "★₊★" (NO. 21) FROM *ALBUM FOR THE YOUNG*, OP. 68

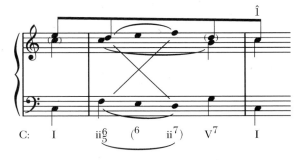

D. (REDUCTION)

C: I   ii$\frac{6}{5}$ (⁶   ii⁷)   V⁷   I

E.

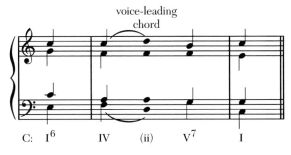

voice-leading chord

C: I⁶   IV   (ii)   V⁷   I

F. THOMAS À BECKET: "COLUMBIA, THE GEM OF THE OCEAN"

G. (REDUCTION)

A♭:   I   IV   (ii)   V⁷   I

A pre-dominant harmony may be extended by using different inversions of the same chord, such as ii⁶–ii (Example 10a), IV–IV⁶, or ii⁷–ii⁶. These inversions are often bridged with a passing ⁶ or ⁶₄ chord, as in Example 10c; note the resulting voice exchange between the supertonic chords in this passage. We will sometimes encounter a movement from IV to ii (the reverse, ii–IV, seldom occurs). This progression results from a 5–6 motion over $\hat{4}$ in the bass, where the 6 (or $\hat{2}$) is then displaced into the bass voice (Example 10e). In such cases the ii chord is sometimes called a **voice-leading chord,** since it is derived from the linear 5–6 motion. An instance of this procedure occurs in "Columbia, the Gem of the Ocean" (Example 10f). The notes in parentheses in Examples 10d and 10g suggest the implied soprano lines.

Pre-dominant function can also be extended by "resolving" certain inversions of the IV⁷ into some form of a ii⁷ (Example 11).

Example 11

A. SCHUBERT: MOMENT MUSICAL NO. 6 IN A♭ MAJOR

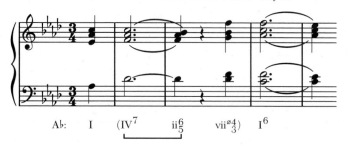

A♭:   I   (IV⁷   ii⁶₅   vii°⁴₃)   I⁶

B. (REDUCTION)

A♭:   ⁷₅   ⁶₅   ⁶₄   ─₃

C. Bach: Prelude in C Major from *Well-Tempered Clavier*, Book I

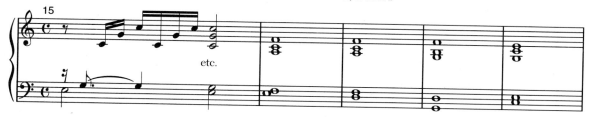

D. (Reduction)

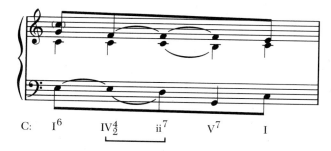

C: I⁶   IV₂⁴   ii⁷   V⁷   I

In the Schubert passage (Example 11a), the IV⁷ moves to a ii⁵₆ through the resolution of a 7–6 suspension; notice how this dissonance (mm. 1–2) is "answered" by the dissonant 4–3 figure (mm. 3–4). The same progression occurs in the Bach Prelude (Example 11b), where the 7–6 "suspension" figure is now displaced to the bass voice, producing a IV₂⁴–ii⁷ succession.

Summary of Partwriting Procedures

Partwriting with II⁷ and IV⁷ and their inversions is not especially problematic, provided that you prepare and resolve the chordal 7th correctly; when using an inverted form of these chords you should include all four notes. Corrections of bad partwriting of these chords in several musical contexts are shown in Example 12.

In the progression ii⁷–V⁷, one of the chords must be incomplete lest parallel 5ths result (Example 12a). Parallels may also arise in the progression IV⁷–V; to prevent them from occurring, double the chordal 5th in the V chord (Example 12b). Parallel 5ths and doubled leading tones are particularly troublesome in the succession IV⁶₅–V⁶₅; observe the solutions in the third model of Example 12c.

Example 12

Melody Harmonization

Using pre-dominant seventh chords and their inversions in melody harmonizations is very much like using the triadic forms of these chords. Though the II_5^6 occurs frequently in authentic cadences, the other types of pre-dominant seventh chords are most effective when used sparingly.

A possible harmonization of the hymn tune "Dix" (by Conrad Kocher) in Example 13 includes a variety of pre-dominant triads and seventh chords. The melody consists of three phrases, each of which is divided into a pair of two-measure subphrases. Though the first two melodic phrases are identical, they have different harmonic settings. Do a roman-numeral analysis of the harmonization, distinguishing between embellishing (unstemmed) and essential (stemmed) chords in the voice-leading reduction that accompanies the harmonization. Do you notice any IV's that act as neighbors to I? Explain the function of each II$^{(7)}$ and IV$^{(7)}$, as well as the treatment of their chordal 7ths.

Example 13   KOCHER: "DIX" (HYMN TUNE)

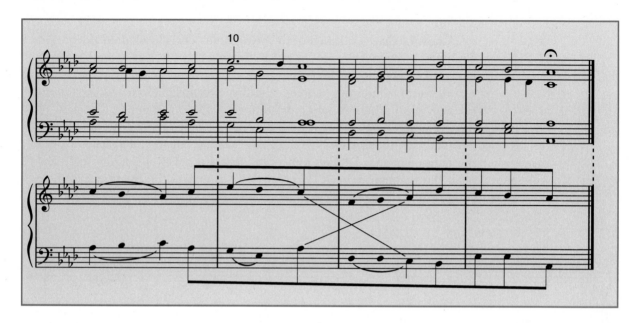

Terms and Concepts for Review

II⁷ chord
IV⁷ chord
treatment of the chordal 7th
cadential *vs.* embellishing pre-dominant
   seventh chords

prolongation of pre-dominant chords
voice-leading chord

CHAPTER 18

The VI, III, and Other Diatonic Chords

IN THIS CHAPTER we will complete our study of diatonic chords. We will first focus on the submediant and mediant harmonies and then discuss the v^6 and VII in minor, and the I^7 in both modes. All of these chords are normally produced by linear motion, and therefore function as embellishing harmonies. In some cases, however, the VI and III may substitute for the tonic triad.

The submediant and mediant chords are minor triads in the major mode (vi and iii) and major triads in the minor mode (VI and III).

THE VI TRIAD AS A VOICE-LEADING CHORD

The submediant triad is almost always found in root position. In this form, it frequently connects the tonic to a pre-dominant harmony, since its bass note ($\hat{6}$) divides the leap from $\hat{1}$ down to $\hat{4}$ into two 3rds, supporting such progressions as I–(vi)–IV or I–(vi)–ii^6 in major, and i–(VI)–iv or i–(VI)–ii^{o6} in minor. See Example 1.[1]

---

1. In the root-position progression I–VI, the submediant is sometimes referred to as a *voice-leading chord*, since it is derived by a 5–6 motion over $\hat{1}$ in the bass, where the 6 (or $\hat{6}$) is displaced into the bass voice. This same principle has already been mentioned in Chapter 17 with regard to the progression IV–ii (p. 234).

Example 1

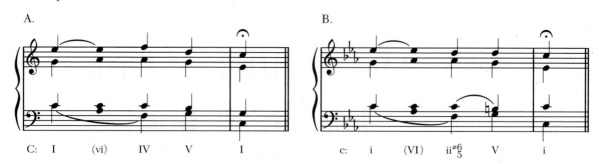

A.   B.

C: I   (vi)   IV   V   I   c: i   (VI)   ii⌀⁶₅   V   i

Observe how we indicate these submediants in reductive notation and roman-numeral analysis. These chords are often interpolated into the progression I–( )–IV–V–I, as shown by the bass stemming in Example 2; the interpolation will often include I⁶ or even iii.

Example 2

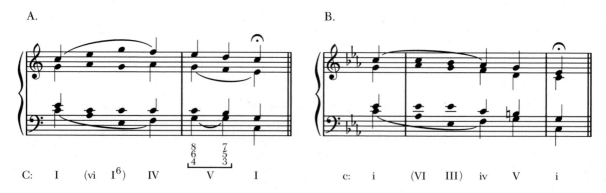

A.   B.

C: I   (vi   I⁶)   IV   V   I   c: i   (VI   III)   iv   V   i

OTHER USES OF THE VI TRIAD

The submediant triad may appear in other contexts (Example 3).

Example 3

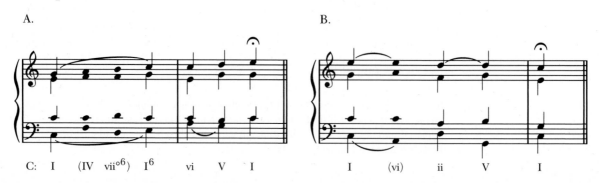

A.   B.

C: I   (IV   vii°⁶)   I⁶   vi   V   I   I   (vi)   ii   V   I

C.

It can substitute for a pre-dominant chord and move directly to V, as in Example 3a; note that the chord tones are stemmed in this context. The submediant triad may also initiate a series of falling 5ths: vi–ii–V–I (Example 3b). A familiar form of this progression, shown in Example 3c, has provided the harmonic basis for innumerable popular songs, such as "Blue Moon" and "The Way You Look Tonight."

How the first inversion of this chord (vi⁶) functions is difficult to define. Since scale degree $\hat{1}$ appears in the bass, the triad is closely related to the tonic chord. The first two beats of the Schubert sonata in Example 4 perhaps are best considered a melodic 6–5 motion over I rather than a vi⁶. In the Schubert song that follows, the soprano G^4 and A^4 fill in a passing motion from $\hat{5}$ to $\hat{8}$, as can be seen in the accompanying reduction.

Example 4

A. SCHUBERT: PIANO SONATA IN A MAJOR, D. 664, II   B. (REDUCTION)

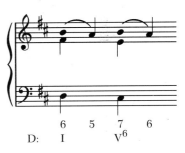

C. SCHUBERT: "DU BIST DIE RUH'"

D. (REDUCTION)

THE VI AS A SUBSTITUTE FOR I: THE DECEPTIVE CADENCE

In our previous melodic analysis of the tune "Old One Hundred" (Example 17 of Chapter 3), we noted the premature arrival of the tonic note at the end of the third phrase. In order to avoid a conclusive-sounding cadence on $\hat{1}$ here, we may substitute a vi chord for the expected I; doing so maintains the sense of harmonic momentum toward the final tonic (Example 5).

Example 5   LOUIS BOURGEOIS: "OLD ONE HUNDRED" (HYMN)

This submediant substitution for the tonic chord in a perfect authentic cadence is called a **deceptive cadence.** The only difference between the normal authentic cadence and its deceptive counterpart is the stepwise ascent in the bass ($\hat{5}$–$\hat{6}$ rather than $\hat{5}$–$\hat{1}$); the soprano retains its usual $\hat{2}$–$\hat{1}$ or $\hat{7}$–$\hat{8}$ motion, as in Examples 6a and 6b. In your partwriting, you should avoid a soprano movement from $\hat{7}$ to $\hat{6}$, since the leading tone's "wrong" resolution would be so audible.

Example 6

Deceptive progressions within a phrase may employ a $\hat{5}$–$\hat{3}$ motion in the soprano (Example 7).

Example 7

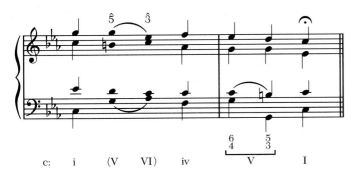

c: i (V VI) iv $\begin{smallmatrix}6\\4\end{smallmatrix}$ $\begin{smallmatrix}5\\3\end{smallmatrix}$ V I

In "America" (Example 8), the dominant $\begin{smallmatrix}6-5\\4-3\end{smallmatrix}$ appears to be leading to an authentic cadence but instead moves to vi, thereby continuing the harmonic flow until the actual cadence arrives two bars later.

Example 8 "AMERICA"

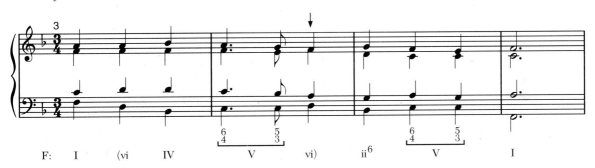

F: I (vi IV $\begin{smallmatrix}6\\4\end{smallmatrix}$ $\begin{smallmatrix}5\\3\end{smallmatrix}$ V vi) ii^6 $\begin{smallmatrix}6\\4\end{smallmatrix}$ $\begin{smallmatrix}5\\3\end{smallmatrix}$ V I

THE VI TRIAD IN MUSIC LITERATURE

Some typical uses of the submediant triad in music literature are illustrated in Example 9. Rossini was especially fond of the "divider vi" (i.e., the vi that divides the $\hat{1}$–$\hat{4}$ descending root movement in two) in his grand final cadences: I–(vi)–ii^6–V–I (Example 9a). Starting with the vi chord, what type of interval occurs between the successive roots of the chords in Meyerbeer's march (Example 9c)? Notice the interpolation of I^6 between the vi and ii$^6_5$ in the quotation from "Rule, Britannia" (Example 9e). The reduction of the Handel aria shows that its basic progression is I–(vii$^{\circ 6}$)–I^6–V (Example 9g); a transient deceptive V^7–vi (shown in brackets) is simply interpolated within this overall progression.

Example 9

A. ROSSINI: OVERTURE TO *L'ITALIANA IN ALGERI*

B. (REDUCTION)

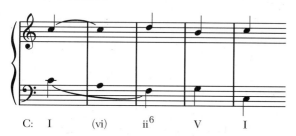

C: I   (vi)   ii⁶   V   I

C. MEYERBEER: MARCH OF THE PRIESTS FROM *LE PROPHÈTE*, ACT IV   D. (REDUCTION)

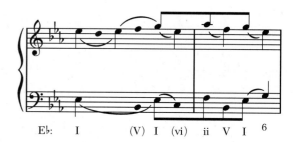

E♭:   I   (V) I   (vi)   ii   V   I   6

E. THOMAS ARNE, "RULE, BRITANNIA"   F. (REDUCTION)

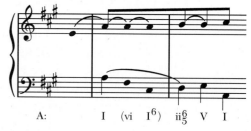

A: I   (vi   I⁶)   ii⁶₅   V   I

G. HANDEL: "VERDI PRATI" FROM *ALCINA*, ACT II

H. (REDUCTION)

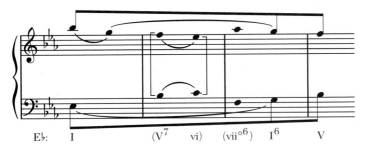

E♭:   I   (V⁷   vi)   (vii°⁶)   I⁶   V

THE DECEPTIVE CADENCE IN LARGER MUSICAL CONTEXTS

Deceptive cadences are sometimes used to link two larger sections of music. One such instance occurs at the end of the Scherzo of Beethoven's Symphony No. 5. Although it is highly unusual for an entire movement to conclude with a deceptive cadence, here Beethoven uses it as a bridge to link the Scherzo with the last movement. After the deceptive VI chord, he holds us in suspense with an extended ambiguous passage before arriving at an emphatic dominant that eventually resolves into the opening C-major chord of the Finale.

Example 10   BEETHOVEN: SYMPHONY NO. 5, III TO IV

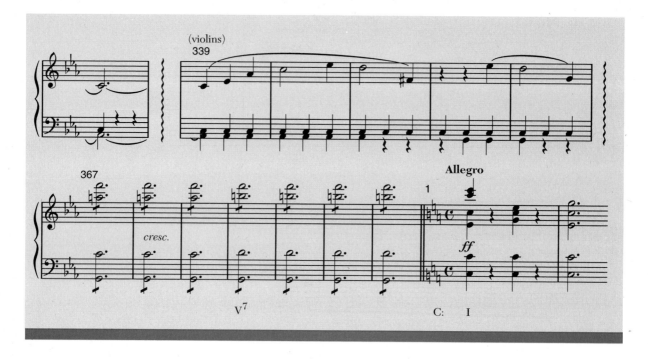

THE III TRIAD WITHIN THE PHRASE

We will now turn to the submediant's companion, the mediant triad, and examine its role in harmonic progressions. In the major mode, the iii chord in root position has taken on idiomatic usages illustrated in Example 11.

The mediant triad can initiate a sequence of falling 5ths—iii–vi–ii–V–I—as in Wagner's familiar bridal chorus. The iii chord can also support a descending $\hat{8}$–$\hat{7}$–$\hat{6}$ motion in the soprano; at the opening of "Chester," the unstemmed iii moves directly to IV in the manner of an incomplete neighbor. The interpolated deceptive progression between measures 2 and 3 in this passage (see the notes in brackets) recalls the procedure found in the Handel aria in Example 9. The mediant chord can even substitute for I[6], as in the Fischer fugue (Example 11e).

Example 11

A. WAGNER: BRIDAL CHORUS FROM *LOHENGRIN*, ACT III

B. (REDUCTION)

C. "CHESTER" (MELODY BY WILLIAM BILLINGS)

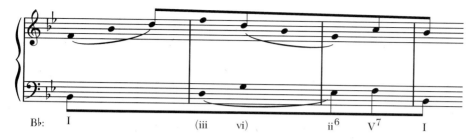

D. (REDUCTION)

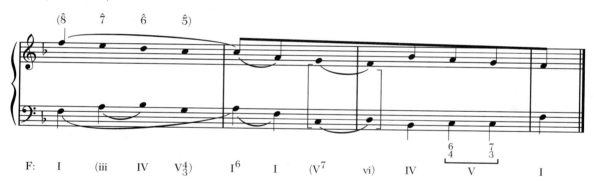

E. JOHANN FISCHER: FUGUE IN F MAJOR FROM *ARIADNE MUSICA*

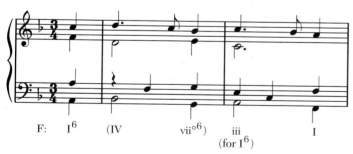

Like the vi⁶, the iii⁶ has a nebulous function. Just as vi⁶ may substitute for the tonic, iii⁶ is often associated with dominant harmony. When we encounter what appears to be a iii⁶, in most cases we are merely seeing a 5–6 or 6–5 soprano motion within a V or V⁷ (see Example 12). It is best to analyze this sonority as dominant harmony, even when the chordal 5th ($\hat{2}$) is omitted.

Example 12

A.

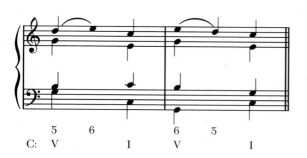

C: V   I   V   I
      5   6   6   5

B. "VATER UNSER IM HIMMELREICH"
(BACH CHORALE HARMONIZATION)

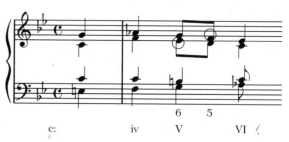

c: iv   V   VI
              6   5

C. CHOPIN: BALLADE IN G MINOR, OP. 23

D. (REDUCTION)

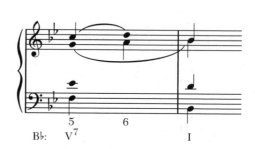

Bb: V⁷   I
        5   6

In the minor mode, the III chord may function as the tonic chord in the relative major key. Therefore, III is tonally stronger than iii, its counterpart in major. In the Mendelssohn excerpt (Example 13a), the root movement by ascending 3rds, producing i–III–V, is analogous to the descending movement from the tonic (I–vi–IV) seen in Example 8. In the i–III–v progression, scale degree $\hat{5}$ is common to all three chords. Although III may support scale degree $\hat{7}$ in the soprano line $\hat{8}$–$\hat{7}$–$\hat{6}$–$\hat{5}$ in minor, it rarely substitutes for i⁶ (Example 13b).

Example 13   MENDELSSOHN: *FINGAL'S CAVE OVERTURE*, OP. 26 (SIMPLIFICATION OF MM. 9–13)

A.

b: i   III

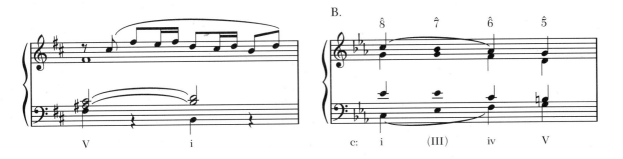

MODAL CHORDS

When the submediant, mediant, and supertonic triads (vi, iii, and ii) are favored over dominant harmony in certain progressions, the sense of normal harmonic function may become less evident, and the music may take on a more "modal" flavor.[2] For this reason, these triads are sometimes referred to as **modal chords.** The Russian and Eastern European composers of the nineteenth century were especially fond of this implied modality. What are we to make of the opening measure of the little *Nutcracker* march?

Example 14   TCHAIKOVSKY: MARCH FROM *THE NUTCRACKER*, ACT I

2. Modal music, such as that from the Renaissance period (1450–1600) or from folk-music repertories, does not show normal harmonic function characteristic of common-practice period music. See Appendix 2 for further information about the diatonic modal scales.

THE VI⁷ AND III⁷ CHORDS

The rare examples of VI⁷ and III⁷ usually occur as part of a sequence of seventh chords by descending 5ths; we will discuss this progression in further detail in Chapter 22.

OTHER DIATONIC CHORDS

Since the diatonic chords that we will discuss in this section are derived linearly, they almost always function as embellishing harmonies. The v^6 in the minor mode contains a subtonic rather than a leading tone, and therefore shows little or no tendency to resolve to the tonic like a normal dominant (Example 15).

Example 15

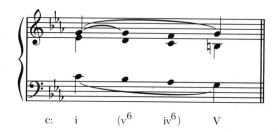

Instead, the $\flat\hat{7}$ tends downward to $\flat\hat{6}$ on the way to $\hat{5}$. The descending tetrachord that results spawns the progression i–v^6–iv^6–V, frequently found in passacaglias and chaconnes of the Baroque period (Example 16). This familiar progression is often elaborated with 7–6 suspensions.

Example 16   JOHANN KUHNAU: CIACONA IN F MINOR

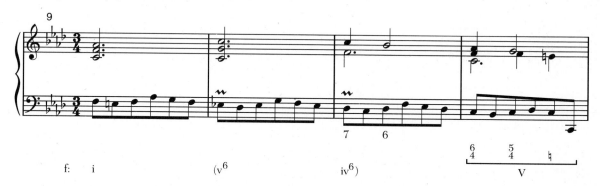

The bass pattern $\hat{8}$–$\hat{7}$–$\hat{6}$–$\hat{5}$ in minor also occurs in Spanish flamenco music, where VII and VI substitute for v^6 and iv^6 (Example 17). Observe the parallel 5ths above the bass, which are typical of this style.

Example 17   FLAMENCO GUITAR PROGRESSION

The VII triad in the minor mode often precedes the III, acting as a dominant to it (see Example 18 of Chapter 25).

The addition of a 7th to the tonic triad transforms the normally stable I into an active harmony. It creates a major 7th in major (I^7) or a minor 7th in minor (i^7). This chord frequently appears in a progression of descending 5ths, as illustrated in Example 18a. What type of sequence does the tonic seventh chord initiate in the Brahms Intermezzo (Example 18b)?

Example 18

A. FRIEDRICH KUHLAU: SONATINA FOR PIANO IN C MAJOR, OP. 88, NO. 3

B. BRAHMS: INTERMEZZO IN B♭ MINOR, OP. 117, NO. 2

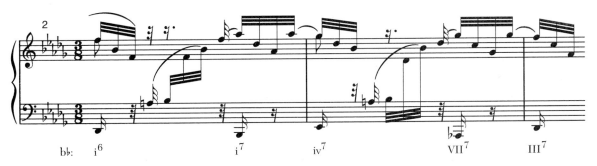

C. RACHMANINOFF: VOCALISE, OP. 34, NO. 14   D. (REDUCTION)

In the Rachmaninoff vocalise (Example 18c), this chord's $\frac{4}{2}$ form is derived by passing motion. We may even encounter a major 7th as an added "color" tone in the final I chord of popular or jazz compositions.

Summary of Partwriting Procedures

The progressions I–vi, vi–IV, IV–ii, and I–iii show a root movement by diatonic 3rd. How you write these particular progressions will depend on the soprano line. The first two models in Example 19 employ common tones. When the upper voice leaps, a change from close to open structure will usually occur (Example 19c).

Example 19

A.

B.

C.

As Example 20 demonstrates, the deceptive progression V–vi can easily foster partwriting mistakes, such as a melodic augmented 2nd or parallel octaves or 5ths. Since the roots ascend by step, two of the upper voices must move contrary to the bass, producing a doubled 3rd in the submediant triad.

Example 20

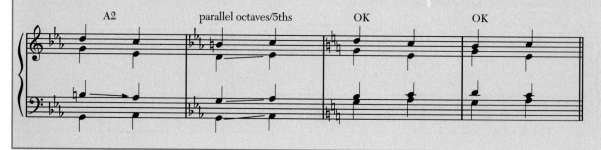

Melody Harmonization

In harmonizing melodies, you should associate the VI triad with the melodic scale degrees $\hat{3}$ or $\hat{1}$ rather than $\hat{6}$, and the III triad with $\hat{3}$ or $\hat{7}$ ($\hat{7}$ will usually continue to descend through $\hat{6}$ to $\hat{5}$). Although these two chords can add harmonic variety to melodic settings, you should limit their use; certainly avoid using too many deceptive cadences. Examine the three short phrases in Example 21 to see where you could effectively employ the submediant or mediant triad. Then sketch an appropriate bass line for each one.

Example 21

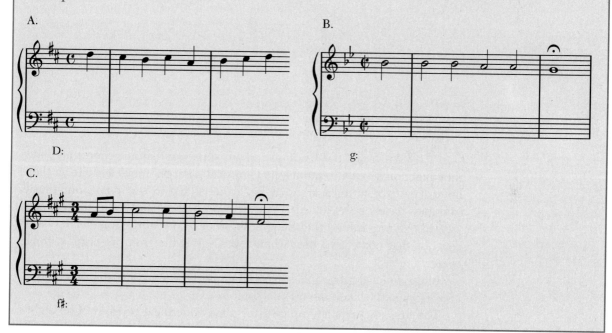

Terms and Concepts for Review

VI as "divider" between I and IV *or* II⁶

"vi⁶" as 5–6 over I

deceptive cadence

III as relative major

modal chords

v⁶, VII, and I⁷

partwriting chords a diatonic 3rd apart

CHAPTER 19

Tonicization and Modulation I

MOTION TO V AND III

Now that we have completed our survey of diatonic chords and how they function,[1] we will examine how musical passages move away from their home key to new tonal areas or key centers. Up to this point, our music examples have rarely exceeded one or two phrases; starting in this chapter we will begin to extend their length, in order to reveal the tonal variety and contrast that come into play when a passage shifts from its original tonal center.

In the following two folk songs (Example 1), we see a temporary motion away from and back to the original tonic key.

The first song is made up of three almost identical versions of an eight-measure period, each phrase of which is bracketed to show the tune's repetitive design. What happens in the middle section (mm. 9–16) to counteract the sense of melodic redundancy? In the second song, the relative key of A♭ major reinforces the contrasting thematic material of the B phrase (mm. 4–8); the A material and the F-minor tonic return simultaneously in the last phrase (mm. 8–12). In these songs, the progression to a new key center, whether using the same or different musical themes, is an important means of achieving tonal variety.

---

1. We will cover the one remaining chord, the vii°⁷ chord, in Chapter 21.

Example 1

A. "ORANGES AND LEMONS" (ENGLISH FOLK SONG)

B. "THE ROSE OF TRALEE" (IRISH FOLK SONG)

THE TONICIZATION OF DIATONIC CHORDS

We use the term **tonicization** to describe the process by which a scale degree or harmony other than the tonic temporarily assumes a tonic function. We have already explored how tonic harmony may be established and prolonged; we will now examine how other diatonic triads may be tonicized, either briefly or at length. The scale degree on which the newly tonicized major or minor triad is built now acts as the momentary tonic. In this chapter, we will concentrate on the two most significant triads to assume a tonic function: the dominant (V) in the major mode, and the mediant or relative major (III) in the minor mode. We will discuss the tonicization of other diatonic chords in Chapters 25 and 26.

THE DOMINANT KEY IN THE MAJOR MODE

To a large extent, tonal harmony revolves around the interaction of tonic and dominant. It is therefore not surprising that V is the most commonly tonicized triad in the major mode. In a typical expansion of the basic progression I–V–I, shown in Example 2, the dominant harmony is temporarily tonicized through the progression ii^7–V^7–I in G major (just before the dotted line). In the next section the harmonic motion leads back to the opening C-major tonic. This movement to the active dominant domain creates a sense of tonal tension that is subsequently resolved by the descent back to the tonic (Example 2).

Example 2

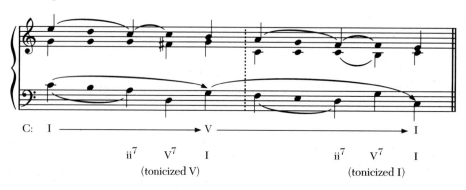

C: I ⟶ V ⟶ I

ii^7 V^7 I   ii^7 V^7 I
(tonicized V)   (tonicized I)

EMBELLISHING TONICIZATIONS

At the surface level of many pieces—that is, the notes that we actually play, sing, or hear, before we strip out the embellishing tones in a reductive analysis—momentary tonicizations that involve only two chords may occur. The second of these chords is a diatonic triad such as V; it is preceded by some member of its own family of dominant chords: its dominant (V/V), its dominant seventh (V^7/V), its leading-tone triad (vii°^{6}/V), its diminished leading-tone seventh (vii°^{7}/V), its half-diminished leading-tone seventh (vii^{ø7}/V), or any inversion of these. We call these new, secondary level of diatonic chords **secondary** or **applied dominants** and always denote them in analysis by a symbol that consists of two roman numerals separated with a slash, the first numeral representing the secondary dominant, the second one its respective tonic—in this case, the original dominant (Example 3).[2]

Any diatonic harmony other than the tonic may be tonicized by coupling it with its own secondary dominant chord.[3] The **embellishing tonicization** that results does not last long enough to give us the sense that we have truly arrived at a new key center. In the Fauré excerpt in Example 4, for instance,

2. In some harmony texts, secondary dominants are indicated in other ways: for instance, "V^7 of V" or "V^7 → V."

3. We will examine applied or secondary dominant chords in some detail in Chapter 25.

Example 3

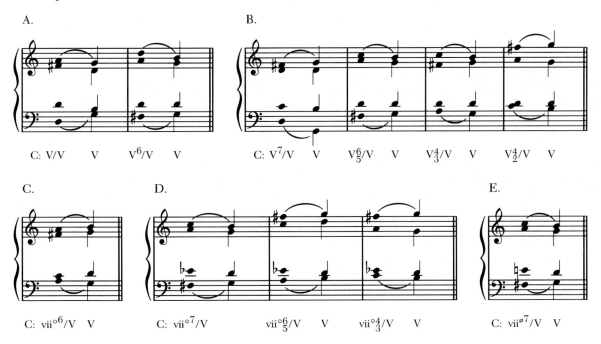

A.

B.

C: V/V   V   V^6/V   V

C: V^7/V   V   V$^6_5$/V   V   V$^4_3$/V   V   V$^4_2$/V   V

C.

D.

E.

C: vii°^{6}/V   V

C: vii°^{7}/V   vii°$^6_5$/V   V   vii°$^4_3$/V   V

C: vii°^{7}/V   V

even though the iv and V are preceded by their respective secondary dominant sevenths, we do not perceive that the C-minor tonic has actually been replaced by either F minor or G major.

Example 4   FAURÉ: PIANO QUARTET IN C MINOR, OP. 15, I

c: i   (iv^6 V$^6_5$/iv   iv)   i   (V^7/V)   V

Temporary tonics such as these pass so quickly that they are never truly heard as I or i but rather retain their function in the original key.

MODULATION

Tonicization may also occur at more fundamental formal or structural levels. When this process involves a distinct aural shift away from the original tonic to some other key center, we designate this larger-scale tonicization as a **modulation.** We will examine how modulation results from the directed motion to the new key and a cadential confirmation of this new key. Our sense of tonic shift will depend on the length of time we spend within the key. For instance, in Example 5 the tonicization of the dominant, C major, is first suggested by the introduction of its leading tone (B♮) in measure 1 and the subsequent stabilization of the new key by a cadence in measure 2.

Example 5 "DAS WALT' GOTT VATER UND GOTT SOHN" (BACH CHORALE HARMONIZATION)

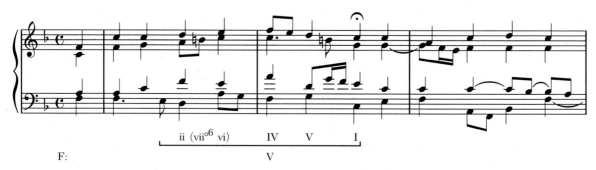

F:

The next phrase, however, immediately returns to the original tonic, and we perceive the tonicized V area as only a **transient modulation** within the basic F tonality. In the analysis of such temporary modulations we place the roman numerals indicating the new area over a bracket and the triad that is tonicized under the bracket, as in the Bach example.

After arriving in the dominant area, the composer may wish to remain in the new key. In such cases we will perceive a definite shift in tonal center, with the new key supplanting the old key. In Classical-period sonatas, the dominant section within the exposition often lasts as long as the initial tonic section.[4] When we analyze these extended tonicizations or modulations, we will enclose the roman numeral denoting the new key within a box. In Example 6, for instance, after the motion to and cadence in boxed V in measures 6–8, the dominant area remains tonicized throughout the remainder of the passage.

---

4. For a discussion of sonata form, see Excursion II: More Complex Forms on p. 439–59.

Example 6   CLEMENTI: PIANO SONATINA IN C MAJOR, OP. 36, NO. 1, I

DIFFERENT METHODS OF CHANGING KEY

How do we bring about a change from one key center to another? Three distinct methods are possible.

After a passage cadences in the original tonic, it may immediately switch to a new key in the new section, with or without a change of key signature. We call this procedure a **sectional modulation.** Here there is no sense of modulatory process. When we analyze pieces that employ sectional modulation, we place the new key designation (such as Ⅴ) right at the beginning of the new, contrasting section. In Example 7, the trio section of Mozart's D-major Minuet abruptly begins in A major, or Ⅴ.

Example 7   MOZART: SYMPHONY NO. 35 ("HAFFNER"), K.385, III

Sectional modulations often occur at junctures between the first and second sections of a *ternary,* or three-part, form (ABA), in which the contrasting middle section is set in a different key. Any sectionalized form may employ this type of modulation and use contrasting keys other than Ⅴ. Not only the minuet and trio, but also waltzes, marches (with their inevitable shift to Ⅳ in the trio), mazurkas, rags, and polkas frequently exhibit sectional modulations.

We may also find an occasional sectional modulation between phrases. In the following Beethoven Menuetto (Example 8), the first phrase simply prolongs an F-minor tonic harmony with embellishing dominant chords. At measures 4–5 the tonality immediately shifts to the relative major key (Ⅲ).

Example 8   BEETHOVEN: PIANO SONATA IN F MINOR, OP. 2, NO. 1, III

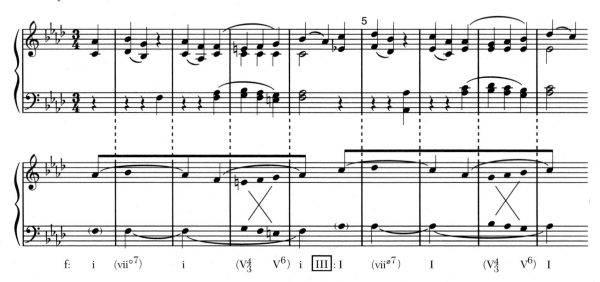

Now look back to the melodies that are given in Example 1. The first one especially shows a sectional modulation between phrases. When modulations occur within a phrase, a **pivot** or **common chord** is usually employed to link the two keys. In this second method of effecting a key change, a diatonic chord in the old key simultaneously functions as a different diatonic chord in the new key. This pivot chord will not be the V(⁷) of the new key, since this secondary dominant will normally contain one or more notes that are not in the original key. The pivot chord, then, must precede the secondary dominant chord and contain no altered notes in either key. Pre-dominant chords in the new key, such as IV, ii, or vi, make excellent pivot chords in modulations to Ⅴ. Thus, the old I becomes the new IV, the old vi becomes the new ii, and the old iii becomes the new vi. Observe how the common chords are vertically aligned in the harmonic analyses in Example 9, with the new-key analysis placed below that of the original key.

Example 9

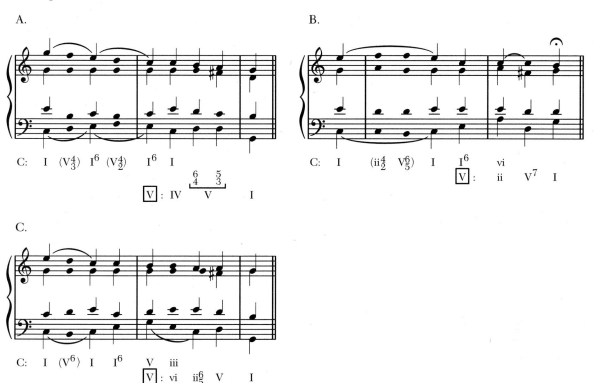

A.

C: I (V$^4_3$) I^6 (V$^4_2$) I^6 I

$\boxed{\text{V}}$: IV $\overset{\overset{6}{4}\;\overset{5}{3}}{\text{V}}$ I

B.

C: I (ii$^4_2$ V$^6_5$) I I^6 vi

$\boxed{\text{V}}$: ii V^7 I

C.

C: I (V^6) I I^6 V iii

$\boxed{\text{V}}$: vi ii$^6_5$ V I

The chromatic alteration of a scale degree within a phrase may signal the start of a **chromatic modulation.** A chromatic modulation to $\boxed{\text{V}}$ will normally utilize $\hat{4}$–$\sharp\hat{4}$–$\hat{5}$ in one of the voices, where the $\sharp\hat{4}$ in the old key acts as the leading tone ($\hat{7}$) in the new key (Examples 10a and 10b). Upon returning to the original key, the $\sharp\hat{4}$ changes back to $\natural\hat{4}$ (Example 10c). Since no common chord is used to return to I, we begin analyzing immediately in the original key. Examine the chromatic motion in the passages in Example 10.

Example 10

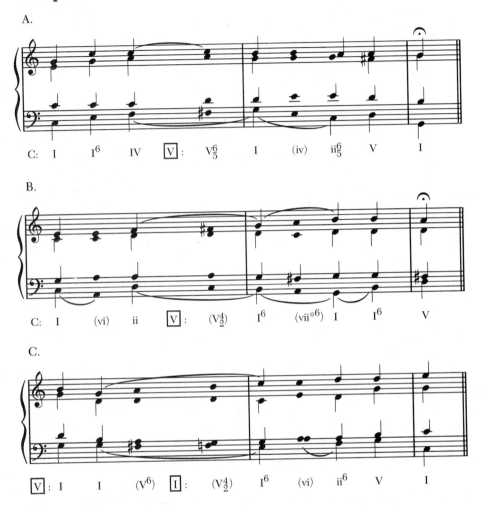

THE MEDIANT KEY IN THE MINOR MODE

Modulation to the mediant or relative major key (III) is the most common modulation in the minor mode. Like modulation to V in the major mode, mediant modulations are found at various levels in music of the common-practice period—as embellishing tonicizations, as transient modulations within a phrase, and as extended modulations that are confirmed by cadences. The mediant key tends not to return directly to the original tonic but rather to continue on to the dominant, resulting in an overall progression of i→III→V→i. This large-scale tonal scheme frequently occurs in minor-mode pieces in binary, ternary, rondo, and sonata form.

Now examine the model key plan in Example 11, which is divided into three sections, denoted by dotted bar lines.

Example 11

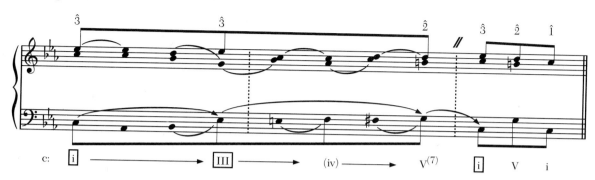

After the movement to III in the first section, the second section makes its way to the dominant through a temporary tonicization of iv. The last section shows the return of the original key. In what way has the beamed soprano motion been "interrupted" here?

Although sectional and pivot-chord modulations to the relative major are frequent, chromatic modulation is rarely encountered in minor mode, since the leading tone of III already exists as a diatonic scale degree. The most common pivot chords between i and III are iv (which becomes the new ii), VI (which becomes the new IV), and i (which becomes the new vi). In addition, the original tonic's VII may be heard as the dominant of III. Some typical common-chord modulations to III are illustrated in Example 12.

Example 12

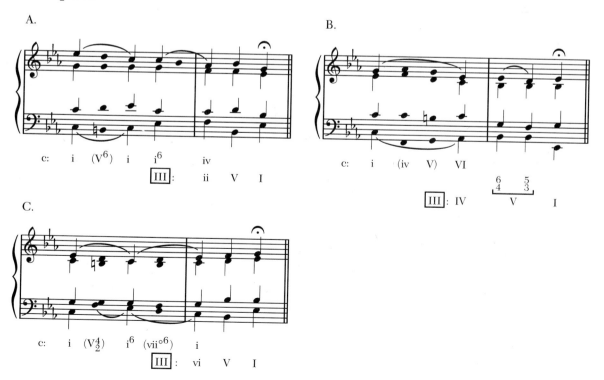

INTRAMOVEMENT TONAL SCHEMES USING DOMINANT OR MEDIANT KEYS

The tonal schemes for many short pieces incorporate modulations to $\boxed{V}$ or $\boxed{III}$. For instance, in the major mode we may encounter a basic tonal scheme of $\boxed{I} \rightarrow \boxed{V} \rightarrow \boxed{I}$, in the minor mode a scheme of $\boxed{i} \rightarrow \boxed{III} \rightarrow \boxed{i}$. In the latter case, a dominant chord is normally used to reroute the tonal motion back to the tonic: $\boxed{i} \rightarrow \boxed{III} \rightarrow (V) \rightarrow \boxed{i}$. We will analyze two short compositions that are based on these plans.

Many dance movements exhibit a two-part structure, called **binary** or **two-reprise form**,[5] in which the two sections are usually set off with repeat signs. The short Haydn Minuet in Example 13 can serve as an example.

Example 13   HAYDN: STRING QUARTET IN D MAJOR, OP. 20, NO. 4, III

The movement to $\boxed{V}$ in the first section is confirmed by an authentic cadence in the new area. While the dominant area is initially extended into

the next section, the appearance of a G♮⁴ in the bass (m. 11) suggests a V⁷ in the original key, so the cadence in measure 12 has the effect of a half cadence in D major. The prolonged V⁷ prepares the return to the original tonic, which in this example is reinforced by a reappearance of the opening thematic idea. Why do you think the tonicization of V in the first section occurs in measures 7–8 and not in measures 5–6?

The two reductions of this excerpt reveal an **interrupted tonal structure,** whose plan can be summarized as ‖: I → V :‖: V⁽⁷⁾ ∥ I V I:‖ (Example 14).

A.

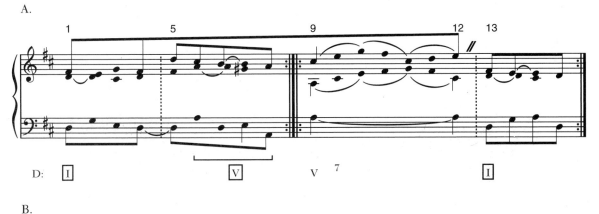

B.

The ∥ sign marks the point of melodic interruption in the soprano line: 3̂–2̂ in measure 12. The 3̂ is regained with the return to the tonic in measure 13 and eventually descends through 2̂ to 1̂. In the second reduction, we have normalized Haydn's registral displacement of the theme at the beginning of the second section by placing the 2̂ an octave lower, in order to show the long-range stepwise voice leading more clearly.

The brief two-reprise piece in A minor that appears, with its tonal reduction, in Example 15 shows a motion to III, followed by the dominant, which leads back to the original tonic. The essential soprano line spans a 5th rather than a 3rd; it is interrupted after reaching 2̂ in measure 12.

Example 15   D. G. Türk: "Abendlied"

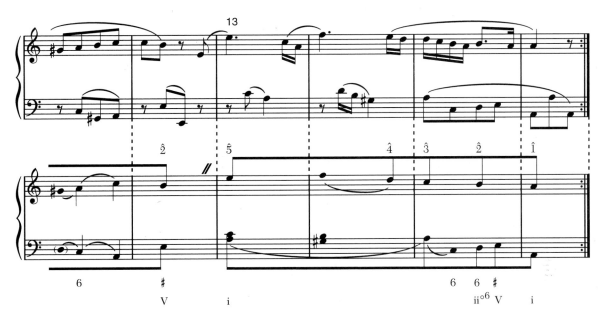

Examples 13 and 15 are complete sections or movements, unlike our previous excerpts. In these pieces, the accompanying analyses not only reduce the surface elaboration to show the more essential voice leading but also illustrate the *overall* linear motion of the entire movement by beaming together the outer voices. In Chapter 23 we will return to the topic of larger-scale voice leading and its relation to the tonal scheme of a whole movement.

Modulation in Melody Harmonization

Modulation is one way to achieve tonal variety in melody harmonizations. While many tunes do not require or even permit a modulation, others will mandate one. For instance, the conclusion of the first melody in Example 16 signals a change in key by the presence of an accidental (F♯). Those in Example 16b suggest a change because they do not form a satisfactory melodic cadence in the original key ($\hat{7}$–$\hat{6}$–$\hat{5}$) but are better heard as $\hat{3}$–$\hat{2}$–$\hat{1}$ in the new key of V. In the minor mode, some melodic cadences may be harmonized either in the tonic or in the mediant key; compare the settings in Examples 16c and 16d. In your melody harmonizations, it is important that you first frame the phrases that modulate with an opening chord in the original key and cadential chords in the new key, as we have done in Examples 16a and 16b; you can then proceed as usual with the harmonization of the phrase's interior.

Example 16

Terms and Concepts for Review

tonicization

secondary *or* applied dominant chord

embellishing tonicization

modulation

transient modulation

sectional modulation

pivot *or* common-chord modulation

chromatic modulation

binary *or* two-reprise form

interrupted tonal structure

EXCURSION 1

Simple Forms

In reading about music we frequently encounter the terms "content" and "form." Musical *content* refers to specific compositional elements or musical materials used within a piece of music; musical *form* pertains to the actual organization of these compositional elements. If we study musical content or musical form alone we will not get a complete picture of a particular piece. For instance, a specific theme in and of itself (one type of musical content) does not tell us anything about the organization of the piece in which it is heard. Likewise, the fact that a composition is in ABA form does not reveal the nature of the themes used in each of its sections. Therefore, when we analyze a piece of music we need to examine musical content and musical form in tandem.

Form itself is made up of two aspects: *formal design* and *tonal structure*. The first includes the similarity or contrast of a composition's themes or motives, texture, dynamics, phrasing and metrical groupings, instrumentation, and the proportional relations between its sections. The second concerns the tonal scheme, melodic characteristics, harmonic language, register, and voice leading.

In this and Excursion 2, which follows Chapter 29, we will examine the design and structure of some of the more familiar forms that composers used during the common-practice period. We will focus on those features that certain pieces have in common, in contrast to our examination of specific pieces of music in the main chapters of this text, where we take into account the individual features that give these compositions their unique character.

In Chapter 12 we discussed forms that arise from various phrase or period groupings. Here, we will concentrate on the formal features of entire movements, noting the interaction of their design and structure. In many of these forms, such as one-part, two-reprise, variation, and rondo form, homophonic texture prevails. We will see that the more contrapuntal forms, such as the chorale prelude, the invention, and the fugue (all covered in Excursion II), often do not have such regular designs.

ONE-PART FORM

Some shorter pieces exhibit a seamless texture that resists being divided into well-defined parts or sections. The texture or figuration of the initial motive usually continues throughout the work, creating a **one-part form.** Brief piano pieces such as the C-major Prelude in Bach's *Well-Tempered Clavier,* Book I, and some of Chopin's Op. 28 Preludes are typical examples. A brief one-part prelude by Bach is quoted in Example 1.

Example 1 BACH: LITTLE PRELUDE IN C MAJOR, BWV 939

BINARY OR TWO-REPRISE FORM

Binary form has a rather ambiguous meaning. In a general sense, it simply describes a composition that is divided into two well-defined sections. One such example is the Brahms excerpt in Example 9 of Chapter 12, which is clearly divided into two parts (AB), each consisting of a period with its own distinct melodic profile. Usually, however, the two-part design takes the form of two *repeated* sections (𝄆 ⫶ 𝄇) and thus is better denoted by the term **two-reprise form.** The theme of the second repeated section generally is not markedly different from that of the first, but instead is often loosely based on it.

The two-reprise scheme may represent an entire movement or only a section of a movement (about the latter, see "Variation Form" and "Rondo," below). The harmonic characteristics of this form, including typical voice-leading models, are discussed in Chapters 19 and 23.

The Two-Reprise Form in the Baroque Period

The tendency to cast short compositions in a two-reprise mold originated in short instrumental dances of the Renaissance. The dances of the Baroque period (including the allemande, courante, sarabande, and gigue), which were often grouped together to form a *suite,* continued to retain this two-section scheme. In Baroque suite movements, the principal theme heard at the opening of the movement is rarely restated in its original version during the second reprise. When a dance's first reprise cadences in the tonic key, the dance's form is called a **sectional two-reprise form.** When its first reprise cadences in or tonicizes a new key area, it is called a **continuous two-reprise form.**

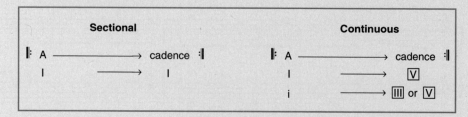

Figure 1

When the first reprise's cadential phrase reappears at the close of the second reprise transposed to the tonic, the form is called a **balanced two-reprise form.**[1]

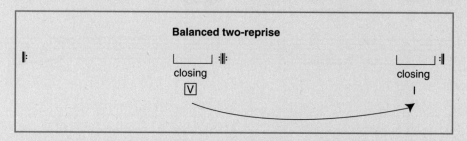

Figure 2

A short two-reprise Minuet by Handel is quoted as Example 2. While the initial theme does not reappear, the identical cadence in the last two measures of each reprise suggests a balanced structure.

Example 2   HANDEL: MINUET IN F MAJOR

1. These terms are based on the discussion of two-reprise form found in Douglass Green's *Form in Tonal Music,* 2nd ed. (New York: Holt, Rinehart and Winston, 1979), 74–79.

The Two-Reprise Form in the Classical Period

Unlike the two-reprise form in the Baroque era, that of the Classical era usually contains an extended preparation for and return of the principal thematic idea toward the end of the second reprise. This creates a scheme that we call a **rounded two-reprise form.**

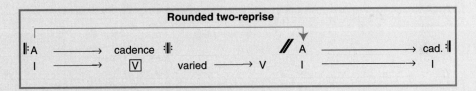

Figure 3

This design is typically found in the Minuet or Scherzo movements of Classical works, where it occurs in both the Minuet proper and the subsequent Trio. The rounded two-reprise form can be seen in Beethoven's Menuetto and Trio, which is discussed in some detail in Chapter 23. For another example, see Example 13 of Chapter 19.

TERNARY FORM

Compositions in **ternary form** show three distinct sections: an opening A section that establishes the initial thematic material and tonic key, a contrasting B section that is usually cast in another key, and a return of the original A section. It may also include a short *introduction* or closing *coda.* Ternary form is commonly found in slow movements (such as the middle movement of Mozart's Piano Sonata in C major, K.330) or short character pieces (such as the Chopin Mazurkas or the Brahms Intermezzi).

The opening A section normally concludes in the tonic key, although occasionally it may end with a short transition that leads to the B section. The B section generally introduces a new melody in a different key or parallel mode and often also includes a brief **retransition,** usually based on dominant harmony, that prepares the return of the A section. In the Classical minuet, however, the contrasting B section or Trio (itself a two-reprise form) usually jumps immediately to the opening A or Minuet section by sectional modulation.

The "Folk Song" from Schumann's *Album for the Young* (Example 3) is cast in a miniature ternary design. Schumann places the return of the A melody in the left hand.

Example 3 SCHUMANN: "FOLK SONG" FROM *ALBUM FOR THE YOUNG*, OP. 68, NO. 9

Most popular songs of the 1930s and 1940s utilized the modified ternary form AA'BA' (the prime signs denote altered versions of the opening A section). In these songs, the A section is called the *chorus* and the B section the *bridge*. This scheme is sometimes called **quatrain form,** since it exhibits four distinct sections. The "Dance of the Reed Pipes" from Tchaikovsky's *Nutcracker* employs an extended quatrain design.

VARIATION FORM

The principle of **variation** is found not only throughout the entire corpus of Western music but also in the musics of other cultures. Since the repetition of a musical idea is essential to the establishment of its identity, it is not surprising that composers modified the musical idea in various ways, either upon its immediate repetition or later on in the piece. "Variation" implies that one or more elements of the original material undergoes change while other elements remain relatively fixed. We may find examples of this procedure within the sections of a single movement, where the immediate repetition of a phrase may be modified, or in the case of a ternary form, where the return of the initial section may be varied. Melodic elaboration is common and can be heard in the ternary *da capo aria,* where the singer frequently embellishes the melodic repetition, or in the *Doubles,* or varied repeats, of Baroque suite movements. In the slow movement of his Piano Sonata in D major, K.311, Mozart embellishes the successive recurrences of the opening melody with increasingly complex elaborations (Example 4).

Example 4   MOZART: PIANO SONATA IN D MAJOR, K.311, II

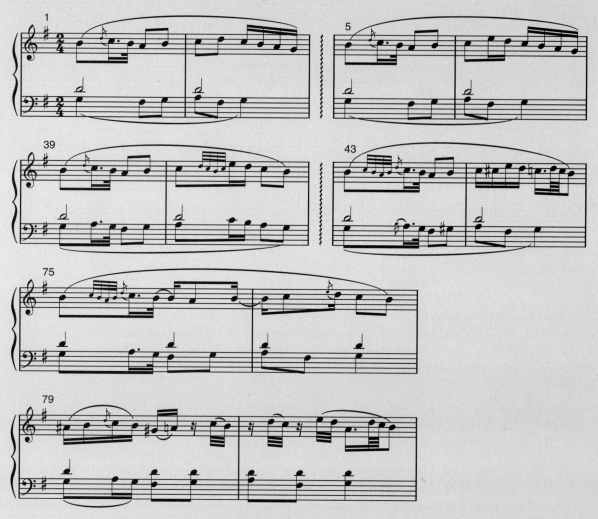

We will focus on two variation procedures that serve as the formal basis for an entire composition: continuous variations and sectional variations, or "theme and variations."

Continuous Variations

Continuous variations follow one other without interruption. They are based on a theme of four to eight measures, usually a reiterated melodic pattern in the bass voice. The names *passacaglia, chaconne,* and *ground bass* were used interchangeably for these pieces. Most are in minor mode, a slow tempo, and triple meter. They tend to remain in the same key throughout, although the middle variations may be set in the parallel major key (for instance, in Bach's D-minor Chaconne for violin) or the relative major (Buxtehude's Chaconne in D minor for organ).

In continuous variations, there are usually a large number of variations on a fairly short theme. Pairings of similar variations or even the repetition of individual variations are common. The bass theme, accompanying harmony, and phrase length are normally retained in each variation, while the texture and rhythm vary. In each variation, the voices above the bass tend to develop a particular motivic idea. If the theme progresses harmonically from i to V, each new motivic idea is confined to a single variation, as in the Bach Chaconne mentioned above. If the harmony concludes on the tonic, the final measure of each variation will often introduce the motivic material of the next, as in Bach's Passacaglia in C minor for organ. The underlying basis of the themes of these two works are quoted in Example 5.[2]

Example 5

A.   BACH: CHACONNE FROM PARTITA NO. 2 FOR SOLO VIOLIN IN D MINOR, BWV 1004

B.   BACH: PASSACAGLIA IN C MINOR, BWV 582

Raison's theme

In some continuous movements, several variations are grouped together to create a greater sense of unity. One common formal design resulting from these groupings is the so-called *double rise*, in which a gradual acceleration of rhythmic motion and increase in textural density occur twice.

The theme and the first several variations of a passacaglia by Handel are quoted in Example 6 (next page). The successive variations follow one another without pause.

Some famous examples of continuous variations from the Baroque period include "Dido's Lament" from Purcell's opera *Dido and Aeneas* (where a two-part aria is supported by a ground bass), Handel's keyboard Chaconne in G major, and the "Crucifixus" from Bach's B-minor Mass. From later periods we may cite Beethoven's *Thirty-Two Variations on an*

2. Bach "borrowed" the first four measures of his passacaglia theme from a three-voice Pasacaille by Phillip Raison.

Example 6 HANDEL: PASSACAILLE IN G MINOR

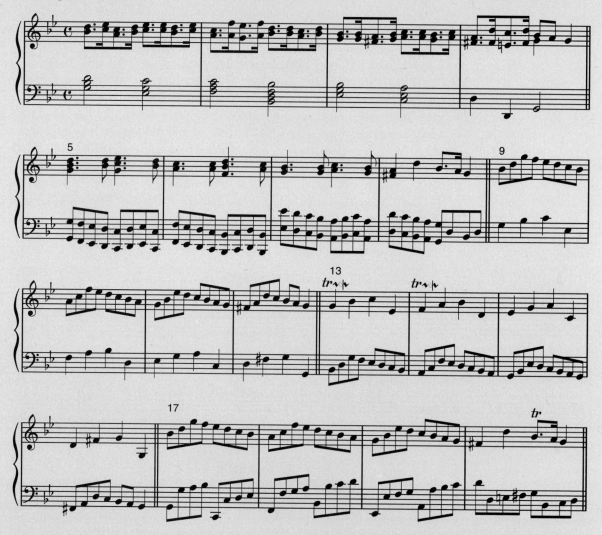

Original Theme in C minor (WoO 80), the Finale of Brahms's *Variations on a Theme of Haydn,* the last movement of Brahms's Symphony No. 4, the Passacaglia from Britten's opera *Peter Grimes,* and the last movement of Hindemith's *Nobilissima Visione.* Jazz improvisations on standard popular songs also represent examples of continuous variations, since they usually retain the harmonies and phrasing of the original tune.

We may also find instances of **ostinato** sections, in which the "theme" is a recurring melodic fragment in either the bass or soprano; see the closing section of Stravinsky's *Symphony of Psalms.* The following excerpt from the Finale of Brahms's Symphony No. 1 uses a descending tetrachord as the ostinato.

Example 7   BRAHMS: SYMPHONY NO. 1, IV (PIANO REDUCTION)

Sectional Variations, or Theme and Variations

Sectional variations, or **theme and variations,** grew in popularity during the Classical period and gradually replaced the older Baroque-period continuous variations. The theme, either an original or borrowed tune, was almost always cast in a rounded two-reprise form or at least consisted of one or more periods (see Mozart's "Ah, vous dirai-je, Maman" Variations in Example 8, below). The entire theme-and-variations set, then, is made up of a series of individual, relatively short pieces, each of which is tonally closed and separated by a brief pause.

The origins of sectional variations go back to dances of the late Renaissance. Each dance in a slow–fast pairing of Renaissance dances, such as the *Pavan* and *Galliard* or the *Tanz* and *Nachtanz,* was usually cast in a two-reprise form, the second dance being a rhythmic variation of the first. Around the beginning of the seventeenth century, keyboard variations on popular dance tunes or airs were frequently written by composers of the English virginal school. The practice of creating sectional variations from a popular tune continues to this day; some of these pieces, including Joseph Arban's *The Carnival of Venice* for trumpet and Arthur Pryor's *The Bluebells of Scotland* for trombone, have become virtuosic showpieces.

During the Baroque era, we may occasionally find theme-and-variations sets in which the theme is cast in a two-reprise form; the most famous example is Bach's *Goldberg Variations,* where the ordering of the thirty-two variations adheres to a precise overall formal scheme. With lengthy theme-and-variations sets, Baroque performers took the liberty of making their own selection of the variations they would actually perform.

In Classical-period theme-and-variations sets, the underlying harmonies, phrasing, and form remained fixed while the melody, texture, register, and rhythm would vary from variation to variation. Each variation was based on a different melodic or rhythmic motive. All variations were normally set in the same key, although the mode could change. The first eight measures of the theme and several variations of Mozart's variations on a well-known tune are quoted in Example 8.

Example 8 MOZART: VARIATIONS ON "AH, VOUS DIRAI-JE, MAMAN," K.265 (FIRST EIGHT MEASURES OF EACH VARIATION)

Variation sets were composed both as separate pieces and as movements of sonatas, quartets, and symphonies. Although in Classical multimovement works a variation set normally appears as the slow movement, it might also occur as the first movement (Mozart's Piano Sonata in A major, K.331) or the last movement (Beethoven's Symphony No. 3).

In keyboard variation sets of this period, the last two variations were often an expressive Adagio and an Allegro Finale; see the last movement of Mozart's Piano Sonata in D major, K.284.

Later composers wrestled with the problem of imposing overall unity or coherence on the variation set. One solution was to divide the pieces into distinct groups, using certain variations as "transitions" to the next group. This approach may be found in Beethoven's *Diabelli Variations* for piano and Brahms's *Haydn Variations* for orchestra.

Other famous sets of sectional variations include the second movement of Haydn's String Quartet in C major, Op. 76, No. 3 (whose theme later became the German national anthem), the slow movements of Beethoven's Fifth and Ninth Symphonies (both of which employ two themes, only the first of which undergoes extensive variation), Brahms's *Variations and Fugue on a Theme by Handel* (which closes with a fugal Finale) and *Variations on a Theme of Paganini,* Elgar's *Enigma Variations,* and Britten's *Young Person's Guide to the Orchestra* (with a fugal conclusion that eventually combines Purcell's theme with Britten's own fugue tune).

RONDO FORM

Rondo *form* takes its basic character from the periodic recurrence of the initial theme, called the **refrain.** The refrain opens the piece and reappears at least twice more. Refrains are separated by contrasting sections that are set in different key areas and often introduce new thematic ideas; these contrasting sections are called **episodes.** Generally only one episode comes after each refrain, creating a formal design of roughly A B A C A D A, where A is the refrain and B, C, and D are the episodes. We will use these letter names in our diagrams of typical rondo schemes below.

The Classical rondo is normally found as the last movement of a sonata, quartet, symphony, or solo concerto. It occasionally appears as the slow movement (Beethoven's Symphony No. 4) or as a separate piece (Mozart's rondos in D major, K.485, and A minor, K.511).

The refrain itself is a self-contained miniature form, usually a two-reprise form (Haydn's Piano Sonata in D major, Hob. XVI:37, third movement) or a ternary form (Beethoven's Piano Sonata in G major, Op. 49, No. 2, second movement). The refrain usually remains in the tonic key. Subsequent recurrences of the refrain are frequently shortened or may even be modified, as in the Finale to Haydn's Symphony No. 101 ("Clock"), where each recurrence uses a new texture. However, just as often it reappears each time exactly in its original version, as in the Beethoven sonata just mentioned.

The episodes employ contrasting themes and textures and usually explore tonal areas other than the tonic. Their formal design tends to be less defined than the refrain. Composers may use sectional modulation to jump from the tonality of the refrain to that of the following episode (see m. 79 of the third movement of Beethoven's Sonata "Pathétique" in C minor, Op. 13), or use a transitional passage to lead to the next episode's new tonality (see mm. 16–23 of the last movement of Mozart's Piano Sonata in B♭ major, K.333). A retransition that typically includes a dominant prolongation normally links an episode to the returning refrain (see mm. 102–110 of the same Mozart movement).

Three basic rondo designs occur in Classical-period compositions: the five-part rondo, the seven-part rondo, and the sonata-rondo. We will discuss the sonata-rondo under "Sonata Form" in Excursion 2.

Five-Part Rondo

The formal design of the five-part rondo is typically A B A C A. The following diagram outlines the key areas of this design in both major and minor keys:

Figure 4

	A	B	(Retrans.)	A	C	(Retrans.)	A	(Coda)
Major	I	V, IV, or vi	(V)	I	V, IV, or vi	(V)	I	
Minor	I	III, v, or VI	(V)	I	III, v, or VI	(V)	i	

Beethoven's G-major Sonata, Op. 49, No. 2, follows this design to the letter; the Finale of Haydn's "Clock" Symphony, on the other hand, contains some extensive transitions, the recurrence of the refrain during the first episode, and some textural modifications of the later refrains. Example 9 quotes another five-part rondo by Haydn.

Example 9   HAYDN: PIANO SONATA IN D MAJOR, HOB. XVI:37, III

Seven-Part Rondo

The seven-part rondo is probably most typical of this period. Its basic structure can be diagrammed as follows:

Figure 5

	A	B	A		C	(Retrans.)		A	B	A	(Coda)
Major	I	V	I		I, IV, or vi	(V)		I	I	I	I
Minor	i	III, v	i		I, iv, or VI	(V)		i	i	i	i

The overall groupings of the sections form a large ternary construction centered around the middle C section, which is usually longer than the B episodes. The return of B is transposed to the tonic and thereby "resolves" its earlier appearance. This scheme was particularly favored by Beethoven, who used it in the finales of most of his solo concertos. The last movement of his "Pathétique" Sonata is a model example; note the amusing reference to the C theme in its coda.

After the Classical period, the rondo waned in popularity, although it continued to be used for concerto finales. Well-known Romantic-period compositions include Mendelssohn's *Rondo Capriccioso,* the last movement of Franck's Violin Sonata, and Saint-Saën's *Introduction and Rondo Capriccio.* Brahms carried on this tradition more than most nineteenth-century composers; see, for example, the "Rondo alla Zingarese" in his Piano Quartet, Op. 25. In the twentieth century the rondo has been featured in works written by composers with strong neoclassical tendencies, such as Hindemith (the Finale to his Clarinet Sonata) and Poulenc (his Trio for Flute,

Terms and Concepts for Review

one-part form
binary form
two-reprise form
sectional two-reprise form
continuous two-reprise form
balanced two-reprise form
rounded two-reprise form
ternary form
retransition
quatrain form

variation form
continuous variations
ostinato
sectional variations (theme and variations)
rondo
refrain
episode (rondo)
five-part rondo
seven-part rondo

Harmonic Sequences I

ROOT MOVEMENT BY
2ND AND 3RD

W ITHIN MOST DIATONIC progressions, the intervals that are produced by the movement of chordal roots vary. The progression shown in Example 1, for instance, is typical. Determine the intervallic distance of the roots from one root-position chord to another; how many intervals do you find?

Example 1   SETTING OF "OLD ONE HUNDRED" (HYMN)

Some progressions exhibit a root movement that employs only one interval. In this chapter we will examine these progressions and determine the harmonic role they play in passages of music.

NONSEQUENTIAL ROOT MOVEMENT

There are two kinds of harmonic progression that feature a single type of intervallic root movement. In the first, the regularity of root movement in the bass does not influence the linear movement of the upper voices, which trace their individual melodic contours. For example, the two passages below exhibit a series of triads that descend by 3rds (Example 2a) and ascend by 2nds (Example 2b), respectively.

Example 2

A. WAGNER: PRELUDE TO *PARSIFAL*, ACT I

B. "PAX" (HYMN TUNE)

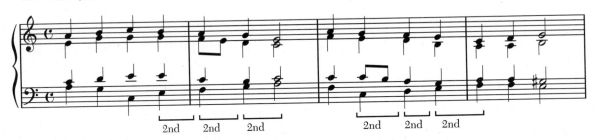

Their upper voices, however, display a variety of other types of intervallic movement. We say that such passage exhibit **nonsequential root movement.**

SEQUENTIAL ROOT MOVEMENT

In many of the passages that employ root movement by a single interval, the melodic motion of the upper voices is coordinated with the bass pattern. This collaboration between melody and harmony characterizes what we call **sequential root movement.** Here, all voices display a strict regularity of movement, restating a particular motivic figure and harmonic progression one or more times on other scale degrees. For example, the regular repetition of a two-measure melodic figure at descending pitch levels in Example 3 is supported by a sequential root movement of descending 5ths: I–IV–vii°–iii–vi–ii–V–I, creating what we call a **harmonic sequence.**

Example 3   "Vive la Compagnie" (French folk song)

In this chapter and in Chapter 22, we will examine the most common types of harmonic sequences and the root movements on which they are based.

All diatonic root movements, which may ascend or descend, fall into three basic categories, each defined by both the interval and its inversion: movement by 2nd (or 7th), by 3rd (or 6th), and by 5th (or 4th). Beginning with a given pitch, these root movements theoretically will eventually cycle through all seven diatonic tones. Figure 1 shows interval cycles of descending 2nds, 3rds, and 5ths starting on the pitch C (this principle applies to ascending motion as well).

Figure 1

By 2nd	C	B	A	G	F	E	D	C	B	A	G	F	E	D	C	B	A	G	F	E	D	C	B	A	G
By 3rd	C		A		F		D		B		G		E		C		A		F		D		B		G
By 5th	C				F				B				E				A				D				G
By 2nd									B								A								G

These root movements coincide to form different levels of harmonic activity. Alternate tones in the series of 2nds produce a pattern of 3rds; alternate 3rds result in a succession of 5ths. Alternate 5ths then produce another cycle of 2nds, although now at a different hierarchical level.

Harmonic sequences in music literature will often show these interlocking patterns, but in many passages they stop far short of cycling through all seven diatonic tones. The embedded 3rd/5th pattern in the Brahms excerpt (Example 4) is one instance of this. In the reduction that follows the excerpt, the upper beams connect the surface root movement by 3rd and the lower beams the larger harmonic motion by 5th. Here, the pattern completes less than half of its full intervallic cycle. We will see a model of a 2nd/5th pattern in Chapter 22, Example 5.

Example 4   BRAHMS: INTERMEZZO IN E MAJOR, OP. 116, NO. 6

A.

B.   (REDUCTION OF BASS LINE ONLY)

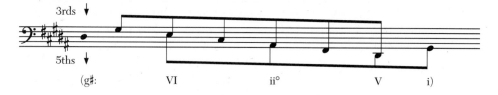

In this chapter we will limit our discussion to sequences that use root movement either by 2nd or by 3rd; we will cover root movement by 5th in Chapter 22. We must be careful to focus on the root movement of the chords, which we determine by extracting the roots of the basic harmonies—even if these harmonies are found in inversion. It is the movement of chordal roots that will define the type of harmonic sequence that is featured. We will find that since all of the voices in such passages are sequential, there is an ever-present danger of creating parallel octaves or 5ths. Therefore, it is necessary in many cases for the composer to find ways to prevent or stagger these parallels, which is usually done by putting some or all of the chords basic to the sequential progression in inversion or by inserting other "filler" chords into the sequence. The purely voice-leading connections between consecutive triads that result should not be confused with the basic root movement inherent within the sequential pattern. This will become clear as we discuss the voice leading of the individual sequences that follow.

Because the harmonies involved in sequential root movement adhere to the basic pattern of the sequence, the chord progressions that result may not obey standard harmonic tendencies, such as our cadential pre-dominant–dominant–tonic motion. In fact, it usually makes little sense to label the separate chords in a sequence with roman numerals, since the harmonic succession is more correctly viewed as a particular linear pattern. Many sequences simply prolong a specific chord, often the tonic.

In the following models, we will dispense with functional labeling and indicate with roman numerals only the framing chords of the sequential passage. We will denote the contrapuntal motion within the sequence with figured-bass symbols, as in Example 5.

Example 5

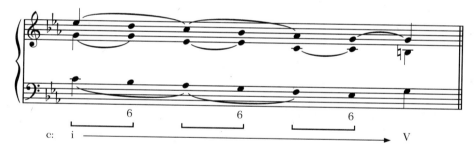

ROOT MOVEMENT BY 2ND: SUCCESSIVE SIXTH CHORDS

In root movements that progress by 2nds, we may find a series of consecutive root-position or first-inversion triads in sequential stepwise motion. First-inversion triads can be arranged in two different ways: either as a $\frac{6}{3}$ with a 4th between the upper voices, or as a $\frac{10}{6}$ (which we would still conventionally label as $\frac{6}{3}$) with a 5th between the upper voices (Example 6a).

In the two sequences using $\frac{6}{3}$ triads in Example 6b, the roots of all the chords are in the soprano voice. The soprano, alto, and bass voices present no partwriting difficulties, since the consecutive 4ths between the soprano and alto are permissible. The tenor, however, must alternately double the soprano and alto to avoid parallel octaves and 5ths.

Example 6

A.

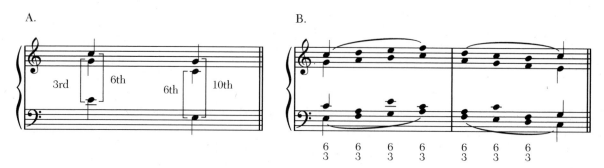

B.

Two elaborated versions of sequential $^6_3$ movement appear in Examples 7a and 7b; the first occurs in a witty Haydn scherzo whose main theme is little more than an ascending and descending major scale. How are the $^6_3$ chords embellished in the second excerpt?

Example 7

A.   HAYDN STRING QUARTET IN E♭ MAJOR, OP. 76, NO. 6, III

B.

Debussy's lovely "Arabesque" (Example 8a) incorporates a falling sequence of $^6_3$ triads, Beethoven's piano sonata in D minor a rising sequence. Complete the reductions that follow each excerpt in Example 8.

Example 8

A. DEBUSSY: "ARABESQUE NO. 1"

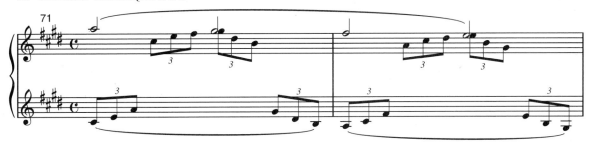

B. (REDUCTION)

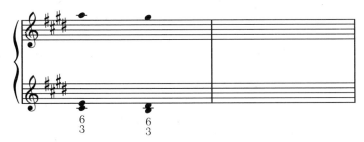

C. BEETHOVEN: PIANO SONATA IN D MINOR ("TEMPEST"), OP. 31, NO. 2, I

D. (REDUCTION)

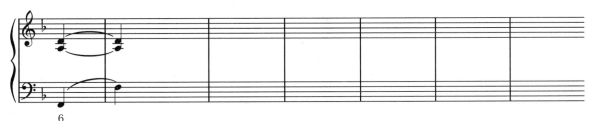

Consecutive $^{10}_{6}$'s will produce parallel 5ths in the upper voices (Example 9a) unless they are staggered in some way to disguise them. The customary way of staggering successive 5ths is to use a series of 7–6 suspensions to shift the 5ths to the offbeats. Compare the four chords in Example 9a with the staggered version of the same chords in the last two measures of the Haydn symphony (Example 9b).

Example 9

A.

$$\begin{array}{cccc} 10 & 10 & 10 & 10 \\ 6 & 6 & 6 & 6 \end{array}$$

B.   HAYDN: SYMPHONY NO. 104 ("LONDON"), I

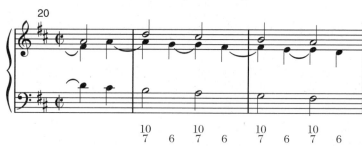

$$\begin{array}{cccccccc} 10 & & 10 & & 10 & & 10 & \\ 7 & 6 & 7 & 6 & 7 & 6 & 7 & 6 \end{array}$$

Complete the reduction that follows the Fux excerpt in Example 10. Why is the chain of suspensions in this excerpt necessary?

Example 10   J. J. FUX: GRADUS AD PARNASSUM

A.

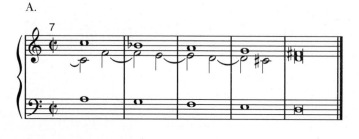

B.   (REDUCTION)

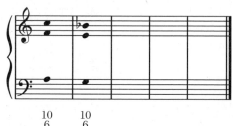

$$\begin{array}{cc} 10 & 10 \\ 6 & 6 \end{array}$$

The sequences of sixth chords in Examples 7 and 9 above prolong the tonic harmony. The two phrases of Example 7 begin and end with a I⁶. We have seen that root movement by 2nd need not cycle back to the first chord through all seven diatonic tones, as these phrases do. In fact, we may use the sequence to modulate to other keys. While the movement to $\boxed{V}$ in Example 11a requires an accidental to create a new leading tone, the movement to $\boxed{III}$ in Example 11b is accomplished through the use of diatonic tones only.

Example 11

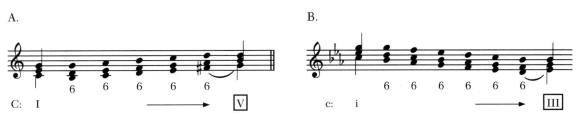

A.

C: I ⟶ V

B.

c: i ⟶ III

SUCCESSIVE ROOT-POSITION TRIADS IN STEPWISE MOTION

Successive root-position triads often ascend stepwise; stepwise-descending root-position triads are rare. Since parallel 5ths occur naturally between the bass and an upper voice in such progressions (Example 12a), it is necessary to use some voice-leading technique to prevent their occurrence.

Example 12

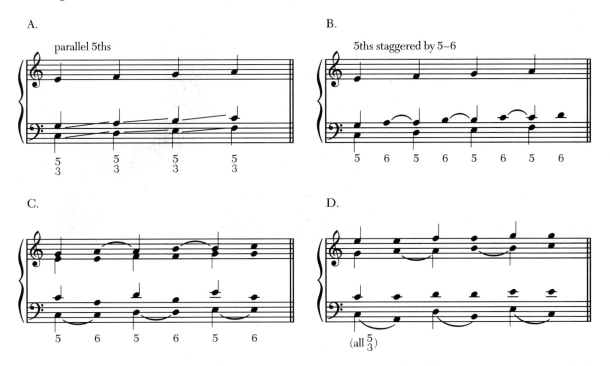

A.

parallel 5ths

$\begin{smallmatrix}5\\3\end{smallmatrix}$ $\begin{smallmatrix}5\\3\end{smallmatrix}$ $\begin{smallmatrix}5\\3\end{smallmatrix}$ $\begin{smallmatrix}5\\3\end{smallmatrix}$

B.

5ths staggered by 5–6

5 6 5 6 5 6 5 6

C.

5 6 5 6 5 6

D.

(all $\begin{smallmatrix}5\\3\end{smallmatrix}$)

Haydn inserted 7–6 suspensions in stepwise $\begin{smallmatrix}10\\6\end{smallmatrix}$ triads to prevent parallels between the upper parts (see Example 9b). In our ascending progression, we must stagger the upper voice that forms the 5ths with the bass. We do this by using a 5–6 motion above the bass, as illustrated in the three- and four-voice settings of Examples 12b and 12c. In addition, in Example 12c, we alternate the doublings (now in the tenor and bass, now in the tenor and soprano) to avoid parallel 5ths, octaves, or both. In Example 12d, the 6 in the alto's 5–6 motion is also transferred to the bass, producing a root-position triad on every chord.

In the first two measures of the Palestrina passage in Example 13, what would result if we omitted the second and fourth half notes in the middle voice? What interval pattern does this middle voice make with the bass part in these two bars?

Example 13   PALESTRINA: AGNUS DEI II FROM *MISSA SANCTORUM MERITIS*

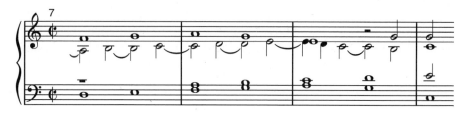

ROOT MOVEMENT BY 3RD

Root movement by descending 3rds usually originates with the tonic and rarely moves beyond the supertonic before breaking the pattern to leap to the dominant: I–vi–IV–ii–(V–I). In such sequential passages, successive root-position triads by descending 3rds can also easily produce parallel 5ths between the bass and an upper voice, as shown in Example 14a. These parallels can be staggered by inserting a sixth chord (or $\frac{6}{3}$) after every root-position harmony (Example 14b). This first-inversion triad, which serves as a passing chord to stagger the 5ths, produces an inverted 5–6 voice-leading pattern with stepwise motion in the bass part. Compare this falling 5–6 pattern with the rising 5–6 pattern in the root-position triads in Example 12b.

Example 14

A.   B.

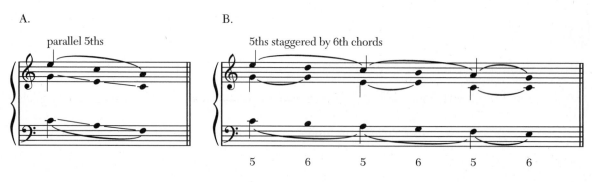

The first two four-voice settings in Example 15 illustrate some variants of the 5–6 pattern within descending 3rd progressions. In Examples 15a and 15b, the bass remains the same but the soprano and tenor voices switch places. The exclusive use of root-position triads in Example 15c reflects the change-of-bass procedure shown in Example 12d.

Example 15

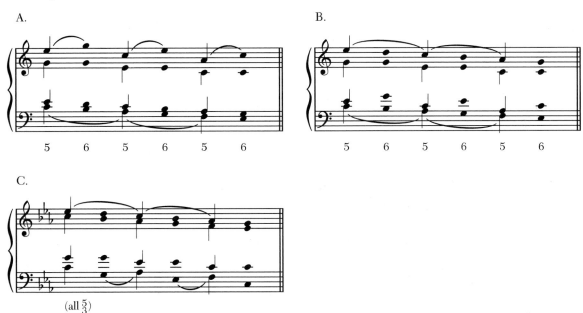

A.   B.

5   6   5   6   5   6   5   6   5   6   5   6

C.

(all $\frac{5}{3}$)

Example 16

A. MOZART: QUINTET FROM *THE MAGIC FLUTE*, ACT II, K.620 (VOCAL PARTS OMITTED)

B. (REDUCTION)

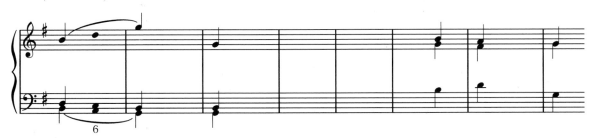

6

C.   MASCAGNI: INTERMEZZO FROM *CAVALLERIA RUSTICANA*

D.   (REDUCTION)

E.   GLIÈRE: SAILORS' DANCE FROM *THE RED POPPY*   F.   (REDUCTION)

All of the three brief excerpts cited in Example 16 (see the previous page for the first) employ root movement by descending 3rd. Continue the underlying pattern for each passage to illustrate its sequential nature. How is the final excerpt different from the first two?

Harmonic sequences that use root movement by ascending 3rds are less common. Once again we must insert a passing chord to prevent the occurrence of parallel 5ths, as shown in Example 17a; notice that the inserted chords here are secondary dominants. Example 17b quotes a more extended upward sequence in the minor mode; what is the nature of the inserted chords?

Example 17

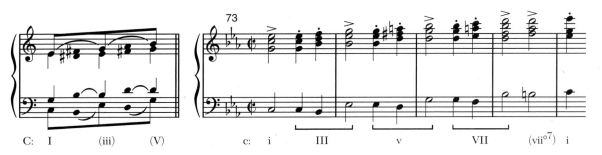

A.

B. WEBER: OVERTURE TO *DER FREISCHÜTZ*

C: I   (iii)   (V)

c: i   III   v   VII   (vii°⁷) i

Since chordal settings of simple tunes rarely exploit extended sequences by 2nds or 3rds, we will postpone the topic of melody harmonization using harmonic sequences until the conclusion of Chapter 22.

Terms and Concepts for Review

nonsequential root movement

sequential root movement

harmonic sequence

root movement by 2nd

consecutive $^6_3$ and 5–6 progressions

root movement by descending 3rd

inverted 5–6 progression

root movement by ascending 3rd

The Leading-Tone
Seventh Chord

I N THIS CHAPTER we will explore the main characteristics of the leading-tone seventh chord (vii°⁷), an embellishing harmony that is formed by adding a chordal 7th to the vii° triad. We will then examine its close relation to the dominant seventh chord.

To begin, play the two passages in Example 1 and note how the vii°⁷'s in the second phrase substitute for the V⁷'s in the first phrase.

Example 1

A.

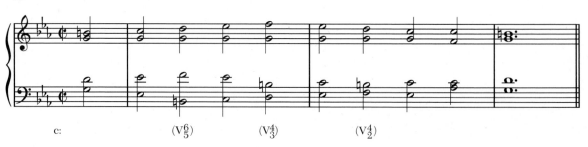

B.

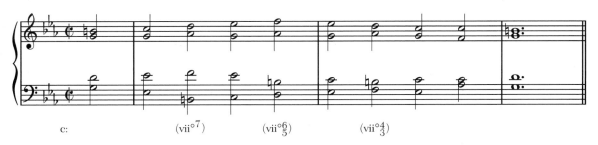

THE LEADING-TONE SEVENTH CHORD IN THE MINOR MODE

The vii°7 in the minor mode is a diminished seventh chord built on the raised 7th, or leading tone. This chord shares three scale degrees ($\hat{2}$, $\hat{4}$, and $\sharp\hat{7}$) with both the vii°6 and the V7; as a result, we usually consider it a member of the family of dominant chords (Example 2a). The ambiguous sonic properties of the vii°7, with its weak sense of root and pair of tritones, convey a greater sense of tonal tension than does the more tonally directed V7.

Example 2

A.

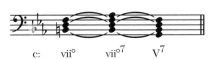

B.

The various inversions of the vii°7 are shown in Example 2b; notice how their bass notes are neighbors to the notes of the tonic triad.

The vii°7 functions as an embellishing harmony within the phrase; in our models and voice-leading reductions, we will therefore leave it unstemmed. The 7th of the chord ($\flat\hat{6}$) and the leading-tone root ($\sharp\hat{7}$) form the interval of a diminished 7th, which contracts to a perfect 5th upon resolution to tonic harmony. (See Example 3.) The diminished 7th's inversion, the augmented 2nd, will expand to a perfect 4th in the upper voices. You might wish to review the spelling of diminished seventh chords in Chapter 4.

Example 3

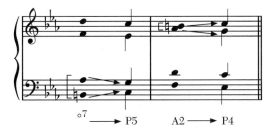

The vii°⁷

As we have noted, the vii°⁷ differs from the V⁷ by only one tone ($\hat{5}$ vs. $\flat\hat{6}$); this factor enables composers to easily interchange the chords. For instance, both the root-position vii°⁷ and the V$^6_5$ have the leading tone in the bass (Example 4).

Example 4

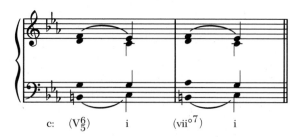

c: (V$^6_5$)   i   (vii°⁷)   i

The three models in Example 5 illustrate some idiomatic uses of the vii°⁷ chord. How is its chordal 7th ($\flat$6, or A$\flat$) approached and resolved in each case? The bass may leap downward to $\sharp\hat{7}$ from either $\hat{4}$ or $\flat\hat{6}$, producing a diminished 5th or diminished 7th, respectively.

Example 5

A.   B.   C.

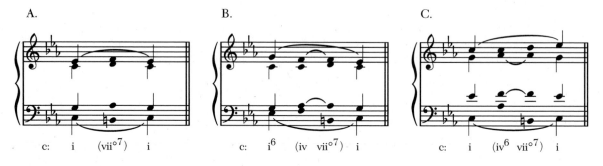

c: i   (vii°⁷)   i   c: i⁶   (iv vii°⁷)   i   c: i   (iv⁶ vii°⁷)   i

The vii°$^6_5$

The vii°$^6_5$ is closely related to the vii°⁶ and V$^4_3$ (Example 6).

Example 6

A.   B.

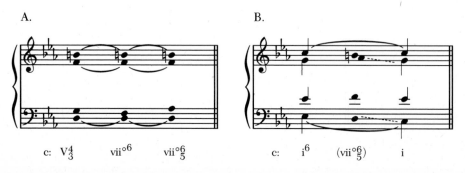

c: V$^4_3$ vii°⁶   vii°$^6_5$ c: i⁶   (vii°$^6_5$)   i

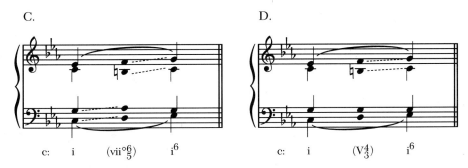

All three employ scale degree $\hat{2}$ in the bass and usually function as passing chords between i and i⁶. Similar 5ths (indicated with dotted lines in Example 6), which frequently occur with the vii°⁶ and V⁴₃ (see Example 20 of Chapter 13), are also characteristic of progressions involving the vii°⁶₅.

The vii°⁴₃

Scale degree $\hat{4}$ appears in the bass of both the vii°⁴₃ and the V⁴₂ (Example 7).

Example 7

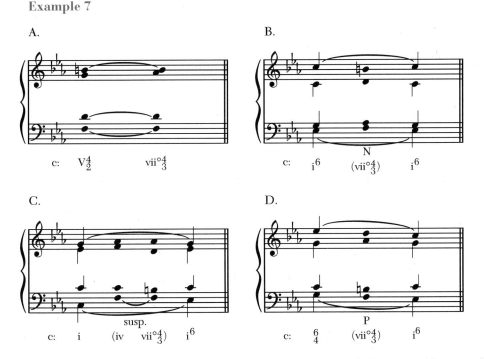

The vii°⁴₃ is most commonly used as a neighboring chord or treated as a suspension. It can also occur as a passing chord when moving from a ⁶₄, in the manner of a V⁴₂. The vii°⁴₃ can also suggest an extension of the plagal cadence, which is typical of closing sections, as in the Bach excerpt in Example 8. Here, the upper G♯₄ acts as an inverted pedal.

Example 8   BACH: PRELUDE IN G♯ MINOR FROM *WELL-TEMPERED CLAVIER*, BOOK I

A.

B. (REDUCTION)

$$g\sharp: \quad iv \quad (vii^{\circ 4}_3) \quad I$$

The vii°⁴₂

The vii°⁴₂ is less commonly found than the other inversions, because it can only be resolved in one way. Since its chordal 7th (♭6̂) is in the bass, it must resolve downward to 5̂, the root of either a V⁷ or a ⁶₄ (Example 9).

Example 9

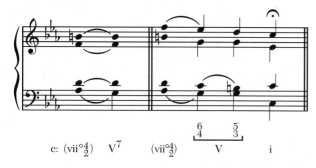

$$c: \quad (vii^{\circ 4}_2) \quad V^7 \quad (vii^{\circ 4}_2) \quad V \quad i$$

Leading-tone seventh chords are often used to prolong a particular harmony. In Example 10a, the tonic harmony is extended by successive inver-

Example 10

A.

B.

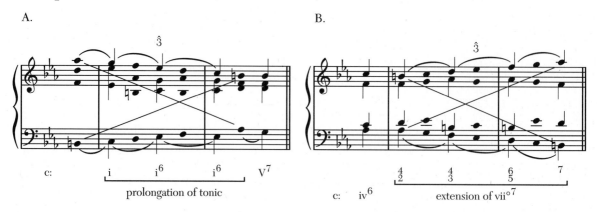

C. MENDELSSOHN: VIOLIN CONCERTO, I

sions of embellishing vii°⁷'s. In Example 10b, the accentuated positions of the vii°⁷ chord within the bar indicate that it is the leading-tone 7th itself that is prolonged.

The symmetry of the diminished seventh chord is apparent if we look at how the bass and soprano lines mirror each other around scale degree $\hat{3}$ (E♭) in these two examples, producing the effect of a long voice exchange (indicated by crossed lines). The vii°⁷, consisting of three superposed minor 3rds, thus divides the octave into four equal segments. What melodic interval is bracketed in the Mendelssohn excerpt? The augmented 2nd, generally forbidden as a melodic interval, is permissible only when it occurs within the vii°⁷ harmony, not when it links two different chords.

In Example 11, three short quotations from music literature employ the leading-tone seventh chord; each is accompanied by a voice-leading reduction. Study the bass line, the chord's inversions and functions, and the treatment of the chordal 7ths in each passage. What relationship do you observe between the pairs of voices in the Bach fugue? Why is this possible?

Example 11

A. BACH: FUGUE IN B♭ MINOR FROM *WELL-TEMPERED CLAVIER*, BOOK II

B. (REDUCTION)

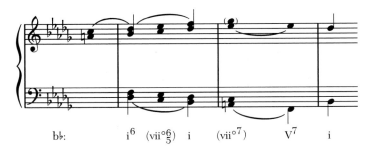

b♭:   i⁶ (vii°⁶₅) i   (vii°⁷)   V⁷   i

C. HAYDN: PIANO SONATA IN E♭ MAJOR, HOB. XVI:38, II

D. (REDUCTION)

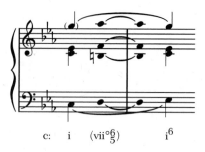

c: i   (vii°$^6_5$)   i^6

E. TCHAIKOVSKY: SYMPHONY NO. 6 ("PATHÉTIQUE"), I

F. (REDUCTION)

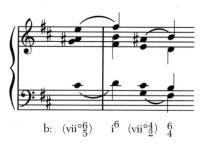

b: (vii°$^6_5$)   i^6 (vii°$^4_2$) $^6_4$

THE LEADING-TONE SEVENTH CHORD IN THE MAJOR MODE

Two forms of the leading-tone seventh chord are found in compositions written in the major mode. The first represents a "borrowing" of the vii°[7] from the minor mode. One approach to the chordal 7th (♭$\hat6$) is through the unaltered form of the scale degree, which results in a chromatic movement from ♮$\hat6$ to ♭$\hat6$, as shown by the arrow in the following Mozart excerpt.

Example 12   MOZART: SONATA FOR TWO PIANOS IN D MAJOR, K.448, I

A.

B. (REDUCTION)

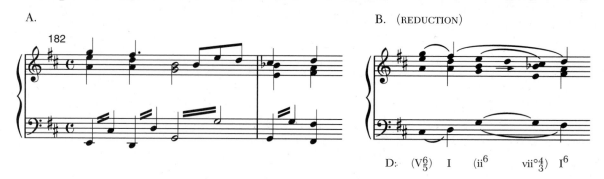

D: (V$^6_5$)   I   (ii^6 vii°$^4_3$) I^6

The second form is a half-diminished seventh chord (vii^{ø7}), built on the leading tone and containing a minor 7th between root and chordal 7th (Example 13).

Example 13

A. "JESU, MEINE FREUDE"
(BACH CHORALE
HARMONIZATION)

B. SCHUBERT: MOMENT MUSICAL NO. 6 IN A♭ MAJOR

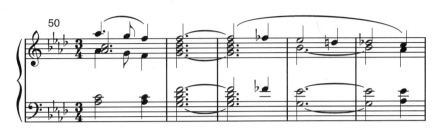

G: IV⁶ (vii°⁷) I

C. (REDUCTION)

D. WAGNER: *DAS RHEINGOLD*, SCENE I

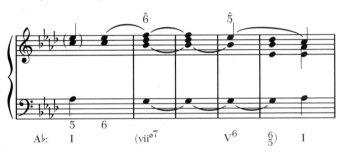

In compositions from the Baroque period, the vii°⁷ usually appears as a passing chord (Example 13a). In Example 13b, Schubert first extends the chordal 7th ($\hat{6}$) and then resolves it to $\hat{5}$ in a V⁶, as can be seen in the reduction (Example 13c). In Example 13d, the joyful cry of the Rhinedaughters employs a neighboring vii°⁷ over a tonic pedal.

THE USE OF LEADING-TONE SEVENTH CHORDS IN TONIC PROLONGATIONS

The following passage (Example 14) relies heavily on the embellishing character of the vii°⁷. A voice-leading reduction is provided directly under the score. Beethoven begins the first movement of his sonata with a large-scale prolongation of the opening tonic chord (mm. 1–18), utilizing various inversions of the vii°⁷.

Initially arpeggiated up to $\hat{3}$ (mm. 1–3) and eventually reaching $\hat{5}$ (m. 9), the tonic harmony is extended by passing and neighboring motion through i⁶ (m. 8) and then back to i (m. 18) before reaching the final cadence, ii°⁶–V–1 (mm. 19–22). The entire passage suggests a stepwise descent in the soprano from $\hat{5}$ to $\hat{1}$): G–F–E♭–D–C, as shown in the summary reduction given in Example 15. The F^4 is indicated with a dotted stem in Example 15 since it belongs to an embellishing vii°7. The last note of each triplet group fills in the upper voice ($\hat{3}$ $\hat{2}$ $\hat{1}$ $\hat{7}$ $\hat{1}$) starting in measure 17. Notice that the original $\hat{5}$ is displaced an octave (G^5 to G^4) before it descends to $\hat{1}$.

Example 14   BEETHOVEN: PIANO SONATA IN C MINOR, OP. 10, No. 1, I

Example 15

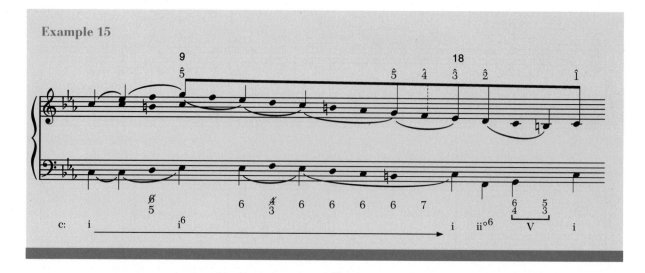

Partwriting Procedures and Melody Harmonization

Some principles for partwriting with the vii°⁷ and vii⌀⁷ are illustrated in Example 16.

You should focus on treating the chordal 7th correctly by using suspension or neighboring figures to precede and resolve the 7th, as outlined in the models in Examples 4 through 9. Avoid similar or parallel 5ths (Example 16a). As long as similar 4ths appear in the upper voice, your partwriting will proceed smoothly, through stepwise motion exclusively (Example 16b). When resolving the root-position vii°⁷ or vii⌀⁷ to tonic harmony, avoid similar or parallel 5ths by doubling the chordal 3rd in the chord of resolution (Example 16c). Remember, however, that similar 5ths are allowed when resolving the vii°⁶₅ (Example 16d), as we have seen in Example 6.

In melody harmonizations, using the leading-tone seventh chord presents an alternative to using inversions of the V⁷. In addition, we may now harmonize ♭6̂ in a minor-mode melody with a vii°⁷ rather than the more usual iv. On what basis does a composer choose between a vii°⁷ and a V⁷? Refer back to Example 1: the first harmonization uses inversions of the dominant seventh chord, for which the second substitutes leading-tone seventh chords, making its character more intense, dark, and foreboding.

Example 16

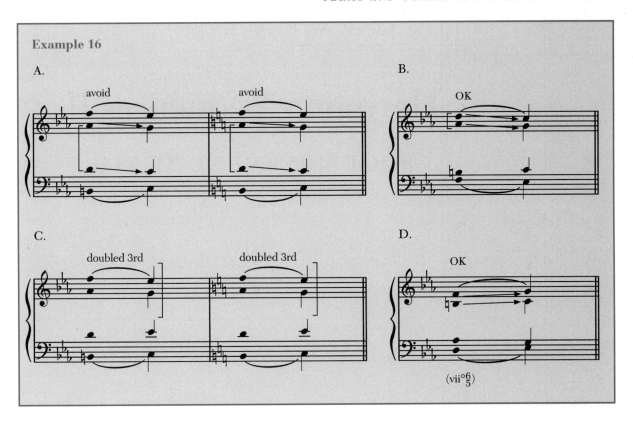

Terms and Concepts for Review

vii°⁷ *vs.* V⁷

inversions of vii°⁷

vii°⁷ as an embellishing chord

vii°⁷ *vs.* viiø⁷ in major

vii°⁷ as an alternative to V⁷

Harmonic Sequences II

ROOT MOVEMENT BY 5TH

Iɴ ᴛʜɪs ᴄʜᴀᴘᴛᴇʀ we will continue our study of diatonic harmonic sequences. We will first examine sequential passages that employ root movement by successive 5ths, and then passages that employ sequential movement by other intervals. Finally, we will explore ways to elaborate our sequential models and apply sequential patterns to our melody harmonizations.

The opening measures of Jerome Kern's lovely song in Example 1 display both melodic and harmonic sequences. What type of root movement controls the succession of seventh chords?

Example 1 Jᴇʀᴏᴍᴇ Kᴇʀɴ: "Aʟʟ ᴛʜᴇ Tʜɪɴɢs Yᴏᴜ Aʀᴇ" (sɪᴍᴘʟɪꜰɪᴇᴅ)

TRIADIC ROOT MOVEMENT BY DESCENDING 5TH

Motion by descending 5th is the most common root movement in functional harmony. In Chapter 18 we briefly discussed this type of root movement in the progression III–VI–II–V–I in both major and minor keys. We can extend this root movement through all seven diatonic tones back to the tonic (for instance, C–F–B–E–A–D–G–C) and thereby achieve a long-range prolongation of tonic harmony. This **cycle of 5ths** can be especially useful in restoring a sense of tonal stability after a change of key.

The consecutive roots of such cycles of 5ths in both the major and minor modes are illustrated in Example 2.

Example 2

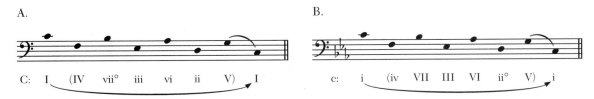

A.   B.

C: I   (IV   vii°   iii   vi   ii   V)   I   c: i   (iv   VII   III   VI   ii°   V)   i

A diminished 5th must occur somewhere in the progression to prevent the series of perfect 5ths from moving outside the tones of the diatonic system or scale (see Figure 1 in Chapter 3). Between which two scale degrees does this tritone occur in each mode?

In our four-voice realizations of complete diatonic cycles of 5ths, we will again (as in Chapter 20) denote only the two framing chords with functional roman numerals and designate the interior linear motion of the sequence with figured-bass symbols (Example 3).

Example 3

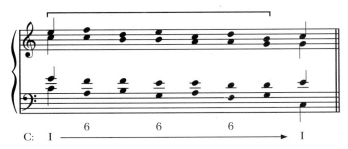

C: I   6   6   6   I

Because we retain the exact pattern created by the opening two chords throughout the rest of the sequence, we may create certain irregularities of doubling, such as the doubled leading tone in Example 3. These are tolerated within sequential writing, whereas in normal partwriting they are not.

We need not cycle through all seven diatonic triads when writing a passage that employs this root movement. If we wish to modulate to another key, we can "get off the train early" by inserting an appropriate accidental to create the leading tone in the dominant of the new key (Example 4).

Example 4

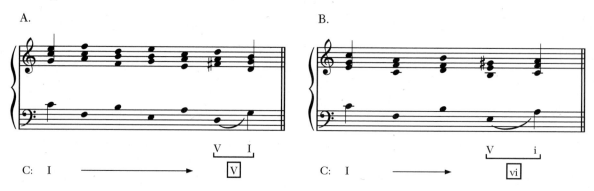

TRIADS IN DESCENDING 5TH SEQUENCES

In a cycle of root-position triads progressing by 5ths, the soprano-bass dyads of alternate chords will often produce a stepwise succession of descending 10ths, as shown by the beaming in Example 5. In Example 5a the succession begins with the first chord, while in Example 5b it begins with the second. When such a progression begins with the tonic, its metrically accented chords will form one of two descending tetrachords in the bass, ending either on the dominant ($\hat{8}-\hat{7}-\hat{6}-\hat{5}$) or on the tonic ($\hat{4}-\hat{3}-\hat{2}-\hat{1}$).

Example 5

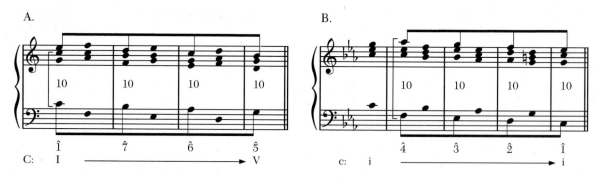

This span of a 4th is also the basis for the two models in Example 6, which employ only root-position triads and exhibit two of the most commonly found soprano lines. The partwriting in both models proceeds very smoothly; why does Example 6b require a continued alternation of close and open structure?

Example 6

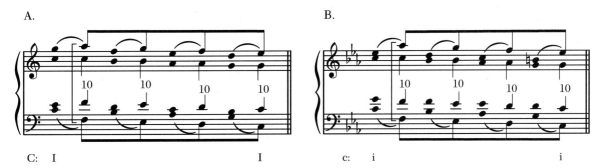

A.   B.

C: I   I   c: i   i

The "Storm" theme from Rossini's *William Tell* (Example 7) employs a succession of root-position triads descending by 5ths, with the chromatic motive alternating between bass and soprano. Complete the voice-leading reduction that has been begun for you below, beaming the stepwise 10ths in the outer voices.

Example 7   ROSSINI: OVERTURE TO *WILLIAM TELL*

A.

B. (REDUCTION)

e: i

The two models in Example 8 illustrate descending 5th sequences that alternate $\frac{5}{3}$ and $\frac{6}{3}$ triads to create smoother voice leading in the outer parts. Example 8a features a series of stepwise 10ths; the succession of harmonic 6ths in Example 8b results from switching the soprano and bass scale degrees of Example 8a. As usual in the minor mode, the leading tone does not appear until the last V chord.

Example 8

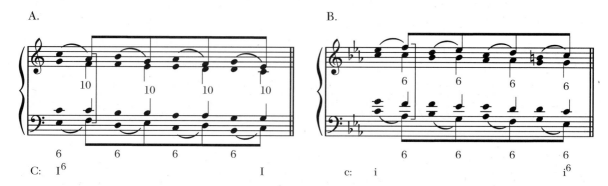

Determine the root movement in the Geminiani excerpt (Example 9) and complete its voice-leading reduction, continuing the beaming of the descending 10ths.

Example 9   GEMINIANI: SONATA FOR VIOLIN AND CONTINUO IN E MINOR, LARGO

TRIADS IN ASCENDING 5TH SEQUENCES

Triadic sequences using ascending 5th motion are less common, since they direct the harmonic motion away from the tonic harmony. Such sequences are restricted to the major mode and rarely progress past the mediant harmony: I–(V–ii–vi)–iii. Why do you think this is so? (To answer this, determine what the next two chords in Example 10a ought to be.) In the most common voice-leading models (Examples 10a and 10b), the beamed soprano and bass ascend stepwise in 10ths.

Example 10

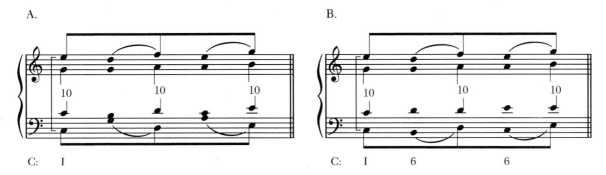

Finish the reduction of Bach's "Little Prelude" that has been started for you below. The dissonant notes within 4–3 suspensions are circled.

Example 11   BACH: LITTLE PRELUDE IN C MAJOR FROM *CLAVIERBÜCHLEIN*, BWV 924

SEVENTH CHORDS IN DESCENDING 5TH SEQUENCES

Diatonic seventh chords in descending 5th sequences are extremely common. The number of popular songs based on this progression is legion; in addition to that featured in Example 1, we might mention "The Windmills of Your Mind" or the Beatles' "You Never Give Me Your Money." The sequence of root-position seventh chords originates from a chain of descending 7–6 suspensions.

Example 12

In the series of $^{10}_{6}$ chords in Example 12a, the 7–6 suspensions in the alto serve to avoid the parallel 5ths by staggering the stepwise descents. If we support each suspension resolution with a note a 10th lower in the bass (Example 12b), creating a change of bass when the suspension resolves (refer back to Example 3 of Chapter 14), the model now resembles a sequence of root-position seventh chords. As each chordal 7th in the soprano or alto resolves, the held note in the other upper voice in turn becomes a new 7th, producing a pattern of overlapping dissonance and resolution. (The preparations and suspensions are not tied together in these models.) In the four-part setting shown in Example 12c, why must we omit the 5th of every other seventh chord?

Analyze the root movement of the Brahms excerpt in Example 13.

Example 13 BRAHMS: *EIN DEUTSCHES REQUIEM*, VI

A.

B. (REDUCTION)

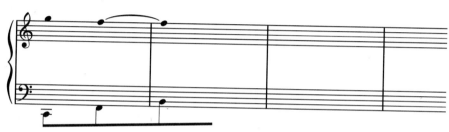

C:

Composers often employ chordal inversions when composing sequences of seventh chords. Two different successions are preferred: either ^{7} alternating with $^4_3$, or $^4_2$ alternating with $^6_5$ (Example 14).

Example 14

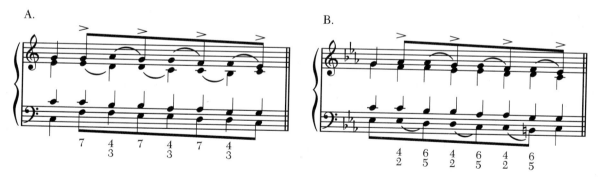

A.

B.

Example 15 shows two models that alternate triads with seventh chords. In such cases, the dissonant seventh chord usually occurs on an accented beat, corresponding to the normal placement of suspensions.

Example 15

A.   B.

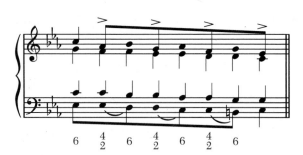
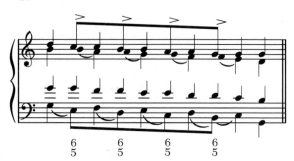

In the two excerpts in Example 16, determine the pattern of seventh-chord inversions, filling in the figured-bass symbols for each excerpt. The brackets indicate the sequential motion.

Example 16

A. GRIEG: MUSETTE FROM *HOLBERG SUITE,* OP. 40

B. BUXTEHUDE: "JESU CHRISTUS, UNSER HEILAND"

OTHER DIATONIC SEQUENCES

We may occasionally encounter harmonic sequences that do not fall within the basic categories discussed in this chapter and in Chapter 20. In the Rameau passage in Example 17, you will note that the root-position triads in the first, third, and fifth measures form a stepwise ascent with similar 10ths in the outer voices, which are beamed in the reduction. If the triads in measures 2 and 4 were G and A minor, respectively, the progression would resemble an ascending 5th sequence: C–G–D–A–E. However, the chords in these two measures instead ascend a 4th from the preceding triad, producing a regular bass pattern of C–F–D–G–E.

Example 17   RAMEAU: GAVOTTE AND VARIATIONS

Can you determine the root-movement succession on which the beautiful Fauré piece in Example 18 is based? Consider both the root movement within each measure and the motion from measure to measure. What is the long-range linear movement in the bass and soprano?

Example 18   FAURÉ: PAVANE, OP. 50

THE ELABORATION OF SEQUENCES

The abstract voice-leading models for each of the sequences that we have presented have been devoid of any surface melodic embellishment. In actual musical passages, however, an underlying sequential movement is normally elaborated by a prominent motivic idea. In the Mozart symphony in Example 19, for instance, this elaboration takes the form of imitation between the soprano and bass.

Example 19

A.

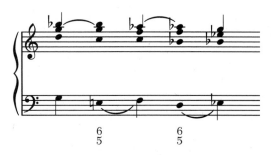

B.   Mozart: Symphony No. 41 ("Jupiter"), K.551, I (string parts only)

In deducing the voice leading of sequences that are melodically embellished, we should not try to determine the framework of the outer voices too hastily. At first glance, the essential tones in the bass and soprano in Example 20 appear to be the initial notes of each measure.

But this is not entirely the case. If we look at this example more closely, we will see that the notes that begin some measures are simply the result of voice exchanges. In fact, voice exchanges permeate this example; the first starts right in measure 50. These voice exchanges suggest a kind of compound melody, some notes of which appear in an inner voice and others of which appear as more structural, outer-voice tones (Example 20b). The implied soprano and bass voices, which are stemmed outward, constitute the underlying sequential voice leading: alternating $\frac{5}{3}$ and $\frac{6}{3}$ triads (Example 20c).

Example 20   HANDEL: ORGAN CONCERTO IN G MINOR, OP. 4, NO. 3, II

A.

B. (REDUCTION 1)   C. (REDUCTION 2)

UNUSUAL TREATMENT OF SEVENTH CHORDS IN SEQUENTIAL MOVEMENT

The following two examples show a more unusual handling of seventh chords in harmonic sequences. The Schumann excerpt (Example 21) represents a rare usage of consecutive seventh chords in a series of root-position chords descending by 3rds.

Example 21   SCHUMANN: "ICH GROLLE NICHT" FROM *DICHTERLIEBE*

A.

B.

C: I

In the voice-leading reduction, we have incorporated octave transfers of structurally important notes (some are from the right-hand piano accompaniment) to help set off the underlying stepwise motion inherent in the upper voices. Thus, starting in measure 2 the outer voices of the alternating seventh-chord inversions (^{7} and $^4_3$) outline a stepwise descent in 10ths. While the chordal 7th of each $^4_3$ resolves properly in the reduction's soprano part, the 7th of each root-position chord is switched into the bass, as shown by the arrows. This transference of the chordal 7th simultaneously prolongs the seventh harmony of the first half of each measure and creates a new passing seventh-chord harmony in the second half of the measure.

Even freer resolutions of the chordal 7th are typical of Debussy, as can be seen in Example 22.

Example 22   DEBUSSY: "CLAIR DE LUNE" FROM *SUITE BERGAMASQUE*

The opening of this famous piano miniature shows descending stepwise motion with 6ths occurring between the outer parts. This intervallic framework is filled out by a series of partially sequential seventh chords; the irregular alternation between $\frac{4}{3}$'s, $\frac{4}{2}$'s, and $\frac{6}{5}$'s keeps the passage from being fully sequential. This progression produces a somewhat static sense of harmonic motion that is finally broken in measure 7 with the ii$\frac{6}{5}$–V^7–I cadence.

Harmonic Sequences in Melody Harmonization

When employing harmonic sequences in melody harmonization, we must first examine the original tune for any melodic sequences. Regular stepwise descents and ascents, as well as skips by 3rds alternating with another interval, present opportunities for creating such sequential patterns. The guidelines below may serve as a summary to our study of harmonic sequences in Chapter 20 and the present chapter. The numbers above the staves show the scale degrees that begin and end the melodic sequence.

1. If the melody descends by step, try a succession of first-inversion triads (Example 23a), root movement by descending 3rds on alternate chords (Example 23b), or a cycle of 5ths with seventh chords (Examples 23c and 23d).

Example 23

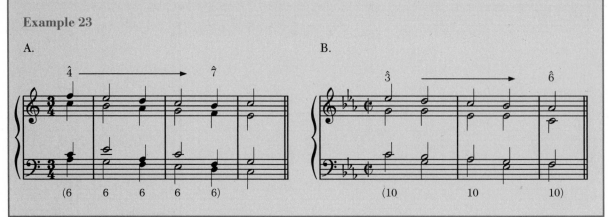

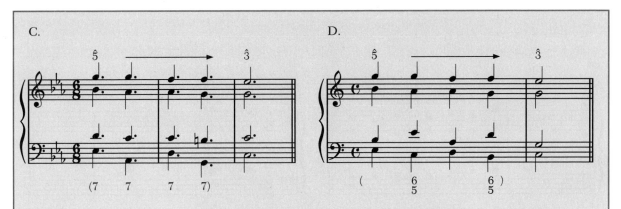

2. If the melody ascends by step, try a succession of rising first-inversion triads (Example 24a), a rising 5–6 series (Example 24b), a series of ascending 5ths (Example 24c), or even a sequence of ascending 3rds in root position (Example 24d).

Example 24

3. If the melody consists of 3rds alternating with another interval, try a series of falling 5ths (Examples 25a), a series of rising 5ths (Example 25b), or a series of falling 3rds alternating with ^{6} chords (Example 25c).

Example 25

A.

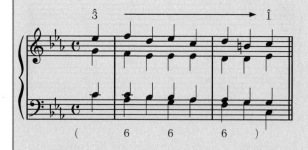

B.

C.

You might wish to apply some of these principles to the melodic phrases given in Example 26.

Example 26

A.

B.

C.

D.

A particular melody may allow several different sequential possibilities. When it repeats, we can choose to harmonize it another way. The second phrase of a very familiar tune is given in Example 27. Contrast a nonsequential harmonization (Example 27a) with one that employs a cycle of 5ths with alternating $\frac{5}{3}$ and $\frac{6}{5}$ triads (Example 27b).

Example 27

A.

B.

Example 28 quotes two phrases from Bach's chorale harmonizations that employ sequential motion. Can you determine the basic sequential models on which these two passages are based? Observe Bach's expressive use of suspensions in his elaborations of both melodies.

Example 28

A. "HEUT IST, O MENSCH, EIN GROSSER"
    (BACH CHORALE HARMONIZATION)

B. (REDUCTION)

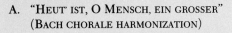

C.   "IN DULCI JUBILO" (BACH CHORALE HARMONIZATION)

D.   (REDUCTION)

F: IV   V⁶

Terms and Concepts for Review

root movement by 5th (sequential and
    nonsequential)
cycle of 5ths
seventh chords in descending 5th motion

elaboration of sequential models
unusual treatments of seventh chords in
    sequential movement

Analytical Comments on a Menuetto and Trio by Beethoven

Until now we have largely confined the length of our music examples to a two-phrase period. In this chapter we will conclude our study of diatonic harmony by examining a complete movement from a larger work: the Menuetto and Trio of Beethoven's Piano Sonata in F minor, Op. 2, No. 1. This short movement illustrates a variety of tonal and formal idioms that we have covered in the preceding chapters, and thereby provides an excellent summary of the principles of diatonic harmony. The way we analyze this piece can serve as a model for your future analyses.

LARGER FORMAL CONSIDERATIONS

We will begin by briefly discussing the formal design of this **Minuet and Trio.** The minuet often appeared as a stylized dance in suites of the late Baroque period; in the Classical era it occurred more frequently as the third movement of symphonies, string quartets, and even solo sonatas, as is the case with this Beethoven movement. The stately nature of this dance in the Baroque era was occasionally replaced in later years by a more playful or "scherzo-like" quality, partly the result of a faster tempo; the Beethoven movement is a typical example.

By the time of Mozart and Haydn, the minuet had assumed a three-part or **ternary form** (ABA), consisting of the Minuet proper (A), a succeeding Trio (B), and a subsequent return (*da capo*) of the Minuet proper. Each of these larger units was divided in turn into two well-defined sections demarcated by repeat signs, producing a binary or two-reprise form.[1]

Classical composers superimposed a relatively rigid thematic design and tonal structure onto this binary form. This scheme is diagrammed in Figure 1 in both major and minor modes.

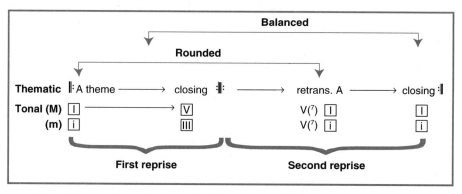

Figure 1

The first reprise opens with the principal theme (A) in the tonic key. Minuets in a major key usually modulate to the dominant key ($\boxed{V}$), while those in minor normally modulate to the relative major key ($\boxed{III}$).[2] Melodic phrases are usually four measures long; however, composers of the Classical period sometimes indulged in remarkably irregular phrasing.

The second reprise often opens with a development or elaboration of the initial theme, during which other scale degrees may be temporarily tonicized. This process leads to a **retransition,** where a brief prolongation of V tonally prepares for the synchronized return of the A theme and the tonic harmony. Two-reprise pieces that include a return of the complete original theme in the tonic are said to be in **rounded binary form.** If the original theme does not return, and the second reprise simply concludes with a transposition of the first reprise's cadence to the tonic key, it is in **balanced binary form.** The second reprise section is normally longer than the first.

Rounded binary forms frequently exhibit an interrupted tonal structure that consists of (1) tonal movement from the initial tonic at the opening of the first reprise to the dominant at the retransition in the second reprise, then (2) a reiteration of the initial theme and tonic harmony that leads to the final authentic cadence at the end of the second reprise: ‖: I :‖: V ∥ I–V–I :‖. Note that this very basic harmonic scheme applies equally to major- and minor-mode movements. This interrupted harmonic structure is often

1. For a discussion of binary, two-reprise, and ternary forms, see Excursion I: Simple Forms.
2. In the minor mode, the first reprise may also modulate to the minor dominant key ($\boxed{v}$).

reinforced by the overall voice leading of the soprano line: $\hat{3}$–$\hat{2}$ **//** $\hat{3}$–$\hat{2}$–$\hat{1}$ (typical of major keys) or $\hat{5}$–$\hat{4}$–$\hat{3}$–$\hat{2}$ **//** $\hat{5}$–$\hat{4}$–$\hat{3}$–$\hat{2}$–$\hat{1}$ (typical of minor keys).

FORMAL CHARACTERISTICS OF BEETHOVEN'S MENUETTO AND TRIO

With few exceptions, the Menuetto and Trio sections of this movement adhere to the form we have outlined above. Schematic diagrams of both the Menuetto and the Trio are given in Figure 2, with measure numbers.

Menuetto				Trio									
1	5	11 – 14	15	25 – 28	28	35 – 40	41 – 44	45 – 50	51	61	65	66	70 – 73
‖: A	A → closing	:‖	A → retrans.	A → closing	‖:A	→closing	‖	‖:(extended dominant)				A → closing	:‖
f: i	III	III	iv	V⁷	i	i	F:I	V	V	(IV⁶)	V⁷	I	I

Figure 2

Compare these diagrams with the actual score (Examples 1 and 3) while you listen to the movement.

MOTIVES AND PHRASE GROUPINGS IN THE MENUETTO

We will now examine the Menuetto's motivic content and phrase grouping. For the moment, please disregard the analytical reduction below the score in Example 1; we will return to this reduction later when we consider the voice leading.

Example 1   BEETHOVEN: PIANO SONATA IN F MINOR, OP. 2, NO. 1, III, MENUETTO

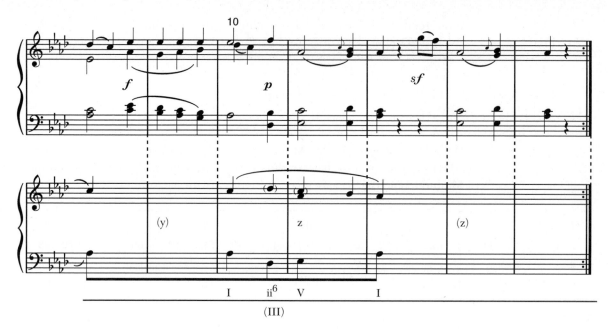

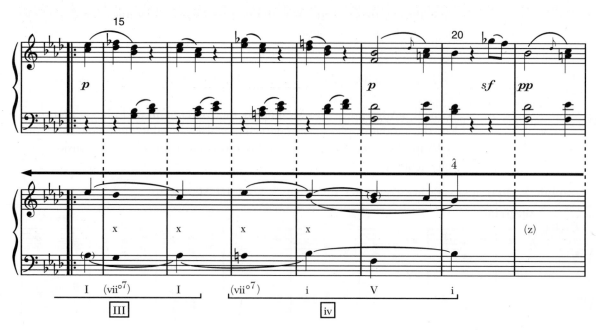

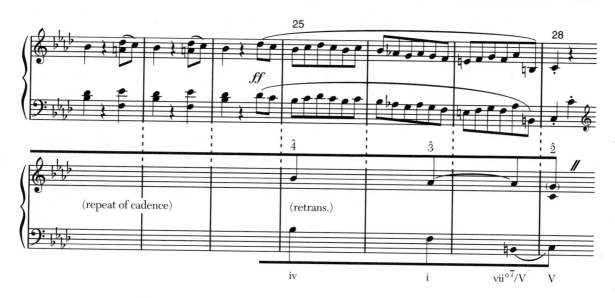

In surveying the Menuetto's first reprise, you will notice three distinct melodic motives (Example 2).

Example 2

A.   B.

The *x* motive (and its immediate partial sequence a step lower) initiates each phrase; the *y* motive continues the melodic flow. The *z* motive forms part of a $^6_4$ cadence (I–ii^6–$\overset{6-5}{\underset{4-3}{}}$V–I) in measures 10–12. The latter portion of this cadence is repeated in measures 13–14.

We may outline the motivic succession of the first reprise (mm. 1–14) as in Figure 3.

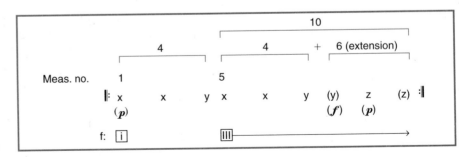

Figure 3

Since the *x x y* of the opening phrase (mm. 1–4) prolongs the F-minor tonic triad with a single embellishing dominant (V^6), the phrase lacks a strong root-position cadence. As we have seen in Example 8 of Chapter 19, the tonality immediately shifts to the relative-major key of A♭ at measure 5 for a repetition of the opening material. We might expect Beethoven to introduce the cadential *z* after this reiteration of *x x y*, in order to provide a more conclusive close in the new key. However, the composer first interpolates an additional *y* (note the *forte* marking) before doing so, and then extends the cadence with another statement of *z*, which emphasizes its finality (mm. 5–14). This interpolation and extension produce an overall phrase grouping of 4 + 10 in the first reprise.

We may diagram the second reprise (mm. 15–40) in a similar fashion (Figure 4).

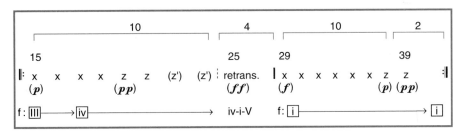

Figure 4

This section commences with a fourfold statement of *x*, supported by a tonal motion from III to iv, or B♭ minor (mm. 15–18). The subdominant key is reinforced by reiterations of the cadential *z* motive, the last two of which are compressed to a single measure z^1. The resulting 4 + 6–measure grouping recalls the ten-bar phrase in the latter part of the first reprise. At this point, we might anticipate a retransition on a prolonged dominant to prepare for the return of the original theme and tonic key. Instead, Beethoven inserts a three-measure passage of running eighth notes in octaves, which spans the harmonies iv–i–V (mm. 25–28) and is played *fortissimo*. The return of the opening tonic theme (m. 28) occurs in the left hand. Since this final section must remain in F minor, the composer avoids any reference to A♭ major and instead embellishes the tonic harmony with vii^{o7} chords (mm. 28–34). A pair of cadential *z*'s lead to the final cadence. This concluding tonic section (mm. 29–38) again reiterates our previous ten-measure grouping. Why do you think Beethoven added the last two measures?

HIERARCHICAL LEVELS OF TONAL STRUCTURE AND VOICE LEADING

In preceding chapters we have occasionally provided both foreground and middleground analyses of particular passages, the first of which strips away surface elaboration and highlights basic musical events, and the second of which shows larger-scale tonal motion. A foreground reduction of the first ten measures of this movement appeared in Example 8 of Chapter 19. Here, we will examine the Menuetto in light of the middleground voice leading, which is provided below the score in Example 1. As we go through the analysis, you might note how it highlights the Menuetto's interrupted tonal structure ($\hat{5}-\hat{4}-\hat{3}-\hat{2}$ ∥ $\hat{5}-\hat{4}-\hat{3}-\hat{2}-\hat{1}$). You might try to fill in this middleground reduction by inserting surface or foreground events.

Following the opening prolongation of tonic harmony (mm. 1–4), the second phrase immediately shifts to $\boxed{\text{III}}$ by means of sectional modulation. A similar prolongation of A♭ major leads to a $^6_4$ cadence in measures 11–12 and again in measures 13–14. Meanwhile, the soprano moves from $\hat{3}$ (A♭⁴) to $\hat{5}$ (C⁵; $\hat{3}$ of the new key),[3] and then returns stepwise to A♭⁴ via B♭⁴. Although the actual soprano notes in measures 10–11 are F⁵ and A♭⁴, we have inserted an implied D♭⁵ and C⁵ (in parentheses) so that the upper line will descend stepwise ($\hat{4}-\hat{3}-\hat{2}-\hat{1}$) to the tonic of the new key. In compositions from the Classical era, this stepwise descent is generally found in the soprano within $^6_4$ cadences (see Chapter 16); here, Beethoven varies this cadential formula by placing one of the pitches (C) in a lower voice and omitting another (D♭) altogether, instead creating the leap from F to A♭.

The second reprise opens with a chromatic bass motion (mm. 15–18) that takes us from $\boxed{\text{III}}$ to $\boxed{\text{iv}}$. The music tonicizes these areas with a pair of passing vii°⁷ chords. The soprano descends from E♭⁵ to B♭⁴, which is $\hat{4}$ in the original key (mm. 16–24); the implied D♭⁵'s in measures 19 and 21 (the D♭'s are actually found in the tenor voice) again supply the $\hat{3}-\hat{2}-\hat{1}$ $^6_4$ cadence in B♭ minor. The running-eighth-note passage (mm. 25–28) continues the upper-voice descent through $\hat{3}$ (A♭⁴) to $\hat{2}$ (G⁴) at the concluding V (m. 28); note that the $\hat{2}$ is only implied by the voice leading and is not actually present, since Beethoven resolves the B♮ in measure 27 to C but not also the A♭ ($\hat{3}$) to G ($\hat{2}$)—this to preserve the octave texture.

The soprano regains the original $\hat{5}$ (m. 30) immediately after the restatement of the opening theme and tonic key, and makes an uninterrupted stepwise descent to $\hat{1}$ (mm. 30–36) at the conclusion of the Menuetto.

Just as a foreground voice-leading reduction eliminates the surface melodic figuration, a middleground reduction eliminates lesser details of the foreground reduction, such as surface harmonic prolongations, in order to

---

3. The soprano E♭⁵'s in measures 9–10 are actually tones that temporarily cover the melody.

give us a clearer picture of the large-scale voice leading within a complete composition. This permits us to see at a glance the piece's overall tonal structure. This is particularly helpful if we intend to play the piece, since we can thereby plan our performance to better reflect the composer's underlying melodic and harmonic scheme.

OVERALL VOICE LEADING IN THE MENUETTO AND TRIO

Further reduction of the middleground brings us to the **background,** which can be thought of as the underlying foundation for the interplay of readily audible musical events. The soprano line of the background will usually descend stepwise to the tonic from either $\hat{3}$ ($\hat{3}$–$\hat{2}$–$\hat{1}$) or $\hat{5}$ ($\hat{5}$–$\hat{4}$–$\hat{3}$–$\hat{2}$–$\hat{1}$); the bass line of this two-voice contrapuntal framework supports the soprano. In Examples 1 and 3, the scale degrees over the pitches that are beamed in the soprano line represent the long-range soprano descent of the background voice leading.

MOTIVES AND PHRASE GROUPINGS IN THE TRIO

The Trio of Beethoven's third movement (Example 3) is set in the parallel major key.

Example 3

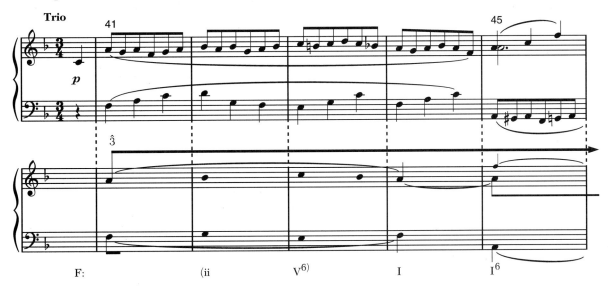

F: (ii   V⁶)   I   I⁶

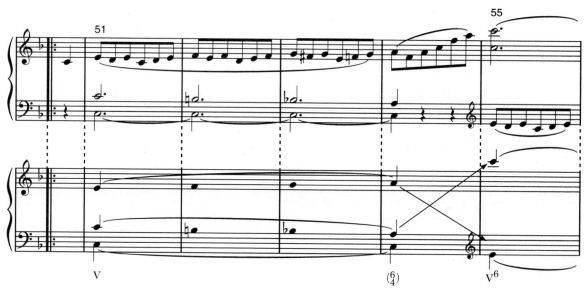

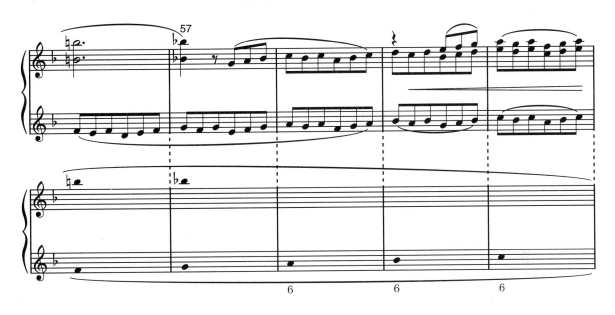

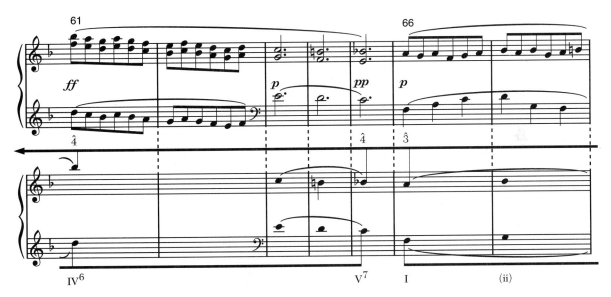

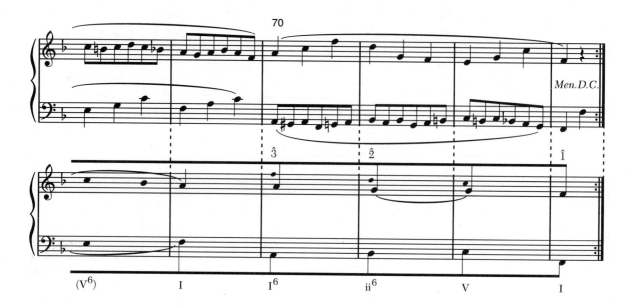

Its main theme consists of running-eighth-note figuration that prevails almost throughout the Trio. The phrasing of the first reprise (mm. 41–50) suggests a 4 + 6 grouping, in which the second phrase is extended by two measures (4 + 2)—much as in the first reprise of the Menuetto—to establish a cadence in the dominant key. The emphatic close compensates for the lack of strong cadential punctuation in the opening phrase, which consists largely of harmonies that linearly embellish the F-major tonic: I–ii–V⁶–I.

Figure 5

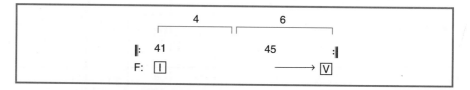

The second reprise begins on the dominant but quickly seems to return to F major via the stepwise motion in the upper and middle voices (E^4–F^4–G^4–A^4 and C^4–$B\natural^4$–$B\flat^4$–A^4) over a $\hat{5}$ pedal (mm. 51–54). The next phrase appears to follow the same plan, but with the outer parts switched (indicated by arrows). Upon reaching the upper $B\flat^5$ in measure 57, however, Beethoven inserts a lengthy interpolation (mm. 57–64) that "extends" the third bar of the four-measure grouping. This internal extension ends at measure 65, which takes the place of the final bar of the original four-measure grouping, with a $B\flat^4$ in the upper voice instead of the A^4. The return to the tonic in measure 66 is coupled with a restatement of the initial theme, which concludes the Trio with a pair of four-measure phrases.

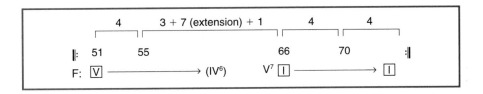

Figure 6

MIDDLEGROUND STRUCTURE IN THE TRIO

The reduction below the score in Example 4 reveals the middleground tonal structure of the Trio. The opening phrase (mm. 41–44) prolongs the $\hat{3}$ (soprano) and $\hat{1}$ (bass) of the F-major tonic. The $\hat{3}$ is then transferred to the middle voice, which moves downward by step to $\hat{5}$ (m. 50) over an authentic cadence in the dominant key. The upper soprano voice is super-imposed over this descent, creating a series of descending ^{6} chords that leads to the $^6_4$ cadence.

Following the dominant pedal that opens the second reprise (mm. 51–54), the soprano moves chromatically from C^5 to $B\natural^4$ to $B\flat^4$ (m. 57), at which point the interpolation occurs. The $B\flat^4$ (scale degree $\hat{4}$) is reinforced by a IV^6 in measure 61 and provides the chordal 7th of the V^7 at measure 65. This middle section of the second reprise represents a large-scale pro-longation of dominant harmony that eventually leads to the restatement of the original tune and tonic of F major in measure 66. The remainder of the Trio represents an extension of the all-important soprano $\hat{3}$ (mm. 66–69) before the final $\hat{3}$–$\hat{2}$–$\hat{1}$ descent in the last phrase (mm. 70–73).

UNIFYING FACTORS IN THE MOVEMENT

Like every great composer, Beethoven strove to unify the different musical elements in each of his compositions. This is evident not only within individual movements but even between the different movements of longer works.[4] These unifying features are not always obvious; sometimes they lie disguised beneath the surface of the music.

For instance, the initial phrases of both the Menuetto (mm. 1–4) and the Trio (mm. 41–44) avoid a strong cadential punctuation. The first convincing cadence of the Menuetto appears in the relative key of A♭ major. What standard cadential formula is employed in measures 11–12? Now turn to the phrase in measures 45–50 of the Trio. What type of cadence is

---

4. For instance, the four movements of his Ninth Symphony reveal a recurring relation between D and B♭ at both superficial and deeper levels.

employed here? Does this section modulate? Do either or both of these cadences exhibit phrase extensions?

The switching of voices in the musical texture, such as when the soprano and bass exchange parts, is called **double counterpoint.** This device plays an important role in the Trio; it is first suggested in the initial pair of four-measure phrases (mm. 41–44 and 45–50). Another instance of double counterpoint occurs at measures 51–58. Can you locate yet another instance in the Trio? The use of this device has already been anticipated in the Menuetto; study the first theme in measures 6–10 and its return in measures 28–30.

We have seen that the thematic material of the Menuetto is constructed almost entirely of three short motives. Can you find one notable exception to this? What is its formal and harmonic function? And how does this brief passage relate to the Trio? Now find the single exception to the continuous running figuration in the Trio. Where does it occur, and what is its formal and harmonic function?

We have already mentioned the lack of a strong dominant-oriented retransition (mm. 25–28) prior to the return of the initial motive in the Menuetto. How do you think Beethoven compensated for this abbreviated $V^{(7)}$ in the second reprise of the Trio?

Similar musical relationships abound in this movement. If you take a few minutes to examine it a bit more closely, you will be amply rewarded.

Terms and Concepts for Review

Minuet and Trio
ternary form (ABA)
retransition
rounded binary form

balanced binary form
background voice leading
double counterpoint

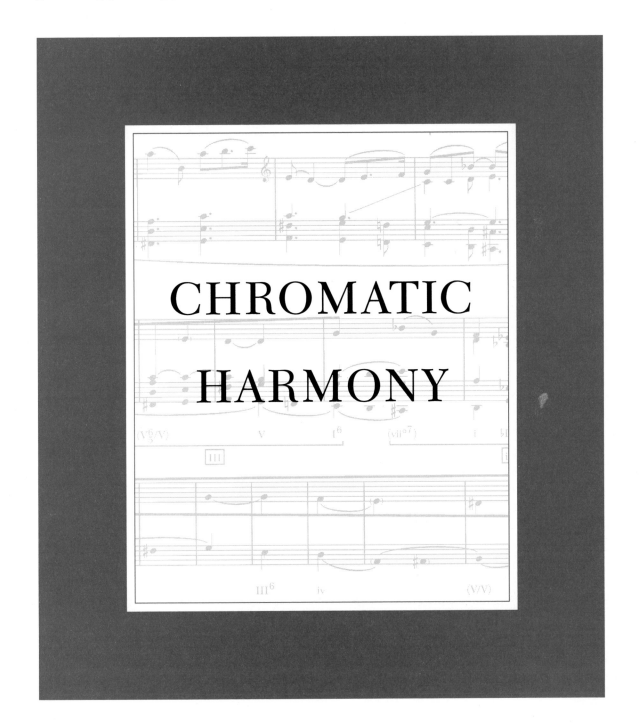

PART THREE

CHROMATIC

HARMONY

Introduction to Chromatic Harmony

Now that we have completed our examination of how diatonic triads and seventh chords operate in the music of the common-practice period, we are ready to explore the topic of **chromatic** or **nondiatonic harmony**—that is, the way in which **altered** scale degrees and chords are introduced in the major and minor modes.

Let us begin by contrasting the two C-major settings in Example 1. We can see that while the first phrase is completely diatonic, the second phrase contains four nondiatonic pitches in the bass line.

The altered notes in the latter passage illustrate several important features of chromatic harmony:

1. It provides an enlarged tonal palette with which to enrich or "color" diatonic melodies and diatonic harmony. (The term *chromatic*, in fact, is derived from the Greek word *chroma*, meaning "color.")
2. It intensifies the tendency of certain scale degrees and chords to resolve. For instance, in the motion to the dominant (Example 1b), the B♭ and A♭ (♭$\hat{7}$ and ♭$\hat{6}$) strengthen the descent of the original $\hat{8}$–$\hat{7}$–$\hat{6}$–$\hat{5}$. Likewise, the inserted G♯ acts as a secondary leading tone to the A (♯$\hat{5}$–$\hat{6}$).

Example 1

A.

B.

3. When a pitch changes its spelling enharmonically, its scale-degree function also changes. In Example 1b, the descending A♭ is matched by the ascending G♯. Observe how the two pitches have opposite tendencies: the A♭ pulls down toward G (♭6̂–5̂), while the G♯ pulls up toward A (♯5̂–6̂).

The chapters in Part Three will explore the wide scope of chromatic harmony, which ranges from individual chromatic chords and notes to large-scale tonal schemes. Chapters 27, 28, 29, 31, and 32 concentrate on specific altered harmonies. Other chapters take up topics already introduced in Part Two: tonicization and modulation, dominant prolongation, and sequences. Chapter 30 explores the relation of aesthetics to music. The final chapter deals with analytical issues within the Prelude to Wagner's *Tristan and Isolde*, which provides a summation of the various facets of chromatic practice, much as our discussion of the Beethoven Menuetto served as a summation of diatonic practice.

THE HISTORICAL EVOLUTION OF NONDIATONIC TONES

The introduction of nondiatonic tones in Western music evolved gradually. Western ecclesiastical chant and early secular songs were simple melodies that employed the natural diatonic or "white-key" notes, with an occasional B♭. Since there was no standard pitch reference such as our present A⁴ = 440 hertz at that time, these melodies were sung at various pitch levels.

However, they were always notated with natural pitch classes, as shown in the two tunes of Example 2.

Example 2

A. EPITAPH OF SEIKILOS (EARLY GREEK MELODY)

B. KYRIE "CLEMENS RECTOR" (GREGORIAN CHANT)

Ky - ri - e _____ e - le - i - son.

With the introduction of polyphony, or music with several individual voice parts, composers began to focus attention on the harmonic aspect of their music. By the mid Renaissance (about 1500), a number of additional notes—particularly B♭, F♯, C♯, G♯, and E♭—were being used to adjust harmonic cadences. Composers were using them to create major triads on the final chord of pieces whose natural $\hat{3}$ was minor. Performers were inserting them at appropriate points, including cadences, to supply leading tones; since they did not appear in the score, these accidentals were called **musica ficta,** or "fictitious music."[1] In Example 3, the sharp above the staff indicates that the note below it should be performed as a G♯.

Example 3 PALESTRINA: "QUIA FECIT MIHI MAGNA" FROM *MAGNIFICAT*

By the time of Bach and Handel, composers were employing a variety of altered scale degrees to expand the tonal resources at their disposal (Example 4).

1. In most modern editions, these *musica ficta* accidentals are usually written above the affected note.

Example 4   "Es ist genug" (Bach chorale harmonization)

A: V

Example 5 illustrates the range of common chromatic scale degrees that came to be used in the common-practice period; they appear in the bass line supporting various altered chords. Observe that the enharmonically equivalent notes C♯/D♭, D♯/E♭, and G♯/A♭ tend to belong to completely different chordal harmonies within the chromatically extended key of C major.

Example 5

CHROMATIC MELODIC MOTION

In a general sense, the term **chromaticism** refers to the presence of numerous altered pitches in musical passages, where diatonic tones have been raised or lowered by accidentals. These altered notes may be approached by means of diatonic melodic motion. For instance, in Example 6a the altered note F♯ in the key of C major is approached from the diatonic tones E and A. On the other hand, we can also approach the F♯ from an F♮ by a half-step chromatic motion; as you might suspect, the F♯ will then progress to G (Example 6b). Altered notes may occur as either nonharmonic tones, such as passing or neighboring tones (Example 6c), or as the chordal member of a particular harmony. In Example 6d, we have labeled the passing chord that contains the altered note with "(P)."

We also use the term *chromaticism* in a general sense to describe musical passages that display extensive half-step motion in the same voice or between parts. In a more specific sense, chromaticism involves the use of *augmented primes*, such as F♮–F♯—that is, diatonic notes that are raised or lowered by an accidental. (*Prime* is another term for unison.) Here, the note

Example 6

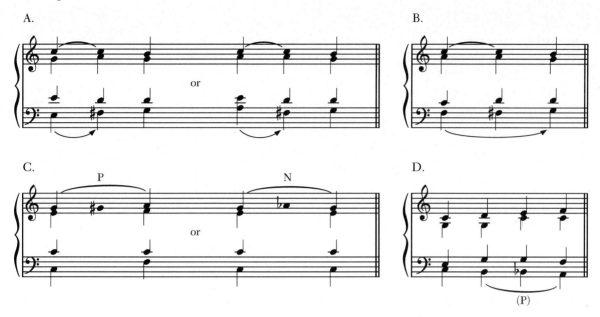

keeps its letter name; contrast this with the motion F♯–G (a minor 2nd), where two different letter names are involved. In chromaticism, the altered or chromatic version of the scale degree will then "resolve" to another scale degree: C–C♯–D, B♮–B♭–A, and so forth. Example 7 illustrates the usual treatment of melodic augmented primes: diatonic notes that are raised by an accidental will normally resolve upward by half step, and those that are lowered by an accidental will normally resolve downward by half step.

Example 7

The bass line in Example 8 proceeds entirely by half-step motion: A–G♯–G♭–F♯–F♮–E. Which intervals are minor 2nds and which are augmented primes? While chromaticism often involves nondiatonic scale degrees, we can see that this is not the case in Example 8, since all of the notes actually belong to the composite A-minor melodic scale.

Example 8   SWEELINCK: *CHROMATIC FANTASY*

The Brahms variation in B♭ major illustrates a concentrated use of chromaticism (Example 9). Circle each chromatic or altered-note scale degree and determine the diatonic degree from which it is derived and the diatonic degree to which it moves or "resolves."

Example 9   BRAHMS: *VARIATIONS AND FUGUE ON A THEME BY HANDEL*, OP. 24 (VAR. 20)

DECORATIVE VS. STRUCTURAL CHROMATICISM

Most surface chromaticism in tonal music is **decorative** in nature, since it involves half-step elaborations of an underlying diatonic framework. As early as the Baroque period, music theorists were already demonstrating the diatonic basis of chromatic passages. The reduction of the "royal theme" from Bach's *Musical Offering* by the theorist Johann Marpurg is one example among many (Example 10).

Example 10

A.   FREDERICK II: "ROYAL THEME," USED BY BACH IN HIS *MUSICAL OFFERING*

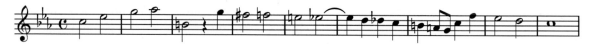

B. JOHANN MARPURG'S REDUCTION OF FREDERICK'S THEME

The decorative nature of nondiatonic pitches is apparent in Kuhnau's chorale prelude in Example 11, where the augmented primes are chromatic passing tones. The resulting altered tones, however, do not form dissonances within the existing diatonic chords.

Example 11   JOHANN KUHNAU: VARIATIONS ON "JESU, MEINE FREUDE" (VAR. 9)

Some instances of chromaticism cannot be reduced to a diatonic basis. For example, the middle section of Chopin's B♭-major Prelude, which opens with a direct modulation from B♭ major to G♭ major (I – ♭VI), juxtaposes two diatonically unrelated keys (Example 12).

Example 12   CHOPIN: PRELUDE IN B♭ MAJOR, OP. 28, NO. 21

Because the "altered" key of ♭VI is not equivalent to the diatonic key of vi, this represents the use of chromaticism at a **structural** level, creating a chromatic key relation that extends beyond the musical foreground. Here, the D♮ in B♭ major forms an augmented prime with the D♭ in G♭ major.

Situations may even arise where the density of the chromaticism obscures our sense of tonality. Play Example 13. What do you think is the basic key? Do you even perceive a tonic?

Example 13 WAGNER: PRELUDE TO *PARSIFAL,* ACT III

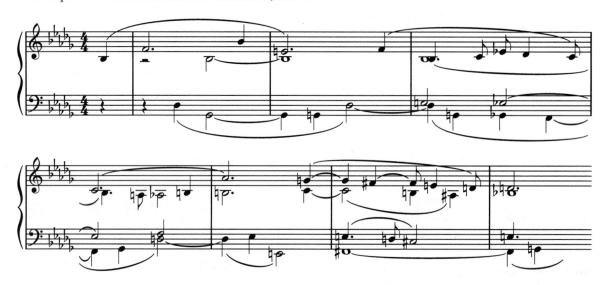

Although most examples of nontonal or atonal procedures are confined to the twentieth century, we may encounter isolated instances in the common-practice period. We will examine some of these occurrences in Chapter 39, which deals with harmonic relations based on equal divisions of the octave.

USING ROMAN NUMERALS TO DESIGNATE CHROMATIC HARMONIES

Along with the standard roman numerals, we will need to use additional and sometimes modified indicators to denote the altered nature of the chromatic chords. Most of these symbols fall into three categories, which are illustrated in Example 14.

Example 14

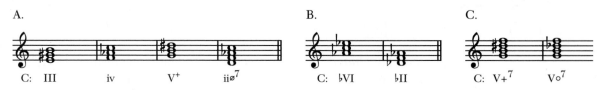

A.

C: III   iv   V$^+$ ii^{ø7}

B.

C: ♭VI   ♭II

C.

C: V+^{7} V○^{7}

1. We designate the chord type by the appropriate lowercase or capital roman numeral and by other symbols, such as ° for diminished and + for augmented. In the major mode, for instance, the diatonic versions of iii, IV, V, and ii^7 may be changed to III, iv, V$^+$, and ii^{ø7}. Refer to Example 14a.

2. We indicate the altered root of a chord by a flat (or rarely a sharp) before the roman numeral: ♭VI, ♭III, and ♭II in major, or ♯iii in minor (Example 14b).

3. We denote seventh chords that have certain raised or lowered chord members, such as the 5th, in the following way: V+^{7} or V○^{7} (Example 14c).

In later chapters we will introduce symbols appropriate to the function of other altered chords.

Terms and Concepts for Review

nondiatonic, altered, *or* chromatic harmony

musica ficta

melodic chromaticism

enharmonic notation of altered scale degrees

decorative *vs.* structural chromaticism

use of roman numerals in nondiatonic harmony

Tonicization
and Modulation II

SECONDARY DOMINANTS

IN CHAPTER 19, WE discussed the tonicization of $\boxed{V}$ in major and of $\boxed{III}$ in minor. We also examined the various degrees of tonicization, from transient modulations that last only a few beats and involve only a few harmonies, to confirmed modulations of extended length. In this chapter we will explore the use of secondary or applied dominants more fully, noting the various diatonic triads in both the major and minor modes that they momentarily tonicize.

Play Example 1 (p. 359) and observe the different harmonies that are tonicized, as indicated by the brackets. What is the relationship of each tonicized chord in the original tonic?

Any diatonic major or minor triad may be preceded by its own secondary or applied dominant chord, in root position or in inversion: V^6/V, V^7/ii, vii^{o6}/vi, vii^{o7}/iv, and so forth. These applied chords[1] usually function as embellishing harmonies, and in our models and reductive analyses we will leave them unstemmed and place parentheses around their roman

---

1. Music theorists use the terms *secondary dominant* and *applied dominant* interchangeably. The latter expression denotes that the altered chord is "applied" or attached to the diatonic triad that immediately follows it. Be careful not to confuse the terms *applied* and *implied*; while the former refers to secondary dominants, the latter refers to a note absent from the actual music but included in a reductive analysis (enclosed in parentheses) to indicate the expected voice leading.

Example 1   "COMBE MARTIN" (HYMN TUNE)

numerals. (See Example 3, below, and Example 4 in Chapter 19.) The actual function of applied chords always depends on their context within a given passage; thus, when we encounter applied chords that function in a more structurally significant manner, we will notate them differently in our analyses. Finally, after a discussion of the role of secondary dominants in sequential passages, we will examine how to incorporate these chords into melody harmonizations.

THE APPROACH TO ALTERED NOTES IN SECONDARY DOMINANTS

An applied dominant will normally contain one or more altered scale degrees. One is usually the leading tone ($\hat{7}$) to the temporarily tonicized triad that follows (Examples 2a and 2b), but other altered notes may also occur (Examples 2c and 2d).

Example 2

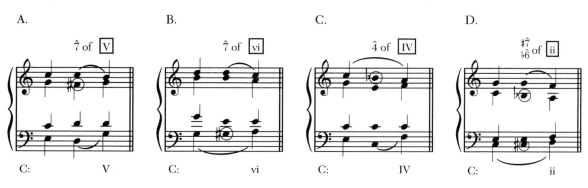

The altered tone or tones may be approached by diatonic melodic motion (Examples 3a and b), or they may be derived chromatically—that is, by adding an accidental to the immediately preceding note (Example 3c). The altered note can occur within the same chord as the preceding unaltered note (Example 3d) or appear as a member of a completely new harmony.

Example 3

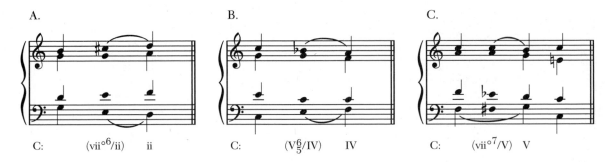

D. EDWARD PURCELL: "PASSING BY"

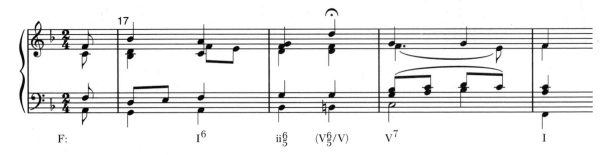

CROSS-RELATIONS

When the chromatic motion occurs between two different voice parts, a **cross-relation** results. Example 4 gives several instances of cross-relations, shown by the line connecting the two chromatic pitches. Notice that cross-relations always occur between two notes with the same letter name.

Example 4

Cross-relations between the soprano and bass are normally avoided. In our partwriting we should try to soften any cross-relations by involving an inner part.

A **chromaticized voice exchange,** such as the one shown in Example 5, sometimes occurs. A passing chord usually connects the chords containing the chromatically related tones. What is the nature of the passing chord in this excerpt?

Example 5   MOZART: KYRIE FROM MASS IN C MAJOR ("CORONATION"), K.317

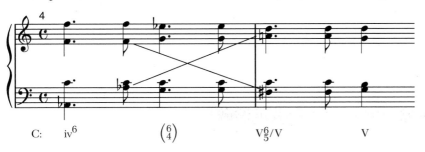

SURFACE TONICIZATIONS OF V AND IV (iv) IN THE MAJOR AND MINOR MODES

Surface tonicizations of the dominant and subdominant triads are very common in both modes. Tonicization of the dominant frequently occurs at cadences. The applied dominant of V includes the raised fourth scale degree (♯$\hat{4}$), enhancing its tendency to resolve to $\hat{5}$. When the secondary dominant substitutes for a diatonic IV or II in an authentic cadence, we stem the applied chord in our analyses and do not enclose its roman numeral in parentheses, in order to show its essential pre-dominant function (Example 6).

Example 6

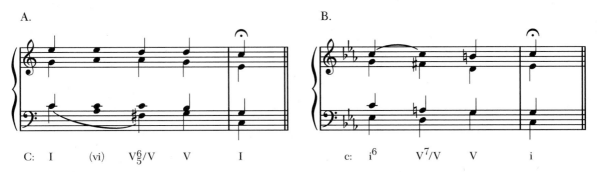

When the applied chord is chromatically inserted between a diatonic IV or ii⁶ and the V in an authentic cadence, we do not stem its chord members, in order to make its passing or embellishing nature clear (Example 7).

Example 7

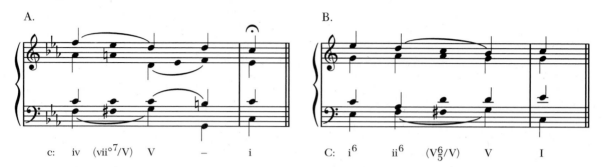

c: iv (vii°⁷/V) V — i   C: i⁶ ii⁶ (V⁶₅/V) V I

When encountering secondary dominants, we must be careful to distinguish between this use within a half cadence that remains in the original key and within an actual modulation to $\boxed{V}$ at the conclusion of a phrase. Example 8a clearly shows a half cadence, with the soprano ending on its customary $\hat{2}$.

Example 8

A. ROBERT FRANZ: "WIDMUNG," OP. 14, NO. 1

hab' ich sie treu - lich, ab - ge - le - sen.

G: (V⁷)   I   V⁷/V   V

B. HAYDN: STRING QUARTET IN D MAJOR, OP. 20, NO. 4, III

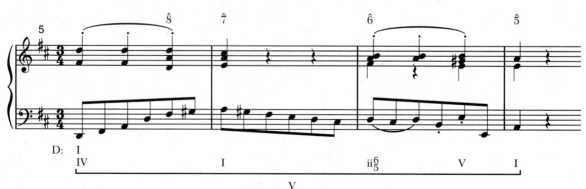

D: I
IV   I   ii⁶₅   V   I
              V

Example 8b, however, is best considered as showing a transient modulation to the dominant area, or $\boxed{V}$. Observe the pivot chord in measure 5 and the descent from $\hat{8}$ to $\hat{5}$ in the soprano. You may wish to compare this excerpt with the complete movement, found in Example 13 of Chapter 19.

As we have seen above and in Chapter 19, secondary dominants of V within the phrase have an embellishing function, often originating in passing motion or suspensions (Example 9).

Example 9

A.   B.

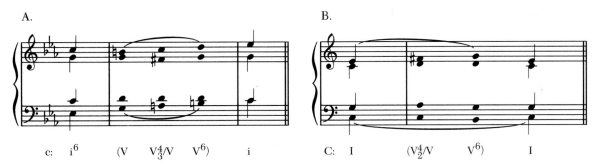

In Example 10 the altered note in the passing applied chords is derived chromatically and resolved diatonically.

Example 10

A.   B.

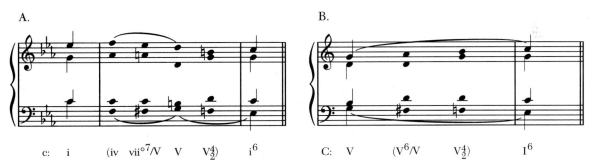

In subdominant tonicizations, the altered $\flat\hat{7}$ in the tonic harmony forms a tritone with $\hat{3}$ that impels the normally passive tonic toward IV, where they resolve to $\hat{6}$ and $\hat{4}$ respectively (Example 11a).

In the minor mode, the raised mediant ($\sharp\hat{3}$) is usually derived chromatically, as in the vii°7/iv of Example 11b. What is curious about the resolution of the bass leading tone (B♮) in Example 11c?

Example 11

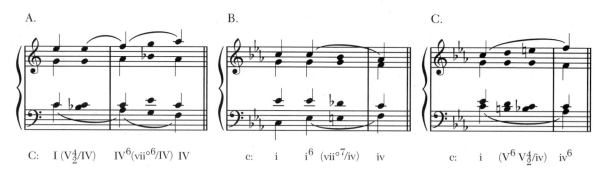

C: I (V$\frac{4}{2}$/IV)   IV^6(vii°^{6}/IV)   IV   c: i   i^6 (vii°^{7}/iv)   iv   c: i   (V^6 V$\frac{4}{2}$/iv)   iv^6

Applied dominants of IV in major frequently occur in opening progressions. In Example 12a, the subdominant functions as an embellishing or neighboring harmony to the tonic.

Example 12

A. THOMAS MOORE: "BELIEVE ME, IF ALL THOSE ENDEARING YOUNG CHARMS"

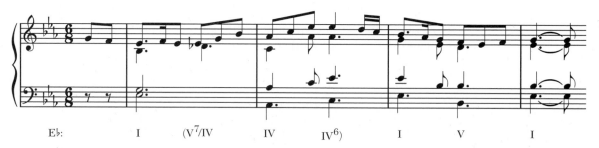

E♭:   I   (V^7/IV   IV   IV^6)   I   V   I

B. BACH: LITTLE PRELUDE IN C MAJOR, BWV 939

C: I   (V^7/IV   IV   V^7)   I

The Bach Prelude (Example 12b) opens with a tonic pedal under the progression I–V^7/IV–IV–V^7–I, which establishes the key of C major. This same progression is frequently seen in closing passages or codas, which prolong the tonic in a similar manner. Two typical instances are quoted in Example 13. What occurs in the bass voice of both excerpts?

Example 13

A. HAYDN: SYMPHONY NO. 101 ("CLOCK"), IV

D: I (V⁷/IV)   IV   V⁷) I (V⁷/V IV   V⁷)   I

B. TCHAIKOVSKY: *ROMEO AND JULIET*

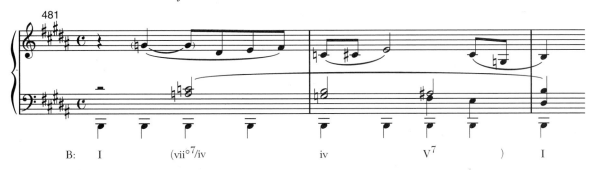

B: I   (vii°⁷/iv)   iv   V⁷   )   I

SURFACE TONICIZATIONS OF ii, vi, AND iii IN THE MAJOR MODE

Secondary dominants of the supertonic triad in major contain scale degree
♯$\hat{1}$ of the original key; vii°⁷/ii also contains ♭$\hat{7}$ (Example 14a and 14b).

Example 14

A.   B.   C.

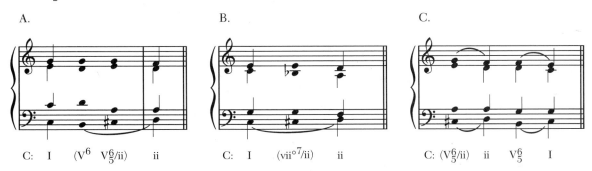

C: I   (V⁶ V⁶₅/ii) ii   C: I   (vii°⁷/ii) ii   C: (V⁶₅/ii) ii V⁶₅ I

The sequential progression in Example 14c commonly appears at the beginning of the second reprise of Classical minuets; Mozart had already assimi-
lated it (Example 15) by the tender age of four!

Example 15   MOZART: MINUET IN G MAJOR, K.1

A.   B.   (REDUCTION)

G: V^7/ii   ii   V^7 I

The third phrase of Diabelli's waltz (Example 16), immortalized in Beethoven's piano variations on the same tune, employs a sequence that moves from IV^6 to V^6; both are tonicized by their V$^4_2$.[2]

Example 16   ANTON DIABELLI: WALTZ IN C MAJOR

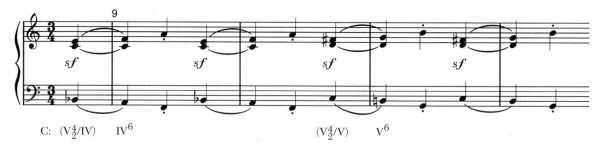

C: (V$^4_2$/IV)   IV^6 (V$^4_2$/V)   V^6

Applied dominants to vi and iii (Example 17) require no special treatment. Chromatic motion of $\hat{5}$–$\sharp\hat{5}$–$\hat{6}$, is characteristic of the former.

Example 17

A.   BRAHMS: INTERMEZZO IN E MINOR, OP. 119, NO. 2   B.   (REDUCTION)

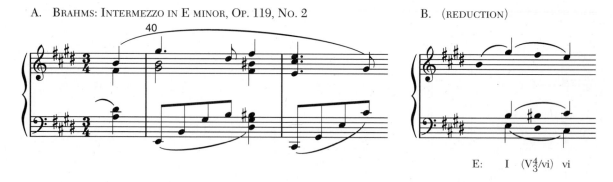

E: I   (V$^4_3$/vi)   vi

[2]Such a strict sequence up a whole step is referred to as a *Rosalia* in Italian and a *Schusterfleck* ("cobbler's patch") in German.

C. "AMERICA"

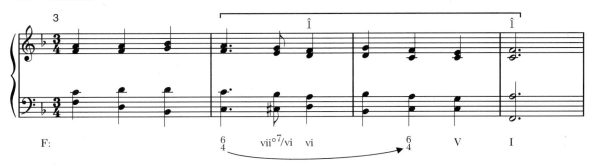

F: $^6_4$ vii°^{7}/vi vi $^6_4$ V   I

D. SCHUBERT: SYMPHONY NO. 8 ("UNFINISHED"), II   E. (REDUCTION)

E: I   (V^7/iii)   iii

The Brahms excerpt involves motion from I to vi by way of a passing secondary V$^4_3$. The excerpt from "America" shows the insertion of a vii°^{7} in a deceptive cadence; we might also consider this passage as an expanded $^6_4$ cadence ($^6_4$–V–I, as indicated by the bracket). What altered scale degrees are used in the V^7/iii in the Schubert excerpt?

SURFACE TONICIZATIONS OF III, VI, AND VII IN THE MINOR MODE

Tonicizations of the three major triads in the natural minor mode (III, VI, and VII) usually employ secondary V's or V^7's. The V^7/III contains no altered scale degrees (Example 18).

Example 18

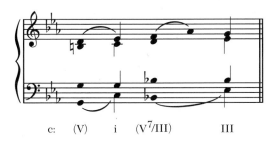

c: (V)   i   (V^7/III)   III

Tonicizations of VI and VII often occur in sequential progressions. (Chromaticism in diatonic sequences will be taken up in detail in Chapter 35.) In the passage from Handel's *Messiah,* these tonicizations form part of a descending tetrachord in the bass: G–F–E♭–D.

Example 19   HANDEL: 34A. "HOW BEAUTIFUL ARE THE FEET OF THEM" FROM *MESSIAH*

A.

B.   (REDUCTION)

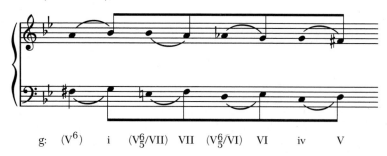

g: (V⁶)   i   (V⁶₅/VII)   VII   (V⁶₅/VI)   VI   iv   V

DECEPTIVE RESOLUTIONS OF SECONDARY DOMINANTS

Secondary dominants may also resolve in a deceptive manner, much like V⁽⁷⁾–vi. This occurs most often in the progression V⁷/vi–IV (or iv).

Example 20   PAUL DRESSER: "BY THE BANKS OF THE WABASH"

G: I   (V⁷/vi)   IV

THE USE OF SECONDARY DOMINANTS IN HARMONIC SEQUENCES

Secondary dominants are often found in sequences built on 5ths, 3rds, and 2nds. In descending-5th sequences, the insertion of secondary dominants will not alter the basic voice leading, but it will provide additional harmonic color and possible chromatic motion that could lead to other key centers. Example 21 quotes some typical 5th sequences in the major mode.

Example 21

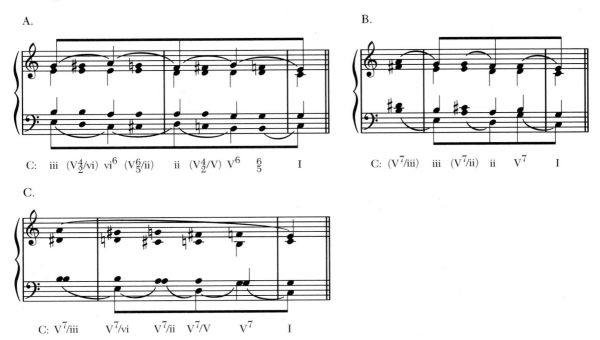

A.

C: iii (V_2^4/vi) vi^6 (V_5^6/ii) ii (V_2^4/V) V^6 $\begin{smallmatrix}6\\5\end{smallmatrix}$ I

B.

C: (V^7/iii) iii (V^7/ii) ii V^7 I

C.

C: V^7/iii V^7/vi V^7/ii V^7/V V^7 I

In Example 21a, applied dominant 7ths are inserted between the chords in the sequence (notated with stems); in Example 21b, they substitute for diatonic harmonies. Example 21c includes a succession of consecutive applied V^7's, in which the chromatic approach to the next chordal 7th and the resolution of the last occur simultaneously. This device, often associated with "barbershop" harmony, produces parallel tritones, which here occur between the soprano and alto. What types of sonorities appear in the Mendelssohn quotation in Example 22?

Example 22   MENDELSSOHN: TARANTELLA FROM *LIEDER OHNE WORTE*, OP. 102, NO. 3

In sequences by descending 3rds, inversions of secondary V⁷'s will usually alternate with temporarily tonicized $\frac{5}{3}$ triads. In the Schubert excerpt in Example 23a, the chordal 7ths result from descending passing motion in the soprano. In his famous C♯-minor Waltz (Example 23b), Chopin incorporates secondary dominants in a pattern of ascending thirds: i–III–v.

Example 23

A. SCHUBERT: PIANO QUINTET IN A MAJOR ("TROUT"), III

$$\text{A:} \quad \text{I} \quad (\text{V}^4_3/\text{vi}) \quad \text{vi} \quad (\text{V}^4_3/\text{IV}) \quad \text{IV} \quad (\text{V}^4_2/\text{ii}) \quad \text{ii} \quad (\text{vii}^{ø7}/\text{V}) \quad \text{V} \quad \text{I}$$

B. CHOPIN: WALTZ IN C♯ MINOR, OP. 64, NO. 2

C. (REDUCTION)

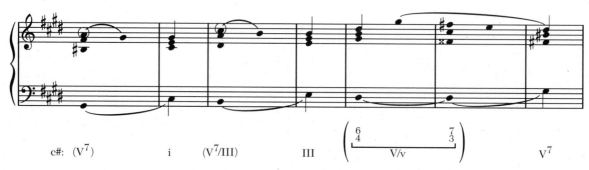

$$\text{c♯:} \quad (\text{V}^7) \quad \text{i} \quad (\text{V}^7/\text{III}) \quad \text{III} \quad \left(\overset{\frac{6}{4}}{\underset{\text{V/v}}{}} \overset{\frac{7}{3}}{} \right) \quad \text{V}^7$$

The Beethoven excerpt in Example 24 shows a series of stepwise-ascending triads that are preceded by applied V^7's. Why is it not possible to extend this sequential pattern past the iii chord?

Example 24   BEETHOVEN: PIANO SONATA IN G MAJOR, OP. 14, NO. 2, II

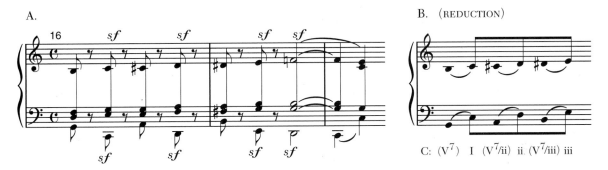

C: (V^7)   I   (V^7/ii)   ii   (V^7/iii)   iii

AN EXTENDED USE OF SECONDARY DOMINANTS

The closing section of the scherzo in Schumann's Symphony No. 1 in B♭ major employs an extended succession of applied vii°^{7}'s (Example 25).

The reduction shows that this excerpt opens with an implied cadential $^6_4$, whose resolution to the usual $^5_3$ is delayed by the neighboring motion of vii°^{7}/vi–VI but finally arrives on V with the customary $\hat{2}$ in the soprano (mm. 390–94). Schumann delays the resolution to $\hat{1}$ by inserting a remarkable succession of vii°^{7} tonicizations (three of these precede the arrival on V, and three follow it) while continuing the soprano descent through an octave span to A^4. Once the tonic is finally attained (I^6), a simple cadential formula (ii^6–V^7–I) closes the movement. (The upper voice remains suspended on A, $\hat{5}$ of D major. A glance at the finale of the symphony explains this imperfect cadence: the last movement opens with an A, the leading tone of the symphony's B♭ tonic.)

Example 25   SCHUMANN: SYMPHONY NO. 1 ("SPRING"), III

A.

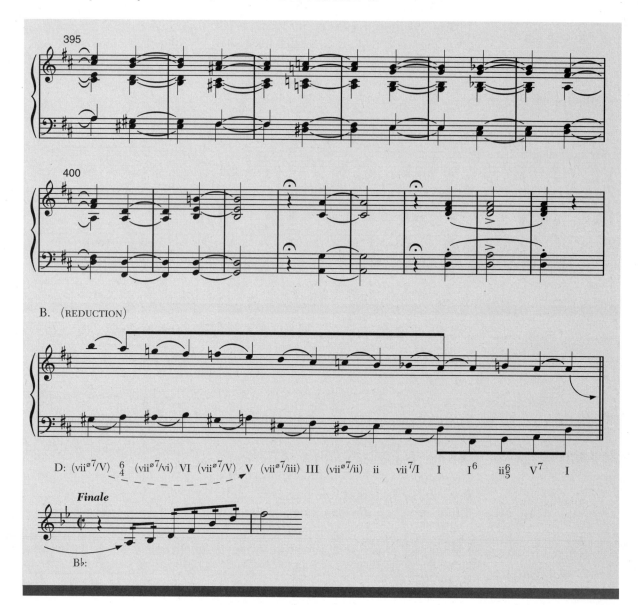

B. (REDUCTION)

D: (vii°⁷/V) $\frac{6}{4}$ (vii°⁷/vi) VI (vii°⁷/V) V (vii°⁷/iii) III (vii°⁷/ii) ii vii⁷/I I I⁶ ii$\frac{6}{5}$ V⁷ I

Finale

Bb:

Melody Harmonization

Since most chorale or hymn melodies are diatonic, we must relegate the altered pitches of secondary dominant chords to the lower voices—especially to the bass. For any given tune, you should try to work out several different harmonic settings. Compare the three versions in Example 26.

Example 26

A.

B.

G: (V$^4_2$/IV)   IV   (V^6/ii)   ii   (V$^6_5$/V)   V

C.

G: (V$^6_5$/ii)   ii   (vii°^{7}/vi)   vi   (III)

The first is completely diatonic and contains no tonicizations. The last two insert applied dominant chords in several places; study them carefully. Observe that, with the exception of the inserted altered notes, the bass line of the passage in Example 26b is basically the same as that in Example 26a; the bass of Example 26c is completely different. Remember: the secret to good harmonization and partwriting often lies in first composing an interesting bass line.

Terms and Concepts for Review

cross-relation
chromaticized voice exchange

harmonic sequences with applied dominants

Tonicization
and Modulation III

MODULATION TO CLOSELY
RELATED KEYS

IN THIS CHAPTER WE will explore the process of modulation more fully. First we will look at the reasons why composers in the common-practice period preferred to modulate to only a small group of tonal areas. Then we will examine the various scale degrees to which a piece can modulate and discuss the different ways in which these modulations are carried out.

Starting from a specific key in a tonal composition, it is possible to modulate to no fewer than twenty-two other major and minor keys, not counting modulations to enharmonic keys and the parallel major or minor key. Some of these key relations, however, appear only rarely during the common-practice period. From about 1700 on, composers begin to display a decided preference for remaining within a much smaller group of keys, namely those whose signatures differ by only sharp or flat from the original key. It is easy to modulate to these keys, since the new keys' tonic chords appear as diatonic major or minor triads within the original key.[1]

---

1. During the time of Bach and Handel, the tuning systems favored modulations to a limited number of keys. In most earlier tuning systems, especially those used during the seventeenth century, enharmonic notes (e.g., F♯ and G♭) were not equivalent in pitch, but instead sometimes varied by as much as one eighth of a tone.

CLOSELY RELATED KEYS

To look more closely at the nature of **closely related keys,** let us begin by diagramming the major and minor triads that are common to the key of C major and its relative minor, A minor. Each of the five scale degrees or triads shown in the diagram below may be tonicized as a new key in both the major and minor modes. You will note that the diminished chord on B, either as vii° in the major mode or ii° in the minor mode, is missing from the diagram. Because of its lack of a perfect 5th, this triad's unstable nature prevents it from functioning as a potential tonic.

Figure 1

C major:		I	ii	iii	IV	V	vi	(vii°)	I
Keys:		C	d	e	F	G	a		
A minor:	(ii°)	III	iv	v	VI	VII	i		

The close kinship between the keys in Figure 1 is implicit in their signatures, which differ by only one sharp or flat from the original key. We can see this more easily when we group them into pairs according to relative major-minor relationships:

C major/A minor: no accidentals
G major/E minor: one sharp
F major/D minor: one flat

The keys closely related to both an original major and minor key are given in Example 1; notice the difference in mode of the members of each set in comparison with one another.

Example 1

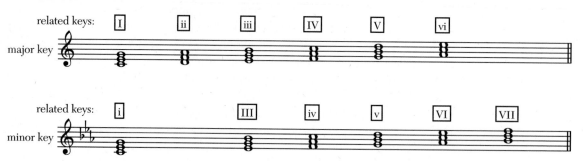

The **change of mode** from a major to a minor tonic (I to i) or vice versa is not considered a "modulation," because no tonic shift is involved. In fact, these two parallel keys are not even closely related, since their signatures differ by three accidentals.[2]

In many common-practice-period compositions that modulate, all of the new key centers are closely related to their original tonic key, regardless of where they occur in relation to one another. As we progress through a piece, we may find that each new key center is also closely related to the last that was heard. In Example 2, for instance, which shows a bass line and harmonic progression, D minor is closely related to the previous G minor, F major to the previous D minor, B♭ major to the previous F major, and so forth.

Example 2

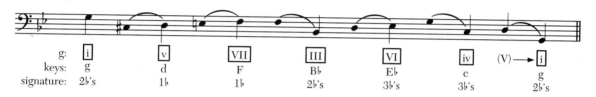

However, this affinity between successively tonicized key centers is not always present. In Example 3, the third and fourth keys, A minor and D major, are not closely related to each other because they are two sharps apart, but both are closely related to the original tonic of G major.

Example 3

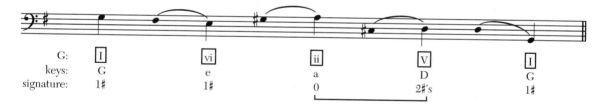

In this chapter we will explore some characteristics of closely related keys, such as the relative frequency with which they occur, their comparative length, the methods used to modulate to them, their role in the overall tonal scheme of a movement, and their use in melody harmonizations.

RELATIVE FREQUENCY OF CLOSELY RELATED KEYS

The two most common modulations in the major mode are to V̅ (the dominant) and v̅i̅ (the relative minor). Motion to the dominant is favored be-

---

2. Modal exchange and even change-of-mode modulations will be discussed in Chapters 27 and 34, respectively.

cause it logically leads back to the tonic; motion to the submediant is favored because it shares the same pitch-class content with the original key. Modulations to IV, ii, and iii are less favored but are also possible. In the case of a root movement to the subdominant, the descent of a perfect 5th may cause us to hear a return to the original tonic as V of the subdominant area. How does this root movement by 5th differ from a modulation to the dominant?

Compositions in the minor mode more commonly modulate to III (the mediant) and v (the dominant minor). We must be careful to distinguish between the dominant *harmony* (V) in minor, which is always major, and the dominant *key* (v) in minor, which is minor. Other possible goals of modulation in the minor mode include the keys of iv, VII, and VI.

THE EXTENT OF THE TONICIZED AREA

In **extended modulations** the sense of the new key is firmly established; the sheer length of such key changes may even cause us to temporarily forget the original tonic. In **closed tonal forms,** which are those that begin and end in the same key, we should still consider these areas as extended tonicizations of diatonic triads. When we do so, we never lose sight of their function in terms of the overall tonal scheme of the entire movement. To this end, we will continue to indicate the goal of diatonic modulations according to their scale degree and triadic function and not according to the designation of keys by pitch-class: for example, c: i → III → iv → v → i and not c→E♭→f→g→c. In our analyses, the new key area, which is enclosed within a box and followed by a colon, is next followed by roman numerals that designate chordal functions in the new key; for example, III: I–ii⁶–V–I (see also the models in Example 7 below).

Modulations to a new key area are sometimes temporary or transient, as we have seen in Chapter 19. Although we may sense a tonal shift toward a

Example 4

A. "ICH DANKE DIR, O GOTT, IN DEINEM THRONE" (BACH CHORALE HARMONIZATION)

B. Saint-Saëns: Piano Concerto No. 4, III

new key at the cadence, this shift is not always confirmed by a continuation in the new key. The next phrase may either immediately return to the original tonic or move to yet another key, as in the Bach and Saint-Saëns quotations in Example 4. For **transient modulations,** use a bracket to show the extent of the tonicization, with a roman numeral below it to denote the key area that is being tonicized.

In movements where long stretches of music occur in the new key, we may even encounter temporary tonal shifts within the secondary key area. Here we are literally in "a key within a key." In Example 5, for instance, Haydn has modulated from his original tonic of G major to V (D major) and confirmed this new key with an authentic cadence (m. 65). In measure 66 he begins a sequence by descending 3rds that leads to a ii chord of the dominant area (m. 72). The composer then proceeds to tonicize this harmony by means of its own dominant, giving us the sense of a transient tonal shift to E minor, or ⅱ of Ⅴ (mm. 72–77). This temporary tonic now acts as a pivot chord to bring us back to the V of D major via a B♭⁵ chromatic passing chord (B–B♭–A in the top voice); see mm. 77–83.

Example 5   HAYDN: STRING QUARTET IN G MAJOR, OP. 33, NO. 5, I

The Process of Modulation

Modulations to closely related keys employ the same processes that we discussed in Chapter 19: sectional modulation, modulation by pivot or common chord, and chromatic modulation. Sectional modulations (that is, shifts in key at significant formal divisions) usually progress from $\boxed{\text{I}}$ to $\boxed{\text{V}}$, $\boxed{\text{vi}}$, or $\boxed{\text{IV}}$, or from $\boxed{\text{i}}$ to $\boxed{\text{III}}$ or $\boxed{\text{VI}}$. In Example 6, what is the key relationship between the two sections of the Joplin rag?

Example 6   JOPLIN: "THE ENTERTAINER"

Six typical pivot-chord modulations are illustrated in Example 7. Note that we have stemmed the pivot chords only if they show a pre-dominant function.

Example 7

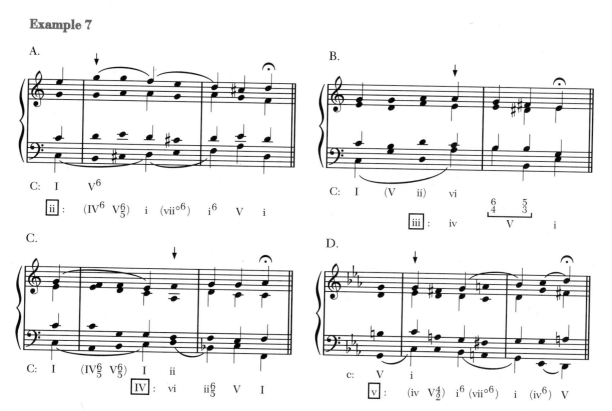

E.

F.

c: (V⁶) i (vii°⁶) i⁶ iv

$\boxed{\text{VI}}$: vi ii⁶₅ V I

c: i (ii⁰⁴₂ V⁶) i

$\boxed{\text{VII}}$: ii V I

Finally, Example 8 demonstrates five possible ways of moving to related keys through chromatic voice leading.

Example 8

A.

C: I

$\boxed{\text{ii}}$: (vii°⁷) i iv ₄⁶ ₃⁵ i

                 V

B.

C: I V

$\boxed{\text{vi}}$: (V⁶₅) i iv⁶ V

C.

C: I (V⁶)

$\boxed{\text{iii}}$: (V⁴₂) i⁶ i ii⁰⁶₅ V i

D.

c: i iv

$\boxed{\text{V}}$: (V⁶) i (VI) ii⁰⁶₅ V i

E.

c: i (V) i⁶

$\boxed{\text{iv}}$: (V⁶₅) i iv⁶ V

Additional excerpts from music literature that contain short-term modulations to closely related keys are supplied in the accompanying Workbook.

TONAL SCHEMES WITHIN A MOVEMENT

We have seen that the tonicization of different scale degrees allows a composer to extend the tonal scheme of a movement beyond a single key center. Modulations to closely related keys not only can reinforce contrasting thematic material but also can infuse previously stated musical ideas with fresh meaning. Within movements that begin and end in the same key, we usually find the following general scheme: (1) the establishment of the original tonic, (2) a move to a closely related key area or areas, and (3) a return to the initial key. A retransition section that includes prolonged dominant harmony often precedes the return. The choice and order of keys affords a wide range of possibilities to the composer. The selection of a particular tonal plan contributes to the distinctive character of the piece. Some musical forms, such as the minuet we discussed in Chapter 23, usually display a fairly predictable key scheme; others will feature one chosen specifically by the composer.

The tonal structures of three movements by Loeillet, Mozart, and Beethoven are diagrammed in Examples 9–11. In the voice-leading reduction of the short Loeillet piece (Example 9b), a middle voice has been added that realizes the figured bass and fills out the harmonies.

Example 9 LOEILLET: SOLO FOR FLUTE AND CONTINUO IN F MAJOR

A.

B. (REDUCTION)

The first reprise concludes with a cadence in $\boxed{\text{V}}$. At the opening of the second reprise, the chromatic C♯ defines the opening A-major triad as a secondary dominant of vi, which becomes a secondary dominant in turn and immediately leads to a more extended $\boxed{\text{ii}}$ area. This supertonic key is cadentially confirmed in measure 15. The descending root movement by 5ths that commenced at the beginning of the second reprise continues through dominant harmony to the original tonic key in measure 18. Observe how this motion actually overshoots the I on the way to IV in measure 19 before turning back via the V$_5^6$ to the final tonic chord. After the four-measure groupings in the first reprise, what happens to the phrasing in the last section?

The beamed soprano notes in the reduction (Example 9b) reveal the overall voice leading in the upper voice. Following the initial $\hat{3}$ (A^5) in the soprano, the neighboring $\hat{4}$ (B♭^{5}) resolves back to $\hat{3}$, which then descends via $\hat{2}$ to the final $\hat{1}$.

The tonal scheme of the Trio to the Minuet of Mozart's "Dissonant" string quartet (Example 10) demonstrates an ascending succession of keys leading to the dominant: $\boxed{\text{i}}$– $\boxed{\text{III}}$ –($\boxed{\text{iv}}$)–V. The return of the tonic is preceded by a retransition based on V^7 harmony.

Example 10   MOZART: STRING QUARTET IN C MAJOR ("DISSONANT"), K.465, III, BASIC TONAL SCHEME

While the modulation to $\boxed{\text{III}}$ is confirmed by a cadence, the motion to $\boxed{\text{iv}}$ may be considered as a transient modulation.

Often the tonal scheme of a piece or movement may give us a clue to its thematic design. For instance, many popular songs of the 1930s and 1940s display a thirty-two-measure quatrain form of A A' B A'. The contrasting B section (or bridge) is frequently differentiated by a change of key. Another example can be found in the key scheme of the last movement of Beethoven's Piano Sonata in G major, Op. 49, No. 2, given in Example 11. The periodic recurrence of the tonic key suggests that the original theme also reappears, while the contrasting keys suggest where different thematic ideas occur.

Example 11   BEETHOVEN: PIANO SONATA IN G MAJOR, OP. 49, NO. 2, II, BASIC TONAL SCHEME

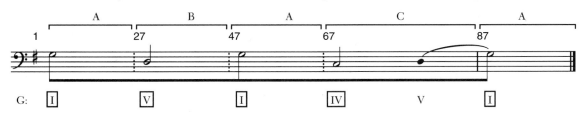

This, in fact, is true. The movement is in rondo form, in which the first theme, or refrain, alternates with contrasting ideas, or episodes.[3] The underlying key scheme corresponds to this melodic plan.

Our discussion of these movements suggests that the process of tonicizing scale degrees elevates them to a higher level of structural importance. The succession of key areas, however, does not always reflect the progression of chords at the surface of the music. In other words, the succession of key areas through a movement does not always produce chord progressions that are typical of measure-to-measure harmony. Thus, we must never confuse the various levels of the tonal hierarchy.

Melody Harmonization

Modulations to closely related keys provide a significant resource for tonal variety and contrast in melody harmonizations. They are especially good at accommodating different types of melodic motion at cadences.

Since one function of cadences is to stabilize new keys, potential cadence tones should be examined first to ascertain whether they reflect a move to a different tonal center. Each pair of soprano scale steps in Example 12 suggests several different cadences.

Example 12

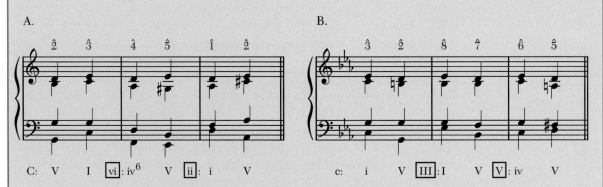

For instance, scale degrees $\hat{2}$–$\hat{3}$ in major could support not only the familiar imperfect cadence (V–I) but also a Phrygian cadence in the submediant key (vi̅: iv⁶–V) or even a half cadence in the supertonic key (ii̅: i⁶–V); see Example 12a. The succession $\hat{3}$–$\hat{2}$ in the minor mode suggests settings in

---

[3]For additional information on rondo form, see Excursion I: Simple Forms.

the tonic ($\boxed{i}$) or mediant ($\boxed{III}$), or an inverted Phrygian cadence on scale degree $\hat{5}$ ($\boxed{v}$); see Example 12b.

When harmonizing melodies and seeking to incorporate modulations to closely related keys, first examine the melodic lines leading to the cadence as well as the beginning of the following phrases. Label potential related keys and then fill in the remainder of the setting, trying to work out smooth transitions between the various keys. Example 13 illustrates this method; the

Example 13   "BRISTOL" (HYMN TUNE)

cadential tones, with their tonicizing harmonies, are sketched in first, then the inner voices and the remaining harmonies are filled in. What do you observe about the overall progression of keys?

Bach's different settings of the chorale tune "O Haupt voll Blut und Wunden" illustrate his ingenuity in harmonizing this melody.[4] Play the three harmonizations of the first two phrases of the chorale and contrast the settings.

Example 14   "O HAUPT VOLL BLUT UND WUNDEN" (THREE BACH CHORALE HARMONIZATIONS)

4. Donald Martino's edition of the Bach chorales transposes multiple harmonizations of the same tune to one key to compare them more directly; see his *178 Chorale Harmonizations of J. S. Bach: A Comparative Edition for Study* (Newton, MA: Dentalian, Inc., 1984).

In Example 14a, a chromatic motion (G^3–$G\sharp^3$) provides the means of modulation from $\boxed{I}$ to $\boxed{vi}$. In Example 14b, the submediant key starts earlier, with a pivot chord (ii in C major = iv in A minor), allowing the first phrase to end in a Phrygian cadence in $\boxed{vi}$. The last setting (Example 14c) is more adventuresome, since after the first two chords within the key of A minor, the phrase makes a transient modulation to D minor ($\boxed{iv}$). The $C\natural^5$ in the third measure produces a cross-relation with the $C\sharp^4$ in the preceding cadence. Bach harmonizes the C with an ambiguous diminished seventh chord to soften the jarring effect of the cross-relation and to modulate back to the original key. Even in measure 2, the partwriting has its share of pitfalls; observe the leap G^3–D^3 in the tenor to avoid parallel 5ths and the curious melodic 7th in the bass on beats 3 and 4.

Terms and Concepts for Review

closely related keys
change of mode

closed tonal forms
extended *vs.* transient modulations

CHAPTER 2 7

Modal Exchange
and Mixture Chords

I N THIS AND THE following two chapters we will focus on specific chromatic chords that are used in tonal music. The altered scale degrees within these chords allow us to expand the spectrum of harmonic color in our diatonic progressions. To illustrate this, let us examine the passage in Example 1, which starts in C minor and then changes mode to C major following the cadence on V in measure 4.

While the second phrase is clearly in the major mode, the music still retains certain scale-degree inflections that remind us of the parallel minor key of the first phrase. These inflections produce three different chords, each of which contains at least one altered scale degree; these are marked with arrows.

Example 1

In this chapter we will examine the relations between parallel major and minor keys and learn about the various types of chromatic chords, such as the three given in Example 1, which are produced when particular harmonies are borrowed from one mode to the other.

MODAL EXCHANGE

The major and minor modes were clearly delineated from each other in tonal compositions of the later Baroque period (ca. 1670–1750). A movement or entire piece of music would normally start and finish in the same key and mode and thereby exhibit tonal closure, although interior modulations were possible. Later, composers began to experiment with a blurring of the modes by introducing passages in the parallel major or minor key. This technique, called **modal exchange,** was frequently employed by Beethoven and Schubert during the opening decades of the nineteenth century. The increasing use of modal exchange throughout this century eventually created some doubt about whether a given passage was in major or minor. Modal ambiguity became a distinguishing trait of music composed in the late Romantic period, one element of its heightened expressiveness. The later music dramas of Richard Wagner typify this tendency.[1]

In vocal compositions, modal exchange is often introduced to highlight the effect of contrasting passages of text: major to minor ("brighter" to "darker"), or minor to major ("darker" to "brighter"). The French national anthem, "La Marseillaise" (Example 2), contains an example of this practice,

1. We will examine this aspect, among others, in an analysis of the *Tristan* Prelude in Chapter 36.

which vividly supports the text. The change to minor during the third phrase (m. 16) heightens the effect of the following major-mode call to arms.

Example 2   ROUGET DE LISLE: "LA MARSEILLAISE" (FRENCH NATIONAL ANTHEM)

Ils viennent jusque dans nos bras
Égorger vos fils, vos compagnes.
Aux armes citoyens!

They are practically in our midst, coming
To slaughter your sons, your dear ones.
To arms! Citizens!

The alternation of modes in Schubert's famous "Der Lindenbaum" (Example 3) likewise reflects the changing moods of the wandering lover as he remembers his girlfriend while beholding the linden tree in the winter snow.

Modal exchange is especially effective in instrumental pieces that are based on a narrative or story, such as nineteenth-century program music. During his pictorial odyssey on the Moldau, Smetana associates this river

Example 3   SCHUBERT: "DER LINDENBAUM" FROM *WINTERREISE*

Ich musst' auch heu - te wan - dern vor - bei in tie-fer Nacht,

e:

Am Brunnen vor dem Thore	By the well before the gate
da steht ein Lindenbaum;	There stands a linden tree
Ich musst' auch heute wandern	I had to pass by it now
vorbei in tiefer Nacht,	In the deep night

with a recurring minor melody (Example 4a). As the river finally surges into the open sea, the mode triumphantly switches to major (Example 4b).[2]

Example 4 SMETANA: "THE MOLDAU" FROM *MÀ VLAST*

A.

e:

B.

E:

2. Also refer to the alternation of minor and major modes in the excerpts from Bizet's Farandole in Chapter 5.

Modal exchange is a useful tool for modulating to more distant or non-diatonic keys, a topic we will cover in Chapter 34.

MIXTURE CHORDS

We will now direct our attention to individual **mixture** or **borrowed chords,** harmonies that contain chromatic inflections or pitches borrowed from the parallel major or minor mode. Example 5 compares the scale steps of the major and natural minor scales. The major scale is marked with upward stems, and the minor scale with downward stems. The differing degrees are $\hat{3}$, $\hat{6}$, and $\hat{7}$; these are the pitches that can be borrowed from one mode to the other. (Remember, however, that the raised 6th and 7th scale degrees in minor are already present in the major mode.)

Example 5

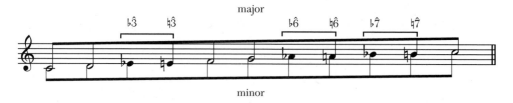

MIXTURE CHORDS IN THE MAJOR MODE

Most modal borrowing within individual chords involves minor scale degrees transferred to the major mode. The primary mixture chords in major, then, feature the lowered scale steps ♭$\hat{3}$, ♭$\hat{6}$, and to a lesser degree ♭$\hat{7}$; these degrees impart a darker, more somber harmonic color to passages in a major key. Example 6 lists these chords with their roman numerals. Carefully observe how we denote each harmony: a lowercase or capital roman numeral indicates the chord type, and a flat sign before the roman numeral denotes when the triadic root is lowered.

Example 6

Identify the borrowed modal scale degree in each chord. As you can observe, all of the diatonic chords in the minor mode may occur as mixture chords in the parallel major; because of its characteristic $\flat\hat{6}$, the $vii°^7$ may be considered a mixture chord as well. You should avoid doubling the altered scale degrees in these chords unless they act as the root of the triad.

We will now separately discuss each of the various mixture chords and their different harmonic functions.

The i Chord

The minor tonic (i) normally occurs as a transient harmony. It may follow the normal I as a chromatic inflection, as in the following Beethoven excerpt, or momentarily substitute for the major tonic, as in the Brahms quotation (Example 7).

Example 7

A. BEETHOVEN: KYRIE FROM *MISSA SOLEMNIS*

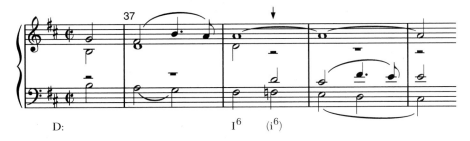

B. BRAHMS: *EIN DEUTSCHES REQUIEM, IV*

The iv and ii^{ø7} Chords

The iv and ii^{ø7} may function as pre-dominant mixture chords at cadences, appear in embellishing progressions within the phrase, or act as neighboring harmonies to the tonic. Examine each of the four models in Example 8 and determine which use applies to each model. What altered scale degree appears in each phrase, and how does it resolve?

Example 8

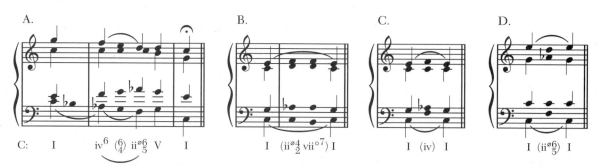

A.
C: I   iv⁶ (⁶₄) ii°⁶₅ V   I

B.
I   (ii°⁴₂ vii°⁷) I

C.
I   (iv)   I

D.
I   (ii°⁶₅) I

The ♭VI Chord

The lowered submediant (♭VI) is used in a variety of contexts. It usually occurs in a deceptive progression: V–♭VI (Example 9a). Notice that the chordal 3rd (1̂) of the ♭VI is doubled to avoid either an augmented 2nd or parallels in the partwriting (Examples 9a and 9b). Since the progression I–♭VI features an awkward chromatic motion of ♮3̂–♭3̂, it is somewhat rare (Example 9c); when ♭VI appears within the phrase, it normally moves to iv (Example 9d).

Example 9

A.   "Vater unser im Himmelreich" (Bach chorale harmonization)

F: I   (vi)   ii⁶₅ V   ♭VI

B.

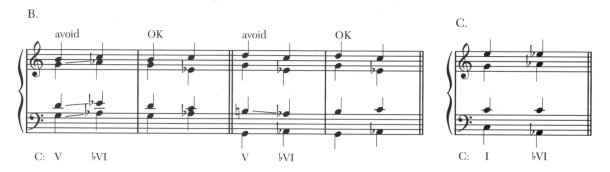

avoid   OK   avoid   OK

C: V   ♭VI   V   ♭VI

C.

C: I   ♭VI

D.

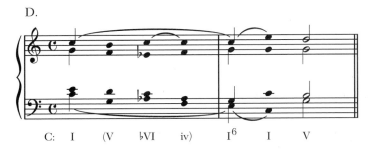

C: I   (V   ♭VI   iv)   I⁶   I   V

In the scherzo of Beethoven's Sixth ("Pastoral") Symphony (Example 10), the tonicized ♭VI, coming out of a deceptive cadence, abruptly interrupts the "Merry Gathering of the Country Folk" with a premonition of the impending F-minor "Storm." Here, the appearance of ♭VI at the opening of the new section initiates a series of modulations to distantly related keys (not shown here).

Example 10   BEETHOVEN: SYMPHONY NO. 6 ("PASTORAL"), III TO IV

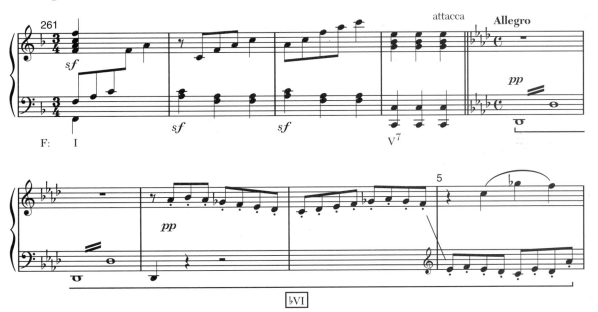

The ♭III and ♭VII Chords

The ♭III and ♭VII harmonies are less commonly used.[3] The familiar aria in Example 11 substitutes a ♭III⁶ for a cadential ⁶₄; the V⁷ that follows resolves deceptively to ♭VI.

---

3. The foreign keys of ♭III and ♭VI frequently are the goal of modulations in major movements of the Romantic period; see the discussion in Chapters 34 and 38.

Example 11 WAGNER: "HYMN TO THE EVENING STAR" FROM *TANNHÄUSER*, ACT III

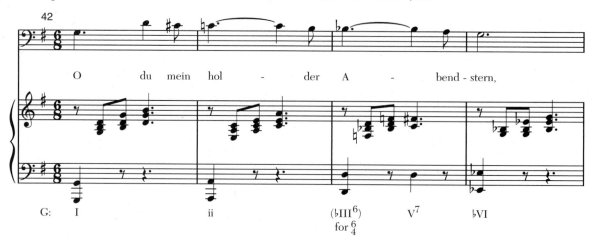

Example 12

A. GEORGE HARRISON: "SOMETHING"

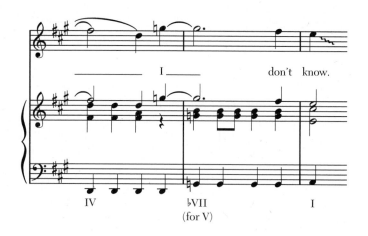

B. LENNON AND MCCARTNEY: "YOU NEVER GIVE ME YOUR MONEY"

C: I   ♭VII   IV   I
                       (or IV/IV)

In popular music, the ♭VII sometimes functions as a modal substitute for
V or as an embellishing IV/IV, producing an ascending 4th progression
(Example 12; see previous page).

    In the three excerpts in Example 13, identify the mixture chords and
determine their function.

Example 13

A. SAINT-SAËNS: "MON CŒUR S'OUVRE À TA VOIX" FROM *SAMSON ET DALILA*, ACT II

Ah! _____ ré - ponds _____ à __ ma _____ ten - dres - se,

B. MOZART: STRING QUARTET IN B♭ MAJOR ("HUNT"), K.458, III

E♭:   V   IV

C.   BEETHOVEN: SYMPHONY No. 7, I

In the exquisite Mozart passage, the areas of V and IV are successively
tonicized. In the Beethoven introduction, what is the eventual cadential goal
and what role does the bass line play in the overall voice leading?

MIXTURE CHORDS WITHIN PLAGAL CADENCES

During the Romantic period, composers extended the plagal cadence to
incorporate a pre-dominant mixture chord. This procedure is shown in
three successive steps in Example 14.

Example 14

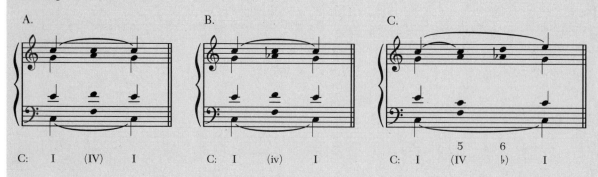

The first progression (IV–I) in Example 14a is altered in Example 14b
through the introduction of ♭6̂, turning the subdominant into a mixture

chord. Then the soprano traces a passing 5–6 motion above $\hat{4}$ in the bass, on its way to the 3rd of I. This progression often served as an alternative to the timeworn authentic cadence (V–I). In the coda-like progression of the Brahms excerpt in Example 15, the mixture chord is a ii$^{ø4}_3$, occurring over a tonic pedal.

Example 15 BRAHMS: "DIE MAINACHT," OP. 43, NO. 2

E♭:　　I　(V$^4_2$/IV　IV^6　ii$^{ø4}_3$)　I

Wagner associated this cadence with "transfiguration" in the concluding harmonies of several of his operas (*Der fliegende Holländer, Tristan und Isolde,* and *Götterdämmerung*).

When used as pre-dominant harmonies, mixture chords are particularly well suited to interject a sense of ominous foreboding in the major mode. In nineteenth-century opera, pre-dominant mixture chords were frequently

Example 16 VERDI: "AVE MARIA" FROM *OTELLO,* ACT IV

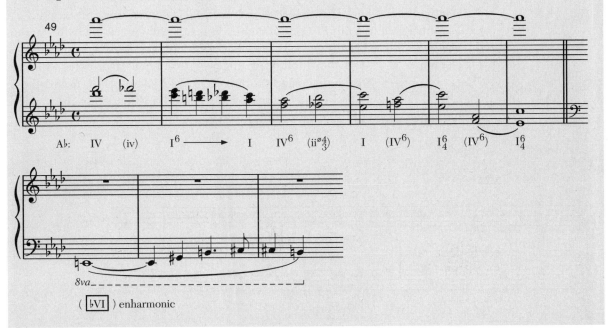

A♭:　IV　(iv)　I^6 ⟶ I　IV^6　(ii$^{ø4}_3$)　I　(IV^6)　I$^6_4$　(IV^6)　I$^6_4$

(♭VI) enharmonic

and effectively exploited in arias where the composer wished to project a feeling of dread. A typical example occurs in the final act of Verdi's *Otello*, where Desdemona sings her aria "Ave Maria," as she prays before the Virgin Mary (Example 16). The pronounced ♭6̂ (F♭) at its ethereal close anticipates the enharmonic modulation to ♭VI at Otello's entry; this is depicted by the deep tones of a solo double bass, which suggests that his intentions are other than making love.

MIXTURE CHORDS IN THE MINOR MODE

We have focused primarily on those mixture chords in major that have been borrowed from the minor mode. The use of mixture chords in the minor mode borrowed from the parallel major is quite rare. We can hardly regard the major tonic (I) as one such example, since it either occurs as a Picardy third at the end of minor-mode compositions or as a secondary dominant to iv. The use of the minor mediant and submediant is restricted to key centers rather than individual harmonies.

THE III TRIAD IN MAJOR

The altered mediant (III) triad is a mixture chord within major-mode compositions. This chord is "borrowed" from the dominant harmony (V) of the relative minor key. This chord (E G♯ B in C major) is often used as the cadential goal of a phrase. In this context it is normally preceded by ii⁶, suggesting a Phrygian cadence in the relative minor key: ii⁶–III = vi: iv⁶–V (Example 17a). The chord following this progression will usually be a tonic chord or a V⁽⁷⁾ that immediately returns to I. In Example 17b, notice the typical 1̂–2̂–3̂ motion in the soprano. How is the III extended in the Verdi quotation (Example 17c)?

Example 17

A. "ST. ANNE" (HYMN TUNE)

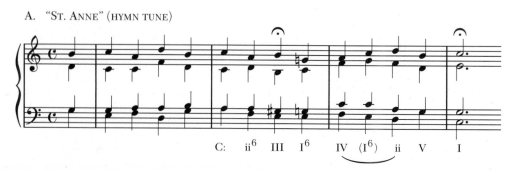

C: ii⁶   III   I⁶   IV   (I⁶)   ii   V   I

B. "ANNIE LAURIE" (SCOTTISH FOLK SONG)

G: I   ii⁶   III   V⁷   I

C. VERDI: "CELESTE AIDA" FROM *AIDA*, ACT II

mi - sti - co   ser — to   di   lu - ce e fior,   del

B♭:   IV   (ii⁶)   III   V/III   III   I

MIXTURE CHORDS NOTATED ENHARMONICALLY

Mixture chords may result from spelling certain structurally important pitches enharmonically. For instance, the enharmonic conflict between ♯$\hat{5}$ (C♯) and ♭$\hat{6}$ (D♭) throughout the introduction to Sousa's march "Hands across the Sea" spawns two completely different harmonies: a secondary dominant (the C♯ implying V$^6_5$/vi) and a mixture chord (the D♭ implying ii$^{ø4}_3$). Play the excerpt in Example 18 and then examine the accompanying reduction; note the voice-leading tendencies of both pitches.

A similar instance occurs in the opening of the Finale of Beethoven's Symphony No. 8 (Example 19). The *forte* unison in measure 17 is heard in the context of F major as a ♭$\hat{6}$ but it is notated as a ♯$\hat{5}$ (C♯). Later in the movement, this same C♯ eventually functions as the dominant of F♯ minor (mm. 376–79).

Example 18 SOUSA: "HANDS ACROSS THE SEA"

A.

B. (REDUCTION)

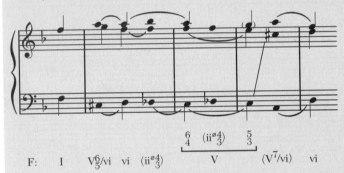

F: I   V⁶₃/vi   vi   (ii⌀⁴₃)   V   (V⁷/vi)   vi

Example 19 BEETHOVEN: SYMPHONY NO. 8, IV

The interplay of ♯5̂ and ♭6̂ also plays a significant structural role in many German lieder of the nineteenth century.

Melody Harmonization

Since most melodies do not employ lowered scale degrees, these altered notes must be inserted into other voices when harmonizing a melody. Be discriminating in your use of mixture chords—overuse can make your harmonization sound trite. If your tune has a text, you may wish to use altered chords to set particular words with appropriate musical "text painting."

Cadencing on the III triad provides an alternative to using an imperfect authentic cadence, especially when the soprano moves 1̂−2̂−3̂ (see Example

17b). Remember that partwriting with the III chord in this context is similar to using a Phrygian cadence.

Several examples of mixture chords are illustrated in the melody harmonizations of Example 20. In the initial setting (Example 20a), the melody and its harmonic support are entirely diatonic. The following three passages (Examples 20b–20d) incorporate various mixture chords, which change the underlying harmonies and the bass lines. Make a roman-numeral analysis of these last three settings, especially noting the ways in which the different mixture chords are employed.

Terms and Concepts for Review

modal exchange
mixture *or* borrowed chords

III as a cadential goal

The Neapolitan Chord

P LAY AND CONTRAST the pair of pre-dominant–dominant–tonic progressions in Example 1. What is the only note that is changed?

Example 1

A.

B.

Despite this minimal alteration in the pre-dominant harmony of the second passage, the musical effect is altogether different. The Db (b$\hat{2}$) engenders an altered triad that we call a **Neapolitan sixth** chord. We will examine the properties and uses of this chord in this chapter.

The Neapolitan sixth is a major triad built on the lowered supertonic (Db F Ab in C minor). Its half-step relation to the tonic gives it a peculiarly dark quality that is unique among chromatic chords.[1] Because of its

---

1. If we progress downward by perfect 5ths from the tonic in minor ($\hat{1}$, $\hat{4}$, b$\hat{7}$, b$\hat{3}$, b$\hat{6}$, b$\hat{2}$, b$\hat{5}$), the Neapolitan b$\hat{2}$ is the most distant relation before the tritone (b$\hat{5}$) is reached.

geographical designation, the Neapolitan sixth has acquired a fame that is disproportionate to its actual use in tonal music. The origin of the term is obscure. While "sixth" refers to the fact that the chord is ordinarily found in first inversion (⁶), "Neapolitan" probably alludes to its use in the operas composed in the Italian city of Naples in the seventeenth century.

The ♭II⁶ as a Cadential Pre-dominant Chord

We typically find the Neapolitan sixth in the minor mode, where it usually substitutes for a diatonic pre-dominant (iv or ii°⁶₅) in authentic cadences. When partwriting with the Neapolitan sixth in this type of cadential progression, we should double the bass ($\hat{4}$) rather than the more active ♭$\hat{6}$ or ♭$\hat{2}$ scale degree. In addition, we should never move from ♭$\hat{2}$ (of the Neapolitan) to ♮$\hat{2}$ (of the V chord) in the same voice part (Example 2).[2]

Example 2

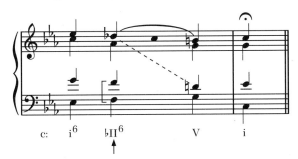

c: i⁶ ♭II⁶ V i

The soprano line often bridges the melodic diminished 3rd between the lowered supertonic and leading tone with stepwise motion: ♭$\hat{2}$ – ($\hat{8}$) – ♯$\hat{7}$. The tonic scale degree may be harmonically supported by either a cadential ⁶₄ or an applied chord, usually vii°⁷/V, as in Example 3.

Example 3

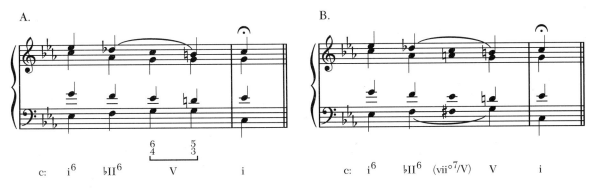

A.

B.

c: i⁶ ♭II⁶ ⁶₄ ⁵₃ V i   c: i⁶ ♭II⁶ (vii°⁷/V) V i

2. Composers did not consider the cross-relation between ♭$\hat{2}$ and ♮$\hat{2}$, in different voices a problem, however.

This passing motion is often missing, as the excerpt in Example 4 from the "Moonlight" Sonata demonstrates.

Example 4   BEETHOVEN: PIANO SONATA IN C# MINOR, OP. 27, NO. 2 ("MOONLIGHT"), I

When harmonizing an upper-voice descent of $\hat{5}-\hat{4}-\hat{3}-\hat{2}-\hat{1}$ that incorporates a $\flat II^6$ chord, we should avoid the troublesome similar 5ths that could occur between the vii°^{7}/V and V by doubling the chordal 5th in the dominant triad (Example 5).

Example 5

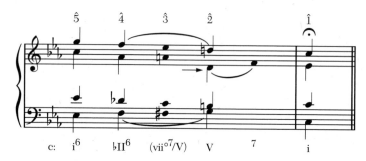

THE $\flat II^6$ AS AN EMBELLISHING PRE-DOMINANT CHORD

Although the Neapolitan normally occurs at cadences, it may assume an embellishing role within the phrase. In this capacity the dominant harmony normally resolves to a weaker form of tonic, such as a i^6 (Example 6). What is the function of the circled tones in the upper voice of this excerpt?

Example 6   SCHUMANN: *PAPILLONS*, OP. 2, NO. 10

C: (♭II⁶   vii°⁴₃)   i⁶   (V⁴₃)

An embellishing ♭II⁶ may also move directly to i⁶, as in Mozart's stepwise sequence of sixth chords in Example 7.

Example 7   MOZART: PIANO SONATA IN D MAJOR, K.284, III

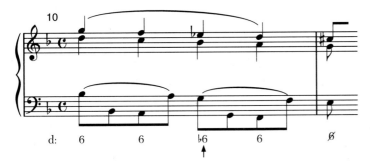

d: 6   6   ♭6   6   ∅̸

In order to emphasize its particularly dark quality, composers will sometimes elaborate the Neapolitan chord with some kind of melodic flourish or gesture, as in the excerpt from Mozart's Fantasia (Example 8a), or extend it through several beats or even measures, as in the passage from Beethoven's "Moonlight" Sonata (Example 8b).

Example 8

A. MOZART: PIANO FANTASIA IN D MINOR, K.397

d: VI   ♭II⁶

B. BEETHOVEN: PIANO SONATA IN C♯ MINOR, OP. 27, NO. 2 ("MOONLIGHT"), III

They may also consciously exploit the foreboding or sinister nature of the tritone relation between ♭II and V. In the excerpt in Example 9, Saint-Saëns employs a tritone leap in the top voice (C^6–$F\sharp^5$) that reinforces the demonic character of his *Danse macabre*.

Example 9   SAINT-SAËNS: *DANSE MACABRE*

The Neapolitan harmony is also employed in the crucial Curse motive of Wagner's *Ring* cycle, where ♭II–V^7 is set over a dominant pedal in B minor, producing a tritone relation between the sustained F♯ and the C Neapolitan triad; see Example 4c in Chapter 28 of the Workbook.

Examine the excerpts in Example 10 and identify the Neapolitan harmony in each. Observe the prevailing use of the minor mode; the ♭II in major is less common.

Example 10

A.   "ACH GOTT, VOM HIMMEL SIEH' DAREIN" (BACH CHORALE HARMONIZATION)

B.   BACH: PASSACAGLIA AND FUGUE IN C MINOR, BWV 582

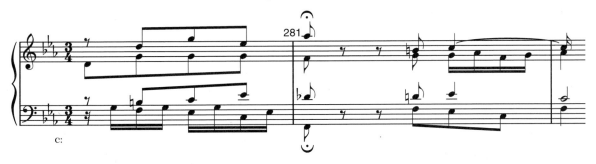

C. Brahms: *Tragic Overture*, Op. 81 (reduction of mm. 126–30)

f:

D. Haydn: Piano Sonata in C♯ minor, Hob. XVI:36, I

c♯:

The first passage is the only instance of a ♭II⁶ in all of Bach's chorale harmonizations. In Example 10b, the ♭II⁶ serves as the climax of a triple fugue; how does Bach emphasize this chord? Do these first two passages by Bach exemplify cadential or embellishing functions? What is peculiar about the Neapolitan and its voice leading in the Brahms reduction given in Example 10c? Explain what happens in the first two beats of the second measure of the Haydn passage.

OTHER USES OF THE NEAPOLITAN CHORD

The Neapolitan harmony may appear in other settings. In a few instances we find it in root position rather than its customary first inversion, so that ♭$\hat{2}$ rather than $\hat{4}$ occurs in the bass. The final cadence of Chopin's funereal C-minor Prelude is frequently cited as an instance of **♭II in $\frac{5}{3}$ position** (Example 11b).

FOR FURTHER STUDY

An interesting use of the Neapolitan as an initial harmony occurs in the first three measures of Chopin's G-minor Ballade, Op. 23. At the other extreme, the B-major conclusion of Strauss's *Also sprach Zarathustra* continually reiterates a ♭$\hat{2}$ (C) in the bass, harking back to the "Nature" motive—C⁴–G⁴–C⁵ in the trumpet—that opens the work.

Example 11 CHOPIN: PRELUDE IN C MINOR, OP. 28, NO. 20

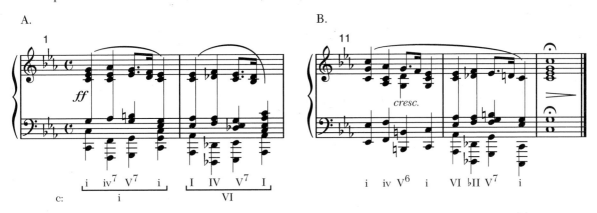

The opening two measures of the piece (Example 11a) reveal its origin. After the initial i–iv⁷–V–i, the same progression is repeated in ⃞VI (A♭ major), where the D♭ triad functions as IV. The return of this material in the last measures (Example 11b) sets up the expectation that a cadence in the submediant area will again follow the cadence in i, but the dominant of i substitutes for V/VI, instead directing us back to the tonic.

A poignant instance of the root-position ♭II may also be found in Wotan's touching Farewell, where the Neapolitan extends the pre-dominant function: iv⁶–♭II.

Example 12 WAGNER: WOTAN'S FAREWELL FROM *DIE WALKÜRE*, ACT III (SIMPLIFIED)

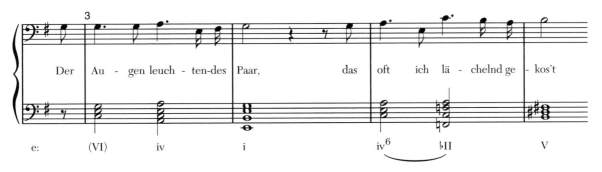

Der Augen leuchtendes Paar,
das oft ich lächelnd gekos't

The radiant pair of eyes,
which I often caressed with a smile

The Neapolitan may also serve as a **neighbor to the tonic,** substituting for an embellishing subdominant, as demonstrated by the excerpts in Example 13.

Example 13

A. BRAHMS: *VARIATIONS ON A THEME OF HAYDN*, OP. 56A (VAR. 6)

B. (REDUCTION)

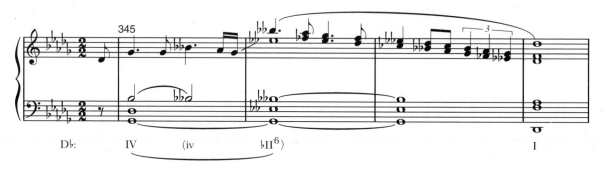

B♭:   I   (♭II⁶)   I   (iv⁶)   I

C. WAGNER: IMMOLATION SCENE FROM *GÖTTERDÄMMERUNG*, ACT III (SIMPLIFIED)

D♭:   IV   (iv   ♭II⁶)   I

D. SCHUBERT: "DER DOPPELGÄNGER" FROM *SCHWANENGESANG*

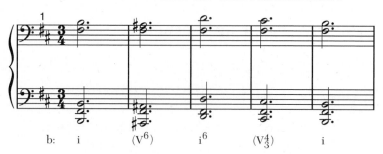

b: i   (V⁶)   i⁶   (V₄³)   i

E.

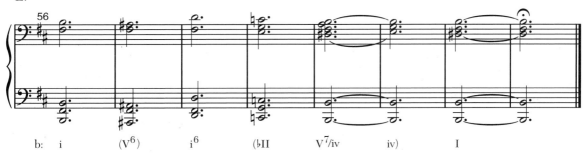

$$b{:} \quad i \qquad (V^6) \qquad i^6 \qquad (\flat II \qquad V^7/iv \qquad iv) \qquad I$$

The major tonic of the Brahms passage is embellished first by a $\flat II^6$ and then by a mixture iv^6 (Example 13a and 13b). The conclusion of Wagner's *Ring* cycle features an extended plagal motion of IV–$(iv$–$\flat II^6)$–I (Example 13c). The quotations from "Der Doppelgänger" (Examples 13d and 13e) exemplify Schubert's sensitivity to harmonic color. The accompaniment to this haunting song is based on a two-voice motive doubled in octaves; this can be seen in the first measures of this excerpt. In the brief piano coda (mm. 56–63), a Neapolitan chord in root position is now exchanged for the V^4_3 that was heard earlier and initiates a conclusion to the piece with a plagal gesture: $(\flat II$–$V^7/iv)$–iv–I. How does the composer avoid parallel 5ths in the i^6–$\flat II$ progression?

A careful study of Schubert's songs reveals how closely he associated the Neapolitan harmony with subjects of grief or death in the texts. For instance, the Neapolitan is tonicized in the closing measures of his "Erlkönig," when the child is found dead in his father's arms. This chord is especially prominent in the depiction of tragic wandering in Schubert's song cycle *Winterreise*.

PROLONGED NEAPOLITAN HARMONY

Measures 75–88 of the sixth of Schumann's *Davidsbündlertänze* contain an interesting example of prolonged Neapolitan harmony; listen to the excerpt while following the reduction in Example 14.

Following the opening $\flat II^6$, a sequence of applied $^4_2$ dominants initiates a descending succession of sixth chords. This sequential motion continues through the passage, arriving at another $\flat II^6$ preceded by its V^4_2. The octave span in the soprano (see the beamed $E\flat^5$–$E\flat^4$) prolongs the Neapolitan, which then resolves in a typical $^6_4$ cadence.

Example 14   SCHUMANN: *DAVIDSBÜNDLERTÄNZE*, NO. 6

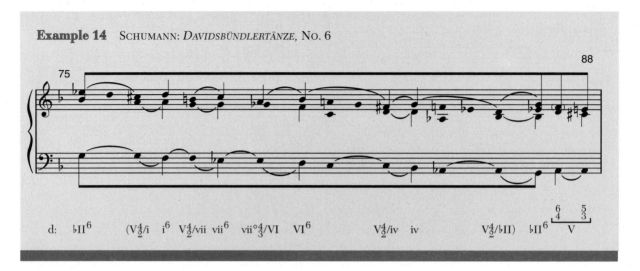

TONICIZATION OF THE NEAPOLITAN TRIAD

When the Neapolitan chord is tonicized in the minor mode, it is preceded by its dominant, the VI chord (Examples 15 and 17, below). The association between VI and ♭II in minor may be summed up in the adage "The dominant of the Neapolitan is the Neapolitan of the dominant."

Example 15

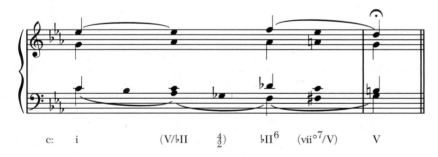

Neapolitan tonicizations are less common in major. The Mozart excerpt in Example 16 includes brief tonicizations of ii, I, and ♭II⁶. In this case, the dominant of the Neapolitan (V/♭II) is a ♭VI triad.

Example 16   MOZART: CLARINET QUINTET IN A MAJOR, K.581, IV

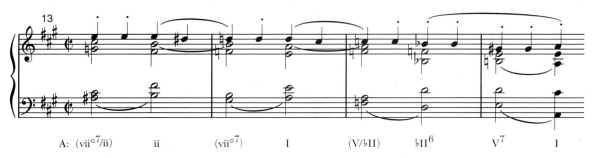

A: (vii°⁷/ii)   ii   (vii°⁷)   I   (V/♭II)   ♭II⁶   V⁷   I

We may also encounter extended tonicizations of ♭II. In the Chopin passage in Example 17, the ♭II is tonicized and prolonged for several measures before it moves to I⁶ via a V⁴₂. Study the approach to and departure from the Neapolitan in the voice-leading reduction, which shows that the whole passage is actually prolonging the tonic chord in a simple embellishing progression with a very slow harmonic rhythm.

Example 17   CHOPIN: PRELUDE IN B MINOR, OP. 28, NO. 6

A.

B.   (REDUCTION)

b: i   (V/♭II   ♭II⁶   V⁴₂)   i⁶

FOR FURTHER STUDY

In several of his works, Beethoven follows the opening tonic statement of the theme with its repetition a semitone higher, which anticipates the important role that the Neapolitan will play in the remainder of the movement.

BEETHOVEN: STRING QUARTET IN E MINOR, OP. 59, NO. 2, I

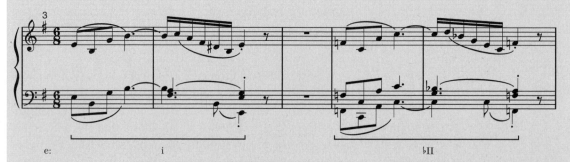

Beethoven resorts to this procedure in other works, such as the openings of his "Appassionata" Sonata, Op. 57, and his String Quartet, Op. 95, both in F minor. Another excellent instance of this tonal premonition of ♭II occurs in the initial unison theme of the first movement of Brahms's Clarinet Sonata in F minor, Op. 120, No. 1. The curious ♭$\hat{2}$ used at the cadence of this tune spawns a series of Neapolitan relations at both lower and higher structural levels throughout the movement. The theorist Edward Cone uses the term "promissory note(s)" to describe such anticipatory gestures.

Melody Harmonization

Unless the given tune actually employs a ♭$\hat{2}$, scale step $\hat{4}$ must occur in the soprano to permit the use of the Neapolitan chord. Its function is normally that of pre-dominant harmony in an authentic cadence; refer back to Example 3. Always double scale degree $\hat{4}$ in the bass.

Examine the first two passages in Example 18. The descending soprano ($\hat{5}-\hat{4}-\hat{3}-\hat{2}-\hat{1}$) would usually be harmonized with a $^6_4$ cadence, as shown in Example 18a. Contrast this with the alternative setting in Example 18b; the use of the ♭II^6 and secondary diminished seventh imparts an entirely different character to the passage. Now play the cycle-of-fifths progression in Example 18c, first with a D♮ in the bass of the third measure and then with the D♭, noting the contrasting musical effect.

Example 18

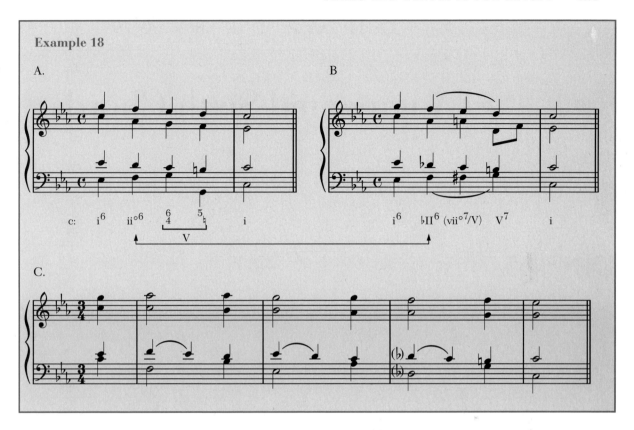

A.

c: i⁶   ii°⁶   ⁶₄   ⁵₃   i
                         V

B.

i⁶   ♭II⁶ (vii°⁷/V)   V⁷   i

C.

Terms and Concepts for Review

Neapolitan sixth (♭II⁶)
♭II in ⁵₃ position

Neapolitan as neighbor to the tonic
tonicization of the Neapolitan (V⁷/♭II)

Augmented Sixth Chords

LET US BEGIN OUR study of another family of chromatic chords by examining the two half cadences in Example 1.

Example 1

a: i   iv⁶   V   i   V

The initial Phrygian cadence employs the customary iv⁶–V progression. What pitch is changed in the second cadence? How does this note intensify the pull to scale degree $\hat{5}$?

The new sonority in the second half cadence contains the interval of an augmented 6th (F–D♯); we call this harmony an **augmented sixth chord** (or **Aug6th**). Although Aug6th chords came into limited use during the Baroque period, their frequency greatly increased in the Classical era, when they were frequently employed to emphasize the approach to V at half cadences. Examine the two excerpts in Example 2 and identify the augmented 6th interval in each. Do you find any use of suspensions? If so, where?

Example 2

A. "ICH HAB' MEIN' SACH' GOTT HEIMGESTELLT"
   (BACH CHORALE HARMONIZATION)

B. MOZART: SYMPHONY NO. 40, K.550, I   C. (REDUCTION)

In this chapter, we will examine the treatment of Aug6th chords in some detail. The sonority E♭ G C♯ illustrated in Example 2 is something of a harmonic maverick. It is not constructed entirely of major and minor thirds since the interval C♯–E♭ is a diminished 3rd (the inversion of an augmented 6th). The Aug6th chord is often derived from contrapuntal motion, and therefore can be called a **chromatic linear chord**—that is, an embellishing harmony that results from passing or neighboring melodic motion. The tendency of the interval of an augmented 6th to resolve outward to the dominant octave (♭$\hat{6}$–$\hat{5}$ in the lowest voice and ♯$\hat{4}$–$\hat{5}$ in an upper voice) is its chief characteristic. Do not confuse this interval with the minor 7th that appears within a major-minor chord, even though in isolation they sound the same (both contain ten semitones). The resolution tendencies of the two intervals are opposite (Example 3): the former pulls outward to the octave, the latter pulls inward to a 3rd (or 10th).

Example 3

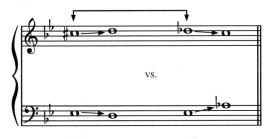

A6   m7

Aug6th chords occur more frequently in the minor mode, since they contain scale degree ♭6̂ and sometimes ♭3̂. At cadences, the Aug6th chord may substitute for an essential pre-dominant harmony such as iv or ii°⁶. To show this function, we stem the Aug6th's chord tones; see Example 4a. When the Aug6th chord is derived from linear passing or neighboring motion (usually from iv⁶), we leave its chord members unstemmed (Example 4b). What types of melodic figures occur in Examples 4c and 4d?

Example 4

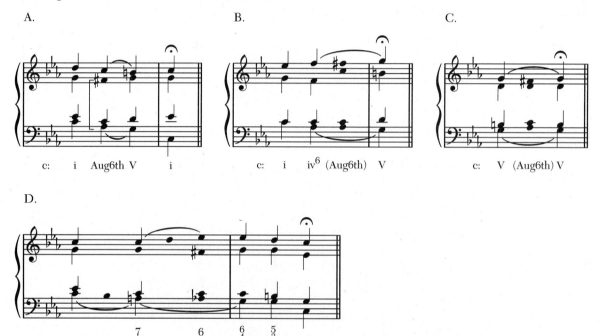

A.

B.

C.

c: i   Aug6th V   i

c: i   iv⁶ (Aug6th) V

c: V (Aug6th) V

D.

7   6   6   5
           4   3

c: i   IV⁶   (Aug6th)   V   i

Three forms of Aug6th chords generally occur in common-practice period music. In analysis they are normally labeled with abbreviations of geographical titles: *It* for Italian, *Fr* for French, and *Ger* for German.[1] Because of their linear derivation, using functional roman numerals to label these chords hardly seems appropriate. We therefore will use the abbreviations given above, with figured-bass symbols to indicate the various inversions.

You should practice spelling these chords upward from the ♭6̂ scale degree, which customarily appears in the bass. We will now treat each form of the Aug6th chord in detail, beginning with the ways in which each occurs in the minor mode.

1. These terms were coined by John Calcott in *A Musical Grammar* (London, 1806), on the basis of nothing more than a highly subjective correlation between the chords' supposed characters and his notions of the various national characters: "the elegance" of the Italian, the "strength" of the German, and the "feebleness" (!) of the French.

AUGMENTED SIXTH CHORDS IN THE MINOR MODE

The **Italian sixth** (**It^6**) consists of only three different scale degrees: $\flat\hat{6}$, $\hat{1}$, and $\sharp\hat{4}$.

Example 5

A.

B.

C.

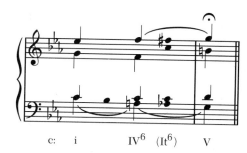

In your partwriting, you should not double the $\sharp\hat{4}$ and $\flat\hat{6}$, since both are active degrees. In four-voice texture, double instead the tonic note ($\hat{1}$), which resolves to both the 3rd and the 5th of the dominant chord that follows (Example 5a). Contrast the soprano neighboring motion of Example 5b with the double-chromatic approach from IV^6 of Example 5c, in which the unstemmed It^6 functions as a passing chord.

Adding scale degree $\hat{2}$ to the It^6 produces a **French $\frac{4}{3}$** (Fr$^4_3$) chord (often called the *French sixth*); see Example 6.

Example 6

A.

B.

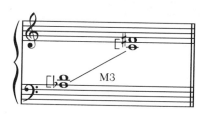
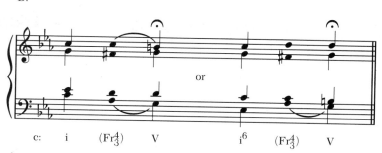

The construction of this exotic chord is curious; it contains two tritones separated by a major 3rd. Partwriting with the Fr$^4_3$ is not particularly difficult, since the $\hat{2}$ is common to both the Fr$^4_3$ and the V chord, and the suspended 7th ($\hat{8}$, or $\hat{1}$) of the former resolves to $\sharp\hat{7}$.

The **German $\frac{6}{5}$** (Ger$^6_5$) chord (often called the *German sixth*) substitutes a $\flat\hat{3}$ for the $\hat{2}$ of the French sixth (Example 7).

Example 7

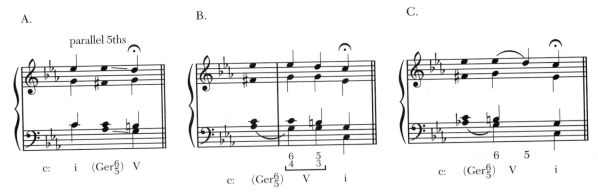

A.

B.

C.

c: i   (Ger$_5^6$)   V

c: (Ger$_5^6$)   V   i

c: (Ger$_5^6$)   V   i

Partwriting with the Ger$_5^6$ is trickier since a direct resolution to V will produce parallel 5ths (Example 7a). There are two ways to avoid parallel 5ths, both of which delay the motion from ♭$\hat{3}$ to $\hat{2}$: you may either progress to a cadential $_4^6$ (Example 7b) or use an accented 6–5 suspension over the dominant (Example 7c).

AUGMENTED SIXTH CHORDS IN THE MAJOR MODE

In the major mode, most of the chord members of Aug6th chords are altered scale degrees (♭$\hat{6}$, ♯$\hat{4}$, and ♭$\hat{3}$). A common way to approach an

Example 8   BEETHOVEN: STRING QUARTET IN G MAJOR, OP. 18, NO. 2, III

A.

B. (REDUCTION)

C: I   (V$_5^6$ V$_2^4$/IV)   IV^6 (It^6)   V   (V^7/V)   V

Aug6th chord in major is from a IV^6 via a double chromaticism, as shown in Example 8 (compare with Example 5c, above). Here the It^6 results from a chromatic descent in the bass that precedes the tonicized V at the cadence.

In the major mode, the $\sharp\hat{4}$ of an Aug6th may occasionally resolve to the 7th of a V^7 ($\hat{4}$) rather than to the dominant octave ($\hat{5}$), as in Example 9.

Example 9   BEETHOVEN: "THE GLORY OF GOD IN NATURE," OP. 48, NO. 4

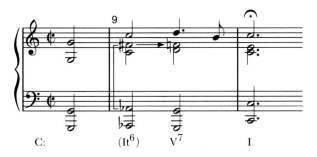

C: (It^6)   V^7 I

DOUBLY AUGMENTED FOURTH CHORDS

When a Ger$^6_5$ chord is used in the major mode, we may write the $\flat\hat{3}$ as a $\sharp\hat{2}$, producing a triply chromatic approach to the $^6_4$ harmony that usually follows it. This sonority is sometimes called a **doubly augmented fourth chord** (AA4th); in C major, this doubly augmented 4th is the interval A♭–D♯. This enharmonic notation, however, does not negate the parallel perfect 5ths that we hear between the tenor and bass in measure 3 of the Beethoven sonata in Example 10.

Example 10

A.

B.   BEETHOVEN: PIANO SONATA IN F MINOR, OP. 57
     ("APPASSIONATA"), II

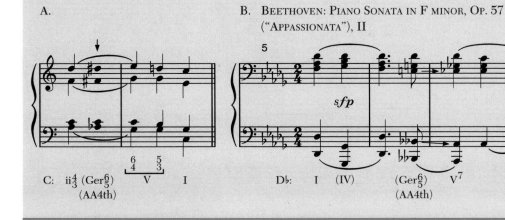

C: ii$^4_3$ (Ger$^6_5$)   V   I   D♭:   I   (IV)   (Ger$^6_5$)   V^7 I
    (AA4th)   (AA4th)

DIMINISHED THIRD CHORDS

Although the ♭$\hat{6}$ of an Aug6th chord normally occurs in the bass voice, we may sometimes find other chord members there. When the ♯$\hat{4}$ appears in the lowest part, a diminished 3rd (the inversion of the augmented 6th) results between it and the upper ♭$\hat{6}$. Since this inversion, known as the **diminished third chord,** usually employs the German form of the Aug6th chord, it will be denoted as Ger°3. Using it often eliminates the danger of creating parallel 5ths inherent in the Ger$^6_5$ (Example 11).

Example 11

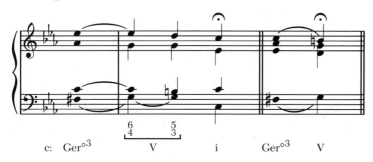

Example 12 illustrates two instances of Ger°3 chords.

Example 12

A. BACH: CRUCIFIXUS FROM *B-MINOR MASS*, BWV 242

B. CHOPIN: PRELUDE IN E MINOR, OP. 28, NO. 4

The "Crucifixus" of Bach's *B-minor Mass* is based on the reiteration of a descending chromatic tetrachord in the bass. Near the end of the movement the music begins to modulate to the relative major key of the triumphant "Et resurrexit" that follows (Example 12a). Rather than descend to the dominant of E minor, the C♮³ in measure 3 of Example 12a pulls upward to C♯³, producing a Ger°³ chord that prepares the authentic cadence in G major. Near the conclusion of Chopin's E-minor Prelude (Example 12b), the composer inserts what appears to be a V$^4_2$/♭II. This harmony actually functions as an enharmonic Ger°³, pulling back to V.

OTHER INVERSIONS OF AUGMENTED SIXTH CHORDS

On occasion we will encounter other inversions of various Aug6th chords. Examples 13a and 13b are voice-leading reductions of the opening twenty-five measures of Brahms's Piano Concerto No. 1 in D minor.

Example 13

A. BRAHMS: PIANO CONCERTO NO. 1, I (MM. 1–25) (REDUCTION 1)   B. (REDUCTION 2)

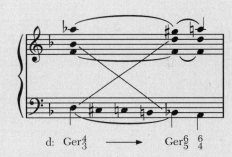

C. CHOPIN: NOCTURNE IN G MINOR, OP. 15, NO. 3

The prolonged first chord, which Brahms spells as a $V^6_5/\flat II$ (B♭ D F A♭), actually turns out to be an enharmonic Ger6th in $\frac{4}{3}$ inversion! Its resolution to a V^6 initiates a chromatic descent in the bass voice, eventually reaching a normally spelled Ger^6_5 that moves on to the $^6_4$ half cadence. The excerpt from Chopin's Nocturne extends a dominant triad in F♯ minor (Example 13c). Compare the pre-dominant chords in measures 1, 3, and 5; what inversions of the Ger6th are employed?

SECONDARY OR ENHARMONIC AUGMENTED SIXTH CHORDS

Aug6th chords can appear in other guises, as the result of either transposition or enharmonic spelling. For instance, the voice leading within an Aug6th–V progression may be transposed to other harmonies, spawning a family of **secondary Aug6th chords** that can resolve to I, IV, or some applied dominant. The series of secondary It⁶'s in Example 14 form a sequence by descending 5ths.

Example 14

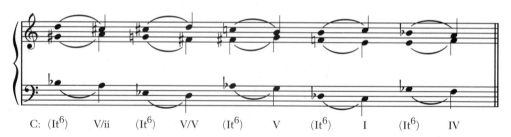

C: (It⁶)   V/ii   (It⁶)   V/V   (It⁶)   V   (It⁶)   I   (It⁶)   IV

An ingenious elaboration of this pattern occurs in the Finale of Mozart's "Jupiter" Symphony (Example 15). Notice the use of a chromatic motive in the upper voice (C♮–C♯–D, F♮–F♯–G), which by moving chromatically up—first to D^6 and then to G^5—rather than down (to B^5 and then to E^5), effectively avoids parallel 5ths.

Example 15   MOZART: SYMPHONY NO. 41 ("JUPITER"), K.551, IV

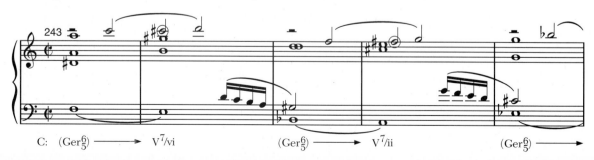

C: (Ger⁶₅) ──────► V⁷/vi   (Ger⁶₅) ──────► V⁷/ii   (Ger⁶₅) ──────►

An isolated Ger$^6_5$ sounds identical to a V^7 (in another key), despite its different spelling; see Example 16.

Example 16

c: Ger$^6_5$ D♭: V^7

Composers have exploited this sonic relation in various ways. The Ger$^6_5$ (in C major: A♭ C E♭ F♯) can be spelled enharmonically as a V^7/♭II (A♭ C E♭ G♭); as such, it is closely related to Neapolitan harmony. The poignant passage in Example 17 appears to prolong ♭II in F minor via a cadential $^6_4$ figure (mm. 1–3 in the excerpt). The applied dominant seventh (D♭ F A♭ C♭) suddenly resolves to V of the original key via this chord's enharmonic spelling as a Ger$^6_5$ (D♭ F A♭ B♮).

Example 17   Schubert: "Gefror'ne Thränen" from *Winterreise*

. . . zerschmelzen desganzen Winters Eis   . . . would melt all of Winter's ice.

Example 18 provides three passages that employ various Aug6th chords. Analyze each excerpt and identify the type and inversion of the Aug6th chord and its function within the passage.

Example 18

A. DONIZETTI: SEXTET FROM *LUCIA DI LAMMERMOOR*, ACT II (VOCAL PARTS OMITTED)

D♭:

B. VERDI: "DIES IRAE" FROM *REQUIEM*

C. FRANCK: *SYMPHONIC VARIATIONS*

f♯:

TRITONE SUBSTITUTION

Both the V^7/V and Ger$^6_5$ tend to resolve to V, and therefore can function in a similar manner. In the opening of his Second Piano Concerto, Liszt precedes the V^7 with both a Ger$^6_5$ and V^7/V, suggesting resolutions in the bass by half step and perfect 5th, respectively. This relation is sometimes called a **tritone substitution,** where the aural bass of two chords that function similarly are exchanged at the tritone, in this case F♮ and B♮. The voice leading in the reduction shows an octave displacement of the B in the last chord; note that the D♯ of the Ger$^6_5$ becomes the 3rd of the V^7/V, which then resolves to the 7th of the V^7.

Example 19   LISZT: PIANO CONCERTO NO. 2

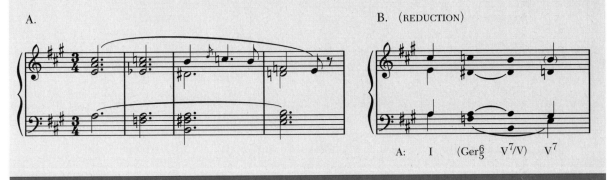

OTHER RESOLUTIONS OF AUGMENTED SIXTH CHORDS

During the late Romantic period, composers experimented with other ways to resolve Aug6th chords. While the augmented 6th interval itself normally resolves to scale degree $\hat{5}$ of a particular key, it is possible to construct other Aug6th chords whose augmented 6th resolves to scale degrees $\hat{1}$ or $\hat{3}$: in C major, D♭–B (to $\hat{1}$), or F–D♯ (to $\hat{3}$). See Example 20.

Example 20

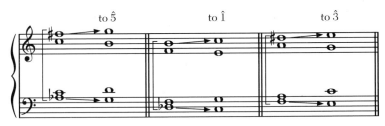

The concluding cadence of the last movement of Schubert's C-major Quintet (Example 21a) employs a Fr$^4_3$ on $\flat\hat{2}$ that resolves directly to the tonic: $\sharp\hat{7}$–$\hat{8}$ and $\flat\hat{2}$–$\hat{1}$. A basic blues progression adds another twist; in Example 21b the F^7 (in C major) may be considered as a transposed Ger$^6_5$ in which the $\hat{4}$ and enharmonic $\sharp\hat{2}$ (F–D$\sharp$) move to the 3rd of the tonic chord. But instead of resolving to a I^6 chord, this "American" sixth (if we can call it that) flouts tradition and resolves to a root-position tonic (Example 21c)!

Example 21

A. SCHUBERT: STRING QUINTET IN C MAJOR, IV

B. TYPICAL "BOOGIE" BLUES

C. (REDUCTION)

MORE EXOTIC CHORD TYPES CONTAINING AN AUGMENTED SIXTH

The defining interval in Aug6th chords is the crucial augmented 6th itself; the other notes in the chord merely produce variants of this basic sonority. In rare instances composers experimented with adding different pitches to the augmented 6th; some of these instances are illustrated in Example 22.

Example 22

A.   WAGNER: PRELUDE TO *TRISTAN UND ISOLDE*, ACT I

B.   RICHARD STRAUSS: *TILL EULENSPIEGEL'S MERRY PRANKS*, OP. 28

C.   SCHOENBERG: *CHAMBER SYMPHONY* NO. 2   D.   (REDUCTION)

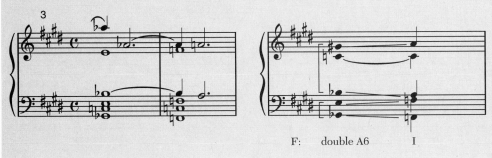

E. BILLY STRAYHORN: "TAKE THE A TRAIN"

C: I   (Aug6th)   I

In the so-called "Tristan" chord,[2] the F–D♯ is accompanied by a B and G♯, producing the sound of a half-diminished chord; in this case the D♯ resolves to the 7th of the following V[7] (Example 22a). The "Till Eulenspiegel" chord uses the same half-diminished seventh sound, but now its augmented 6th (B♭–G♯) resolves to the 3rd of the tonic F-major triad (Example 22b). How many augmented 6ths occur in the Schoenberg progression (Example 22c)? Do they resolve correctly? What type of sonority does Billy Strayhorn employ in Duke Ellington's famous theme song "Take the A Train" (Example 22e)?

2. We will discuss this chord in more detail during our analysis of the *Tristan* Prelude in Chapter 36.

SUMMARY ANALYSIS

We sometimes encounter composition in which one particular altered chord plays a highly significant role. In his G-minor Prelude, Chopin returns to the sonority C♯ E♭ G B♭ three times (Example 23).

Example 23   CHOPIN: PRELUDE IN G MINOR, OP. 28, NO. 22

A.

B. (REDUCTION)

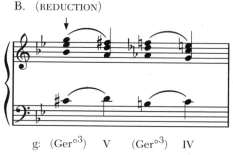

g: (Ger°3)   V   (Ger°3)   IV

The sonority first appears as a noncadential Ger°3 to V in measures 5–6, which is sequenced a step lower (Examples 23a and 23b). The composer then (mm. 17–18) respells it enharmonically, where it acts as a V_2^4 in a tonicized A♭ Neapolitan progression (Examples 23c and 23d). Finally (mm. 38–41), it serves as the essential pre-dominant harmony in the last cadence, substituting a Ger°3 for the diatonic iv⁷ (Example 23e).

Melody Harmonization

In harmonizing diatonic melodies in the minor mode, we can use Aug6th chords to support scale degrees $\hat{1}$ (It⁶), $\hat{2}$ (Fr$_3^4$), and $\hat{3}$ (Ger$_5^6$). They will usually occur as part of the cadence, whether an authentic or half cadence. The three passages in Example 24 illustrate how these chords may be put to effective use in setting diatonic notes in the soprano voice. Play each progression first with only diatonic harmonies, then play the suggested F♯, turning each chord into an Aug6th.

Example 24

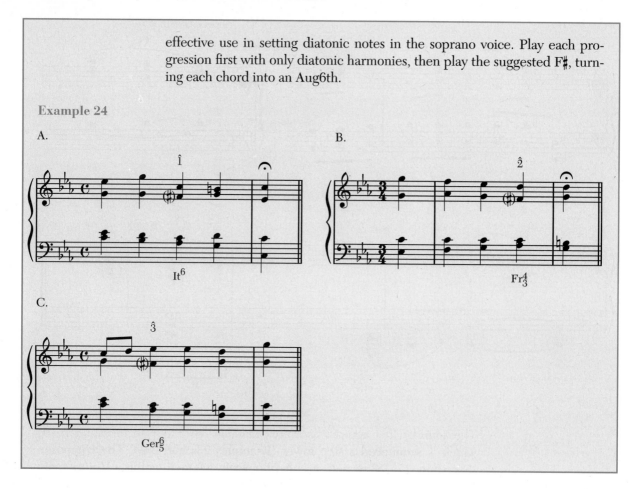

Terms and Concepts for Review

augmented 6th (diminished 3rd)

augmented sixth (Aug6th) chords

chromatic linear chords

Italian sixth (It^6)

French $\frac{4}{3}$ (Fr$\frac{4}{3}$)

German $\frac{6}{5}$ (Ger$\frac{6}{5}$)

doubly augmented fourth chord (AA4th)

diminished third chord (Ger$^{\circ 3}$)

secondary Aug6th chords

enharmonic relations between the Ger$\frac{6}{5}$
  and V^7

tritone substitution

More Complex Forms

In Excursion 1 we discussed some of the simpler formal designs and tonal structures that are found in homophonic music. In Excursion 2 we will conclude our examination of homophonic forms by examining some more complex designs, such as sonata, sonata-rondo, and concerto forms. In addition, we will introduce several genres typical of works that employ contrapuntal texture; these include the chorale prelude, invention, and fugue.

SONATA FORM

We will use the term **sonata form** to refer to the design and structure of a single movement. The sonata-form scheme may be found in first, last, and even slow middle movements of multimovement works. In works from the Classical period, the tonal structure and design of sonata form is based on rounded two-reprise form. The following figure shows how sonata form expands the key scheme and proportions of two-reprise form. The top of the figure outlines a two-reprise from with its continuous,

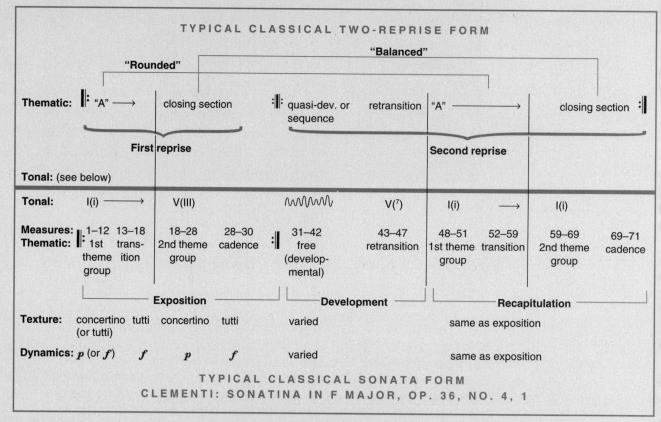

Figure 1

rounded, and balanced characteristics. The basic features of sonata form are aligned directly beneath their counterparts in two-reprise form. Observe that the first repeated section of the two-reprise form has become the **exposition,** the section following the double bar the **development,** and the "rounded" section the **recapitulation.** Typical thematic and tonal characteristics are specified in the middle of the diagram; typical textural and dynamic characteristics appear at the bottom. Its model is the first movement of Clementi's Sonatina in F major, Op. 36, No. 4, the score of which is given in Example 1. Although this piece is actually in **sonatina form,** a diminutive version of sonata form, it includes all the salient attributes of a full-blown sonata movement. (Note that if this movement were in the minor mode, the tonality of the exposition would typically move from $\boxed{i}$ to $\boxed{iii}$ rather than $\boxed{I}$ to $\boxed{V}$.)

Example 1   MUZIO CLEMENTI: SONATINA IN F MAJOR, OP. 36, NO. 4, I

We will treat the formal design of each of the three major divisions of sonata form in some detail. Then we will outline sonata form's basic tonal structure and discuss some of the modifications that composers made to this form when adapting it to other genres, conflating it with other forms, or altering it to suit their own taste.

Exposition

In addition to presenting the principal themes of the movement, the exposition sets up a polarity between two key centers: in major, $\boxed{\text{I}}$ and $\boxed{\text{V}}$, and in minor, $\boxed{\text{i}}$ and $\boxed{\text{III}}$ (or occasionally $\boxed{\text{v}}$). The tonal tension created by the motion to the contrasting key is finally "resolved" by the return to the tonic in the recapitulation section. The exposition is usually repeated.

1. In sonata form, the opening theme of the original two-reprise form is often expanded into a **first theme group,** which contains several different musical ideas. This theme group appears in the tonic key.
2. A **transition** directs the tonal motion away from the tonic toward the new key. In symphonic movements it is usually played *forte* by the full orchestra, and it normally concludes with a half or authentic cadence in the new key area.
3. The **second theme group** is set in the contrasting key. Its phrase groupings are often more regular, it is typically quieter and more lyrical, and in symphonies it often employs a smaller instrumental force than the first theme group. Although its theme or themes are usually new, it may instead consist largely of a transposition of the first theme, producing a **monothematic sonata form.** Haydn was especially fond of using only one theme or theme group for both key areas; see the opening movement of his Symphony No. 100 in G major ("Military").
4. The **closing section** of the exposition serves to confirm the contrasting key and is thus largely cadential. It normally consists of arpeggios, scales, and trills, and it is almost always played *forte.* Following the cadence of this *forte* section, a brief new **closing theme** or **codetta,** usually played *piano,* may occur as a final appendage to the exposition.

Development

The term *development* suggests that the material of the exposition will now undergo expansion, fragmentation, sequencing, or other developmental procedures. While such techniques are usually employed in the development, the most significant characteristic of the development is its modulatory nature. The composer generally uses the development to freely explore various key relations; as a result, it follows no fixed design, and irregular phrase groupings and striking contrasts of texture, register, and dynamics are typical. Perhaps the term *fantasia section* would be more appropriate; the German word for this section, *Durchführung* ("leading through"), more clearly stresses its transitory nature.

Toward the end of the development, a **retransition** based on a dominant prolongation usually prepares the return of the original thematic material in the tonic key at the beginning of the recapitulation.

Recapitulation

The musical events heard in the exposition return in their original order in the *recapitulation*. There is one significant difference: the dominant or mediant key, used for the second theme group and closing section in the exposition, is now replaced by the tonic. This creates an interesting problem in the transition between the two theme groups: in the exposition this transition effected a modulation to the new key area; here, it must now give a sense of "modulating" somewhere while still remaining in the tonic key. Thus, the transition frequently tonicizes IV, which then returns to I via V. The closing section—including the closing theme, if any—serves to reinforce the movement's conclusion in the tonic. In sonata-form movements from the early Classical period, the development and recapitulation are repeated, harking back to the two-reprise form on which sonata form is based.

Tonal Structure of Sonata Form

We may view the tonal structure of sonata form in terms of the intersection of its harmonic scheme with its long-range, or background, voice leading. This voice leading typically forms a descending pattern in the upper voice that is interrupted. We have already seen this type of structure in shorter excerpts (Chapter 19, pp. 264–65, and Chapter 23, Example 1). In a major key, the harmony within the exposition, development, and dominant retransition usually progresses from I to V, and the long-range movement of the soprano line from $\hat{3}$ to $\hat{2}$; within the recapitulation, the harmony moves from I to V to I, and the upper line from $\hat{3}$ to $\hat{2}$ to $\hat{1}$. In a minor key, the long-range harmony within the exposition to the retransition generally incorporates the III key area (i–III–V), the soprano's long-range descent to $\hat{2}$ usually beginning with $\hat{5}$ rather than $\hat{3}$ so that the voice leading can better incorporate this new key area ($\hat{5}-\hat{4}-\hat{3}-\hat{2}$). The recapitulation then outlines a i–V–i harmony, with the long-range stepwise motion beginning anew on $\hat{5}$ and descending to 1. Example 2 shows how the three-part design of sonata form is reconciled with its two-part tonal structure, in both major and minor key areas.

Example 2

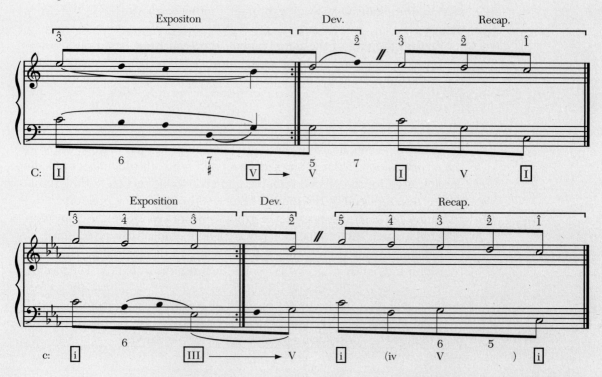

For some typical treatments of sonata form, see the first movement of Mozart's Symphony No. 40 in G minor, the second movement of Beethoven's Symphony No. 1 in C major, and the Finale to Haydn's Symphony No. 92 in G major ("Oxford").

Introduction

First-movement sonata forms are sometimes preceded by a slow **introduction.** Most introductions consist of three parts: (1) a tonic opening, (2) a tonal transition, which often includes sequences or applied dominants, and (3) a dominant prolongation, which prepares the tonic key that begins the most briskly paced exposition. Introductions to major-key movements are frequently in the parallel minor mode. Motivic ideas stated in the introduction may reappear in the allegro section as in Haydn's Symphony No. 100 in G major ("Military") and Beethoven's Piano Sonata in C minor, Op. 13 ("Pathétique").

SONATA FORM **447**

Later composers gave their introductions grander proportions; see, for instance, the extended opening of Beethoven's Symphony No. 7 in A major.

Coda

A **coda** is sometimes appended to the closing section of the recapitulation. In early sonata-form movements, the coda consists of little more than an extension of the closing section but with much fanfare, rhythmic activity, and tonic affirmation. Beethoven pioneered the conception of the coda as a kind of second development section, although with less daring key relations. The first movement of his Symphony No. 3 in E♭ major ("Eroica") and the opening movement of his Symphony No. 5 in C minor, in which the coda actually develops a new theme, are good examples of developmental codas.

Concerto Form

The opening movement of solo concertos from the Classical period alter the typical design and structure of sonata form in the following ways to produce what is often known as **concerto form:**

1. The exposition is largely repeated, but not by means of a repeat sign. In the "first exposition," called the **orchestra exposition,** the orchestra alone plays, remaining in the tonic key. In the "second exposition," called the **solo exposition,** the solo instrument is introduced; after playing the first theme group, the soloist and orchestra progress together to the secondary key. The alternation of "solo" (or "concertino," in the case of a group of soloists) and "tutti" sections indicates a historical link with the *concerto grosso* of the Baroque period.
2. A **cadenza** displaying the soloist's technical prowess is usually inserted before the principal cadence preceding the coda.

The initial movement of Mozart's G-major Flute Concerto, K.285c, represents a traditional handling of concerto form.

Sonata-Rondo Form

In some seven-part rondos (see Excursion I: Simple Forms), the middle or C section does not present a new theme but instead assumes the character of a development section, exploiting prior material through modulatory procedures. Such pieces (for example, the last movement of Mozart's Piano Sonata in B♭ major, K.333) exhibit **sonata-rondo form.**

Modifications of Sonata Form

Later composers modified sonata form in other ways. For instance, the second tonal center within the exposition sometimes employs a **dominant substitute**—that is, a foreign key instead of the usual $\boxed{\text{V}}$ (in major movements) or $\boxed{\text{iii}}$ (in minor movements). A famous example is the opening movement of Beethoven's Piano Sonata in C major, Op. 53 ("Waldstein"), where the exposition's second key area of $\boxed{\text{iii}}$ (E major) appears as $\boxed{\text{VI}}$ (A major) in the recapitulation. In both places, once the second theme has been presented in its foreign key area (both of which are related by a third to the original key center), it modulates back to the customary $\boxed{\text{V}}$ and then $\boxed{\text{I}}$ to close each section. This second theme also occurs in the tonic within the movement's coda.

Other changes may include the following: (1) the repeat of the exposition may be omitted (Brahms's Symphony No. 4 in E minor, first movement); (2) the development section may introduce either a completely new theme, which is then also expanded (Beethoven's Piano Sonata in E major, Op. 14, No. 1, first movement), or a **false recapitulation,** where the opening theme returns in the wrong key (Beethoven's Piano Sonata in C major, Op. 2, No. 3, first movement); (3) the retransition may be abbreviated or omitted altogether (Brahms's *Tragic Overture,* Op. 81), or may even prolong the dominant of a key other than the tonic (Haydn's Symphony No. 104 in D major ["London"], fourth movement); (4) the recapitulation may begin in a key other than the tonic (Mozart's Piano Sonata in C major, K.545, first movement) or may reverse the order of the first and second theme groups (Mozart's Piano Sonata in D major, K.311, first movement); (5) a "double development" or "double recapitulation" may be introduced (Beethoven's Symphony No. 8 in F major, Finale); or (6) sonata form may be given a programmatic character (as in Tchaikovsky's overture-fantasy *Romeo and Juliet,* where the thematic ideas are patterned around the basic narrative of Shakespeare's drama).

UNIQUE FORMAL DESIGNS

Composers generally accepted the prevalent forms of their time and cast their works in patterns similar to those discussed in this and the previous Excursion section. Sometimes they did not adhere rigorously to such models. Beethoven, for instance, continually modified the Classical forms he inherited; compare the Scherzo section of the third movement of his Symphony No. 5 in C minor to the stranded two-reprise form of the period. Other innovative composers either "deformalized" the standard formal models or else created new designs with ingenious tonal schemes. The **symphonic poems** or **tone poems** of Liszt and Richard Strauss offer a rich field for exploration in this area.

CONTRAPUNTAL FORMS

In contrapuntally oriented compositions, the term *form* often refers more to a genre rather than a fixed design. We will examine three specific examples that emanate from the Baroque period: the chorale prelude, the invention, and the fugue.

Chorale Prelude

The Lutheran **chorale** was the traditional hymn of Protestant Europe in the Baroque period. While the congregation sang the tune in unison, the organist provided differing harmonic accompaniments, depending on the text of each verse. Chorale melodies were often cast in **bar form** (AAB), in which the first phrases were repeated as a group, followed by different phrases. Four-voice chorale harmonizations, including many of Bach's 371 chorale harmonizations, may be found as the final movement in numerous cantatas of the era.

In the Lutheran service the organist would play a verse of the chorale to remind the congregation of the tune, since the hymnals contained only the texts. As time went on, these preliminary performances became increasingly elaborate. The resulting contrapuntal settings of the chorale are usually called **chorale preludes.** These are cantus-firmus compositions that contrapuntally set the preexisting chorale melody in a variety of ways. The tune customarily appears in the soprano or bass voice. In simple chorale preludes the melody continues throughout, while in more complex pieces the tune is segmented into individual phrases that are separated by sections of contrapuntal writing called **interludes.** Bach's well-known "Jesu, Joy of Man's Desiring" is a fine example of the latter; in fact, the famous melody that opens this chorale prelude itself is an elaboration of the first chorale phrase!

In a ***vorimitation* chorale prelude,** one or all of the phrases are preceded by imitation in the voices, based on the succeeding chorale tune. When the thematic material in the interludes between the chorale phrases returns periodically, we refer to the chorale prelude as a **ritornello chorale prelude;** this technique occurs in the opening of Bach's familiar cantata *Wachet auf.* A brief chorale prelude based on the "Vom Himmel hoch" tune is quoted in Example 3; the cantus appears in the upper voice.

Example 3   FRIEDRICH ZACHAU: "VOM HIMMEL HOCH" (CHORALE PRELUDE)

Invention

In 1722 Bach composed a collection of keyboard pieces for his eldest son Wilhelm Friedemann, a child prodigy. Included in this "little keyboard book" (*Clavierbüchlein*) were a series of two- and three-voice pieces called *preambles* and *fantasias.* Bach later published these short works under the title *Inventions and Sinfonias,* rearranging their key schemes and revising some of the **inventions.** Their original purpose was pedagogical; they were intended to explore such practical issues as fingering and the increasing difficulty of key signatures as well as, more importantly, to teach the art of composing short imitative compositions. The inventions display great economy of means, most or all of the musical material being derived from the original theme or themes. Though they are not based on a particular formal model but rather exhibit considerable diversity of organization, we can pinpoint some of their general characteristics:

1. Most begin with imitation, either at the octave or the upper 5th. The opening statement that is imitated may consist only of a brief motivic idea (C-major and E-minor Inventions), or it may constitute a longer theme (D-major Invention). Some open with a **double theme,** the two voices being written so that they can switch between soprano and bass; this technique is called **invertible** or **double counterpoint.**
2. After the initial imitation, the theme or themes recur throughout the piece in other keys. Thus, the general tonal scheme is tonic–related keys–tonic. Each of these tonally stable thematic occurrences is usually separated by episodes (see below); in some cases they may be paired together in a kind of "tonic–dominant" relation, such as III followed by V/III.
3. These recurring thematic statements are often separated from each other by modulatory sections called **episodes.** The episodes may be based on motivic fragments from the original thematic idea or may introduce new material. They usually employ sequential patterns and frequently conclude with a well-defined cadence in a new key.

In their original order within the *Clavierbüchlein,* the compositional techniques gradually increase in complexity. The two-part set concludes with a **canon,** a piece that displays strict imitation throughout. We may find examples of other devices in the three-part pieces, such as stretto (B♭ major) and triple counterpoint (F minor); see the discussion of each of these below. Bach's Invention in E♭ major, quoted in Example 4, stresses double counterpoint, as exemplified in the opening double theme.

Example 4 BACH: TWO-PART INVENTION No. 5 IN E♭ MAJOR, BWV 776

Fugue

The **fugue** was the prevailing imitative genre of the Baroque period, and it appears in both instrumental and vocal works. The fugue is a contrapuntal and basically monothematic composition that opens with imitation. Fugues exhibit strict three- or four-voice texture (two- and five-voice fugues are less common) in which each voice is strictly accounted for. Unlike the principal formal models of the Classical period, such as the two-reprise form and the rondo, the fugue is actually more a compositional procedure than a form, since design and tonal structure tend to vary considerably from one fugue to another. Nevertheless, it is possible to generalize about some aspects of fugue construction.

In the **fugal exposition,** or opening imitative section, the voices enter in a predetermined tonal scheme of tonic–dominant–tonic–(dominant, etc.). Those entering in the tonic key are called the **subject,** and those entering in the dominant key are called the **answer.** The answer may feature **real imitation** in which the original melodic intervals of the subject are strictly retained, or **tonal imitation,** in which one or more intervals are modified so that they fit into the prevailing tonal scheme. If the accompanying counterpoint set to the thematic answer is retained throughout the fugue, it is called the **countersubject;** in this case, the subject and countersubject are always written in invertible counterpoint, a technique that allows the voices to be switched. A short **bridge** sometimes links the end of the answer entry (in V) to the tonic of the following subject (in I).

There is no set pattern for the entry of the different voices or the time interval between their entries. In Bach's *Well-Tempered Clavier* the subjects are relatively short, while in some of his larger organ fugues they may extend up to eight measures. Once the final entrance of the subject is completed, the exposition ends. Some composers choose to repeat the exposition with modifications; this is called a **counterexposition.**

The continuation of a fugue after the exposition is difficult to codify. Some theorists have divided the typical fugue into three sections: the "exposition" (see above), a middle "development," where the subject recurs in other keys, and a "final section," where the tonic key is reaffirmed along with the last entries of the subject. The C-minor fugue in Bach's *Well-Tempered Clavier,* Book I, is often cited as a model. However, a careful examination of the literature reveals that there are just as many exceptions to this design. For instance, the D♯-minor fugue in the *Well-Tempered Clavier,* Book I, is constructed on an entirely different plan. This fugue is divided into three distinct sections, each of which emphasizes a different contrapuntal device (see definitions below): (1) imitation and stretto, (2) inversion or mirror and stretto, and (3) augmentation. Each section begins in the tonic key.

Subsequent entries of the subject (in contrasting keys or in the tonic) tend to alternate with episodes that employ sequential writing; these episodes often modulate to and cadentially confirm a new key prior to the subject's next entry in the new key. This is analogous to the concerto grosso, the subject reentries corresponding to the latter's *tutti* or *ripieno* sections, the episodes to its *concertino* sections.[1]

Various contrapuntal techniques may be employed in the course of a fugue. We may find examples of **inversion** or **mirror technique,** in which the melodic intervals of the subject are literally turned upside down;

---

1. See Edward Cone, *Musical Form and Musical Performance* (New York: W. W. Norton, 1968), 71.

triple counterpoint, in which three voices may be switched, producing six different arrangements between the voices; short passages of strict canonic imitation; augmentation and diminution, in which all the note values of the subject are proportionately lengthened or shortened, respectively; and stretto, in which the temporal distance between the original entries of the theme is subsequently shortened.

The F-major Fugue from the *Well-Tempered Clavier*, Book I, is quoted in Example 5. Examine its design and tonal structure, identifying any notable contrapuntal devices.

Double fugues combine two distinct subjects. They may be presented at the opening of the exposition (as in the Finale to Haydn's String Quartet in F minor, Op. 20, No. 5, where both immediately occur together), or each subject may be accorded its own exposition, with the thematic combination occurring later in the piece (see Contrapunctus X in Bach's *Art of the Fugue*).

Fugues continued to be written well beyond the Baroque period. In the Classical period we may cite the "Kyrie eleison" from Mozart's Requiem (a "Handelian-sounding" double fugue) and the opening movement of Beethoven's String Quartet in C♯ minor, Op. 131. Even later instances include the Finale to Brahms's *Variations and Fugue on a Theme by Handel*, the concluding number in Verdi's *Falstaff*, Wagner's "riot" fugue in the last scene of Act II of *Die Meistersinger* (which actually turns out to be a vast chorale prelude), the set of fugues in Hindemith's *Ludus Tonalis*, and the last movement of Stravinsky's *Concerto for Two Pianos*.

Example 5   BACH: FUGUE IN F MAJOR FROM *WELL-TEMPERED CLAVIER*, BOOK I

Terms and Concepts for Review

sonata form
exposition
development
recapitulation
sonatina form
first theme group
transition
second theme group
monothematic sonata form
closing section
closing theme
codetta
introduction
coda
concerto form
orchestra exposition
solo exposition
cadenza
sonata-rondo form
dominant substitute
false recapitulation
symphonic or tone poem
chorale
bar form

chorale prelude
interlude
vorimitation chorale prelude
ritornello chorale prelude
invention
double theme
invertible (double) counterpoint
episode (invention or fugue)
canon
fugue
fugal exposition
subject
answer
real imitation
tonal imitation
countersubject
bridge
counterexposition
inversion (mirror technique)
triple counterpoint
canonic imitation
stretto
double fugue

Implication
and Realization

Throughout this text we have directed our attention to technical aspects of music—harmony, voice leading, phrase grouping, and so forth. While this approach provides us with detailed information about what makes music work, in order to understand music more fully we must also take into account those *affective* or emotional responses that music may arouse.[1] Topics such as the sense of beauty, artistic merit, and satisfaction that we derive from music fall within the realm of **music aesthetics,**[2] which attempts to explain the meaning and significance of music in our culture.

Few people question the ability of music to induce emotional responses in the listener. The ways in which this affective process takes place have been the subject of speculation and debate throughout the history of Western music. The noted author Leonard Meyer has written extensively about how music conveys meaning; his ideas form the basis of the discussion that follows.[3]

1. The historical-social background of compositions, another rich field for study, lies outside the scope of this text.
2. From the Greek word *aisthesis,* meaning "feelings or sensations."
3. These basic premises are found in the first three chapters of his *Emotion and Meaning in Music* (Chicago: Univ. of Chicago Press, 1956). Also see his *Music, the Arts and Ideas* (Chicago: Univ. of Chicago Press, 1967), *Explaining Music* (Chicago: Univ. of Chicago

MUSIC AS COMMUNICATION

The familiar expression "music is an international language" is misleading in several ways. There are similarities between the "syntax" and "grammar" of language and music, as we noted in Chapter 3, but the way in which they convey meaning is different.[4] We cannot combine individual musical stimuli, such as an eighth note, an F$\sharp^4$, and a C-major triad, to form musical "words" with specific embedded meanings in the same way that language combines letters of the alphabet to form words of specific meaning. While music does communicate meaning to us, it does so in a different and less concrete manner. Nor are these communicated meanings perceived in the same way by different cultures. When we hear the familiar wedding music of Wagner or Mendelssohn, we immediately associate it with a well-defined social function. This association is based on a learned response that is common to our culture. On the other hand, when we hear a piece of Ethiopian or Tibetan music, our ignorance of their respective customs prevents such intimate musical–social connections. We can only guess what purpose or even general character such pieces have within their social context. The Wagner bridal chorus would be as meaningless to an Australian bushman as a piece of his hunting music would be to us. Nor can we rely on some common theoretical system that underlies all world musics, for the pitch and rhythmic organization of various musical cultures are often vastly different.

REFERENTIALISM VS. ABSOLUTISM

Meaning in music originates from two basic sources. On the one hand, music may communicate **referential meanings,** that is, those that relate to extramusical sources or references. These meanings may be of a personal nature—for instance, the romantic memories awakened by hearing "our song." They also may be of a broader cultural nature, based on common, acquired associations, such as the wedding music referred to above. When we listen to the closing passage of William Walton's score for the film *Richard III* (1955), our reactions may consist largely of images or impressions that originate outside of the music itself: "It sounds like a procession," "It sounds English," "It sounds like the triumphant ending to a movie," and so on. In distinction to this referential viewpoint is the notion that meaning arises from relations between forces within the music itself. In the remainder of this chapter we will focus on this latter, **absolutist** view.[5]

Press, 1973), and *Style and Music* (Philadelphia: Univ. of Pennsylvania Press, 1989), as well as Eugene Narmour's *Beyond Schenkerism* (Univ. of Chicago Press, 1977).

4. The relation of linguistics to music is explored in Fred Lerdahl and Ray Jackendoff's *A Generative Theory of Tonal Music* (Cambridge: MIT Press, 1983).

5. *Absolute*, when applied to music, means independent of anything outside itself.

EMOTION IN MUSIC

Psychologists point out that emotion is aroused when our tendency to respond to a particular stimulus or situation is inhibited. For instance, we do not ordinarily attach any particular emotional significance to habitual actions of everyday life, such as removing clothes from a coat hanger. If, however, the hangers become tangled, our customary response is delayed and we may experience irritation, an emotional reaction.

Meyer observes that affective experiences in music usually differ from nonmusical experiences in the amount of aesthetic consequence each type portrays. Daily events in our life that impede the expression of a normal reaction to a stimulus, such as our encounter with the coat hangers, may be relatively accidental and therefore produce little aesthetic consequence. In the arts, however, and music in particular, inhibitions such as the type that we will discuss below take on a more explicit meaning. Therefore, in order to be aesthetically relevant in the arts, tendencies that are consequently inhibited must be provided with meaningful resolutions. For instance, our enjoyment of a typical swashbuckling or horror movie is derived from the extended inhibitions produced by a succession of escalating crises. Nevertheless, even in the most hopeless predicament, we always sense that the hero or heroine will eventually dispatch the villain or monster.

IMPLICATION AND REALIZATION

The common-practice period may be considered as a particular **style system**—that is, a collection of preferred tendencies within musical compositions. Each of the different style systems that have evolved throughout the history of Western music consist of standard, or *normative,* procedures that occur over and over. The voice-leading models in this text are good examples of these recurrent tendencies within common-practice period style. Each model sets up a harmonic and melodic **implication,** or expectation, which is followed by its **realization** or resolution in one or another way. Due to their frequent occurrence, these familiar models imply a predictable realization. Deviations from these norms are largely limited to either irregular procedures (such as the transferred resolution of a seventh chord) or outright errors (such as parallel 5ths). Because of their relative improbability and more individuality, these deviations are less predictable. If the deviations are so extreme that they cannot be rationalized in terms of the established norms of a style, we may respond with amusement; the "wrong notes" in the horn parts of the Trio to the Minuet from Mozart's *Musical Joke* are a case in point.

Certain inhibitions momentarily block or delay the tendencies of our normative models. We can accept these deviations as musically valid, provided that they can be rationalized within the accepted style. Example 1a illustrates a typical harmonic model of the common-practice period. Even when heard out of context, we can identify it as an authentic $^6_4$ cadence. The tonic goal, or realization, is clearly implied by the pre-dominant IV and suspended dominant ($^{6-5}_{4-3}$). We will now supply this familiar progression with four different resolutions that deviate more and more from the established norm. Which of these deviations can we readily accept, and which ones cause us to question our sense of continuation?

Example 1

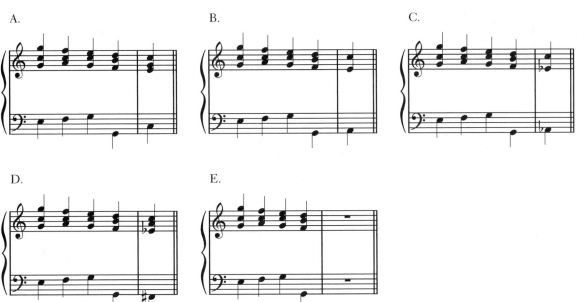

In Example 1b the substitution of vi for I, which creates a deceptive resolution, is not as common as the final tonic in Example 1a but nevertheless implies a continuing harmonic motion toward a more stable goal, such as I or V. In Example 1c the ♭VI is slightly more puzzling, since it raises the possibility of modal mixture and its future role in the ensuing music. The diminished seventh chord in Example 1d is stranger still, since it leaves us even more unsure of what tonal course it may take. And finally, the absence of any resolution in Example 1e opens up a host of future possibilities. In the last four progressions, our expectation of a tonic resolution has been blocked or delayed, and we sense that normative harmonic continuation is progressively less certain or predictable. In each case these inhibitions have aroused our emotional curiosity. The extent to which affective inhibition and its eventual outcome play a significant role in musical meaning will become evident as we continue to listen.

Now play the harmonic progression in Example 2.

Example 2

Since the normative tonic resolution of the $\frac{6}{4}$ cadence has been circumvented, there is some doubt about our final goal. Nevertheless, a roundabout succession of tonicized chords does bring us back to the opening $\frac{6}{4}$, which finally resolves to I. It is as though we have taken a ramp off the expressway for a brief detour through the countryside before getting back on the highway to our destination. We do not begrudge the additional time since our more extended journey has proved rather enjoyable. One might hypothesize that a "straight line" is not necessarily the most gratifying route between two points in music. Thus, our sense of immediate aesthetic pleasure results from "the arousal and suspension or fulfillment of expectation, which are products of many previous encounters with works of art."[6]

Procedures that block or delay a tonal goal may occur in melodic writing as well. Example 3 quotes the opening eight-measure phrase of a waltz tune from Richard Strauss's *Der Rosenkavalier*.

Example 3   RICHARD STRAUSS: WALTZ MELODY FROM *DER ROSENKAVALIER*, LAST PART OF ACT II

6. H. D. Aiken, "The Aesthetic Relevance of Belief," *Journal of Aesthetics* 9 (1950), 313.

The melody outlines a stepwise descent from $\hat{3}$ down to $\hat{4}$ against a framing harmonic background of I–V^7. Drawing on our innate knowledge of the style, we anticipate a continuation of $\hat{2}$ down to $\hat{3}$ (V^7–I) in the succeeding eight bars by means of a melodic sequence (Example 4).

Example 4 IMPLIED CONTINUATION

However, after beginning the consequent phrase on $\hat{4}$, the composer suddenly veers off in such an unexpected manner that the eventual tonal goal is in jeopardy (Example 5). At the last moment, he regains our "original" course, leading to the "anticipated" $\hat{3}$ over tonic harmony. The stepwise motion of the first phrase is still apparent in the second, although it has been cleverly disguised in the inner voice (some notes are implied) with $\flat\hat{7}$ and $\flat\hat{6}$ degrees.

Example 5 STRAUSS'S CONTINUATION

Play these versions consecutively and note your affective response to each.

Another instance of this process occurs in the phrase periodicity of the Minuet in Haydn's "*London*" Symphony No. 104 in D major (Example 6). With the exception of one six-measure extension in the second reprise, practically all of the phrases are based on a recurring 4 + 4-measure pattern. The return of the original theme in the tonic (m. 35) appears to signal the final eight-bar period of the piece. At this crucial moment, the composer inserts a harmonic motion to the subdominant (mm. 43–48) that completely disrupts our sense of regular measure grouping; observe the effect of the two measures of silence. The final phrase then restores the previous four-measure periodicity.

Example 6 HAYDN: SYMPHONY NO. 104 ("LONDON"), III

The climax of the development section in the first movement of Beethoven's "Eroica" Symphony No. 3 in E♭ major (Example 7) provides a wonderful example of how simultaneous deviations in several different musical aspects (harmony, rhythm, phrasing, and dynamics) work together to create an overpowering emotional experience.

Example 7 BEETHOVEN: SYMPHONY NO. 3 ("EROICA"), I

E minor (new theme)

The passage that opens this excerpt establishes a sequence of rising 5ths (F minor–C minor–G minor–D minor). A strict continuation of this sequential pattern would bring us through A minor to E minor, the minor enharmonic Neapolitan of the tonic E♭ major. But at this point (m. 248), Beethoven breaks off the sequential motion by introducing a host of deviant elements: a change in the basic harmonic rhythm from four to six measures, extensive syncopation and hemiola that conflict with the established triple meter, and increasingly ambiguous chordal progressions (mm. 248–71). The passage culminates on the C$^6_4$ in measure 274 and its move to F$^6_5$ in measure 278; note the emphasis on the minor-2nd dissonance in this last chord. Following a sudden rhythmic break (with a quarter rest), we perceive the chord on B (m. 280) as a dominant, which finally leads us to our goal of E minor.[7] With the gradual relaxation of tension, Beethoven now introduces a new theme in measure 284 to complement his new tonal center. In hindsight, we may understand the progression F$^6_5$–B^7–Em as ♭II$^6_5$–V^7–i in E minor. But the combined tonal, metric, and periodic elements that deviate from the normal course of this piece give us a very different impression as we initially listen to the passage.

Beethoven is not the only composer who will sometimes toy with our sense of expectation. In the opening measures of his C-minor Piano Fantasia, K.475 (Example 8), Mozart presents a two-measure statement that moves from i to V^6.

Example 8 MOZART: PIANO FANTASIA IN C MINOR, K.475

Based on our familiarity with Classical phrasing, we anticipate a consequent phrase that will return to the tonic: V^6–i (Example 9).

---

7. Observe that the bass line in this excerpt finally reaches the destination of E^2 by descending stepwise motion: D^3–C^3–B♮^{2}–A♯^{2}–A♮^{2}–G^2–(F♯^{2})–E^2.

Example 9   IMPLIED CONTINUATION

c: V^6 i

Instead Mozart avoids this expected progression in favor of a descending chromatic sequence (Example 10).

Example 10   MOZART'S CONTINUATION

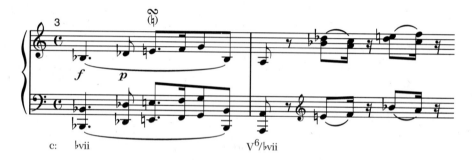

c: ♭vii V^6/♭vii

We now readjust our expectations and opt in the third phrase for a Ger^6_5, which with the first two phrases outlines a chromatic descent from $\hat{1}$ to $\hat{5}$ in the bass: C–B♮–(B♭–A♮–A♭–G).

Example 11   IMPLIED CONTINUATION

c: Ger^6_5 V^7 i

Though the third phrase indeed begins with A♭ (m. 5), the note instead functions as the dominant of ♭II, resulting in a complete evasion of our expected dominant goal (Example 12).

Example 12   Mozart's continuation

The composer has not completely forsaken this G, however, since after a second chromatic descent from B to F♯ (mm. 10–17), the G harmony reappears as an extended VI in B minor (Example 13).

Example 13

In the return of this theme near the end of the work (mm. 167–74), Mozart dispenses with his prior setting in favor of a more direct approach to the tonic, employing the previous D♭ triad (see m. 5 of Example 12) as ♭II⁶, which eventually resolves via V to i (Example 14).

Example 14

vii°⁷/V   V   i

The Mozart excerpt above is typical of musical situations where we are forced to reevaluate our expectations of what direction the music will actually take as it continues. This process of reevaluation can operate in terms of musical form and design as well. Any Chopin waltz with repeated sections, such as his G♭-major Waltz, Op. 70, No. 1 (Example 15), can serve as an illustration. We have labeled the first four sections of this waltz A, B, C, and D.

Example 15 CHOPIN: WALTZ IN G♭ MAJOR, OP. 70, NO. 1

As we hear each successive section (without repeats), we continually project possible continuations of the piece, guessing which section we will hear next. For instance, after the first period (mm. 1–8), we may hear one of three possible continuations: an exact repetition (A A), a modified repetition (A A'), or new material (A B). Progressing through the composition, however, the number of possible ways it can continue increases almost geometrically. For instance, on reaching the C section, we could anticipate that it might be followed by A, A', B, B', C, C', or D. However, because we draw on previously established patterns in making our future predictions, the number of musically logical continuations actually becomes more limited. The information we receive and process as we listen to the composition is coupled with the knowledge we bring to our hearing. In this case, the more

Chopin waltzes in sectionalized form that we have already heard, the more certain we may be about our ability to predict the continuation of the music.

SURPRISE AND AMBIGUITY

An abrupt, unexpected change of dynamics, texture, register, or harmony in a passage qualifies as a musical **surprise.** In instances of musical surprise, we must quickly reevaluate the new situation and reconcile it to the events that immediately preceded it. Although the "surprise" *forte* chord in the slow movement of Haydn's "Surprise" Symphony hardly raises an eyebrow today, the unexpected *fortissimo tutti* chord that opens the development section in the first movement of Tchaikovsky's Sixth Symphony always succeeds in catching a few concertgoers off guard.

Extended **ambiguity** is another matter. The suspense created by our ignorance of a clearly defined path to the tonal goal can powerfully influence the way we perceive the achievement of that goal. The ingenious transition between the last two movements of Beethoven's Fifth Symphony in C minor is a classic example (see Example 10 in Chapter 18). The composer wishes to build up to the triumphant C-major triad that opens the symphony Finale. But the usual *tutti* ending to the scherzo is normally followed by a pause between movements, which would hardly prepare the listener for the last movement's dramatic entry that Beethoven has in mind. He therefore concludes the scherzo *pianissimo* with a deceptive cadence (m. 324). The A♭ and C of the VI chord are extended for some fifteen measures, underpinned by little more than a monotonous timpani rhythm. The tentative entry of the violins fails to clarify our sense of tonal goal. Thus we are held in suspense until a belated V^7 finally propels us toward Beethoven's intended C-major resolution. The ambiguity generated by this transition is what makes the sun-filled opening of the Finale so effective.

FOR FURTHER STUDY

This same tonal goal of C major also plays a significant role in the tonal schemes of at least two other works as well. The introduction ("Chaos") to Haydn's *Creation* provides the appropriate psychological suspense, which is finally dissipated in the magical C-major setting of the words "Let there be light." Likewise, the somber and ambiguous diminished seventh harmonies at the opening of the Finale to Brahms's First Symphony give way to the famous horn solo in C major, with its strong suggestion of Westminster chimes.

APPLICATION TO MUSICAL ANALYSIS

We may apply some of the principles discussed above to the analysis of musical compositions. In addition to considering harmony, voice leading, rhythm, and form, we may also direct our attention to the ways in which stylistic norms or deviations from these norms operate within individual pieces. One such work is quoted in the Workbook, with accompanying suggestions for its analysis.

Terms and Concepts for Review

music aesthetics
referential *vs.* absolute
style system
implication and realization
tendency and expectation *vs.* resolution

the interplay of norms and deviations in
  harmony, melody, periodicity, and form
reevaluation of expectations
surprise and ambiguity

Ninth, Eleventh, Thirteenth, and Added-Note Chords

In their quest for more expressive means, composers of the Classical and Romantic periods—and in this century jazz and rock musicians—gradually enlarged their chordal vocabulary. We are already familiar with some of these harmonies: seventh chords and certain altered sonorities such as applied dominants, mixture chords, Neapolitan chords, and Aug6th chords. Another means of expanding the harmonic vocabulary involved the continued superimposition of 3rds beyond seventh chords, producing **extended tertian harmonies.** Example 1 presents a typical jazz progression.

Example 1

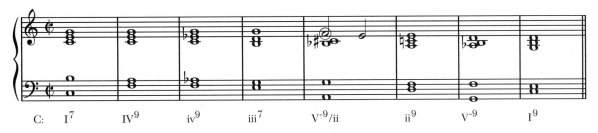

$$\text{C:} \quad \text{I}^7 \qquad \text{IV}^9 \qquad \text{iv}^9 \qquad \text{iii}^7 \qquad \text{V}^{-9}/\text{ii} \qquad \text{ii}^9 \qquad \text{V}^{-9} \qquad \text{I}^9$$

In all but the first and fourth chords, an additional 3rd is superimposed above each seventh chord, producing a **ninth chord.** Locate the 9th above

477

the root in each sonority. If we add another 3rd above a ninth chord, we produce an **eleventh chord.** We will regard these added 3rds as dissonances and treat them as suspension or neighboring figures, much like the chordal 7th in seventh chords. These "tall chords" tend to occur in root position, with the 9th or 11th usually appearing in an upper voice.[1]

After we present the various tertian extensions in this chapter, we will discuss triadic harmonies that contain added notes, such as added 6ths or added 9ths.

DOMINANT NINTH CHORDS

The various ninth chords are determined by the type of triad, 7th, and 9th that appear above a given root; in chord labels, these indications are written in consecutive order. For instance, using D as the root, a major-minor-major (MmM) ninth chord—often known simply as a major ninth chord—would be spelled as D F♯ A C E, where D F♯ A is the major triad, D to C is the minor 7th, and D to E is the major 9th. In a similar fashion, a major-minor-minor (Mmm) ninth chord—usually called a minor ninth chord—would be spelled as D F♯ A C E♭. In order for such a chord to be considered a legitimate ninth chord and not simply a triad with an added 9th, the 7th of the chord should be present.

We will begin by examining **dominant ninth chords,** ninth chords that are built on the dominant. If the interval of a major 9th appears above a V^7, the result is a V^9 (MmM ninth chord); if the interval of a minor 9th appears above the V^7, the result is a V^{-9} (Mmm ninth chord).

Example 2

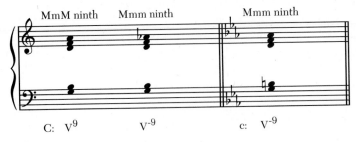

C: V^9 V^{-9} c: V^{-9}

Occasional dominant ninths occurred in the Baroque period as melodic extensions of the V^7 (Example 3).

---

1. The various chord types and commercial chord symbols for ninth and eleventh chords are given in Appendix 4.

Example 3 BACH(?): MINUET IN D MINOR FROM *ANNA MAGDALENA BACH'S NOTEBOOK,* BWV ANH. II:132

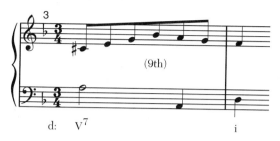

d: V⁷   i

It was not until the Classical era, however, that the 9th became a bona fide member of the V chord. We may generate dominant ninths by adding a 9th to an existing V⁷ (Example 4a), or by inserting a major 3rd below a vii°⁷ (Example 4b).

Example 4

A. KUHLAU: SONATINA IN C MAJOR, OP. 20, NO. 1, II   B.

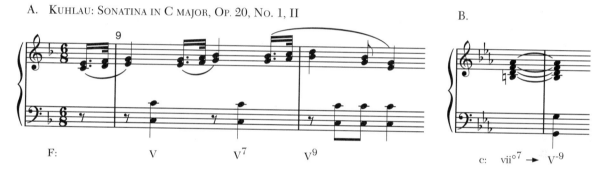

F: V   V⁷   V⁹   c: vii°⁷ ➞ V⁻⁹

By the middle of the nineteenth century, composers were using prolonged dominant ninths quite frequently. Franck's Violin Sonata daringly opens with a prolonged V⁹, which does not resolve until measure 8 (Example 5a). Wagner often lingered on this same chord, as his initial presentation of Brünnhilde's motive illustrates (Example 5b).

Example 5

A. FRANCK: VIOLIN SONATA IN A MAJOR, I

A: V⁹   ⟶

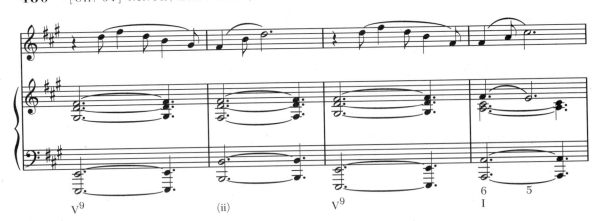

B. WAGNER: PROLOGUE TO *GÖTTERDÄMMERUNG,* ACT I (BRÜNNHILDE'S MOTIVE)

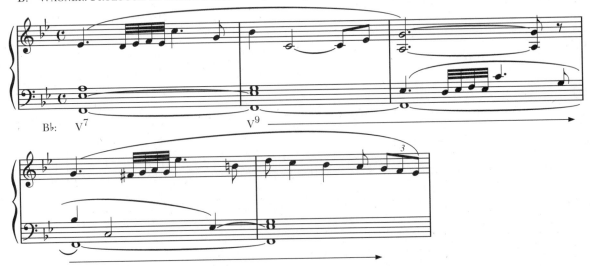

The Aug9th chord (G B D F A♯, for instance) is largely limited to twentieth-century jazz harmony. It can function either as a dominant or not. The 9th is often notated enharmonically, producing a "bluesy" chord with both a major and minor 3rd (in this case, B♮ and B♭).

Ninth chords usually occur in five-voice texture, with each chord member assigned to a different part. In four-voice writing, the chordal 5th is usually omitted. The dissonant 9th (scale degree $\hat{6}$ or ♭$\hat{6}$) will resolve downward to scale degree $\hat{5}$, either within the same chord (Example 6a) or in the tonic triad (Example 6b).

The approach to and resolution of the 9th normally involves a neighboring or suspension figure, as in Examples 7a and 7b. In the Wagner excerpt (Examples 7c and 7d), however, the 9th in the third measure is treated more freely as a chordal arpeggiation within the harmony.

Example 6

A.

B.

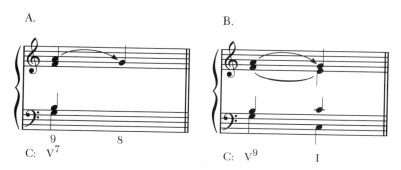

C: V^7

C: V^9 I

Example 7

A.

B.

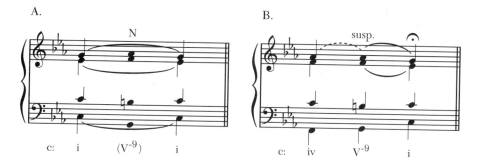

c: i   (V^{-9})   i

c: iv   V^{-9} i

C. WAGNER: *GÖTTERDÄMMERUNG*, ACT I

D. (REDUCTION)

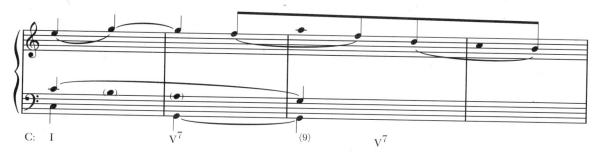

C: I   V^7 (9)   V^7

NONDOMINANT NINTH CHORDS

Nondominant ninth chords lack a tritone. Two types are most frequently encountered: the minor-minor-major (mmM) ninth chord (D F A C E) and the major-major-major (MMM) ninth chord (D F♯ A C♯ E). Examples of the former may be found as the ii⁹ of a major key or the iv⁹ of a minor key, while examples of the latter may be found as the I⁹ and IV⁹ of a major key.

Example 8

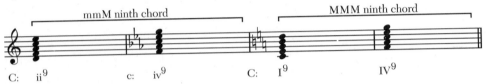

Go back to Example 1 and find all instances of nondominant ninth chords in it. Do you think parallel 5ths occur between measures 2 and 3? Although the treatment of the 7ths and 9ths is rather traditional in this example, in other jazz passages they sometimes occur freely, with little regard for customary approach and resolution.

ELEVENTH AND THIRTEENTH CHORDS

Most **eleventh chords** consist of a perfect 11th suspended over a V⁹ or a V⁻⁹. We can best explain eleventh and even thirteenth chords in terms of nonharmonic tones. Thus, a perfect 11th over a V⁹ (in a major key) or a V⁻⁹ (in a minor key) may be considered as a suspension that resolves to the 10th in the same harmony (11–10, or a compound 4–3). Since most eleventh and thirteenth chords in music literature contain a major 9th, we will assume that interval in our roman-numeral analysis (Example 9a). In those cases where a minor 9th occurs in these chords, we will indicate the minor 9th in the analysis (Example 9b).

Example 9

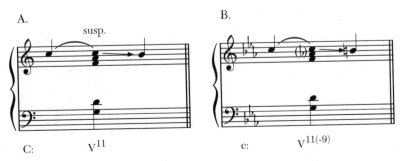

In a typical V^{11} the chordal 3rd is omitted, since it is the resolution note of the suspended 11th: G ( ) D F A C (B). Note, however, that this eleventh chord will always include a 7th and a 9th. In the second act of his opera *Die Meistersinger,* Wagner superimposes the open strings of Beckmesser's lute over an A^2 to produce a V^{11}, which then resolves to a V^7 in D major (Example 10a). On the other hand, the 11th (C^5) in the prolonged dominant of the Grieg excerpt (Example 10b) avoids the expected resolution to B^5.

Example 10

A. WAGNER: BECKMESSER'S SERENADE FROM *DIE MEISTERSINGER,* ACT II

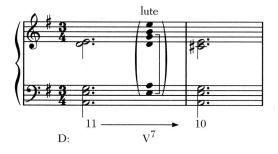

B. GRIEG: PIANO CONCERTO, I

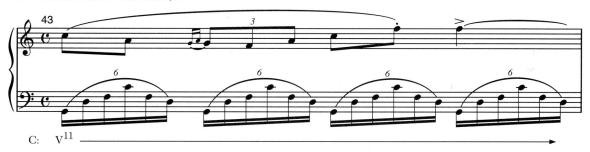

Nondominant eleventh chords are usually complete (see the Ravel excerpt in Example 11a).

Examples of **thirteenth chords** are extremely rare in the music of the eighteenth and nineteenth centuries. The Ravel passage in Example 11a more properly adheres to twentieth-century compositional techniques, yet its tonal language is completely diatonic. The bridge to Victor Young's movie song, shown in reduction in Example 11b, includes chordal 11ths and even a 13th, all of which resolve downward by stepwise motion.

Note the Aug11th chord (F A C E♭ G B) in the Victor Young ballad. Other forms of thirteenth chords may be found in jazz progressions, such as G D F A♭ B E (where the B is the displaced 3rd of the chord) or G B F A♭ D♭ (= C♯?) E, spelled upward from G. These harmonies usually function as dominants.

Example 11

A. RAVEL: "RIGAUDON" FROM *TOMBEAU DE COUPERIN*

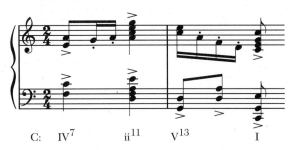

C: IV⁷   ii¹¹   V¹³   I

B. VICTOR YOUNG "STELLA BY STARLIGHT" (REDUCTION)

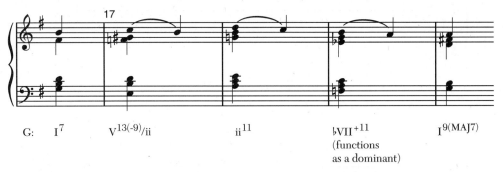

G: I⁷   V¹³⁽⁻⁹⁾/ii   ii¹¹   ♭VII⁺¹¹   I⁹⁽ᴹᴬᴶ⁷⁾
                                              (functions
                                              as a dominant)

At cadences we may encounter what appears to be an incomplete dominant thirteenth chord with its 9th and 11th omitted. In reality, this chord is nothing more than a V⁷ with a melodic 6–5 over the root (Example 12a). The chordal 5th (or scale degree $\hat{2}$) may be missing altogether (Example 12b). Although this 6–5 technique occurs in the Bizet quotation (Example 12c), the harmonies on the third beat of measures 21 and 22 are eleventh chords that are created by neighboring motion, as shown in the reduction. Note the distinction between stemmed and unstemmed noteheads in this and the preceding examples. Remember that chordal 7ths, 9ths, 11ths, and 13ths above the root are always treated as embellishing notes.

Example 12

A.   B.

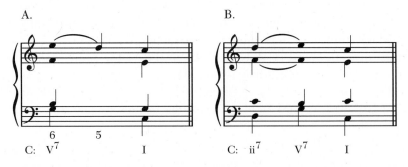

       6   5
C: V⁷   I   C: ii⁷   V⁷   I

C. BIZET: MICAELA'S ARIA FROM *CARMEN*, ACT III

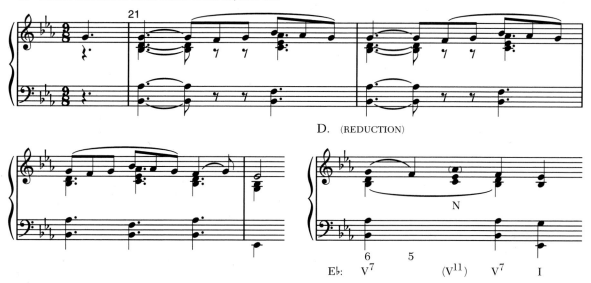

D. (REDUCTION)

Eb: V^7 (V^{11}) V^7 I

ADDED NOTES: 6THS AND 9THS

In Chapter 18 we discussed a 5–6 or 6–5 motion above the tonic triad or tonic root (p. 241). An example of this linear motion occurs in measure 8 of the Franck excerpt above (Example 5). It is also possible to add a major 6th to an existing tonic triad so that the added 6th (D) forms part of the actual harmony. The chordal spacing in Example 13a suggests an F-major triad with an **added 6th** (F A C D), rather than a minor-seventh chord over D (D F A C). Compare this model to the chord in the Wagner excerpt (Example 13b).

Example 13

A.   B. WAGNER: RHINEDAUGHTERS' SCENE FROM *GÖTTERDÄMMERUNG*, ACT III

F$^{(add6)}$ Dm^7 F: I$^{(add6)}$

We may also add a major 9th to a triad (C E G D, or I^{add9}). Do not confuse this **added 9th** with a ninth chord, since no chordal 7th is present here. The addition of a 6th or 9th is not confined to tonic harmony alone. Analyze the cadential progression shown in Example 14, identifying any added notes.

Example 14

The presence of both a major 6th and a major 9th in a major triad (C E G A D, or $I^{add6 \ and \ 9}$) produces a harmony with a distinct pentatonic flavor.[2] Study the two excerpts from Gustav Mahler's *Das Lied von der Erde* in Example 15.

Example 15

A.   MAHLER: *DAS LIED VON DER ERDE*, I

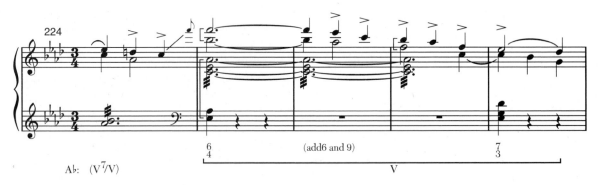

B.   MAHLER: *DAS LIED VON DER ERDE*, V

2.   See Appendix 2, which discusses pentatonic scales.

The climactic harmony in the second measure of Example 15a is an A♭ $^6_4$ chord to which is added a 9th (B♭^{5}) and a 6th (F^6) in the upper voices; both resolve stepwise to the chordal A♭^{5} and E♭^{6} (by parallel 5ths) in the following measure, only to appear once more before the $^6_4$ eventually moves to the V^7 in the last bar. Although both may be explained as nonharmonic tones, their extended length gives them a kind of chordal status. Since this colossal five-movement work continually shifts between the key centers of A minor and C major, the last movement's final C-major triad with an added 6th (C E G A) may represent a melding of the two tonic triads: C E G and A C E (Example 15b).

Terms and Concepts for Review

extended tertian sonorities
ninth chord
dominant *vs.* nondominant ninth chords
preparation and resolution of ninth
 chords

eleventh chord
the suspended 4th in eleventh chords
thirteenth chords *vs.* 6–5 or 5–6 in V^7
 chords
added 6ths and 9ths

Embellishing Chromatic Chords

CERTAIN CHROMATIC CHORDS function as neighboring or passing embellishing harmonies, decorating or elaborating the underlying diatonic voice leading and giving a wider range of tonal color to harmonic progressions. These chromatic harmonies, marked with arrows in Example 1, are unstable chords, such as augmented triads, altered V^7's, diminished sevenths, and Aug6th chords, that need resolution. The slurs in this example emphasize the approach to and departure from the altered note(s) in these chords.

Example 1

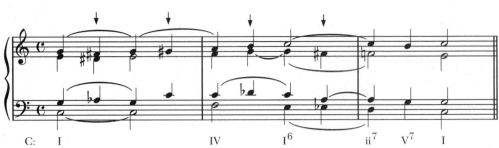

C: I   IV   I^6 ii^7 V^7 I

In this chapter we will examine each of the chords listed above in turn. After discussing some examples of unusual linear chromatic sonorities, we will focus on those altered harmonies in both modes that defy functional categorization.

AUGMENTED TRIADS AS PASSING OR NEIGHBORING CHORDS

Like the diminished triad, the augmented triad is an ambiguous sonority that cannot be tonicized because it lacks a perfect 5th. The augmented triad functions as an embellishing or linear chord in harmonic progressions. We have already discussed its occurrence in the minor mode as a passing chord over V; see Chapter 18, Example 12, and Example 2 below.

Example 2

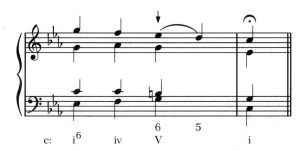

In the major mode, transient augmented triads may result from chromatic passing motion within the progressions V–I and I–IV, or from bridging a 5–6 motion over the tonic. Some theorists prefer to use roman numerals to denote root-position augmented triads, such as that in the progression I–I$^{\sharp 5}$–IV. However, a simple $^{5-\sharp 5}$ given as a figured-bass symbol is sufficient to denote this triad's passing nature (Example 3).

Example 3

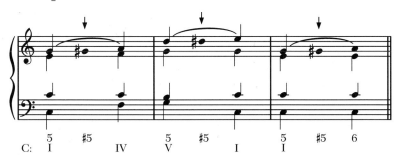

When a first-inversion triad contains a raised chordal 5th, we will use a roman-numeral designation in our analyses I+⁶, which we will enclose in parentheses to show the chord's passing nature; refer to the Schumann passage (Examples 4a and 4b). In the Beethoven quotation (Examples 4c and 4d), we may consider the pair of augmented triads as chromatic applied dominants to IV and V, respectively. In what inversion do the altered chords appear?

Example 4

A. SCHUMANN: "LITTLE STUDY"
FROM *ALBUM FOR THE YOUNG*, OP. 68, NO. 14

B. (REDUCTION)

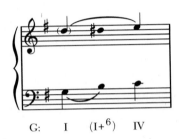

C. BEETHOVEN: BAGATELLE IN C MAJOR, OP. 119, NO. 8

D. (REDUCTION)

Augmented triads may also result from half-step neighboring motion in embellishing progressions.

Example 5

A.

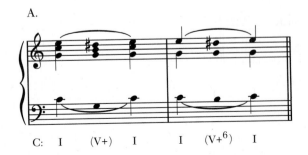

B. WOLF: "DAS VERLASSENE MÄGDLEIN," FROM *MÖRIKE-LIEDER*

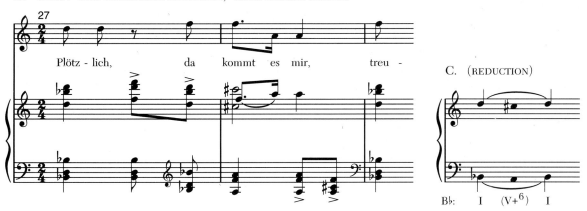

C. (REDUCTION)

Bb: I   (V+⁶)   I

Compare the two models in Example 5a to the passage from Wolf's song (Example 5b), whose forlorn mood is determined to a great extent by the harmonic coloring provided by augmented triads. We will once again use roman-numeral symbols to denote this neighboring motion.

The unique, pungent quality of this chord has often been invoked to depict grief or death, as shown in the elaborated $^6_4$ cadence of the Gibbons madrigal in Example 6. Note that the raised chordal 5th in this excerpt, which is spelled as a lowered 6th, occurs over the word "death" (indicated with an arrow) in the text.

Example 6   ORLANDO GIBBONS: "THE SILVER SWAN"

Wagner, on the other hand, habitually associated the augmented triad with energy, fire, or fear in his operatic *Ring* cycle. In Siegfried's forging song, the V+ resolves deceptively to a VI in D minor; notice the parallel 5ths in its reduction (Example 7).

Example 7 WAGNER: FORGING SONG FROM *SIEGFRIED*, END OF ACT I

A.

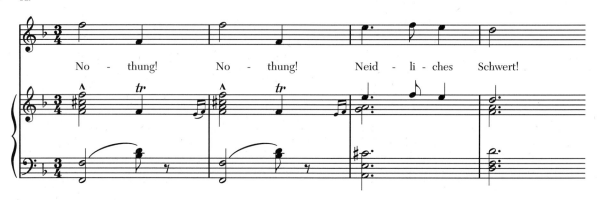

B. (REDUCTION)

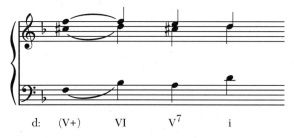

ALTERED V⁷ CHORDS

Another type of embellishing chord results when the chordal 5th of the V^7 is chromatically raised or lowered by a half step ($V+^7$ or $V°^7$), as in Example 8.

FOR FURTHER STUDY

In some of the late works of Franz Liszt, the augmented triad is extended or "composed-out" by various means. For instance, in his song "Blume und Duft" (1860) the keys or significant harmonies of the successive sections arpeggiate an augmented triad: A♭ (a prolongation of an Aug6th chord in mm. 1–4), C (the first section, mm. 5–20), E⁷ (at the end of the next section, mm. 22–27), and A♭ (in the piano coda, mm. 28–31).

Example 8

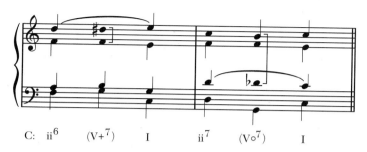

C: ii⁶   (V+⁷)   I   ii⁷   (V∘⁷)   I

In both cases, this chromatic alteration produces an unstable **altered V⁷** sonority that contains the interval of an augmented 6th: F–D♯ in the first model and D♭–B in the second. (Roman-numeral labeling of altered V⁷ chords has never been standardized. The method we will employ expresses the quality of the chordal 5th alone by means of the ∘ and + and then the inversion of the chord by figured bass symbols.) With the V+⁷, the augmented 6th ($\hat{4}$–$\sharp\hat{2}$) must be resolved by moving outward melodically to an octave on the 3rd of the tonic triad. With the V∘⁷ the augmented 6th ♭$\hat{2}$–$\hat{7}$ must melodically expand to the tonic octave. We resolve the upper voices of a root-position altered V⁷ chord by half step and usually derive the altered tone by passing motion. How is this chord approached and resolved in Example 9?

Example 9

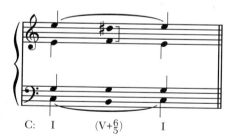

C: I   (V+$\frac{6}{5}$)   I

In the Brahms excerpt in Example 10, we could analyze the V∘$\frac{4}{3}$ as a Fr$\frac{4}{3}$ of I. The recurring theme on which the set of variations in this Finale is based first appears in the soprano. (After the first four statements, this theme reverts to its customary position in the bass voice.) Since the progression that underlies this theme opens with an A-minor chord, we might be tempted to consider the final E-major triad as V in that key. For the remainder of the movement, however, the theme usually begins and ends in the tonic key of E minor.

Example 10   BRAHMS: SYMPHONY NO. 4, IV

The serpentine, chromatic motion of these altered dominants made them a favorite harmony in sentimental and maudlin ballads of the early 1900s, such as the Nevin song in Example 11a. In other pieces they may even function as applied chords. In the Strauss excerpt (Example 11c), for instance, the V+⁷ operates as a secondary dominant to IV.

Example 11

EMBELLISHING OR COMMON-TONE DIMINISHED SEVENTH CHORDS

We have previously treated the diminished seventh chord as an embellishing dominant (vii°[7]) that precedes either the tonic or some other diatonic triad; in such instances all of the chord members resolve by step.[1] We may, however, encounter diminished seventh chords that contain a common tone with the following harmony. We call this family of chromatic chords **common-tone diminished sevenths.** A common-tone diminished seventh is generally spelled by taking the root of its chord of resolution and making it the 7th of the diminished seventh chord; using I in C major, for instance, this would be D♯ F♯ A C.

These **embellishing diminished sevenths** function as either neighboring or passing chords. In the former case, they will usually neighbor either I (Example 12a) or V([7]) (Example 12c); the common tone tends to occur in the bass voice.

Example 12

A. RICHARD RODGERS: "BALI HA'I" FROM *SOUTH PACIFIC*

B. (REDUCTION)

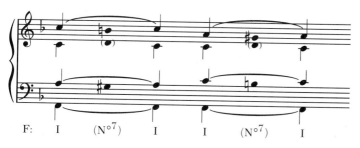

F: I   (N°[7])   I   I   (N°[7])   I

1. The dominant function of this chord is discussed in Chapters 21 and 25.

C. WAGNER: HANS SACH'S MONOLOGUE
FROM *DIE MEISTERSINGER*, ACT II

D. (REDUCTION)

 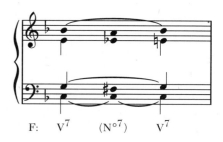

F: V⁷ (N°⁷) V⁷

E. SCHUBERT: STRING QUINTET IN C MAJOR, I

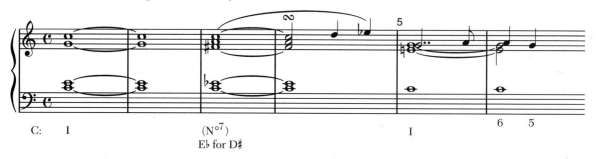

C: I (N°⁷) I
E♭ for D♯ 6 5

We denote these diminished seventh chords by labels that stress their linear derivation. Thus, in Example 12 they are labeled N°⁷, which specifies a neighboring function, and in Example 13 as P°⁷, which specifies a passing function. We usually double the 5th of the tonic harmony that follows a N°⁷; this allows stepwise motion to and from the ♯$\hat4$ (C–B♮–C) and $\hat6$ (C–D–C) in the embellishing neighbor chord. Occasionally, one of the notes in the N°⁷ may be respelled enharmonically, as in the common-tone diminished seventh chord of C major: D♯ (= E♭) F♯ A C. In the quotation from the Schubert Quintet (Example 12e), the E♭ is necessary to maintain a diatonic melodic line in the upper voice: C–D–E♭–G, not C–D–D♯–G.

In Example 13a, the progression I–V$^4_3$–I⁶ is filled in with P°⁷'s. The common tones between these chords and those that follow them are indicated with ties. The outer voices move in parallel chromatic 10ths. Between what two chords does the P°⁷ occur in the Cole Porter song (Example 13c)? In cases where the passing motion descends, the diminished seventh chord shows a common tone with the chord that *precedes* rather than follows it. This progression was a common idiom in popular tunes of the 1930s.

Example 13

A. TCHAIKOVSKY: SYMPHONY NO. 5, III

B. (REDUCTION)

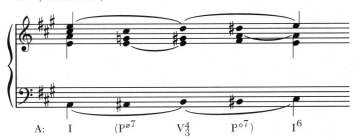

A: I   (P⌀7   V$^4_3$ P°7)   I⁶

C. COLE PORTER: "EV'RY TIME WE SAY GOODBYE"   D. (REDUCTION)

   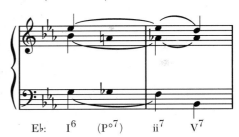

E♭:   I⁶   (P°7)   ii⁷   V⁷

COMMON-TONE AUGMENTED SIXTH CHORDS

If we substitute a ♭$\hat{6}$ for the ♮$\hat{6}$ of a diminished seventh chord that neighbors the tonic, we create an **embellishing German Aug6th chord.** The embellishing German Aug6th may function as either a neighboring or passing harmony. Example 14 illustrates a German sixth that neighbors I; note the half-step voice leading from $\hat{3}$, the doubled $\hat{5}$ in the resolution chord, and the common tone in the bass. The enharmonic notation (♯$\hat{2}$ for ♭$\hat{3}$) is seen frequently in such progressions.

Example 14

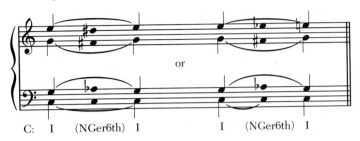

C: I   (NGer6th)   I   I   (NGer6th)   I

In the following Schubert waltz (Example 15a), an embellishing diminished seventh chord is chromatically changed into a Ger$\frac{4}{2}$—that is, a German Aug6th chord in $\frac{4}{2}$ rather than $\frac{6}{5}$ position—which resolves to a I^6. In prolongations of I over a tonic pedal, as in Example 15b, passing motion through ii or iv may also include a common-tone Aug6th chord. In the Verdi excerpt, the upper voices move almost exclusively by half step.

Example 15

A. SCHUBERT: WALTZ IN F MAJOR, OP. 9, NO. 36

F: (CT°^{7} CTGer$\frac{4}{2}$)   I^6 ii^6 V^7 I

B. VERDI: QUARTET FROM *RIGOLETTO*, ACT IV   C. (REDUCTION)

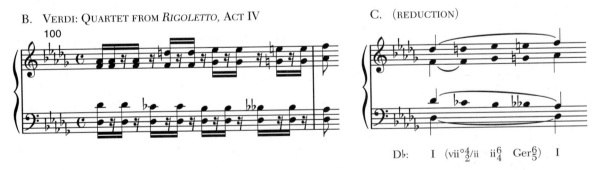

D♭:   I   (vii°$\frac{4}{2}$/ii   ii$^6_4$ Ger$^6_5$)   I

The excerpts in Example 16 exploit either common-tone diminished seventh or German sixth harmonies. Identify the altered chord in each passage and indicate whether it represents neighboring or passing motion.

Example 16

A. OFFENBACH: BARCAROLLE FROM *TALES OF HOFFMANN*, ACT II

B. (REDUCTION)

C. LISZT: "ES MUSS EIN WUNDERBARES SEIN"

D. (REDUCTION)

E. ALBENIZ: "CADIZ" FROM *SUITE ESPAGNOLE*

F. (REDUCTION)

G. WAGNER: "TRÄUME" FROM *WESENDONCK SONGS*

THE USE OF CHROMATICISM TO CREATE MODAL AMBIGUITY

The opening fifteen measures of Brahms's Third Symphony, given in reduction in Example 17, provide an excellent review of the chromatic chords we have discussed thus far in Part Three. Here, the key of F major is infused with chromatic coloring through the use of mixture chords, Neapolitan chords, and embellishing and common-tone diminished seventh chords. The principal motive of the movement (F^4–Ab^4–F^5) is first presented in the soprano (mm. 1–3) and is immediately restated in the bass (mm. 3–5). The motive's Ab ($b\hat{3}$) suggests a modal conflict between F major and its parallel, F minor. This modal duality is extended by other harmonies containing mixture scale degrees ($b\hat{2}$, $b\hat{3}$, $b\hat{6}$, $b\hat{7}$). In the missing blanks between parentheses, supply roman-numeral indications for these chords.

Example 17 BRAHMS: SYMPHONY NO. 3, I (REDUCTION OF MM. 1–15)

The remainder of this movement continues to exploit large-scale mixture tonicizations ($\boxed{\text{III}}$ in the exposition and $\boxed{bVI}$ in the development). Parallel modal relations influence the other movements as well. For instance, a change of mode (from F major to F minor) occurs between the first and fourth movements, and another (from C major to C minor) between the second and third movements. The symphony ends in the tonic major, with a reference to the opening theme that provides a "cyclical" conclusion.

UNUSUAL LINEAR CHORDS

We may encounter occasional passages in which the linear movement of the voices produces a chordal sonority that makes little or no analytical sense when viewed in any other way. You should avoid labeling with a roman numeral any chord that seems to result from chromatic passing or neighboring motion alone. The particular notation or spelling of such chords is determined by the direction in which the melodic lines are moving. Study the sonorities marked with arrows in the three passages of Example 18.

Example 18

A. BEETHOVEN: PIANO SONATA IN D MAJOR, OP. 28, III

B. (REDUCTION)

D: V⁶/vi vi IV⁶ (P) V⁶₅

C. TCHAIKOVSKY: "WALTZ OF THE FLOWERS" FROM *THE NUTCRACKER*

D. (REDUCTION)

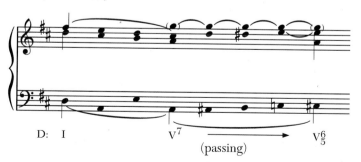

D: I   V⁷ —————————→ V⁶₅
              (passing)

E. MOZART: SYMPHONY NO. 40, I

In the Beethoven excerpt, the chord marked is not a misspelled C-minor triad but rather a passing sonority that result from chromatic motion between IV⁶ and V⁶. The Tchaikovsky waltz involves a chromatic prolongation of the dominant. The strangely dissonant harmonies that appear in the Mozart symphony are all chromatic neighbors to the V⁷.

ADDITIONAL CHROMATIC CHORDS IN THE MAJOR AND MINOR MODES

There remain a number of altered major and minor triads that cannot be said to fall into any clearly defined category of tonal function. These chords are spelled out in Example 19 in both modes (C major and C minor). We have arranged the triads in each mode in a descending-5th progression moving toward the tonic, first on the "sharp" side and then on the "flat" side. (This grouping has little to do with their usage in actual passages of music.)

Example 19

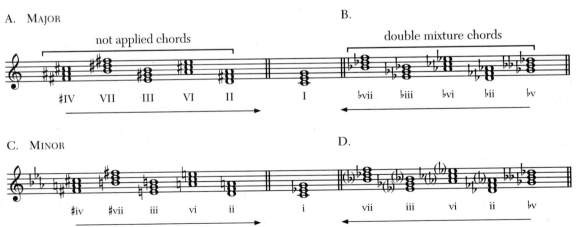

Although the major-mode chords with sharps resemble secondary dominants of diatonic pitches (Example 19a), they may not always function that way. For instance, in Schumann's Fantasy (Example 20a), the composer interpolates an A-major triad between I and IV; this altered chord stands in a chromaticized 3rd relationship to the functional harmonies that surround it.

Example 20

A. SCHUMANN: PIANO FANTASY IN C MAJOR, OP. 17, III

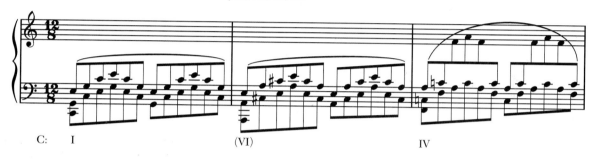

C: I   (VI)   IV

B. CHOPIN: PRELUDE IN E MAJOR, OP. 28, NO. 9

E: I   iv   I   V   I   IV   ♭iii   V/♭III   ♭III   V
                        ♭II

I

C. FRANCK: PIANO QUINTET IN F MINOR, I

C♯:   I   (♭vi)   I

The chords in Example 19b represent mixture harmonies that are mutated into minor triads. These sonorities are sometimes called **double mixture chords** since they represent a two-step borrowing from the minor mode, first the chord itself and then its minor version: thus ♭III becomes ♭iii, and ♭VI becomes ♭vi. In the Chopin excerpt (Example 20b), the tonicization of the Neapolitan (♭II) is followed by a sequential tonicization of ♭iii (indicated by the arrow), before the final cadence in E major. César Franck seemed especially fond of the ♭vi relation (Example 20c).

The two groups of triads in the minor mode in Example 19 include some mixture chords borrowed from the major mode (Example 19c) and diatonic chords that are mutated into minor triads (Example 19d).

The infrequent triads shown in Example 19 occur typically as **vagrant harmonies** that provide a momentary chromatic coloring to diatonic progressions. In some harmonic sequences they may lack any sense of tonal function and may contribute to a temporary suspension of key feeling. For a good example of this, refer to Example 6 in Chapter 39.

Partwriting Procedures and Melody Harmonization

In four-voice texture you should avoid doubling chromatic or altered notes within the chords discussed in this chapter since these notes usually function as tendency or active tones whose resolution would produce parallel octaves. With altered V⁷'s, the resulting augmented 6th must be resolved to an octave (see Example 8). The doubled $\hat{5}$ in I or V provides an anchor note for neighboring diminished seventh and German sixth chords; the bass usually serves as the common tone (refer to Examples 12a, 12c, and 14). To create more diatonic lines, you may wish to respell an altered note enharmonically (see Example 12e).

When harmonizing a melody, examine the tune for points where embellishing chromatic chords could be employed. Half-step motion in the melody, such as $\hat{2}-\sharp\hat{2}-\hat{3}$ or $\hat{5}-\sharp\hat{4}-\hat{5}$, can usually be harmonized with a passing or neighboring altered chord. However, try to resist the temptation to indulge in excessive chromaticism.

A diatonic melodic phrase and its setting are given in Example 21a. In the following harmonization (Example 21b), the tune is underlaid with an assortment of embellishing chromatic chords. Make a roman-numeral analysis of this passage and indicate each altered harmony.

Example 21

A.

B.

Terms and Concepts for Review

passing *or* neighboring motion embellishing chromatic chords
altered V[7] chords
embellishing *or* common-tone diminished sevenths and augmented sixths

linear chromatic chords
double mixture chords
vagrant harmonies

Dominant Prolongation

WE ARE ALREADY FAMILIAR with various ways of prolonging tonic harmony through the use of arpeggiated tonic triads or embellishing passing and neighboring chords. We have also seen how these same techniques may extend dominant and even pre-dominant harmonies. Instances of short-term **dominant prolongation** using embellishing chords appear in Example 9 in Chapter 13 and Example 8a in Chapter 16. In this chapter we will examine some examples of more lengthy dominant prolongations. These prolongations, which may employ various chromatic harmonies, are usually featured in introductory passages, retransitions, $^6_4$ cadences, and passages preceding musical climaxes.

When we protract the dominant function, the psychological effect is quite different from that of a tonic extension. While a prolongation of I results in tonal stability or stasis, a prolongation of V creates tonal suspense, heightening the expectation of an eventual resolution to the tonic.

In this chapter we will first examine two short passages (Example 1) that employ chromatic embellishment in prolonging the dominant; then we will focus on the different musical situations in which dominant prolongation is used. In all of the examples provided in this chapter, you should note the psychological effect produced by this technique.

SHORT-TERM CHROMATIC PROLONGATIONS OF V(7)

The two excerpts in Example 1 illustrate how dominant harmony may be momentarily prolonged by chromatic passing motion.

Example 1

A. MOZART: PIANO SONATA IN B♭ MAJOR, K.333, III

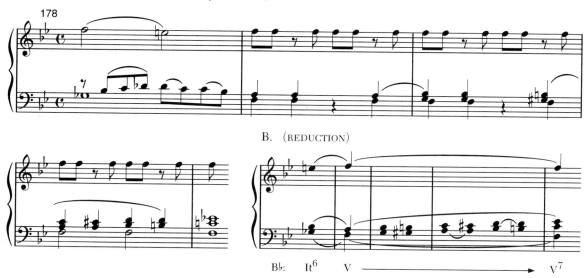

B. (REDUCTION)

B♭:   It⁶   V ⟶⟶⟶⟶⟶ V⁷

C. BRAHMS: CAPRICCIO IN D MINOR, OP. 116, NO. 1

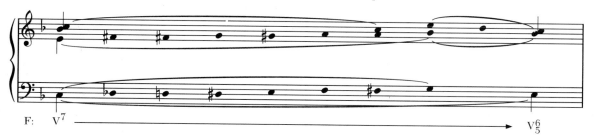

D. (REDUCTION)

F: V⁷ ⟶⟶⟶⟶⟶⟶ V⁶₅

In the Mozart passage (Example 1a) the root of the V⁷ is retained in the bass and soprano while the inner voices exhibit ascending chromatic movement. The Brahms excerpt (Example 1c) rhythmically staggers the chromatic motion between the bass and an upper part; the root and 7th of the V⁷ are held in the two highest voices.

DOMINANT PROLONGATION IN INTRODUCTORY PASSAGES

Some compositions open with an introductory passage that acts as a preparation for the initial tonic theme. Such introductions often include an extended dominant harmony. Sectionalized pieces such as marches, rags, or polkas frequently display an elaboration of dominant harmony in their brief introductions (see Example 9 in Chapter 13). The concert waltzes of Johann Strauss provide more extended examples of this same technique.

An interesting instance of dominant prolongation occurs in the introduction to Chopin's Polonaise in A♭ major. Since this section is rather lengthy, Example 2 provides a reduction of the first seventeen measures; you should listen to the passage while following this reduction.

Example 2 CHOPIN: POLONAISE IN A♭ MAJOR, OP. 53

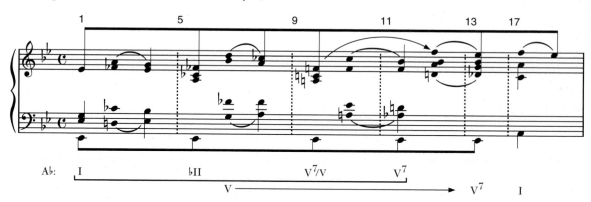

The initial V triad is tonicized and prolonged through a rising chromatic progression through ♭II and V⁷/V, each of which employs an embellishing harmony (Ger°3 and vii°7, respectively). Once the dominant harmony is established by its own applied dominant seventh, it resolves to the tonic in measure 17. Observe that the soprano ascends chromatically E♭⁴–F♭⁴–F♮⁴. The last F (m. 12) then acts as an upper neighbor that anticipates the 6–5 motive of the first A♭-major theme (m. 17).

PROLONGATION OF THE DOMINANT IN RETRANSITION PASSAGES

In many pieces in which the original theme returns in the tonic (within a two-reprise, ternary, or sonata form), the retransition leading to this return frequently includes a prolongation of dominant harmony, often supported by a pedal on $\hat{5}$. The resulting sense of anticipation psychologically prepares us for the return of the tonic and the original theme. (An instance may be found in Example 13 of Chapter 19, where the extended V^7 in mm. 9–12 immediately precedes the return of the initial tonic theme in m. 13.) The methods used for prolonging retransitional dominants are varied, limited only by the imagination of the composer. For instance, in Example 3 of Chapter 23 the dominant prolongation occupies the entire initial section of the second reprise (mm. 51–64).

A typical case of dominant prolongation within sonata form may be found in the retransition of the Beethoven sonata movement in Example 3.

Example 3 BEETHOVEN: PIANO SONATA IN C MINOR, OP. 10, NO. 1, I

The harmonic motion to the retransition is prepared by the chromatic ascent $\hat{3}-\hat{4}-\sharp\hat{4}-\hat{5}$ in the bass (mm. 136–138). Once the V is established in measure 138, a series of $^6_3$ triads descend stepwise over the dominant pedal. After regaining the upper octave, the second sequence of $^6_3$ triads descends to $\hat{2}$, which then resolves to the tonic. The entire passage represents a prolongation of scale degree $\hat{2}$ over V, as the voice-leading reduction illustrates.

PROLONGATION OF THE CADENTIAL $^6_4$ FORMULA

We noted earlier (in discussing Example 6 of Chapter 16) that the improvised cadenza of a Classical solo concerto consists of a "composing-out" of a cadential $^6_4$. Similar extensions of the $^6_4$ are often written out by the composer. In the retransitional passage from Mendelssohn's "Behold a Star from Jacob Shining" (Example 4), the $^6_4$ in the parallel minor (m. 53) is prolonged by a series of mixture and applied harmonies.

Although there are several transient resolutions to i^6 and i (see mm. 56 and 58), the consistent texture and even the text of this excerpt support an arpeggiation of the $^6_4$, spanning the octave E$\flat^5$–E$\flat^4$ in the soprano. The dominant eventually resolves via $\hat{2}$ over a V$^4_2$ to the I^6 (mm. 63–64), which marks the return of the original theme in E$\flat$ major; consult the accompanying reductions. The harmonies that Mendelssohn uses with this change of mode provide a good review of the chromatic chords we have already discussed. Make a roman-numeral analysis of the passage.

Example 4   MENDELSSOHN: "BEHOLD A STAR FROM JACOB SHINING" FROM *CHRISTUS*
(ENGLISH TRANSLATION)

A.

B. (REDUCTION 1)

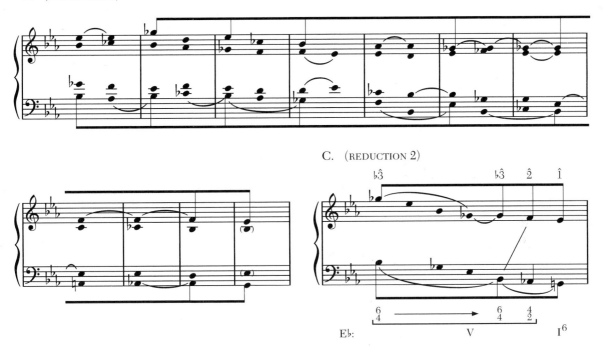

C. (REDUCTION 2)

A more radical handling of this procedure may be found in the first movement of Gustav Mahler's *Das Lied von der Erde* (Example 5).

Example 5 MAHLER: *Das Lied von der Erde,* I

The underlying $^6_4$ cadence that begins in measure 2 of this excerpt is overlaid with exotic linear motion. Note the brief chromatic voice exchange between the vocal part and the upper orchestral voice in the approach to the final resolution, which is temporarily diverted by an embellishing $^6_4$ over I.

DOMINANT PROLONGATION AS CLIMACTIC PREPARATION

Composers in the Romantic period were fond of utilizing a lengthy dominant prolongation to build toward a musical climax. (Beethoven had already realized the potential of this device; for instance, see mm. 99–109 in the initial movement of his "Eroica" Symphony.) After the first presentation of Romeo's theme in *Romeo and Juliet,* Tchaikovsky could not resist employing an extended dominant preparation leading to the theme's impassioned repetition. Observe the rising series of transient tonicizations over the dominant pedal, which the reduction highlights (Example 6).

Example 6   Tchaikovsky: *Romeo and Juliet* (simplified)

Extended dominant prolongations remained common in late Romantic music. In the mature music dramas of Richard Wagner, the role of the tonic chord diminishes to the point that the sense of tonal key feeling is often implied primarily by the dominant function. As we shall see in Chapter 36, the Prelude to Act I of *Tristan und Isolde* contains a prolongation of the V^7 that spans the opening sixteen measures; the first true tonic triad does not appear until measure 24.

Although the tonic and dominant are the most commonly prolonged harmonies, other harmonies are prolonged as well (for example, the Neapolitan triad in Example 19 of Chapter 28). In Chapter 39 we will see how the equal division of the octave gives rise to other types of prolongations.

Terms and Concepts for Review

dominant prolongations:
  by chromatic embellishment
  in introductions

in retransitions
as extensions of cadential $^6_4$
as climactic preparation

Modulation to Foreign Keys I

O UR DISCUSSION OF modulation in the preceding chapters has focused on tonal schemes employing closely related keys, in which all the keys that serve as new tonal goals have signatures with only one accidental more or less than the tonic. Baroque composers such as Bach and Handel were usually content to work within this range of keys.[1] By the Classical era, composers were exploring more remote tonal regions as goals within the modulatory sections of sonatas and other large-scale compositions. The signatures of these **foreign keys** differ from the original tonic key by more than one accidental. The substitution of foreign keys for the traditional closely related keys led to more diverse tonal schemes.

In this chapter we will begin by categorizing the more common foreign key relationships found in the common-practice period. We will then discuss three basic procedures for modulation: by change of mode, by common tone, and by pivot chord. Finally, we will chart the succession of foreign keys in two of Beethoven's development sections. Some additional ways of modulating to foreign keys will be examined in Chapter 38.

---

1. Foreign key relationships are often encountered in fantasias, toccatas, and recitatives of the Baroque period.

CHANGE-OF-MODE MODULATION

Modal exchange, discussed previously in Chapter 27, provides an efficient means of modulating to foreign keys. These **change-of-mode modulations** involve a mutation of the original key from major to minor, or vice versa. By substituting C minor for C major, for instance, we can move to any key that is closely related to the parallel mode but foreign to the original tonic. The possible tonal relations arising from a change-of-mode modulation are summarized in Figure 1; the right-hand diagram shows C as the tonic. The ↕ sign denotes the original mutation between major and minor.

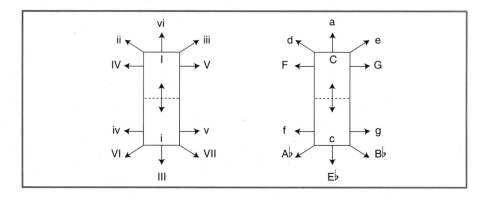

Figure 1

Change-of-mode modulations tend to occur either in a modulatory section that explores a variety of different keys or in a contrasting middle part of a sectional work such as a ternary or rondo form. In Example 1, the exposition section in the first movement of Mozart's familiar sonata closes with

Example 1   MOZART: PIANO SONATA IN C MAJOR, K.545, I

A.

2. The repeated first section of a Classical sonata form is called the *exposition* of the movement. It is characterized by a tonal motion from ⃞I to ⃞V (in major), or ⃞i to ⃞III (in minor). Consult the discussion of sonata form in Excursion II: More Complex Forms.

B. (REDUCTION)

G: I   V⁷   I   V⁷   I   g: i   V⁷   i   V⁷   i

[v]: iv   —   V⁷   i

an arpeggiated flourish in the dominant area.[2] At the beginning of the development section, G major suddenly changes to G minor; a pivot chord (i = iv) then leads to D minor or [v], a key in a foreign tonal relationship to G major.

In Haydn's D-major rondo (Example 2), the switch to the parallel minor occurs abruptly at the opening of the first episode or contrasting section.[3] D minor then moves to F major, with its [♭III] relationship to the tonic.

---

3. In rondo form, the refrain represents the thematic idea or section in the tonic that recurs periodically throughout the movement. It alternates with episodes or contrasting sections that employ other keys or the parallel mode. See Excursion I: Simple Forms for a discussion of Rondo form.

Example 2 HAYDN: PIANO SONATA IN D MAJOR, HOB. XVI:37, III

A.

B. (REDUCTION)

The music later retraces its path back to D minor, and the opening theme of the movement reappears in the original D-major tonic.

In change-of-mode modulations from major to minor, the usual foreign goal is ♭III of the original key. In change-of-mode modulations from minor to major, which are more typical of the Romantic period, a common tonal goal is vi of the original key. In the second strophe of Schubert's "Der Weg-weiser," for instance, after G major replaces the tonic G minor, the music moves to an implied vi (E minor, its relative minor) through two deceptive cadences and a half cadence, marked by brackets in the score (Example 3).

Example 3   SCHUBERT: "DER WEGWEISER" FROM *WINTERREISE*

Habe ja doch nichts begangen
dass ich Menschen sollte scheun,
welch ein thörichtes Verlangen
treibt mich in die Wüsteneien?

I have yet done nothing
that I should shun men,
What foolish desire
drives me into the desert?

Observe the unexpected return to the original key (marked with an arrow) near the end of the excerpt. A literal translation of the German text reveals the correlation of text and music.

MODULATIONS TO FOREIGN KEYS IN THE MAJOR MODE

Modulations to foreign keys tend to occur more frequently in major keys; we will focus our attention only on the more common foreign key relations

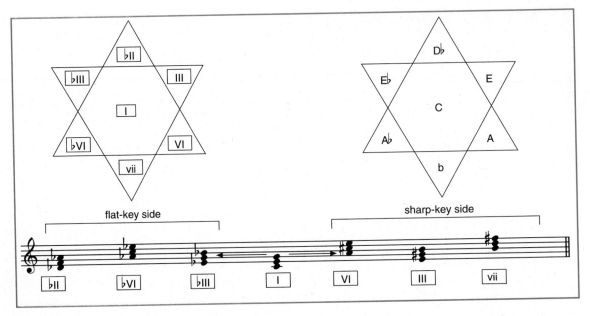

Figure 2

in that mode. These relations can be divided into two groups and charted on a six-point star (Figure 2).

The first group consists of **chromatically 3rd-related keys,** which in Figure 2 form the sides flanking the central tonic: the two sharp-key areas are to the right (III and VI), and the two flat-key areas are to the left (♭III and ♭VI). Both a chromatic and a common-tone relation occur between the chord members of a 3rd-related triad and the original tonic triad.

Example 4

The second group of foreign keys, positioned directly above and below the tonic in Figure 2, are related to the tonic by half step (♭II and vii). Since modulations to the major supertonic or subtonic keys (II or ♭VII) are quite rare except as part of a harmonic sequence, they have been omitted from the chart. We will now concentrate on *how* we modulate to these foreign keys.

3RD-RELATED MODULATIONS BY COMMON TONE

Chromatically 3rd-related keys retain one tone in common with the tonic triad. This common tone may serve as a convenient modulatory link. Four such modulations are possible, depending on which common tone serves as the link; see Example 5.

Example 5

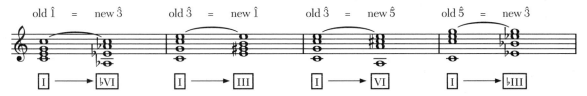

In Example 6, excerpts demonstrate this common-tone modulation technique. In the Beethoven symphony (Example 6a) a sustained A in the violins, held over from the F-major Scherzo, ushers in the D major of the Trio (old $\hat{3}$ = new $\hat{5}$). This common tone then functions as an inverted dominant pedal throughout the new section. Something similar occurs in the Brahms excerpt (Example 6b). Here the tonicized dominant $\hat{5}$ (E♭ in A♭ major) becomes $\hat{3}$ in the enharmonic ♭III key area of B (= C♭) major. Vincent Youmans's perennial "Tea for Two" (Example 6c) shifts to III by repeating the opening phrase a major 3rd higher; the pivot used is $\hat{3}$ = $\hat{1}$. We earlier encountered an instance of this type of modulation in Example 12 from Chapter 24, where the sudden lurch into the ♭VI pentatonic section of Chopin's B♭-major Prelude made use of a common B♭ ($\hat{1}$ = $\hat{3}$). This abrupt manner of changing keys usually occurs at formal junctures such as the end of a section or phrase.

Example 6

A. BEETHOVEN: SYMPHONY NO. 7, III

B. BRAHMS: SYMPHONY NO. 1, III

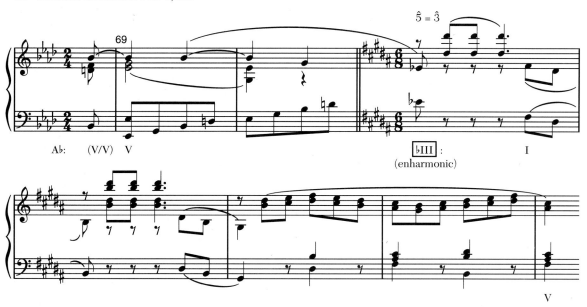

Ab: (V/V) V   bIII :   I
                                    (enharmonic)

                                                         V

C. VINCENT YOUMANS: "TEA FOR TWO"

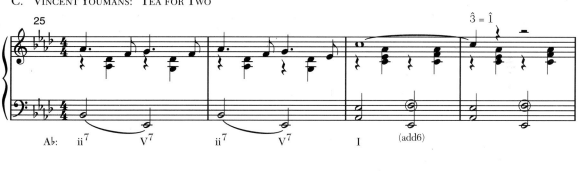

Ab: ii⁷   V⁷   ii⁷   V⁷   I   (add6)

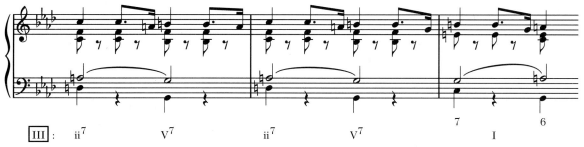

III :   ii⁷   V⁷   ii⁷   V⁷
                                              7   6
                                                    I

FOR FURTHER STUDY

In the Menuetto of Haydn's "London" Symphony, the mode of the Trio appears to change from D major to D minor by retaining the D and changing the F♯ to F♮. However, these two tones actually turn out to be scale degrees $\hat{3}$ and $\hat{5}$ in the key of B♭ major (♭VI). An enharmonic $V^7/IV = Ger^6_5$ is employed to effect a return to the original tonic, which we show in reduction only.

HAYDN: SYMPHONY No. 104 ("LONDON"), III

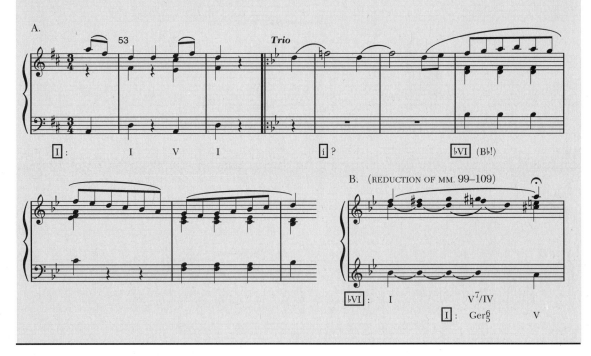

MODULATIONS TO FOREIGN KEYS BY PIVOT CHORD

We have seen that, in common-chord modulations to closely related keys, the chord used as the pivot chord functions as a diatonic harmony in both keys: for instance, vi in I = ii in V . This same method is frequently used to modulate to a foreign key. In such cases, however, an *altered* harmony in one or both keys is usually employed as the pivot chord, as illustrated in Figure 3 using a modulation from C major to E♭ major (I to ♭III).

Old key (C major)		New foreign key (E♭ major)
diatonic (I)	C E G	altered (V/ii)
altered (♭VI)	A♭ C E♭	diatonic (IV)
altered (V^7/V)	D F♯ A C	altered (V^7/iii)

Figure 3

Mixture and Neapolitan chords are frequently used as altered pivot chords. For instance, the dramatic shift in key during the impassioned duet between Carmen and Don José during the final scene of Bizet's *Carmen* (Example 7a) cadences deceptively on the mixture chord of ♭VI (in D♭ major), which becomes I in the enharmonically spelled new key of A (= B♭♭) major.

Example 7

A. BIZET: FINAL DUET FROM *CARMEN*, ACT IV

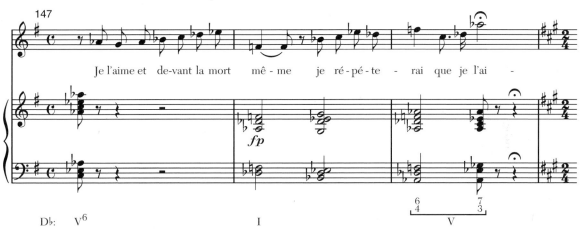

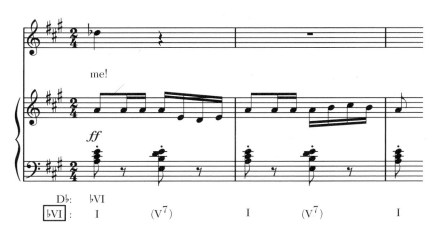

B. VERDI: QUARTET FROM *RIGOLETTO*, ACT IV (VOCAL PARTS OMITTED)

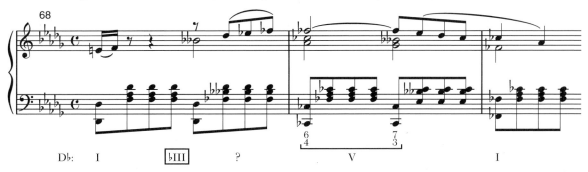

C.

C: I

VII : ♭II   V^7 I

What mixture chord serves as the common harmony from [I] to [♭III] (D♭ major to F♭ major) in the Verdi excerpt (Example 7b)? Even the original tonic can function as a ♭II when the key moves a half step lower to [VII], as shown in Example 7c; this progression may be heard in the practice rooms of almost any music school where singers are vocalizing major scales on successive chromatically descending steps.[4]

Example 8 BEETHOVEN: PIANO SONATA IN C MAJOR, OP. 53 ("WALDSTEIN"), I

A. EXPOSITION (REDUCTION OF MM. 1–35)

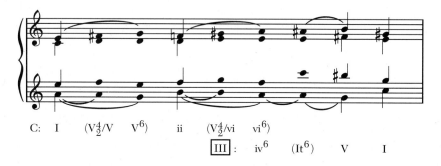

C: I   (V$^4_2$/V   V^6)   ii   (V$^4_2$/vi   vi^6)

III : iv^6 (It^6)   V   I

B. RECAPITULATION (REDUCTION OF MM. 174–196)

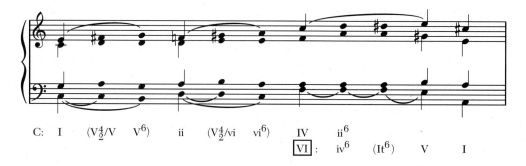

C: I   (V$^4_2$/V   V^6)   ii   (V$^4_2$/vi   vi^6)   IV   ii^6

VI : iv^6 (It^6)   V   I

4. The ascending form of this pattern is illustrated in Example 5 of Chapter 38.

In the opening movement of his "Waldstein" Sonata, Beethoven appends an It^6 to vi^6 to direct the tonal motion toward $\boxed{\text{III}}$ in the exposition, and to ii^6 to direct it toward $\boxed{\text{VI}}$ in the recapitulation, as can be seen in the reductions in Example 8 (see previous page). In each case, the dominant of the new key is prolonged some twelve measures to assure that the ensuing new tonic is adequately prepared in the listener's ear.

MODULATIONS TO FOREIGN KEYS IN THE MINOR MODE

The most commonly used keys that stand in a foreign relation to a minor-mode tonic are illustrated in Figure 4. With the exception of the Neapolitan (whose tonicization we have discussed in Chapter 28), these modulations normally move from a minor key to a minor key.

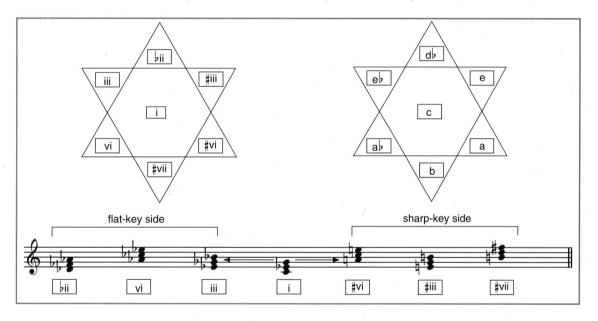

Figure 4

Enharmonically spelled pivot chords normally introduce these rather exotic tonal goals. A particularly dramatic tonal shift from $\boxed{\text{i}}$ to $\boxed{\text{#iii}}$ (C minor to E minor) occurs in the sixth movement of Brahms's *A German Requiem* (Example 9). In measures 4–6 the V^7/iv also serves as an enharmonically spelled Ger$^6_5$ in the new key.

Example 9 BRAHMS, *EIN DEUTSCHES REQUEIM*, VI

FOREIGN KEY RELATIONS IN DEVELOPMENT SECTIONS

The tonal schemes of two of Beethoven's development sections are given in Examples 10 and 11. Both make extensive use of the types of foreign key relationships discussed in this chapter.

Example 10 BEETHOVEN: PIANO SONATA IN G MAJOR, OP. 14, NO. 2, I

In Example 10, after the conclusion of the exposition in $\boxed{V}$, the ensuing development section opens with a statement of the original tonic theme in the tonic's parallel minor. This change of mode introduces a succession of keys that almost exhausts the flat keys distantly related to G major: $\boxed{\flat III}$

(B♭ major), ⌐b̲I̲I̲⌐ (A♭ major), ⌐b̲v̲i̲i̲⌐ (F minor), and ⌐b̲V̲I̲⌐) E♭ major). A lengthy dominant prolongation prepares the return of the original tonic. What do you notice about the overall motion of these foreign keys?

The development section of the first movement of Beethoven's Symphony No. 6 in F major ("Pastoral"), on the other hand, focuses almost exclusively on sharp-key foreign relationships (Example 11).

Example 11   BEETHOVEN: SYMPHONY NO. 6 ("PASTORAL"), I

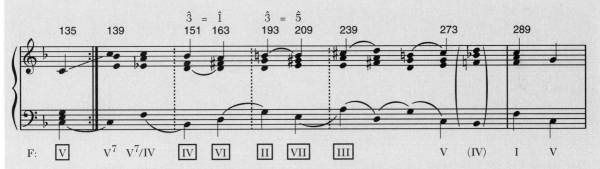

An applied dominant directs the motion from the initial ⌐V̲⌐ to the tonicized ⌐I̲V̲⌐ (B♭ major) in measure 151. The musical material used in the succession of keys that follows is based on the melodic motives listed in Example 22d of Chapter 12. What common-tone scale degrees may be used to shift from B♭ to D major, and from G to E major? A progression by 5ths leads to a prolonged dominant that resolves to the F-major tonic.

Melody Harmonization

You may find it difficult to employ modulations to foreign keys in harmonizing most diatonic melodies. In melodies that contain altered notes, it is possible to create a harmonization that can either remain in the original key or move to a foreign key. In such cases, you should first scan the melody to determine which foreign-key modulation you will employ and how you will change key. The tune in Example 12 suggests two possible settings; one remains in the original key, using a tonicized iv, while the other shifts to ⌐b̲I̲I̲I̲⌐, using an altered pivot chord.

Example 12

A.

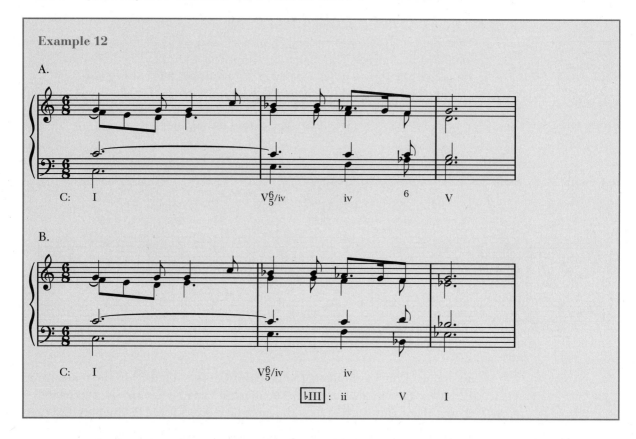

C: I   V$^6_5$/iv   iv ^{6} V

B.

C: I   V$^6_5$/iv   iv

$\boxed{\flat\text{III}}$: ii   V   I

Terms and Concepts for Review

foreign keys
change-of-mode modulation
chromatically 3rd-related keys

modulations to foreign keys by common
tone or pivot chord

CHAPTER 35

Harmonic Sequences III

CHROMATIC ELABORATIONS
OF DIATONIC SEQUENCES

NOW THAT WE HAVE completed our survey of individual altered chords, we can step back and see how chromaticism may influence the voice leading of an entire passage or composition. In this chapter we will discuss how diatonic sequential patterns, such as those presented in Chapters 20 and 22, may be chromatically elaborated. In the four chapters that comprise Part Four of this text, we will examine a range of chromatic techniques—both sequential and nonsequential—that do not have a diatonic basis.

In order to understand the nature of chromaticism in sequential writing, we must first consider some particular characteristics of stepwise motion found in diatonic sequences. Examine the bracketed portion of the first model in Example 1.

Example 1

A.

B.

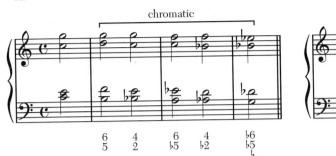

We can see that the bass voice in this sequence of major-minor seventh chords moves exclusively by half step. But if we remove the accidentals (see Example 1b), we reveal a familiar pattern of diatonic seventh chords, in alternating $\frac{6}{5}$ and $\frac{4}{2}$ inversions. This diatonic pattern forms the underlying basis for the chromatic elaboration shown in Example 1a.

THE ROLE OF DIATONIC TETRACHORDS IN CHROMATIC SEQUENCES

Examples of extended chromaticism frequently occur in harmonic sequences. In such cases, the added half-step motion within one or more voices fills in the whole steps that are generally prominent in diatonic sequences. In the bass line of the ascending sequence in Example 2, for instance, the diatonic notes (shown as beamed white notes) are filled in with chromatic notes (shown as stemless black notes).

Example 2

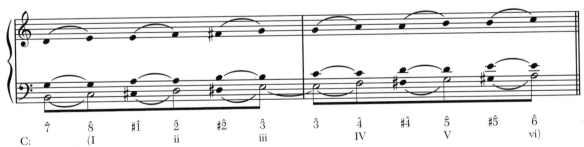

We can extend strict chromatic patterning only so far if we wish to remain within a given key center. In Example 2, for instance, the strict succession of applied V^6's and tonicized root-position triads (I, ii, and iii) can continue only to the mediant harmony; otherwise we would be taken out of the key of C major (in the bass, E♯–F♯, F×–G♯, etc.). The bass-note span within this short sequence (B–E) consists of a diatonic tetrachord—that is, a diatonic pattern of four notes that range a perfect 4th and move by step. Here, the motion is by half step, whole step, whole step (B C D E), which is elaborated chromatically. If we wish to continue the chromaticism within the original key's diatonic framework, we must begin another tetrachord, using our last E as its first note. This new tetrachord has the same intervallic construction: E F G A, as shown in the second measure of Example 2. Thus, the range of the underlying diatonic tetrachord precludes any further continuation of a strict chromatic sequence.

Let us now examine the nature of tetrachords before we proceed to identify how they serve as the foundation for chromatic sequential passages. The major scale consists of two such diatonic tetrachords ($\hat{7}$–$\hat{3}$ and $\hat{3}$–$\hat{6}$), as does the natural minor mode ($\hat{2}$–$\hat{5}$ and $\hat{5}$–$\hat{8}$). Each pair is connected by a common tone: $\hat{3}$ in major = $\hat{5}$ in minor. The two tetrachords of a major key consist of the same pitches as those of its relative minor (Example 3a).

Example 3

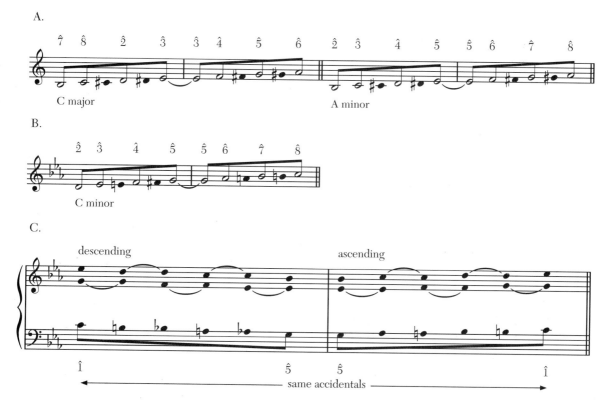

In Example 3b, we have transposed the pitches of the minor-key tetrachords to C minor for comparison's sake. Within a harmonic context, composers tend to use the same chromatic accidentals and chromatic harmonies, regardless of whether the chromatic motion ascends or descends within the tetrachords. Compare the first tetrachord in Example 3c with all the excerpts shown in Example 4.

CHROMATIC ELABORATIONS OF DIATONIC SEQUENCES

Four basic diatonic sequences are frequently chromaticized. As in other harmonic sequences, the first and last chords normally serve as the tonal pillars of the progression. As before, we will label these framing functional chords with roman numerals and indicate the interior contrapuntal motion of the sequence with figured-bass symbols, as in Examples 4b, 4d, and 4f.

Descending Chromatic $\frac{6}{3}$ Sequences

We may chromatically elaborate a succession of $\frac{6}{3}$ triads that descend from tonic to dominant. In this so-called **chromatic tetrachord,** one voice (usually the bass) moves by half step ($\hat{8}$–$\natural\hat{7}$–$\flat\hat{7}$–$\natural\hat{6}$–$\flat\hat{6}$–$\hat{5}$) while the remaining parts (usually the upper voices) are essentially diatonic.

Example 4

A. MOZART: PIANO SONATA IN D MAJOR, K.311, III

B. (REDUCTION)

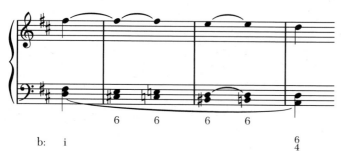

C. HANDEL: CHACONNE IN G MAJOR FROM *TROIS LEÇONS* (G. 230), VAR. 16

D. (REDUCTION)

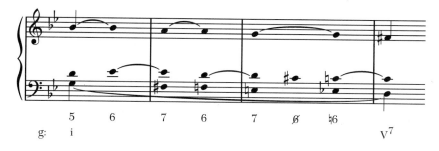

g: i   5   6   7   6   7   ∅   ♮6   V⁷

E. CHOPIN: WALTZ IN E MINOR, OP. POST.

F. (REDUCTION)

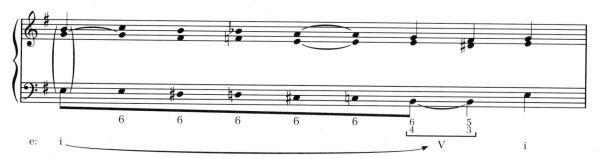

e: i   6   6   6   6   6   6̸₄   5̸₃   V   i

In the Mozart sonata, the retention of the soprano notes in bars 120 and 121 (F$\sharp^5$ and E^5) produces a succession of different chord types (major, diminished, major, minor) to accommodate the chromatic motion in the bass (Example 4a, p. 534). The descending chromatic $\hat{8}$–$\hat{5}$ tetrachord was often used in the Baroque period as the harmonic basis of variation sets in the minor mode, as illustrated by the Handel excerpt (Example 4c); here, the consecutive ^{6} chords are embellished with 7–6 suspensions. In the Chopin example (Example 4e), all the voices proceed chromatically until the $^6_4$ cadence in the penultimate measure concludes the sequential movement. Although parallel 5ths seem to occur between the inner voices in measures 25–28, the tenor line (C^4–B^3–B$\flat^3$–A^3) simply consists of octave doublings of the soprano line; in the reduction, we have eliminated this line.

Ascending Chromatic 5–6 Sequences

The ascending diatonic 5–6 pattern is one of the most commonly chromaticized sequential progressions. In Chapter 20 we discussed this type of sequential movement, which is used mainly to prevent the formation of parallel 5ths. As the underlying roots of the $^5_3$ chords rise by step, the 5–6 voice-leading motion *above* the bass occurs. In such patterns it makes no difference whether the first chord is a $^6_3$ or a $^5_3$, as long as the two continue to alternate throughout the sequence. In Example 5, the diatonic tetrachord from $\hat{7}$ up to $\hat{3}$ (Example 5a) is elaborated with a chromatic bass line (Example 5b). The resulting sequence may be viewed as successive tonicizations of I, ii, and iii by their secondary dominants.

Example 5

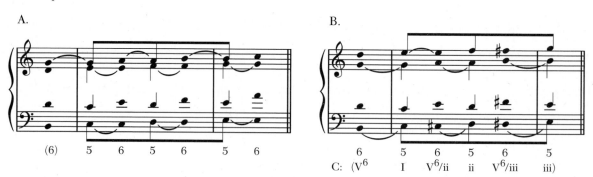

A.

(6)   5   6   5   6   5   6

B.

6   5   6   5   6   5
C: (V^6 I   V^6/ii   ii   V^6/iii   iii)

Chromatic elaborations of 5–6 patterns that feature applied V$^6_5$ or vii$^{\circ 7}$ chords are also possible, as shown in Examples 6a and 6b. In Example 6c, the addition of chromatic motion in the alto and soprano voices (shown with slurs) creates passing augmented harmonies; the underlying $^5_3$ chords (stemmed in the model) are now all major triads.

Example 6

A.

B.

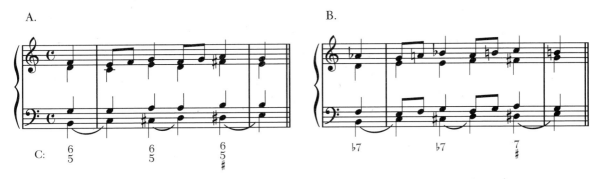

C: 6 6 6
    5 5 5
          ♯

C.

In Example 7, examine the chromatic 5–6 sequences and answer the questions about each excerpt. In the Handel quotation, the bass moves chromatically from 1̂ up to 6̂ in D major. What scale degree acts as the common link between the two underlying diatonic tetrachords? (One of the tetrachords may be incomplete.) The last three measures of the Humperdinck passage are based on an ascending 3̂–6̂ tetrachord in C major; however, the composer has extended the sequence backward by one measure. What altered chords are employed in this extension? In the Vicentino passage, to which voice is the chromatic motion transferred? How does the composer avoid parallel 5ths?

Example 7

A. HANDEL: FUGUE IN B MINOR

B. HUMPERDINCK: PRELUDE TO *HANSEL AND GRETEL*

C:

C. NICOLA VICENTINO: "MADONNA IL POCO DOLCE," FROM *L'ANTICA MUSICA*

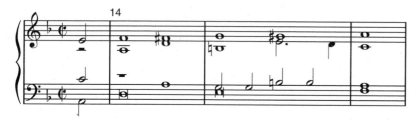

Descending Chromatic 5–6 Sequences

In descending 5–6 sequences, the underlying diatonic triads are followed, rather than preceded, by their attendant dominants.

A tetrachord that descends from $\hat{8}$ to $\hat{5}$ forms the harmonic basis for the Sweelinck excerpt (Example 8a); a D-minor tonic is assumed.[1] The two reductions show how the underlying voice leading within the upper two voices is continually displaced in Sweelinck's realization. Although the incomplete harmony of the pattern suggests either a III⁶ (= V⁶/VI) or a $^6_4$, the latter is unlikely since it does not progress to a dominant chord. If this type of sequence is to effect a return to the tonic, a dominant chord must be introduced on the final bass $\hat{5}$; in his D-minor Quartet (Example 8d), Mozart breaks the strict sequential pattern in measure 5 with a Ger$^6_5$, which leads to an extension of a $^6_4$ authentic cadence.

Example 8

A. SWEELINCK: CHROMATIC FANTASY

1. This excerpt is actually in the Dorian mode on D. Sweelinck's Fantasia exhibits a recurring succession of descending chromatic tetrachords, usually $\hat{8}$–$\hat{5}$ and $\hat{5}$–$\hat{2}$.

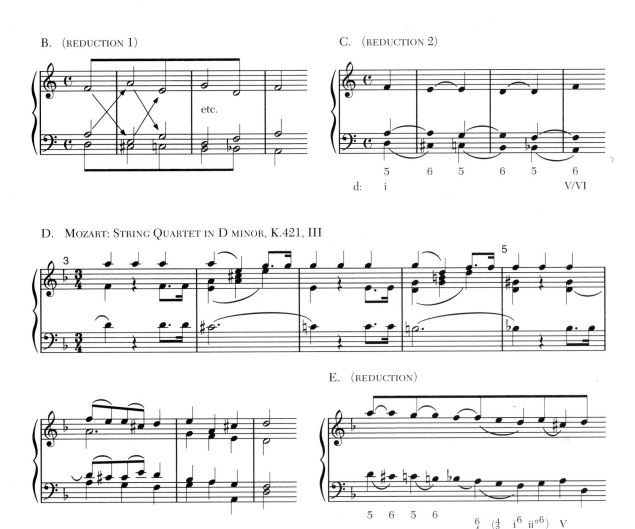

B. (REDUCTION 1)

C. (REDUCTION 2)

D. MOZART: STRING QUARTET IN D MINOR, K.421, III

E. (REDUCTION)

Examples of the descending 5–6 chromatic sequence generally occur in the minor mode. When this sequence appears in a major key, as in the opening of Beethoven's "Waldstein" Sonata (shown in reduction in Example 9), the underlying harmonies pass through the mixture chords of ♭VII and iv⁶. What chord (indicated by the arrows) is interpolated in this progression?

Example 9 BEETHOVEN: PIANO SONATA IN C MAJOR ("WALDSTEIN"), I (REDUCTION OF MM. 1–13)

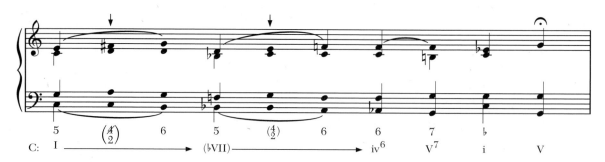

5th-Related Chromatic Sequences

We have observed in Chapters 22 and 25 that sequences by descending 5th may employ consecutive applied V^7's or $vii°^7$'s. When V^7's are used, a pattern of alternating $^6_5$ and $^4_2$ inversions is produced, with resulting parallel tritones. Examine the lower voices of the Beethoven excerpt in Example 10a.

Example 10

A. BEETHOVEN: PIANO SONATA IN C♯ MINOR, OP. 27, NO. 2 ("MOONLIGHT"), II

B. MOZART: PIANO CONCERTO IN C MINOR, K.491, I

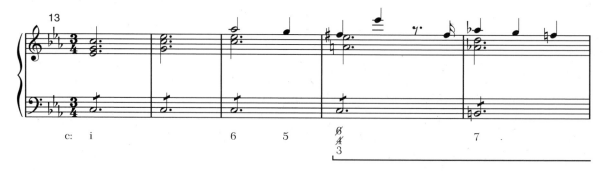

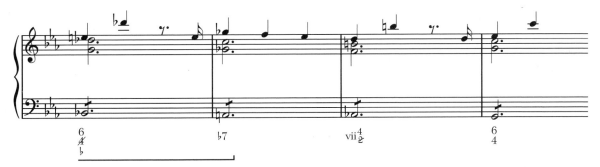

$$\begin{array}{ccc}
\substack{6\\ \sharp\\ \flat} & \flat7 & \text{vii}\substack{4\\2} & \substack{6\\4}
\end{array}$$

The Mozart quotation (Example 10b) shows that sequences of successive diminished seventh chords prefer a pattern of alternating ^{7} and $^4_3$ inversions, which allows the chordal 7th of each harmony to resolve downward by half step.

EXTENDED USE OF CHROMATIC 5-6 SEQUENCES

Two passages can serve to illustrate various treatments of the ascending chromaticized 5–6 sequence. The Trio (*più lento*) of Chopin's Waltz in C♯ minor displays an exquisite elaboration of this pattern. To appreciate the composer's imaginative handling of the opening section, begin by playing the middleground reduction (Example 11a), which represents the underlying diatonic framework.

Now play its chromatic elaboration in the second reduction (Example 11b); the falling 3rds in the soprano artfully disguise the passage's overall stepwise accent. Finally, perform Chopin's own setting (Example 11c), observing how the composer fills out the "double chromatic" motion of the 5–6 sequence in the tenor and bass voices and writes a curiously chromatic soprano over the authentic $^6_4$ cadence.

Example 11   Chopin: Waltz in C♯ minor, Op. 64, No. 2, Trio

A. (MIDDLEGROUND REDUCTION)

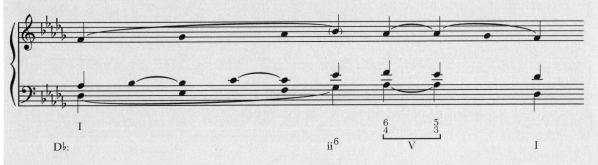

$$\text{D}\flat\text{:} \qquad \text{I} \qquad\qquad\qquad \text{ii}^6 \quad \substack{6\\4} \quad \substack{5\\3} \qquad \text{I}$$
$$\qquad\qquad\qquad\qquad\qquad\qquad\qquad\qquad\quad \text{V}$$

B. (FOREGROUND REDUCTION)

The Beethoven excerpt in Example 12 shows a more innovative use of the ascending 5–6 chromatic sequence.

Example 12   BEETHOVEN: SYMPHONY NO. 1, III

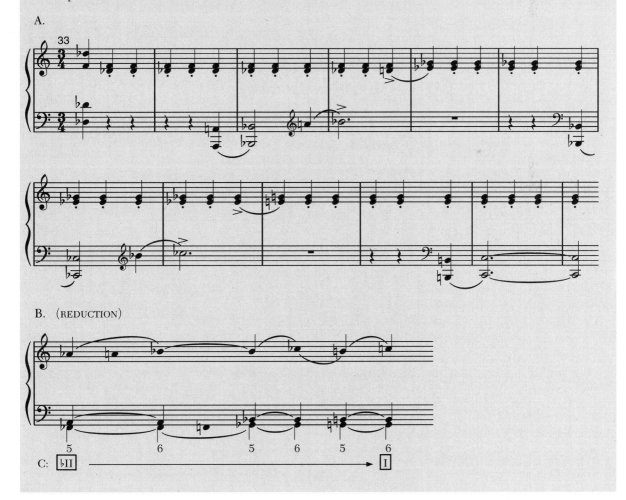

In the development-like second reprise of this Menuetto, the composer has modulated from the original key of C major to the Neapolitan, D♭ major. The tonicization of this remote key, which begins our excerpt, poses the problem of how to return to the initial C-major tonic for the restatement of the opening theme. The composer begins an ascending chromatic sequence from ♭II̲ using a 5–6 technique that alternates between the outer voices. (The reduction in Example 12b uses some octave transpositions to show the underlying voice leading and omits the redundant bass chromatic tones.) On reaching a first-inversion C-major chord, Beethoven achieves a return to tonic without recourse to the usual dominant prolongation that is typical of retransitions.

Terms and Concepts for Review

diatonic tetrachords as limiters in chromatic sequences

chromatic tetrachords

descending chromatic $^6_3$ sequences

ascending and descending chromatic 5–6 sequences

descending 5th-related chromatic sequences

Analytical Comments on Wagner's *Tristan* Prelude

To CONCLUDE OUR REVIEW of the chromatic procedures presented in Part Three, we will examine some passages from the orchestral Prelude to Richard Wagner's opera *Tristan und Isolde.* The harmonic characteristics of this work present a number of interesting analytical issues, not the least of which is its lack of tonal closure.

This music drama is one of the significant watersheds in the history of Western music. In loosely basing his libretto on the medieval epic *Tristram und Yseult,* Wagner drew upon a theme that continually recurs in his operas— the heroine's self-sacrifice for the hero. This theme is filled with various symbolic references, such as the "longing for night" that symbolizes a death wish of the lovers. Completed in 1859, Wagner's *Tristan und Isolde* represents the first major attempt by a composer to sustain a high degree of chromatic voice leading and tonal fluidity over the span of an entire opera. For years to come, its harmonic innovations continued to exert an influence on composers, including such diverse figures as Richard Strauss and Claude Debussy.

The Prelude or Introduction (*Einleitung*) to Act I has fascinated musicians ever since Wagner composed it (1856), before beginning work on the rest of the opera. Some scholars suggest that it represents an orchestral summary of the opera's narrative, portraying the tragic plight of the star-crossed lovers, and Wagner's own program notes reinforce this hypothesis.

Several problems arise in an analysis of the Prelude. The complex interaction of nonharmonic tones and altered seventh chords makes it difficult to extract and determine the exact spelling of individual chords, and the intense linear chromaticism often obscures their tonal function. The frequent use of mixture and applied chords creates an ambiguous sense of modality; it is often unclear whether a specific passage is in a major or minor key. For instance, the passage in measures 25–31 is written with a key signature that implies A minor (see Example 6, below); in its later exact restatement (mm. 45–49), the signature of three sharps implies the parallel key of A major. However, E major is the actual tonic of both passages, as we will see. In addition, there is less sense of tonal stability during the tonicization of a particular key since root-position triads are strangely absent, with one exception. In fact, the tonic harmony of a passage may never even appear, remaining only implied by its dominant seventh. Finally, the piece does not exhibit tonal closure: its opening section (mm. 1–16 in Example 1) suggests the key of A (minor) through a prolongation of its V[7], but the concluding section (mm. 100–110 in Example 8) is an extended half cadence in C (minor), the key that begins Act I.

In this chapter we will examine several illustrative passages within the Prelude and ascertain some of the ways in which the musical material is taken up in the opera itself.[1] The Prelude's initial seventeen measures are given in Example 1.

Example 1 WAGNER: PRELUDE TO *TRISTAN UND ISOLDE*, ACT I

1. A piano reduction of the full score may be found in various music anthologies, including Charles Burkhart's *Anthology for Music Analysis*, 5th ed. (Fort Worth: Harcourt Brace, 1994), which also provides a list of the Prelude's important leitmotives.

This first section consists of a threefold statement of two important themes or *leitmotives* of the opera (themes 1A and 1B), which are linked together.[2] The opening two chords of theme 1B represent one of the most frequently analyzed of all harmonic progressions. Although the E^7 chord in measure 3 suggests V^7 of an implied A (minor), the soprano $G\sharp^4$ in measure 2 obscures the function of the first chord (F B D$\sharp$ G$\sharp$), usually called the "Tristan chord" (abbreviated here as TC1).[3] Does Wagner wish us to hear the G$\sharp$ in this collection of pitches as the essential chord tone, which then creates an enharmonically spelled half-diminished seventh sonority, or does he mean the A to function as the essential chord tone, which then produces a Fr_3^4? This question can only be resolved by consulting the passages that contain these sonorities in the remainder of the Prelude and opera, which confirm that he considers the half-diminished seventh chord to be the essential sonority. Due to the presence of F–D$\sharp$, however, the harmony in measure 2 operates as an Aug6th chord, where the D$\sharp^4$ "resolves" to D$\natural^4$, the 7th of the E^7 chord. Instead of moving to the anticipated tonic of A minor, this progression is sequenced a minor 3rd

FOR FURTHER STUDY

The frequent recurrences of TC1 throughout the opera, often in conjunction with TC2 and TC3, usually retain its original pitch-classes but are often notated enharmonically; in the Prelude, see measure 83 and the bass notes in measures 107–109. For other examples, see the following excerpts in the Schirmer vocal score: measures 11–12 on page 223; measures 2–5 on page 163 (note the upward arpeggiation of TC1 in the upper voice); and measures 16–18 on page 161 (where all three Tristan chords are rearranged in succession).

The motion of a half-diminished seventh chord to a major-minor seventh chord occurs in Wagner's other operas, where the progression is consistently associated with fate, magic, or the supernatural. In *Tristan und Isolde*, the first occurrence of TC1 in Act I (mm. 16–18 on page 8 of the Schirmer score) appears in conjunction with the mention of Isolde's mother, who is a sorceress!

---

2. With one exception, the initial minor-6th leap characteristic of theme 1A turns into a major 6th leap beginning on A$\flat^3$ during the remainder of the opera. The original sketch for the Prelude, interestingly enough, shows the first tone as B^3, forming a tritone with the following F.

3. This chord was discussed briefly in Chapter 29; see Example 22.

higher in measures 5–7, concluding on a V^7 of an implied C-major tonic. The chord in measure 6 is a transposition of the original Tristan chord in measure 2; we will refer to this new collection of pitches as TC2. A third statement of this basic progression (mm. 8–11) likewise suggests a half cadence in E (major). Although not an exact transposition of TC1, the chord in measure 10, which we will call TC3, retains its half-diminished seventh chord quality and moves to a B^7 chord, a major 3rd rather than a minor 3rd higher than the analogous chord in measure 7.

The reduction of this opening passage (Example 2) reveals an ascending-3rd sequence of half-step "sighs" in the bass, which are derived from the F^4–E^4 motion within the original 1A motive (A^3–F^4–E^4–$D\sharp^4$): F^3–E^3, $A\flat^3$–G^3, and C^4–B^3.[4] Although Wagner withholds the resolution of each dominant seventh (on E, G, and B), he nevertheless anticipates the three basic key areas of the Prelude: A minor (or major), C major, and E major or, expressed in terms of the original A minor, $\boxed{i}$–$\boxed{III}$–$\boxed{V}$. In a broader sense, the opening passage represents a prolongation of the V^7 of A (minor), over which the soprano ascends from $\hat{7}$ to $\hat{7}$ ($G\sharp^4$–$G\sharp^5$) by successive half steps before resolving to A^5 in measure 17. The essential tones of this chromatic octave outline the enharmonic spelling of TC2: $G\sharp$ (= $A\flat$) B D $F\sharp$, which is shown by the stemming of the upper voice in the reduction.

Example 2 REDUCTION OF MM. 1–17

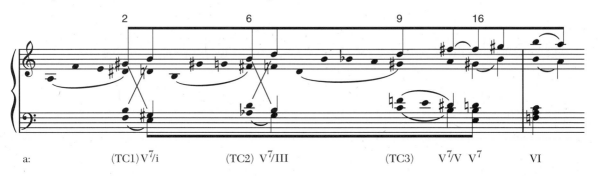

$$a: \quad (TC1)\,V^7/i \qquad (TC2)\,V^7/III \qquad (TC3) \quad V^7/V \;\; V^7 \qquad VI$$

The return to the E^7 chord in measure 16 sets up an expectation of its resolution to the A tonic chord, but instead the semitone motion in the bass reverses direction (E^2–F^2) and leads to a deceptive VI chord. The transient quality of these first seventeen measures masterfully portray the frustrated love that is played out in the remainder of the opera. The intensity of the

---

4. A descending half-step motion that occurs at various pitch levels to represent sighing was well established in Baroque music and was used throughout the common-practice period; one example can be found in Dido's lament, "When I Am Laid in Earth," from Purcell's opera *Dido and Aeneas*.

lovers' desire and longing, depicted by the rising reiterations of the Tristan chord and their attendant dominant sevenths, is continually thwarted by each dominant seventh's lack of resolution.

The F-major chord in measure 17 introduces Theme 2 in the cellos (Example 3); this theme has been called the "Glance" motive by most commentators because in the opera it appears when the eyes of the lovers first meet. Its diatonic melody and setting form a striking contrast to the chromaticism of the previous section.

Example 3

The tonal motion in these measures is now directed toward C major, or $\boxed{\text{III}}$:(IV–(V$_5^6$/V)–V–I^6. D minor, or $\boxed{\text{iv}}$ of the original A minor, is briefly tonicized in the following passage (mm. 20–22) before a V^7/V prepares the Prelude's first and only authentic cadence, in the original key of A (m. 24).

The foreground reduction given in Example 4a extracts the basic chords in measures 17–24 and assigns them possible harmonic functions. The continuing melodic dissonance and the linear derivation of chordal sonorities, however, make some of our chord labels uncertain. For instance, what are the spellings of the chords on the second beats of measures 22 and 23 (denoted in Example 4a with arrows)? The middleground reduction given in Example 4b suggests the large-scale progression (V^7)–VI–III^6–iv–V^7–I in A (minor). The soprano ascends from A to C♯ (if we assume an octave displacement of the initial A). Observe how the upper line splits into two separate melodic strands.[5]

Example 4

A. (REDUCTION 1)

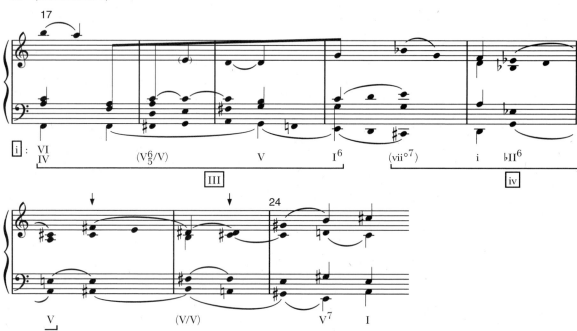

B. (REDUCTION 2)

5. These voice-leading reductions represent modified versions of the elegant reductions given by William Mitchell in his "The *Tristan* Prelude: Techniques and Structure," *The Music Forum* I (1967), 162–203.

In his earlier monograph *On the Overture* (1841), Wagner states that operatic introductions should establish *two* basic themes of contrasting nature that will continue to interact with each other throughout the overture. The *Tristan* Prelude is an excellent example of this principle. The prevailing chromaticism of theme 1(A and B), for instance, is played off against the diatonicism of theme 2. These two thematic ideas generate the subsequent melodic material of the entire Prelude. They are related by an underlying projection of linear thirds: G♯–B–D–F♯–(G♯) in the soprano of measures 1–16 and A–C–E–G in the "Glance" motive of measures 17–20 (Example 5), which, if combined, form an almost complete melodic-minor scale starting on A, the opening key of the Prelude.

Example 5

A.

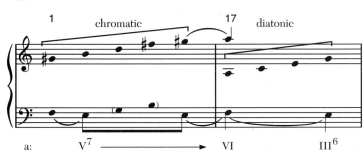

B.

In measure 24 (Example 6), the cadential A-major triad functions as a IV in the dominant key of E major, leading us through a vii$^{\varnothing 4}_{3}$ to a I^6 in the new key, which is then reinforced by a succession of 5th-related seventh chords (F♯^{7}–B^7). Since the voice leading within Example 6 is often obscured by voice exchanges and registral shifts (see the foreground reduction in Example 6b), we have provided a middleground reduction that neutralizes these devices (Example 6c).

Example 6

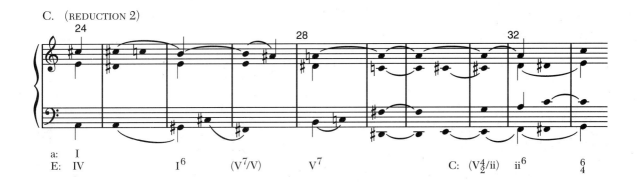

C. (REDUCTION 2)

Thus, the three tonal centers that were implied in the opening statements of Theme 1B (mm. 2–3, 6–7, and 10–11) are now tonicized in succession: A minor/major (mm. 1–16), C major (mm. 17–20), and E major (mm. 25–28), with particular emphasis given to their V^7 harmonies.

The chromatic motion under the sustained soprano A^4 (mm. 28–32) prepares the return of the C-major "Glance" theme via $(V_3^4/ii)–ii^6–(vii^{\circ 7}/V)–V_4^6$ (mm. 31–33). This particular succession of transient tonicizations is typical of the Prelude (and opera) as a whole. Although some of the opera's individual scenes operate within the loose framework of one central tonal center, the harmonies at the surface level of the music never establish a particular key for any length of time.

During the Prelude's climactic section (mm. 74–84), Wagner intentionally emphasizes the tonal ambiguity of the initial TC1 by exploiting its dual enharmonic function. TC1 is enharmonically respelled in measures 81–83 as a $ii^{\emptyset 7}$ in E♭ (minor), moving to V^9.

Example 7

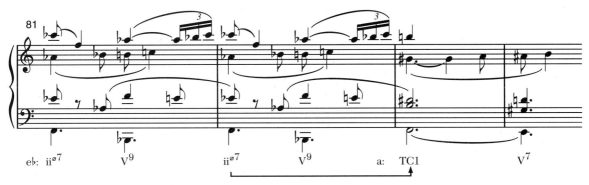

Not only are the principal themes (1A, 1B, and 2) contrapuntally combined (can you find them?), but the repetitive root movement by falling perfect 5th provides a diatonic setting for the tonally ambiguous theme 1B that opens the prelude.[6] At this crucial moment, Wagner renotates the $ii^{\varphi 7}$ as TC1 in measure 83, so that its half-step resolution to E^7 renews the despondent mood of the work's beginning. This ingenious enharmonic change, occurring at the apex of the gradual climactic buildup begun in measure 63, must qualify as one of the most moving and psychologically adroit instances of enharmonic interplay in Western music literature.

The climactic passage discussed immediately above segues into a restatement and extension of the three themes that began the work (mm. 83–94). The deceptive cadence on F (VI) in measure 94 now prepares the final tonal area of C and its subsequent dominant prolongation.

Example 8

6. The clearest reference to this passage occurs in Act III, where the falling perfect-5th motion imparts a sense of renewed hope and deliverance when Tristan's companion discovers that the knight is still alive. See measures 21ff on page 259 of the Schirmer vocal score.

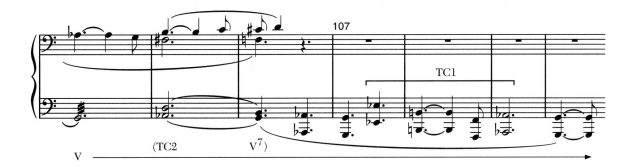

The setting of the ensuing "Glance" motive is now fragmented and underlaid by darker pre-dominant mixture chords in measures 94–97; compare this harmonization with the original in measures 17–21 (Example 3). Theme 2 is transposed to F, or IV/C (mm. 96–100), using the same prominent $ii^{\varnothing 4}_{3}$ in measure 97. The climactic half cadence in measure 100 introduces a prolonged pedal on G^2, over which a final allusion to the opening two statements of 1A and 1B are presented. The earlier E^7 sonority is transformed into a $vii^{\circ 4}_{3}$ of C. An enharmonic melodic reference in the bass to TC1 in measures 107–109 (E♭ B♮ F A♭) resolves instead to the dominant of the implied Ċ (minor).

The fact that the Prelude opens with a dominant prolongation in A and concludes with a dominant prolongation in C raises a crucial theoretical question: How are we to rationalize this obvious exception to the axiom we have given earlier, that movements in the tonal idiom begin and end in the same basic key?

Some theorists have brushed over this anomaly by basing their analyses of the Prelude on the A-major ending that Wagner later composed for the 1860 Paris concerts, although this version is rarely performed today.[7] Other scholars have viewed the primary tonic of the Prelude as C, the key that concludes both the Prelude and Act I.[8] Still others have proposed a more radical solution: a *double-tonic axis* in which the continuous vacillation between A and C sets up a dual tonal system.[9]

Lacking a prolonged tonic, both centers are relatively weak. The case for A lies in its two dominant extensions (the opening mm. 1–17 and its return in mm. 63–73), the authentic cadence in measure 24, and the use of its dominant key of

---

7. See the article by William Mitchell cited in footnote 5.

8. This is the view of Poundie Burstein in his "A New View of *Tristan:* Tonal Unity in the Prelude and Conclusion of Act I," *Theory and Practice* 8/1 (September 1983), 15–41.

9. Robert Bailey, *Richard Wagner's Prelude and Transfiguration from Tristan and Isolde,* Norton Critical Score Series (New York: W. W. Norton, 1985), 113ff. In addition to the draft of the Prelude, Bailey also includes a number of analyses by other Wagner scholars.

FOR FURTHER STUDY

Examples of instrumental movements that lack tonal closure are extremely rare in the common-practice period. Chopin's Scherzo, Op. 31, and Ballade, Op. 38, which conclude in D♭ major and A minor, respectively, actually open in the submediant. The absence of tonal closure is more typical of vocal music, such as certain songs of Schubert and Hugo Wolf, where the dramatic nature of the text may explain the directed motion between different framing keys. In the case of the *Tristan* Prelude, it should be remembered that Wagner intended it as an introduction to the opera proper.

E major. The center of C, on the other hand, gains importance from its association with the "Glance" theme originally heard in measures 17–20 and the final prolongation of its dominant in measures 100ff. The periodic recurrences of theme 2 suggest a kind of C-major "ritornello" that is gradually intensified through higher register, expanded orchestration, louder dynamics, increased harmonic dissonance and chromaticism, the addition of counterthemes, and even phrase overlap (see mm. 32–35, 55–57, 59–62, and 74–76).

Figure 1 outlines the main thematic ideas of the entire Prelude (see the circled numbers), as well as surface tonicizations and important cadential points. The vertical alignment reveals the remarkable similarity of thematic material, tonal centers, and cadences. Partly because all of the Prelude's thematic material grows out of the ideas presented in its initial measures, the piece appears to generate itself. In measures 66–77, however, a modified return of the opening section (mm. 1–20), coupled with the emphasis on the dominant key in measures 25–28 and 45–48, suggest a kind of loose ternary design: Statement = A (mm. 1–24), Intensification and Development = B (mm. 24–65), and a double return of the Statement in the "Climactic Plateau" and "Dissolution" sections = A A' (mm. 66–83 and 83–111).[10]

The melodic material and tonal relations established in the Prelude exert a significant influence on the remainder of the opera. In particular, themes 1A and 1B are constantly transformed to create new motives with related extramusical associations. In the Prelude, the TC1 enharmonically functions as a pre-dominant chord in three different implied key areas: A (minor), E♭ (minor), and C (major/minor).

10. The terms in quotation marks were coined by Robert Morgan and describe the fragmentation of the A themes toward the end of the Prelude.

STRUCTURAL DIAGRAM OF THE *TRISTAN* PRELUDE

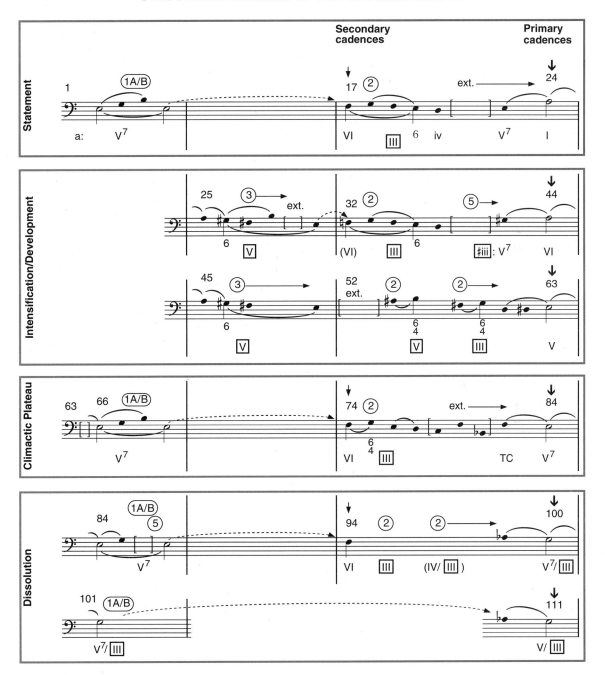

Figure 1

Example 9

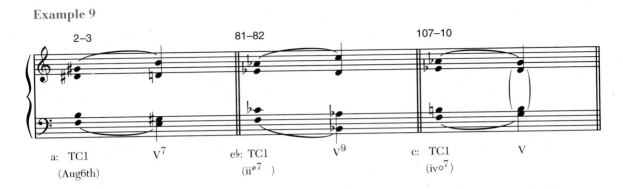

These implied key centers serve as the subsequent tonal basis for Act I, sometimes occurring in a consecutive chain of minor-3rd relations (A–C–E♭). Beginning with the series of love duets in Act II, a new 3rd-chain emerges that continues to the end of the opera: Act II = A♭(=G♯)–B–D (minor), and Act III = F (minor)–A♭(=G♯)–B. The combination of all three 3rd projections produces an almost complete octatonic scale of alternating half and whole steps: G♯–A–B–C–D–E♭–F.[11]

We have touched on several features of this remarkable work, but you may wish to examine other aspects, using a complete piano score. For instance:

1. How is the melodic material in measures 25–26, 36–37, and 63–64 derived from the original themes? (Recall the previous chains of 3rds.)
2. Can you trace the recurrences of the C-major "Glance" theme and indicate how Wagner gradually intensifies each succeeding restatement?
3. Why is there a cadence on a deceptive A-major chord in the temporary area of C♯ minor in measures 42–44?

With this chapter we conclude our basic survey of chromatic harmony in the common-practice period. In Part Four we will discuss some of the advanced chromatic techniques that led to the dissolution of functional tonal harmony that occurred around the beginning of the twentieth century.

---

11. Consult Appendix 2 for information on this scalar formation.

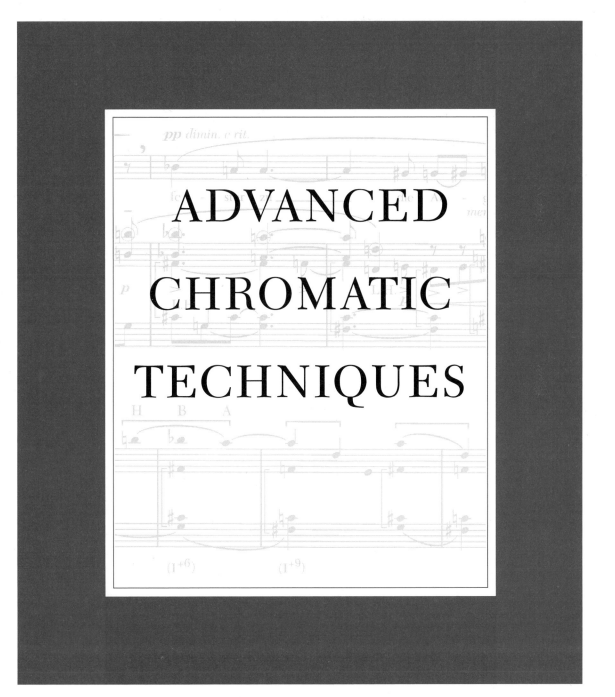

PART FOUR

ADVANCED CHROMATIC TECHNIQUES

Chromatic Voice Leading

I
N PART THREE WE introduced the more prevalent characteristics and
procedures of chromatic harmony. We observed the different ways to tonicize or modulate to new key centers; examined the more commonly used
chromatic chords, chord progressions, and chromatic sequences; and
ascertained the nature of foreign tonal relations and the means by which
music progresses to a foreign key. In this and the following two chapters,
we will discuss techniques that are more exclusively chromatic in nature.
These include the use of strict sequential patterning, purely chromatic
voice leading, and enharmonic spellings to effect modulations to foreign
key centers. Some of these devices may weaken the underlying tonal system to such an extent that our sense of harmonic function or even tonic
harmony is diminished.

In this chapter we will focus on sequences that employ half-step root
movement and study some examples of parallel, contrary, and nonsequential
voice leading within passages of common-practice period music. Then we
will examine the first section of Chopin's Prelude in E minor, Op. 28, No. 4,
a work whose underlying diatonic harmonies are overlaid with an intense
linear chromaticism.

SEQUENCES BASED ON HALF-STEP ROOT MOVEMENT

The harmonic sequences we discussed in Chapter 35 involve chromatic elaborations of diatonic patterns whose underlying root movement proceeds by diatonic 2nds, 3rds, or 5ths. Sequences whose root movement progresses by successive half steps, resulting in **chromatic root movement,** are also possible. Compare the two models in Example 1.

Example 1

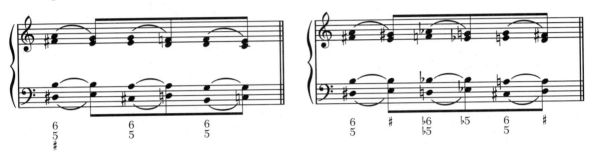

The beamed notes in the first sequence in Example 1a indicate that the overall voice leading in the outer parts proceeds downward by diatonic step-wise motion. Each beamed chord is preceded by its applied $^6_5$. In Example 1b the voice leading is similar but the root movement now proceeds by successive half steps.

Now analyze the two passages in Example 2. For the A♭-major Chopin Prelude (Example 2a) assume that the passage is in the key of E major. How does this excerpt compare to the models in Example 1? Example 2b makes a series of half-step ascending modulations, from C minor through C♯ minor to D minor, using a 5–6 chromatic sequence. What is the pivot chord in each case?

Example 2

A. CHOPIN: PRELUDE IN A♭ MAJOR, OP. 28, NO. 17

B.   Beethoven: Symphony No. 3, ("Eroica"), I

c:

(c#:)

etc.

(d:)

STRICT CHROMATIC PARALLELISM

We have seen how the functional chords that frame sequential patterns are connected by the contrapuntal motion of the sequence itself. These two functional harmonies may also be spanned by an ascending or descending succession of *identical* chord types. When all chord members within these chords move in the same direction in strict half-step motion, they engender what is called **chromatic parallelism.** In passages that exhibit chromatic parallelism, the first and last chords continue to operate as the framing diatonic functions, which we denote with roman numerals. The most common chord types in such passages are major triads and those seventh chords that contain a tritone, such as major-minor, half-diminished, or fully diminished seventh chords.

Several illustrations of this procedure are shown in Examples 3 and 4. In the Ellington excerpt (Example 3a), the "sliding" chromatic motion connects the functional ii^7 and V^7; what type of sonority is employed in the parallel chords? In the Chopin Nocturne (Example 3c), what two essential harmonies (marked with a "?" in the reduction) are linked in the series of chromatic diminished seventh chords? The *Rheingold* excerpt (Example 3e)

Example 3

A. DUKE ELLINGTON: *SOPHISTICATED LADY,* BEGINNING OF CHORUS (SIMPLIFIED)

B. (REDUCTION)

Ab: ii⁷ (chrom. ⁴₂'s) V⁷ I⁷

C. CHOPIN: NOCTURNE IN Db MAJOR, OP. 27, No. 2

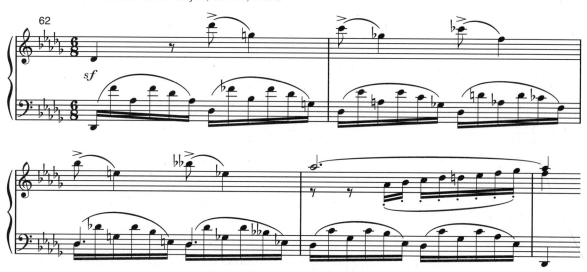

D. (REDUCTION)

Db: ? °7ths ? V⁷ I

E. Wagner: Ascent from Nibelheim from *Das Rheingold*, Scene 4

F. (reduction)

is an interesting example of a **double chromatic parallelism:** the first-inversion major triads that descend chromatically (each is enclosed within a box) are countered by the harmonic root motion that ascends by a half step every two measures (C–D♭–D), all of which occurs over a pedal on G. The reduction of the passage reveals the parallel perfect 5ths between the upper two voices (that is, the two strands within the upper line).

The quotation from Puccini's *La Bohème* in Example 4 is different in one respect from the examples above.

Example 4 PUCCINI: *LA BOHÈME*, ACT II

Although strict parallelism is maintained between the separate chords so that the chord type remains constant, the harmonies do not proceed exclusively by half-step motion at first but rather leap about freely. Name the chord type that is used throughout the passage. What interval remains constant between the bass and soprano?

CHROMATICISM BY CONTRARY MOTION

Sometimes two voice parts will proceed chromatically in opposite directions—that is, in **chromatic contrary motion.** In the diatonic scales of tonal music there are two short melodic successions that can display this strict intervallic mirroring or inversion by contrary motion: from $\hat{7}$ to $\hat{4}$ in the major mode, and from $\hat{2}$ up to $\hat{6}$ in the minor mode, both spanning a melodic tritone. Examine the beamed notes in the C-major model in Example 5.

Example 5

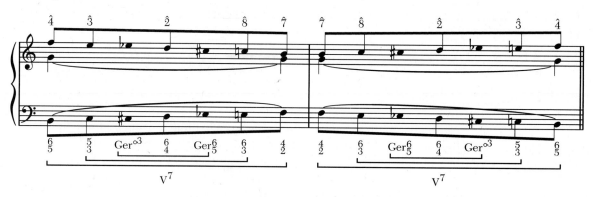

A voice exchange between B and F prolongs a dominant seventh chord by linking its $\frac{6}{5}$ and $\frac{4}{2}$ inversions. The outer voices of this diatonic progression are symmetrically arranged around the central axis note of D (or $\hat{2}$). If we chromaticize the soprano and bass, the third and fifth harmonic sonorities may be explained as enharmonic German Aug6th chords (in $^{\circ 3}$ and $\frac{6}{5}$ positions), while the interior D functions as an implied passing $\frac{6}{4}$ between the two Aug6ths.[1]

---

1. The figured-bass symbols indicate implied chords only, since all chord tones are not present in this model. Starting in Example 7, additional inner voices will be introduced to fill out these suggested harmonies.

This basic tritone exchange can be transposed to other scale degrees when an applied V^7 is being prolonged. For instance, if the basic harmony is V^7/V in C major, it will span F♯–C, with A as the axis tone.

Now let us see how this harmonic model occurs in music literature. Schubert uses a contrary chromatic progression in the final strophe of his "Der Wegweiser" to depict the endless road from which "no traveler returns" (that is, death).

Example 6   SCHUBERT: "DER WEGWEISER" FROM *WINTERREISE*

Einen Weiser seh' ich stehen
unverrückt vor meinem Blick;
eine Strasse muss ich gehen,
die noch keiner ging zürück.

One sign I see standing
fixed before my gaze;
down one road I must go,
from which none have returned.

Here the tritone exchange (B–F), which seems to prolong the V^7 of C major, is not completed but instead breaks off at the bass E^2, which leads back to a cadence in the actual tonic of G minor. If the pattern had continued in strict order, however, it would eventually have cycled back on itself in an "endless" manner. The gloomy Neapolitan chord in the cadence is an appropriate touch in terms of the text (consult the translation in Example 6).

Some compositions may employ only a portion of this progression. In Example 7a the contrary chromatic motion in the outer voices spans a major 3rd, producing a voice exchange between $\hat{5}$ and $\hat{7}$ in F major.

Example 7

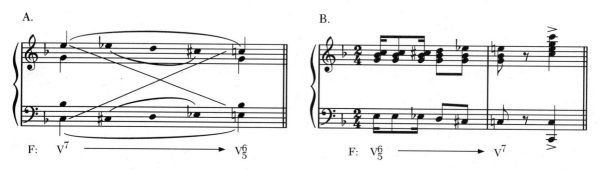

A.

F: V^7 ⟶ V^6_5

B.

F: V^6_5 ⟶ V^7

C. TCHAIKOVSKY: "PAS D'ACTION," *SLEEPING BEAUTY*, ACT I

Eb: I ii^4_2 V^6

V^7

This particular pattern has become almost a cliché, frequently serving as a short "lead-in" or introduction to a composition. A typical example (Example 7b) prolongs a V^7 chord by linking its $^6_5$ and ^{7} positions. Examine the voice leading in Tchaikovsky's lovely "Pas d'action" (Example 7c), noting especially the circled notes of the outer voices. Compare them to Example 7a, allowing for transposition; do you observe any voice exchanges, enharmonic or otherwise?

Another fragment of this chromatic pattern in contrary motion displays a voice exchange between $\sharp\hat{4}$ and $\flat\hat{6}$ (revolving around $\hat{5}$), thus filling in the small interval of a diminished 3rd. This chromatic progression usually neighbors the V, or $^6_4$, with Ger^6_5's and $\text{Ger}^{\circ 3}$'s as shown in Example 8a.

Example 8

A.

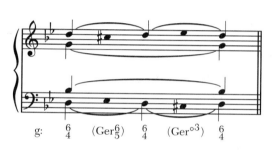

B. BRAHMS: TRAGIC OVERTURE, OP. 81

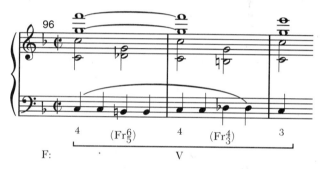

The same principle is operative in the Brahms excerpt (Example 8b), although the individual chord types are different. Note the 4–3 suspension over the C in the bass, which resolves in the upper voice (F^6–E^6) only in the last measure. The neighboring harmonies here include French Aug6ths in rather peculiar $^6_5$ and $^4_3$ inversions. In Chapter 39 we will see how this idiom may be extended by linking together a series of these fragmented chromatic sequences, each one starting a minor 3rd from the last one.[2]

Although passages using chromatic contrary motion may occasionally produce some inexplicable harmonic clashes, our ear tends to accept them as the momentary by-products of the overall linear movement. In Example 9, Wagner daringly juxtaposes parallel major triads in chromatic descent (shown in boxes) over ascending half steps in the bass; do all of the resulting chords form tertian sonorities? Notice how this passage is bisected by the central B-major triad, which is related by tritone to the opening and closing F-major triads.[3]

2. See Example 9 in Chapter 39, as well as the discussion of the "omnibus" progression in that chapter.

3. The key centers of B minor and F major/minor play an important role in the first act of this opera.

Example 9 WAGNER: SIEGFRIED'S RHINE JOURNEY FROM *GÖTTERDÄMMERUNG,* END OF PROLOGUE

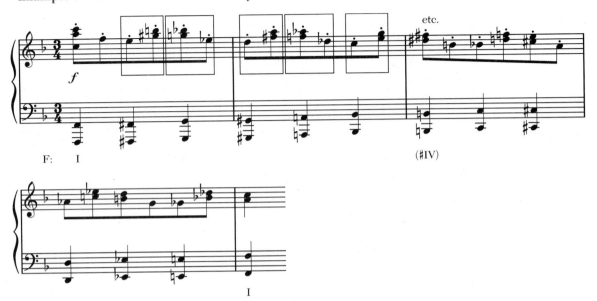

NONSEQUENTIAL CHROMATIC PASSAGES

Chromaticism need not always be associated with the devices of sequence, parallelism, or contrary motion. In music literature, we may encounter numerous nonsequential chromatic passages that are not based on these techniques. In such instances of **nonsequential chromatic voice leading,** the half-step motion results from the use of incidental applied, mixture, or embellishing chords, as in Example 10.

Example 10

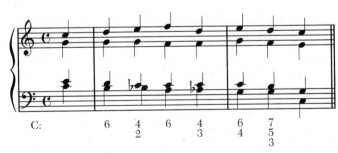

Example 8 in Chapter 29 presents an additional illustration; its underlying progression, i–V⁶–V⁴₂/IV–IV⁶–It⁶–V, is supported by a descending chromatic tetrachord in the bass, but it is not sequential.

In some instances of extreme chromaticism, the half-step motion of the individual parts may become the sole basis for the voice leading, negating any sense of standard harmonic function. The Introduzione from Beethoven's "Waldstein" Sonata provides a case in point; a simplification of the first six measures is given in Example 11a. Notice how the ascent of the upper voices contrasts with the chromatic bass descent.

Example 11 BEETHOVEN: PIANO SONATA IN C MAJOR ("WALDSTEIN"), OP. 53, II (REDUCTION OF MM. 1–6)

A.

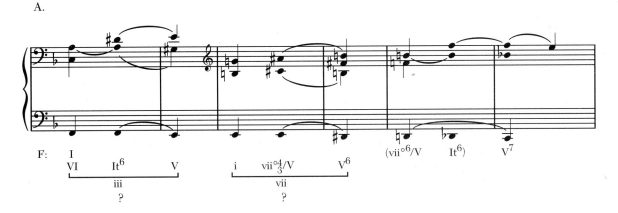

B.

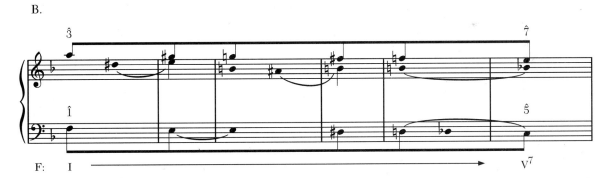

Although we have provided a functional roman-numeral analysis, it raises more questions than it resolves. As an alternative, Example 11b shows a voice-leading reduction that, by assuming several octave displacements, treats the upper parts in a more linear fashion. This reduction suggests a chromatic descent in 10ths, which outlines a descending chromatic tetrachord from $\hat{8}$ to $\hat{5}$ in the bass and from $\hat{3}$ to $\hat{7}$ in the soprano.[4]

4. This graph was suggested by David Beach.

EXTENDED USE OF NONSEQUENTIAL CHROMATICISM

Chopin's Prelude in E minor, Op. 28, No. 4, is frequently cited as an example of extended nonsequential chromaticism. This short piece divides into two sections. The first (mm. 1–10) outlines a tonal motion from i^6 to V^7, which is extended through measure 12. The second repeats this basic progression before reaching an extended dominant, which resolves to the tonic. Only the first section will be considered here.

To acquaint ourselves with this piece, we will reverse our normal analytical procedure of reducing the score to a voice-leading graph and instead examine the underlying diatonic framework first (Example 12a). The fundamental progression, i^6–iv^6–V^7, is overlaid with the drawn-out soprano line B^4–A^4–$F\sharp^4$; see the stemmed notes in Example 12a.[5]

Example 12   CHOPIN: PRELUDE IN E MINOR, OP. 28, NO. 4 (THREE REDUCTIONS)

5. The soprano descent, $\hat{5}$–$\hat{4}$–$\hat{2}$, omits the crucial $\hat{3}$. These three scale degrees are derived from the pitch motive B–A–F$\sharp$, which is found several times, often in disguised form, in the early

Chopin fills in the bass from $\hat{3}$ to $\flat\hat{6}$ (G^3–C^3) with diatonic passing motion, employing dominant and applied chords of iv. In the second reduction (Example 12b), this stepwise movement is chromaticized with embellishing diminished and half-diminished seventh chords. In measure 5, the predominant ii$^{\varnothing\frac{4}{2}}$ (with A^4 in the soprano) is prolonged until the iv^6 of measure 9 (from E^3 to C^3 in the bass). A surface reduction, shown as Example 12c, introduces additional chromatic chords and suspensions. A small-scale sequence by descending step in the bass is bracketed; enharmonic notation is used in mm. 2–3. It is inappropriate to assign functional roman numerals to the harmonies that have been added in this reduction since they arise out of various linear motions. We quote the actual score in Example 13.

Example 13   CHOPIN: PRELUDE IN E MINOR, OP. 28, NO. 4

Students frequently encounter difficulty in the analysis of such pieces when they try to account for every chord with a functional label. The previous excerpts suggest that, in passages of intense chromaticism, we should

preludes of Op. 28 (see Nos. 2, 3, 4, 5, 6, and 8); the notes of the motive are sometimes reordered, but its pitches remain constant. The origin of this motive is unknown.

generally reserve functional roman numerals for the more conspicuous essential harmonies (which are stemmed) and assume a more linear approach to the chromatic harmonies, which usually arise out of embellishing passing or neighboring motion—even in passages that exhibit extended chromaticism. Of course, these embellishing harmonies should be left unstemmed.

Terms and Concepts for Review

chromatic root movement
chromatic parallelism
double chromatic parallelism

chromatic contrary motion
nonsequential chromatic voice leading

Modulation to Foreign Keys II

I̶N OUR PREVIOUS discussion of modulation to foreign keys in Chapter 34, we introduced several ways of effecting these key shifts: by change of mode, common tone, altered pivot chords, or chromatic modulation. In this chapter we will explore some additional means by which a modulation can be achieved; these include enharmonic pivot chords, chromatic alteration of diminished seventh chords, strict sequences, and chromatic voice leading.

ENHARMONIC MODULATION

In modulations to remote key areas that employ a pivot chord, one or more tones of that chord may be notated enharmonically to show its function within the new key. We refer to this process as an **enharmonic modulation.** In some cases only one chord member of the pivot harmony may be respelled enharmonically. For instance, when modulating from $\boxed{\text{I}}$ to $\boxed{\text{VI}}$, the vii°⁷/V in C major (F♯ A C E♭ may be respelled as D♯ F♯ A C to clarify its new function as vii°⁷/V in A major. In other cases the entire chord may have to be respelled. Thus, in modulating from $\boxed{\text{I}}$ to $\boxed{\sharp\text{I}}$, the ♭VI in C major (A♭ C E♭) may be respelled as G♯ B♯ D♯ to clarify its new function as V; refer to Example 2b in Chapter 37. In enharmonic modulations the chord tones are not altered chromatically but are simply respelled. Since in most cases composers cannot employ *both* spellings, they must choose one that reflects either the old or the new key. In our analyses, however, we will continue to indicate the pivot chord with two sets of roman numerals to show its function in both keys.

Enharmonic spellings are sometimes used within modulations to avoid writing awkward double sharps or double flats. In the Act II Love Duet in *Tristan und Isolde,* for example, Wagner spells both the pivot chord and new key center enharmonically as he starts a series of rising half-step tonicizations from A♭ major (Example 1).

Example 1 WAGNER: LOVE DUET FROM *TRISTAN UND ISOLDE,* ACT II (SIMPLIFIED)

B. (REDUCTION)

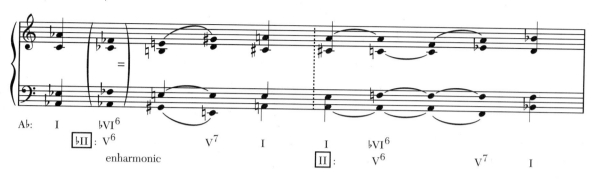

When modulating from the key of A♭ major to its Neapolitan a half-step higher (the ungrateful key of B♭♭), the composer spells the new key A major. To achieve this modulation he uses the pivot chord G♯ B E (= A♭ C♭ F♭) which functions as ♭VI in A♭ major and as V⁶ in the new key. Why is no enharmonic notation required in the succeeding movement from A to B♭ major?

The diminished seventh chord is frequently employed as an enharmonic pivot because it can serve as a $vii^{\circ 7}$ or, more commonly, a $vii^{\circ 7}/V$ in any of four different keys. This sonority's four tones, each a minor 3rd apart, divide the octave into equal segments, which allows each tone to be notated as a potential root. Thus, if we start in C major/minor, the keys that we can attain through different spellings of $vii^{\circ 7}/V$ are A major/minor, F♯ major/minor, and E♭ major/minor. In the excerpt from Schubert's "gravedigger" song given in Example 2b, the transient tonicization of the ♯iv, which is a tritone away from the original tonic, is achieved through an enharmonically spelled diminished seventh chord (marked with an arrow). Note the F–B in the

Example 2

A.

B. SCHUBERT: "TODTENGRÄBERS HEIMWEHE," D. 842

C. (REDUCTION)

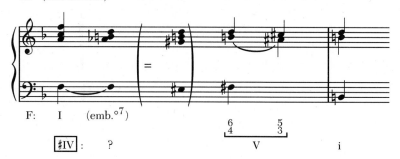

vocal line in measures 2–3, which serves as a link from the old to the new key and reinforces the morbidity of the song's text. This symbolic use of F and B recalls the *diabolus in musica* ("the devil in music"), a medieval term used to describe the sounding relationship between these two pitch-classes. In this excerpt, how does the enharmonic chord in F major function in the new key of B minor?

In modulations to foreign keys, composers of the Romantic period were particularly fond of exploiting the enharmonic relation of the Ger$^6_5$ and V^7, as we have seen in Chapter 29, Examples 18 and following. A striking effect produced by this exchange of harmonies occurs in Tchaikovsky's *Romeo and Juliet* Fantasy, whose tonic key is B minor. An extended dominant prolongation in the key area of $\boxed{\text{III}}$ (D major) that immediately precedes the excerpt given in Example 3 leads us to anticipate a cadence in that key. At the last moment, the A^7 (V^7 of D) instead functions as an enharmonic Ger_5^6 whose resolution to a D♭-major $_4^6$ unexpectedly introduces Romeo's famous theme (Example 3a).[1]

Example 3   TCHAIKOVSKY: *ROMEO AND JULIET*

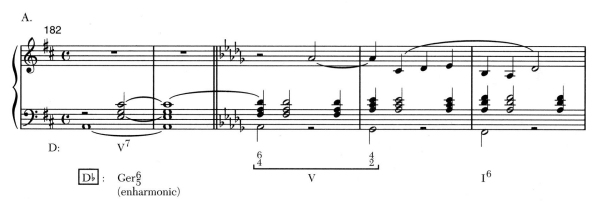

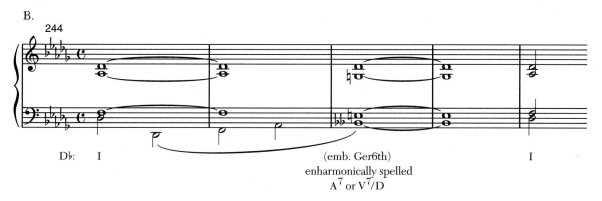

At the conclusion of this D♭ section, the composer repeatedly refers to this previous "A^7," but now it operates as an embellishing common-tone Ger_5^6 in the context of D♭ major (Example 3b).

1. When he wrote this work, the young Tchaikovsky was under the influence of Mily Balakirev, a famous Russian composer and pedagogue who showed a decided preference for pieces written in two sharps or five flats; hence the B minor–D♭ major juxtaposition within *Romeo and Juliet.*

This process may also be reversed, so that a Ger$^6_5$ becomes an enharmonic V^7 in the new key. We are all familiar with the sound of singers vocalizing major scales in ascending half steps, as shown in Example 4. To what key does this model modulate?

Example 4

Saint-Saëns satirized this procedure in *The Carnival of the Animals,* in which his "pianists" practice their scales in ascending chromatic order.

Example 5   Saint-Saëns: "Pianists" (No. 11) from *The Carnival of the Animals*

The enharmonic relation between the Ger$^6_5$ and the V^7 can be drawn on to reroute a series of secondary dominants. For instance, if a seventh chord, which normally resolves by descending-5th root movement, is changed into a Ger$^6_5$, the sonority then can easily resolve by half step (Example 6a).

Example 6

A.

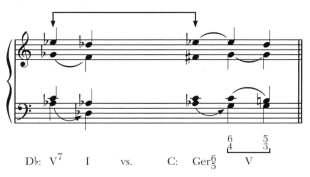

$$\text{D}\flat: \quad \text{V}^7 \qquad \text{I} \qquad \text{vs.} \qquad \text{C:} \quad \text{Ger}^6_5 \qquad \text{V}$$

B. C. P. E. BACH: *SOLFEGGIO*, W. 117/2

c: V^4_3

cycle of secondary dominants

$\begin{pmatrix} \text{V}^7/\flat\text{III} \\ \text{or} \\ \text{Ger}^6_5 \end{pmatrix}$ $\text{Ger}^{\circ 3}$ V   i

In the popular *Solfeggio* of C. P. E. Bach (Example 6b), a cycle of applied seventh chords, all resolving by descending-5th root movement, is by measure 29 in danger of moving outside of the key area of C minor. To prevent this, Bach spells the chord that begins measure 29 not as an A$\flat^7$ (V^7/$\flat$II), which would continue the cycle and move to a D$\flat^7$, but as a Ger$^6_5$, which resolves downward by half step to the $^6_4$ in measure 4. The Ger$^{\circ 3}$ that precedes the $^6_4$ is merely a revoicing of the Ger$^6_5$.

CHROMATIC ALTERATIONS OF DIMINISHED SEVENTH CHORDS

A diminished seventh chord may be changed into a V^7 by lowering one of its notes a half step and, if necessary, respelling some of its other chord members enharmonically. Can you notate the four ways we may mutate the chord F♯ A C E♭ into a V^7? Examples 7a and 7b illustrate this technique as a means of moving to the chromaticized 3rd-related keys of ♭III and VI, respectively.

Example 7

A.   B.

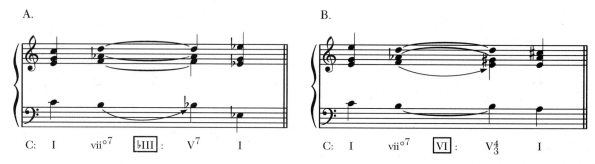

C: I   vii°⁷   ♭III: V⁷   I   C: I   vii°⁷   VI: V⁴₃   I

C.   BEETHOVEN: SYMPHONY NO. 6 ("PASTORAL"), IV

Beethoven frequently employs this procedure; in the tempestuous F-minor Storm movement from his "Pastoral" Symphony (Example 7c) he uses it to modulate from $\boxed{\text{v}}$ to $\boxed{\text{iv}}$.

MODULATION BY STRICT HARMONIC SEQUENCE

One obvious way to introduce a foreign key is to state a phrase in the original tonic and then repeat it verbatim in the new key; this technique is especially effective when the new key is a major or minor 3rd away. Such examples display **sequential modulation** and are akin to those brought about by sectional modulation, as the key change usually occurs between phrases, periods, or sections. In Brahms's G-minor Rhapsody, given in simplified form in Example 8a, the initial phrase begins with an implied V and ends with a G-major triad. This passage is then restated a major 3rd higher, cadencing in B major.

Example 8

A.   BRAHMS: RHAPSODY IN G MINOR, OP. 79, NO. 2 (SIMPLIFIED)

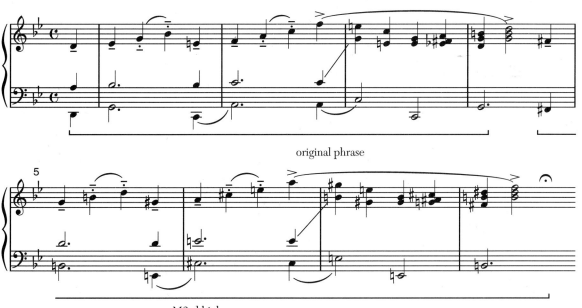

original phrase

sequence a M3rd higher

B. LISZT: "VALLÉE D'OBERMANN" (SECOND VERSION) FROM *ANNÉES DE PÉLERINAGE*

Liszt was especially fond of sequential modulation. What is the harmonic relation between the two phrases in his "Obermann" piece (Example 8b)? What role does the change of mode play?

MODULATION BY CHROMATIC LINEAR PROGRESSION

Some passages modulate to a foreign key through a series of chromatic sequences or other type of linear progression, moving through several transient tonal areas in rapid succession. For instance, the beginning of the Mozart excerpt in Example 9 uses a sequence by descending major 2nds (mm. 73–75) and then one by descending minor 3rds (mm. 76–78) to link the keys of B minor and C major.

Example 9   MOZART: PIANO FANTASIA IN C MINOR, K.475

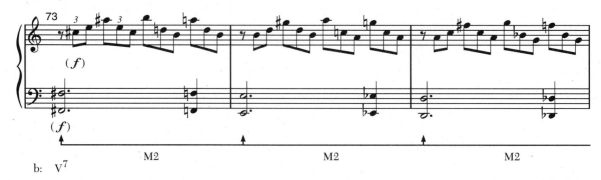

This passage, in fact, also features a modulation to the new key of B♭ major. The F♯ in the bass at the beginning of the excerpt acts as the dominant in B minor; when it reappears an octave lower (m. 78), it is heard in the context of C major, acting as the root of a vii°7/V. But instead of ushering in the key of C major, this diminished seventh chord is transformed into a V7 of B♭ major when its root is lowered one half step (F♯ A C E♭ → F♮ A C E♭).

An Unusual Case of Successive Foreign Modulations

An amazing passage extracted from Bach's "Great" Organ Fantasia in G minor utilizes several of the modulatory techniques we have discussed in this chapter.

Example 10   BACH: FANTASIA AND FUGUE IN G MINOR, BWV 542 ("THE GREAT")

B. (REDUCTION 1)

C. (REDUCTION 2)

The half cadence in the tonic key of G minor at the beginning of Example 10 is followed by a filled-in arpeggiation of its vii°^{7}, which is enharmonically spelled as a vii°^{7}/V in the foreign key of E♭ minor, or $\boxed{vi}$ (F♯ A C E♭ = A C E♭ G♭); see measure 20 in the first reduction (Example 10b). The $^6_4$ that is chromatically prolonged in measure 21 resolves deceptively to VI, or C♭, in measure 22, which initiates an ascending chromatic movement in the bass line that supports a series of tonicized first-inversion triads. Note the displacement of the voices that occurs between measures 23 and 24; this is indicated by arrows in the first reduction. The F-minor ^{6} chord at the beginning of measure 24 is chromatically altered within the upward flourish, turning the F into an F♯ and the A♭ into an A, producing a D^7 by the end of the measure that now functions as V^7 in the original key. We may consider the section that is enclosed within brackets in the middleground reduction (Example 10c) as an extended linear "interpolation" that bridges the pair of dominant sevenths on D. Although we arrive back at our original chord, the tonal motion has implied a transient shift to E♭ minor on the way.

Terms and Concepts for Review

enharmonic modulation
　　using diminished seventh or V^7 chords
　　using a Ger$^6_5$ = V^7, *or vice versa*

sequential modulation
foreign modulation by chromatic voice
　　leading

Symmetrical Divisions of the Octave

Our discussion of diatonic sequences in Chapters 20 and 22 established three basic categories of root movement—by successive 2nd, 3rd, and 5th. Chapters 35 and 37 outlined how these three types of root movement could be chromatically elaborated. As we have seen in these four chapters, a strict intervallic pattern of these three root movements will eventually lead us out of the original key area. In most tonal music, therefore, these strict patterns are broken somewhere within the sequence by one or more "correcting" intervals, so that the music remains in the original key. The diatonic interval projections shown in Example 1 contain such disruptions, which we have bracketed. In the stepwise motion (Example 1a), the whole step B–A disrupts the succession of two major 2nds and one minor 2nd (see also Example 2 in Chapter 35). In Example 1b, the minor 3rd from D to B breaks up the pattern of alternating major and minor 3rds. And a single diminished 5th interrupts the descending perfect-5th progression (Example 1c).

Example 1

A. By M2/M2/m2's

B. By ALTERNATING m3/M3's

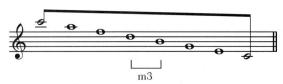

C. By P5's

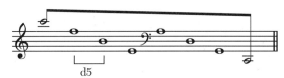

Because of the presence of these "correcting" intervals within the diatonic system, we may consider the diatonic collection as asymmetrical. The dominant scale degree divides the tonic octave into two *unequal* segments, a lower 5th and an upper 4th. The scale steps $\hat{1}$, $\hat{5}$, and $\hat{8}$ define the octave range ($\hat{1}$–$\hat{8}$ or $\hat{5}$–$\hat{5}$) of many diatonic melodies. The division point at the dominant serves to strengthen our sense of gravitational pull toward the tonic, since $\hat{5}$ has a marked tendency to return or resolve to the stable $\hat{1}$ (partly because the root note of a perfect 5th is its lower tone).

In order to loosen the ties with the diatonic tonal system, composers of the common-practice period began to experiment with partitioning the tonic octave into *equal-sized* interval segments, using altered or chromatic notes. The **symmetrical divisions of the octave** that result may occur at various harmonic levels: in a chordal progression, in a harmonic sequence, in temporary tonicizations, in a transient modulation, or even as the underlying key scheme of a complete movement. These symmetrical root movements may or may not complete the interval cycle through the octave. When they do, they often prolong a single basic harmony; when they don't, they may serve as a transition to a foreign key. In all cases, normal harmonic function is momentarily suspended to a greater degree than in most diatonically oriented root movements, resulting in a more pronounced sense of tonal ambiguity. In the continuing quest for harmonic innovation, the increasing practice of basing harmonic schemes on symmetrical divisions of the octave during the nineteenth century contributed to a gradual breakdown of the tonal system.

SYMMETRICAL ROOT MOVEMENTS

The octave may be symmetrically divided by four different intervals: successive major 2nds (two half steps), minor 3rds (three half steps), major 3rds (four half steps), or the tritone (six half steps). The divisions can be seen on the "clock faces" in Figure 1, on which consecutive half steps are marked off. The same patterns will obviously result when these root movements are transposed to other tones.

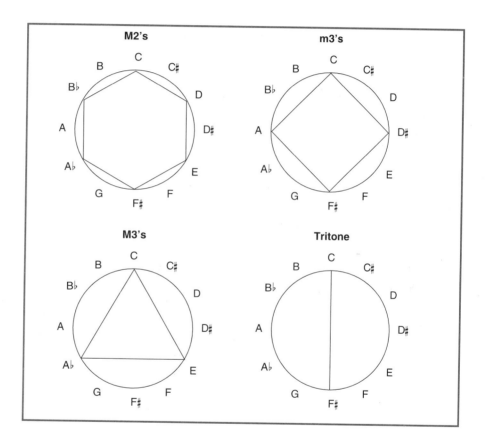

Figure 1

You might note the following interconnections between these symmetrical octave divisions: the major-2nd cycle coincides with the major-3rd cycle; the minor-3rd cycle coincides with the tritone division; the major-2nd cycle is related to the minor-3rd cycle by their common tritone. In this chapter we will examine each of these symmetrical divisions of the octave, or possible symmetrical root movements. In many of the examples below, we have dispensed with roman-numeral analysis and simply indicated the roots of the successive chords.

Root Movement by Major 2nd

We rarely encounter complete cycles of major 2nds, since they would result in a sequence based on the whole-tone scale.[1] One such progression, however, occurs in the "Witches' Sabbath" movement of Berlioz's *Symphonie fantastique*, where the roots of the chromatic triads descend by major 2nd.

Example 2   BERLIOZ: *SYMPHONIE FANTASTIQUE*, V

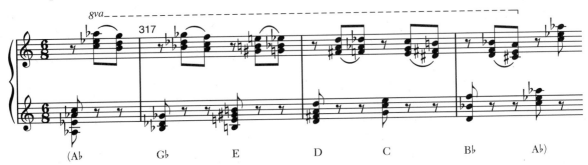

Such patterns normally break off after the fourth or fifth "whole step" and tend to employ applied chords (such as secondary V⁷'s, vii°⁷'s, or even Aug6ths) that tonicize each successive degree. In Chopin's G-minor Ballade, Op. 23, one such sequential passage forms the climax of the middle section in E♭ major, as shown in reduction in Example 3.

Example 3   CHOPIN: BALLADE IN G MINOR, OP. 23 (REDUCTION OF MM. 150–159)

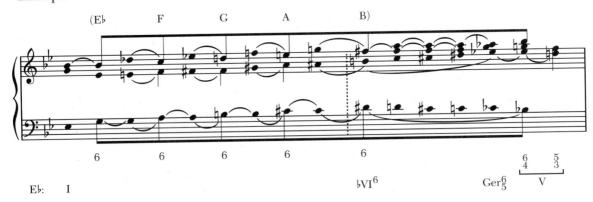

The consecutive $^6_3$ triads starting from G³ that form the underlying ascending root movement by major 2nd (marked with stemmed notes in the reduction) are preceded by secondary vii°$^6_5$ chords. They ascend from I⁶ to an enharmonic ♭VI⁶ (C♭⁶ = B♮⁶) before descending chromatically to a Ger$^6_5$ that ushers in a concluding $^6_4$ cadence back in E♭.

1. Refer to the discussion of scales in Appendix 2.

FOR FURTHER STUDY

Another example of a descending whole-tone root sequence may be found in measures 229–33 of the third movement of Chopin's Piano Concerto in F minor, Op. 21. Not only does this passage transverse the *entire* octave, but each member of the sequence is preceded by its secondary dominant seventh.

Root Movement by Minor 3rd

Root movement by minor 3rd is probably the most common symmetrical progression. The four transpositions that result outline a diminished seventh chord, such as C♯–E–G–B♭–C♯. Instances of both sequential and nonsequential motion occur. Study the illustrative excerpts in Example 4, with their accompanying reductions. In the brief passage from Liszt's famous "Un sospiro" (Example 4a), a series of major triads forms a descending progression of chords related by minor 3rds (B♭–G–E–D♭). The triads are linked by passing tones in the bass. The *Lohengrin* excerpt (Example 4c), on the other hand, features a series of momentarily tonicized keys (A♭–C♭–D–F, or Ⅰ – ♭Ⅲ – ♯Ⅳ – Ⅵ) whose roots ascend by minor 3rds. (This passage is not strictly sequential.)

Example 4

A. LISZT: "UN SOSPIRO" FROM *TROIS CAPRICES POÉTIQUES*

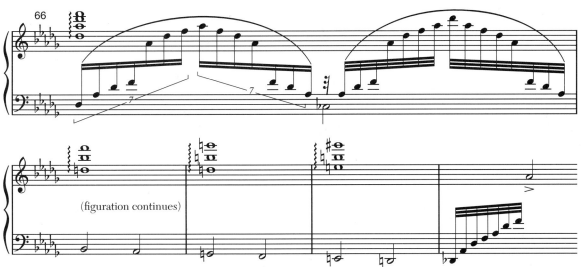

(figuration continues)

B. (REDUCTION)

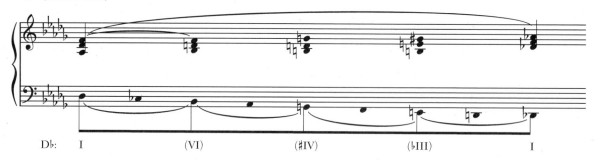

D♭: I   (VI)   (♯IV)   (♭III)   I

C. WAGNER: *LOHENGRIN*, ACT I, SCENE 2

D. (REDUCTION)

Ab: I   bIII   #IV   VI   I

Root Movement by Major 3rd

If we turn back to Figure 1, we can see that strict sequencing by major 3rds permits only three transpositions before returning to the original chord or key: C–E–G♯–C (ascending), or C–A♭–E–C (descending). In the Franck excerpt (Example 5), the descending major 3rds within the brief but complete sequence are linked by a 5–♭6 motion.

Example 5   FRANCK: *CHORAL NO. 1 POUR GRAND ORGUE*

A.

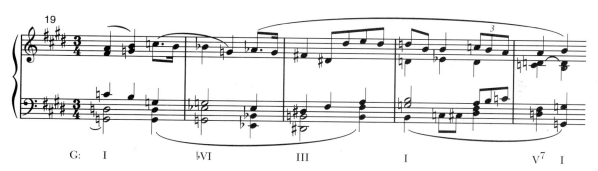

G: I   bVI   III   I   V⁷   I

B. (REDUCTION)

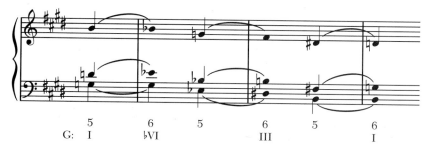

G: I   bVI   III   I

Wagner's "Magic Sleep" motive in Example 6 prolongs a C♯-major harmony. This theme exhibits a complete descending chromatic scale in the upper voice.

Example 6   WAGNER: "MAGIC SLEEP" MOTIVE FROM *SIEGFRIED*, ACT III

A.

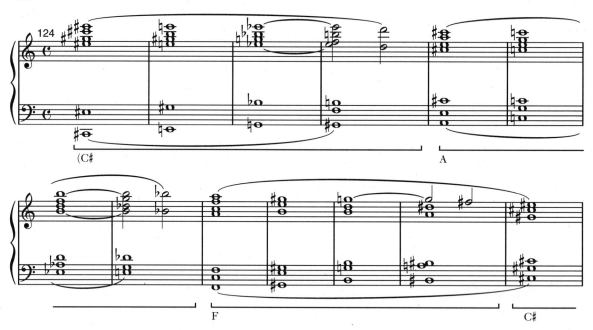

B. (REDUCTION)

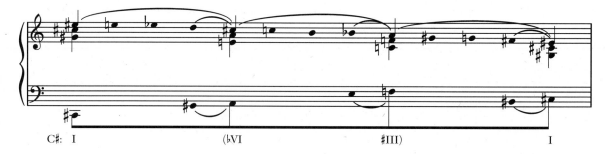

This chromatic descent is supported by major triads on every fifth chord, the bass notes forming a series of falling major 3rds (C♯–A–F–C♯) that outlines an augmented triad, as denoted by the brackets. The harmonies enclosed in each bracket are successively transposed a major 3rd lower. Can you find an exception to this exact transposition? If this progression were extended, it would continue the same pattern endlessly, thus portraying the "eternal sleep" of the earth goddess Erda.

Root Movement by Tritone

The tritone splits the octave exactly in half. In the common-practice period, root movement by tritone is usually reserved for special effects in isolated chordal progressions. In Example 7, for instance, Berlioz depicts Faust's arrival in Hell with a demons' chorus that alternates between B-major and F-major triads (I–♭V), evoking the *diabolus in musica*.[2]

Example 7 Berlioz: "Hell" Scene from *The Damnation of Faust,* Act IV (vocal parts only)

EXTENDED ROOT MOVEMENT BY PERFECT 5TH

A strict series of half steps—that is, the chromatic scale—will eventually cycle through all twelve pitch-classes. Likewise, a series of perfect 5ths without a correcting tritone will also cycle through all twelve pitch-classes. However, composers rarely choose to cycle through the entire chromatic collection. The Bach passage in Example 8 cycles through seven consecutive perfect 5ths (D–G–C–F–B♭–E♭–A♭–D♭) before it abandons the pattern by introducing several diminished seventh chords that lead to the key of E minor. By this time the original key of G minor has been completely obscured.

2. See Chapter 38.

Example 8 BACH: FANTASIA AND FUGUE IN G MINOR, BWV 542 ("THE GREAT")

Occasionally we may find two symmetrical root movements, one of which is nested within the other. The Chopin sequence in Example 9 illustrates an almost-complete cycle of descending perfect 5ths. The downbeat "cadence" that occurs every fourth chord produces a series of tonicizations that divide the 5ths progression into segments marked by descending minor 3rds (G–B♭–D♭–E).

FOR FURTHER STUDY

During a transitional passage in the Scherzo of his Ninth Symphony, Beethoven initiates a series of descending triads that alternates both chord types (major–minor) and root movement (minor– 3rd). Since the succession of two 3rds forms a perfect 5th, the result is an extended cycle of perfect 5ths; consult Example 2 in Chapter 38 of the Workbook.

Example 9 Chopin: Nocturne in G major, Op. 37, No. 2

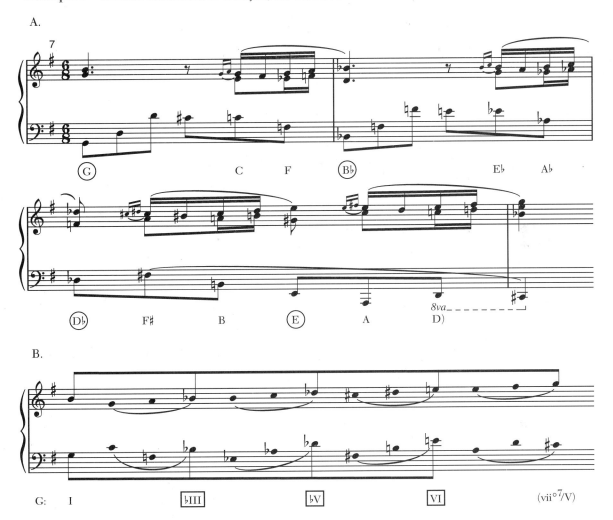

The Omnibus Sequence

The so-called *omnibus sequence* is a symmetrical minor-3rd sequence that employs chromatic voice leading by contrary motion.[3] This type of sequence involves a three-chord pattern that progresses by contrary chromatic motion, which we introduced in Chapter 37; see the discussion associated with Example 8 in that chapter. The pattern is bracketed in Example 10 below. The first chord of each segment may consist of either a diminished seventh chord or an Aug6th chord; the second chord serves as a miniature

3. This term was coined by Victor Yellin.

axis for the neighboring chromatic motion (e.g., A♭–G–F♯). When successive statements of this pattern occur a minor 3rd apart, a complete chromatic scale is produced in one of the voices (usually the bass). The remaining voices retain common tones between each pair of sequential segments (separated by bar lines in Example 10). This sequence may either ascend (Example 10a) or descend (Example 10b).

Example 10

A.

B.

Two pieces that contain this specialized type of sequence appear in Examples 11 and 12. The Beethoven passage, shown in simplified notation (Example 11), prolongs the applied dominant seventh chord (V^7/IV in D major) that frames the sequence.

Example 11   BEETHOVEN: SYMPHONY NO. 2, I (SIMPLIFICATION)

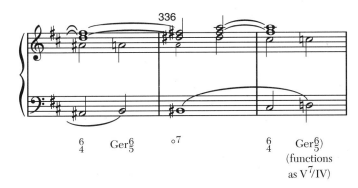

$\begin{smallmatrix}6\\4\end{smallmatrix}$ Ger$\begin{smallmatrix}6\\5\end{smallmatrix}$ $^{\circ}7$ $\begin{smallmatrix}6\\4\end{smallmatrix}$ Ger$\begin{smallmatrix}6\\5\end{smallmatrix}$)
(functions
as V^7/IV)

Within the sequence, the diminished-seventh harmony that begins each sequential segment is held constant, merely enharmonically changing its spelling in measure 336 in relation to the $\begin{smallmatrix}6\\4\end{smallmatrix}$ that follows. The Ger$\begin{smallmatrix}6\\5\end{smallmatrix}$ that ends each sequential segment continues the chromatic bass motion into the following segment. This form of the omnibus usually ascends chromatically in the bass.

The descending omnibus sequence in Example 12 uses both forms of the German Aug6th ($\begin{smallmatrix}6\\5\end{smallmatrix}$ and $^{\circ}3$) exclusively.

Example 12   MUSORGSKY: *BORIS GODUNOV*, ACT III

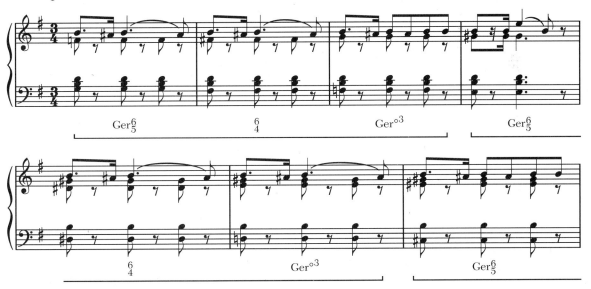

Composers employing the omnibus sequence will often break off the sequential motion before returning to the original chord. How many statements appear in the preceding Musorgsky excerpt? Here the four-measure phrasing conflicts with the three-measure sequential segments. Since the upper voice retains a single tone through most of the passage, the contrary chromatic motion is found between the bass and an inner voice.

TONAL SCHEMES USING SYMMETRICAL DIVISIONS OF THE OCTAVE

Basing the tonal structure of an entire movement on one of the symmetrical patterns discussed in this chapter is rare. Composers were generally reluctant to employ such a tonal scheme because it would omit the dominant key area, the single most important harmonic relation to the tonic. Nevertheless, isolated examples of this technique appear in late nineteenth-century music, including two in Tchaikovsky's Symphony No. 4.

The opening movement of this symphony is based on a progression of key centers by ascending minor 3rds, as shown in the diagram in Example 13.

Example 13   TCHAIKOVSKY: SYMPHONY NO. 4, I

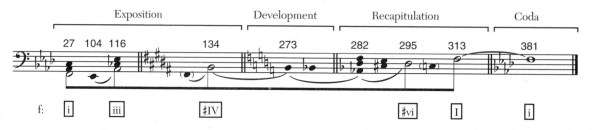

Although each basic key area is preceded by its V chord, dominant harmony plays a decidedly subsidiary role in this movement, and is certainly not an integral part of the overall tonal structure.[4]

The harmonic scheme of the Scherzo (Example 14) is organized around major-3rd relations (F–A–D♭–F)—that is, a long-range arpeggiation of an augmented triad.

---

4. In this symphony's second movement, a harmonic progression by rising minor 3rds in measures 110–16 recalls the basic tonal scheme of the previous movement: A♭–B–D–F.

Example 14 TCHAIKOVSKY: SYMPHONY NO. 4, III

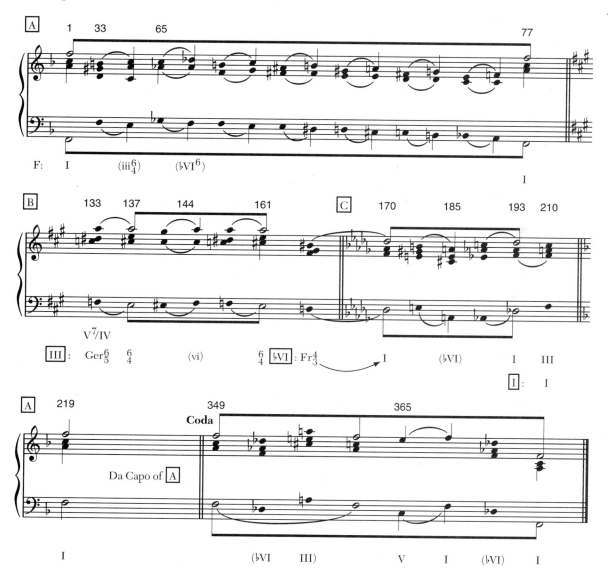

This movement divides into a large ternary form (ABA), with the central keys functioning as a kind of double Trio around the framing F-major pillars of the Scherzo. A different orchestral force is deployed for each key: *pizzicato* strings for the F-major Scherzo, woodwinds for the first Trio in A major, and brass for the second Trio in D♭ major. In the opening F-major section, the tonal centers of A and D♭ are already anticipated in measures 33 and 65, respectively. Observe how Tchaikovsky handles the modulatory links between the basic tonal centers of the movement. In the coda, a series of chromatic 3rd-related triads recalls the principal tonal areas of the piece. This series is followed by the only structural cadential dominant in the piece, which precedes the final tonic harmony.

The principal theme of each section has a different melodic character; however, the same basic motive, a descending diatonic tetrachord ($\hat{8}$–$\hat{7}$–$\hat{6}$–$\hat{5}$), is seen in each of the three themes (Example 15).[5]

Example 15

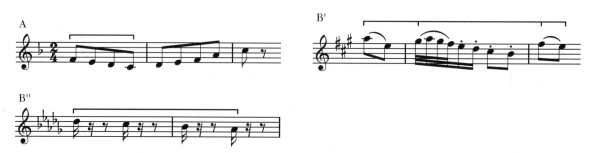

The constant use of symmetrical harmonic progressions and tonal schemes tends to undermine the diatonic tonal system. As certain composers of the late nineteenth century, such as Liszt and Wagner, intensified their use of chromatic voice leading and symmetrical relations, traditional tonal function in their music began to recede. Tonality became increasingly vague and unstable, so that by the turn of the century it was only a small step into the uncharted realms of atonality.

In Chapter 40 we will investigate a composition written around the turn of the century that skirts the very figures of tonality, combining remnants of traditional tonal practice with procedures arising out of purely linear motion that would define the new language of atonality.

Terms and Concepts for Review

symmetrical divisions of the octave
symmetrical root movement by major 2nd, minor 3rd, major 3rd, and tritone

omnibus sequence
tonal scheme using symmetrical relations

---

5. The opening of the Finale employs the same tetrachord that occurred in the F-major Scherzo section: F–E–D–C.

At the Limits of Tonality

BERG'S *FOUR SONGS*, OPUS 2

IN THE LAST FEW CHAPTERS of this text, we have observed how the use of chromatic techniques began to break down the tonal language of common-practice period music. Although a number of early twentieth-century composers, such as Richard Strauss, Giacomo Puccini, Jan Sibelius, Gustav Mahler, and Sergei Rachmaninoff, continued to cultivate the tonal heritage of the 1800s, many others, such as Claude Debussy, Alexander Scriabin, Igor Stravinsky, Béla Bartók, and the composers of the "Second Viennese School," purposefully moved outside the confines of traditional harmonic practice. Stravinsky and Bartók continued to employ diatonic, folk-song–like melodies, but often set them within layers of complex dissonant harmonies that frequently blurred or undermined their tonality.[1] The three composers of the Second Viennese School—Arnold Schoenberg, Alban Berg, and Anton Webern—consciously employed melodic and harmonic materials devoid of any tonal basis, in a quest for what Schoenberg called the "emancipation of the dissonance."

The transition from tonality to what we call **atonality**—that is, the absence or negation of any tonic or functional tertian harmony—was a gradual

1. This technique is especially apparent in Stravinsky's early ballets, such as *The Rite of Spring* (1913).

process. Many compositions written during the early 1900s retain vestiges of traditional tonal techniques interspersed with more atonal procedures. As the melodic and harmonic procedures of the common-practice period were abandoned, they were replaced by new compositional techniques.

In Schoenberg, Berg, and Webern's explorations of new pitch resources, chordal progressions, which were previously controlled by tendencies of harmonic function and careful regulation of consonance and dissonance, became freely dissonant sonorities that were more the product of the linear motion of the individual voices. These "emancipated" pitch elements were often placed within complex textural and rhythmic settings and developed in a process that Schoenberg called "continuous variation."

For the Viennese, these atonal procedures drew upon a novel approach to motives and motivic treatment. Here, a small group of notes might be employed like a traditional motive—that is, a recognizable melodic entity heard in a variety of contexts. It could also be subjected to such techniques as mirror inversion, or could be heard simultaneously—as a chord. The distinction between melody and harmony thus tended to become blurred in this music.

In this chapter we will investigate the juxtaposition of lingering tonal procedures with more radical atonal tendencies in Alban Berg's *Four Songs*, Op. 2 (1908–10; revised 1920). These pieces were written during the period that Berg was courting the affections of Helene Nahowsky, whom he would marry in 1911. The original dedication reads: "To Helene. Alban Berg."

Although Berg drew his texts for the *Four Songs* from two different poetic sources,[2] all of the poems share the common theme of sleep and death. It has been suggested that Berg, in this "psychological exploration of, and journey to, a distant world of 'sleep-death' as an escape from reality," looked to Wagner's *Tristan und Isolde* as a musical source.[3]

The idea of the desire for sleep (= death) as a recurring textual motif is underscored by recurring musical material throughout the *Four Songs*. Some of this material is based in tonal practice; some of it is tonally indeterminate. It is this recurring material that lends the songs much of their fragile and intermittent harmonic stability.

The initial song, "Schlafen, Schlafen, nichts als Schlafen!" ("Sleeping, Sleeping, Nothing but Sleeping!") is a typical example of this merging of tonal and atonal procedures. For instance, the D–A 5th in the lower register

---

2. The text for the first song is drawn from Friedrich Hebbel's "Dem Schmerz sein Recht" (1842). The remaining three songs find their source in Alfred Mombert's *Der Glühende* (1896). In its concentration on a single poetic motif, Berg's Op. 2 set resembles the true song cycles of the Romantic period rather than the collections of textually unrelated songs often gathered under one opus number.

3. Stephen Kett, "A Conservative Revolution: The Music of the Four Songs Op. 2," in *The Berg Companion*, edited by Douglas Jarman (Boston: Northeastern Univ. Press, 1990), 67–87.

(Example 1a), with the F♮ in measure 2, suggests a D-minor tonality at the beginning of the song, as it does when it recurs in later songs. Berg continually associated this key with Helene.[4]

Example 1   BERG: "SCHLAFEN, SCHLAFEN"

A.   MM. 1–12

4. In several of his letters to her during this period he referred to the "most glorious D-minor chords of your soul" and called her "my most glorious symphony in D minor." This key continued to recur as an important tonal center in Berg's later works: the Op. 6 Orchestral Pieces, *Der Wein,* and the final interlude from his opera *Wozzeck.*

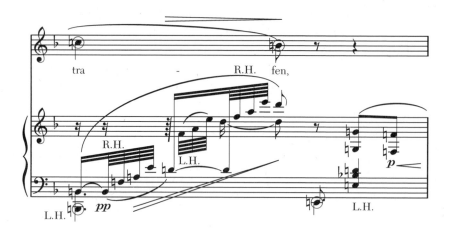

B. (REDUCTION)

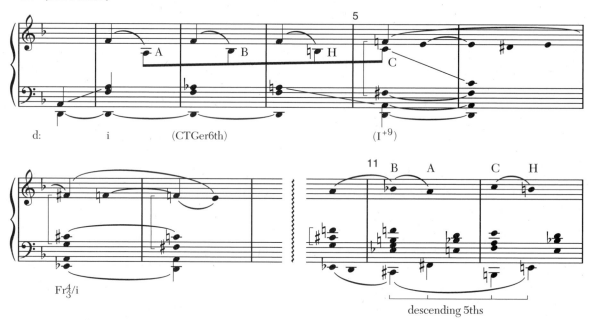

Schlafen, Schlafen, nichts als Schlafen!
Kein Erwachen, keinen Traum!
Jener Wehen, die mich trafen,
Leisestes Erinnern kaum,
das ich, wenn des Lebens Fülle
nieder klingt in meiner Ruh',
nur noch tiefer mich verhülle,
fester zu die Augen tu!

Sleeping, Sleeping, nothing but sleeping!
No awakening, no dream!
Of those griefs that afflicted me,
Hardly the faintest memory,
So that, when the abundance of life
Rings deep into my slumber,
I cover myself still more deeply,
Shut my eyes more soundly.

While the bass maintains its D pedal in measures 1–4, the melodic line heard in the voice part ascends chromatically: A^3–$B\flat^3$–$B\natural^3$; see the circled notes in Example 1a. These pitches probably allude to the initial letters in the names of the composer (*Alban Berg*) and *Helene*; in German, B♭ is called B and B♮ is called H. The practice of basing compositions on motives derived from a person's name was a time-honored procedure; several fugues of J. S. Bach use subjects based on his own last name (B♭, A, C, B♮).[5] In fact, the rising half-step line in these opening measures employs all but one of the B–A–C–H pitches in rearranged order; the piano alone furnishes the remaining pitch (C^4) in measure 5.

A major-minor seventh chord on D with an added F♮ in the upper voice appears in measure 5. The resulting sonority (D F♯ A C F♮ [= E♯]) can be considered an augmented-ninth chord with both a major and minor 3rd (refer back to Chapter 31, p. 480); this chord functions as a kind of referential "tonic" throughout this song and the rest of the cycle. The pitches F♯ C F that lie within it (bracketed in the right-hand piano part in Example 1a) form a three-note nontertian pitch collection called a trichord, which plays a significant role in the song cycle. We will refer to this collection as a ⟨TT–P4⟩, since its intervallic structure, spelled from the bottom note upward, consists of a tritone plus a perfect 4th.[6] Even though this augmented-ninth chord's F♮ "resolves" to E in measure 5, forming a major-ninth chord, the F♮ is continually stressed throughout the song by its metric placement on strong beats. The Aug9th chord first heard in measure 5 alternates throughout measures 5–10 with another Aug9th chord a half-step higher (E♭ G C♯ [= D♭] F♯); this second chord acts as a kind of neighboring harmony and implies a French Aug6th (E♭ G A C♯)—whose A appears in one of the lower voices—with an added F♯.[7] This chord also contains a ⟨TT–P4⟩: G C♯ F♯.

5. This is only the first instance of this procedure in Berg's compositions. The motto theme that opens his *Chamber Concerto* is based on the names of Schoenberg, Webern, and Berg himself. Later, in his *Lyric Suite* for string quartet, Berg derived a four-note motive from his own initials (*A B*) and those of his secret mistress *Hanna Fuchs*.

6. Contemporary theorists classify this sonority as a (0,1,6) set class. The system of classifying and manipulating such recurring pitch collections in twentieth-century music, called *set theory*, arranges the pitch-classes so that they appear in their *normal form*—that is, so that the distance between the outer tones is as small as possible and the smallest of the internal intervals occurs at the bottom of the set. The notes are then assigned numbers, which refer to the intervals within the set, measured in half steps. In order to arrive at the normal form for our trichord, we must therefore displace the F♯ an octave higher, forming C F♮ F♯, and then invert the set around C (F♯ G C) so that the half step occurs at the bottom. Thus, the numbers 0,1,6 represent the first pitch (always called 0), the pitch one a semitone above it (1), and the pitch six semitones above the first (6). The (0,1,6) set class can easily be transposed to any pitch level and can take many musical forms.

7. If we relate both of these chords to the referential D sonority, the first may be considered as a kind of altered thirteenth chord based on the dominant A, while the chord on E♭ lies a half step above the D. These two alternating Aug9th chords curiously anticipate similar

In measures 11–12 the bass moves through a series of perfect 5ths (C♯–F♯–B–E); see the circled notes in Example 1a. Although the harmonies they support do not have a clear tonal function, the overall impression of a descending 5th motion remains. Notice that the upper notes of the vocal line rearrange the previous A–B♭–B♮–C line to form the name B A C H, which is immediately sequenced a step higher in the first two notes of the vocal line in measures 13–14 (Example 2): C–B–D–C♯. (This reference may represent Berg's way of implying that the earlier A–B–H motive is indeed linked to his name and that of Helene.)

The music abandons any sense of tonal reference or function in measures 13–20, where it instead consists largely of complex dissonant harmonies derived by linear motion. The prevailing linear chromaticism in the various voice parts contrasts with the sporadic 5th motion of the bass in measures 13–14 (E♭–G♯–C♯) and 18–20 (A–D–G). A brief passage from this section is quoted in Example 2.

Example 2 "Schlafen, Schlafen" mm. 13–16

harmonic sonorities and relationships that will appear in jazz pieces of the 1940s. In fact, such tritone substitutions (A–E♭) are a common occurrence in jazz harmony of this period.

In measures 20–21 Berg resumes his original A–B–H motive and begins to weave it within the concluding section, which recapitulates much of the opening material, freely reversing the order of its elements (Example 3).

Example 3 BERG: "SCHLAFEN, SCHLAFEN"

A. MM. 21–30

B. (REDUCTION)

Two references to the A–B–H motive (now heard in reverse order: H–B–A) precede the return of the double-3rd D chord in measure 24 (now with F♯ in the bass). The original D–A 5th melodically works its way downward through the texture (see the circled notes in mm. 24–26 and the bracketed notes in the reduction). In the last four measures the A–B–H motive recurs, but again in reverse order (F–B, F–B♭, and F–A), enabling the song to conclude in D minor.

The initial song establishes four important compositional elements: an overall D-minor tonality, a rising half-step motive (A–B♭–B♮–C in mm. 2–5), a descending 5th progression (mm. 11–12), and the double-3rd D sonority with its embedded (TT–P4) (m. 5). The (TT–P4) itself is derived from two of the three other elements, containing both a half step and a perfect 5th (or 4th): F♮ F♯ C. All four elements will recur in later songs of the cycle.

The second song, "Schlafend trägt man mich in mein Heimatland" ("Sleeping, I Am Borne to My Homeland"), carries a key signature of six flats that suggests the key of E♭ minor, representing a half-step relation to the key of the first song. The piece opens with a V°⁷ and concludes with an altered tonic harmony (V°⁷/iv), which leads into the A♭ minor of the following song (Examples 4a–4c). The consistent use of V°⁷ (the French Aug6th sonority) gives a decided whole-tone character to the song.[8]

8. For a discussion of the whole-tone scale, refer to Appendix 2.

Example 4 BERG: "SCHLAFEND TRÄGT MAN MICH"

A. MM. 1–4

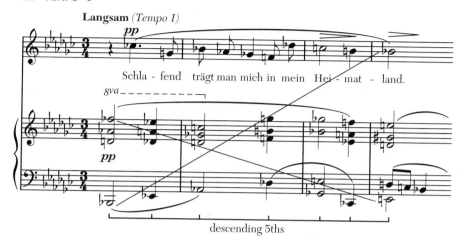

B. MM. 4–8

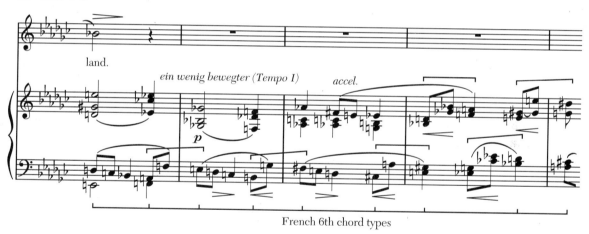

C. MM. 15–18

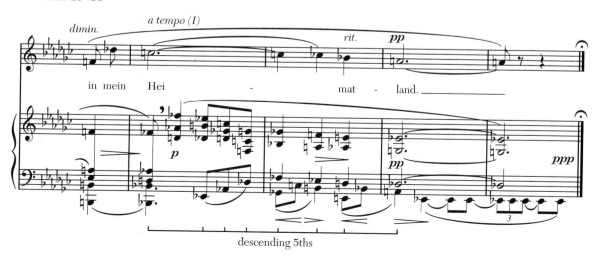

Schlafend trägt man mich in mein Heimatland.	Sleeping, I am borne to my homeland.
Ferne komm' ich her,	I come from far away.
über Gipfel, über Schlünde,	Over peaks, over abysses,
über ein dunkles Meer	Over a dark sea,
in mein Heimatland.	To my homeland.

The opening progression (Example 4a) employs a succession of rising perfect 4ths or falling 5ths in the bass (labeled "descending 5ths" in the music) like that heard in the previous song: B♭–E♭–A♭–D♭–G♭–C♭–E♮. The chords above consist of a series of French Aug6th sonorities (or V°⁷'s), which continue into the middle of the song (Example 4b). The first and last sonorities of Example 4a contain the same pitch-classes, suggesting a return to the opening chord on the word "homeland"; we might consider this progression a prolongation of the opening French Aug6th, with a voice exchange occurring between the B♭ and F♭ (= E♮) in the outer voices. In this song, Berg seems to frequently allude to the opening melodic motive of the *Tristan* Prelude (minor 6th up, half step down), found in Example 1 of Chapter 36. In measures 15–17 (Example 4c) the succession of descending 5ths is repeated and extended before cadencing on the final E♭ dominant sonority (E♭°⁷).

The third song, "Nun ich der Riesen Stärksten überwand" ("Now I Have Overcome the Mightiest of the Giants"), is cast in the key of A♭ minor, heard most clearly in the first four measures of the vocal line, which is built on arpeggiations of the tonic A♭-minor triad (Example 5a). Note, however, the intrusion of the F♮⁴ on beat 3 of measure 2 (see the reduction in Example 5b).

Example 5 BERG: "NUN ICH DER RIESEN STÄRKSTEN ÜBERWAND"

A.

B. (REDUCTION)

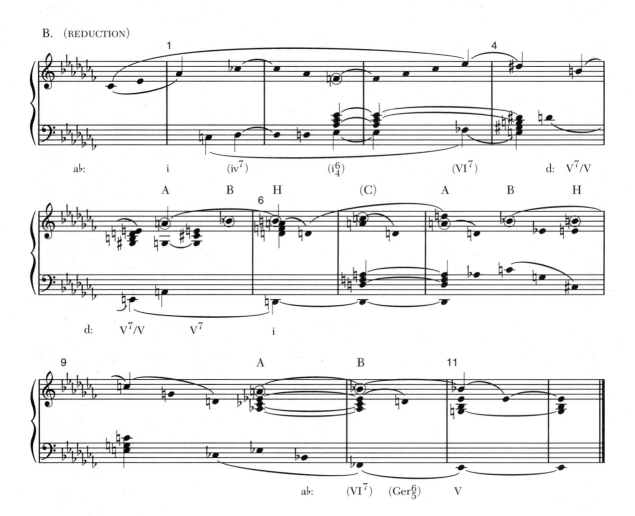

Nun ich der Riesen Stärksten
    überwand,
mich aus dem dunkelsten Land
    heimfand
an einer weißen Märchenhand,
hallen schwer die Glocken;
und ich wanke durch die Gassen
    schlafbefangen.

Now I have overcome the
    mightiest of the giants,
Found my way home out of the
    darkest land,
Guided by a white fairy hand;
The bells resound heavily,
And I stumble through the
    streets, awkward with sleep.

This song recapitulates the elements heard in the opening piece of the
set. The (TT–P4) occurs as the last three notes (a descending perfect 4th

and diminished 5th) of a four-note melodic motive (A♭–C–G–D♭) heard in measure 1, which by its loud dynamics and doubling in octaves alludes to the "giants" ("Riesen") of the text. This motive recurs—usually in transposition—in measures 2, 3, 4, 8, and 9–10 (see the brackets in Example 5a). In measures 1–3 the bass ascends chromatically (D♭–D♮–E♭–E♮), the last pitch acting as an enharmonic pivot (F♭ = E♮ in mm. 3–4) that moves to V⁷/V in D minor (m. 4), the original key of the opening song and a tritone removed from the present tonic of A♭ minor. As the vocal part introduces the syllable "-heim" ("homeward") in measure 4, a descending 5th progression moves to D minor just as the upper voice sounds the A–B–H motive. Notice that Helene's B♮ occurs at the same moment as *her* D-minor harmony on the words "a white fairy hand," possibly representing an allusion to her. The return of the repeating A–D melodic 5th (mm. 6–8) found in the first song indeed brings us "home," although here it also depicts the resounding bells ("hallen . . . die Glocken"). Another iteration of the A–B–H motive in the piano part (m. 8) leads to the C⁵ positioned over and emphasized by a C⁶ chord in measure 9. The motion toward the final half cadence on E♭, the dominant in A♭ minor, repeats the progression found from the end of measure 2 (A♭⁶) through the end of measure 3 (F♭⁷). But rather than moving to D minor, this second F♭ sonority resolves by half step via a German Aug6th to the final E♭ cadence chord.

It is interesting that the last half beat of measure 2 (A♭ C♭ E♭ F) and the last beat of measure 4 (E G♯ B D) employ the same pitch-classes found in the opening harmonies of the *Tristan* Prelude, though the first sonority occurs in a different inversion (Example 6).

Example 6

A. WAGNER, *TRISTAN UND ISOLDE*

B. BERG, "NUN ICH"

This reference to the "Tristan" chord is probably not coincidental, as Berg had already inserted a similar allusion in his Piano Sonata, Op. 1 (mm. 90–101), and later would actually quote the entire *Tristan* passage in the last movement of his *Lyric Suite*.

The three sonorities in this third song that evoke any sense of tonality are stressed by their placement within the piece, at the beginning (mm.

2–3) the Ab-minor $^6_4$, in the middle (m. 6) the D-minor chord, and within the final cadence the Eb triad. The first two sonorities contain an added 6th (F^4 and Bb^4, respectively). Berg's long-range "tonal" organization is demonstrated by the fact that the roots of the three harmonies (Ab D Eb) represent a transposition and rearrangement of the F♯ C F♮ motive in the initial song. In addition, the basic "keys" of the first three songs outline a (TT–P4) with the same pitch-classes: D Eb Ab!

The final song of the set, "Warm die Lüfte" ("Warm Are the Breezes"), is frankly atonal and contains few references to musical material heard in the preceding pieces. As such, it represents the completion of Berg's transition to purely atonal writing. In measures 18–19, however, the first two pitches (Bb and A) of the A–B–H motive occur, coinciding with the word "Stirb!" ("Die!"). The curious harmonic progression that follows summarizes the semitonal motives, the root movement by perfect 5th, and the (TT–P4) heard throughout the set (Example 7a).

Example 7   BERG: "WARM DIE LÜFTE"

A. MM. 19–25

B. (REDUCTION)

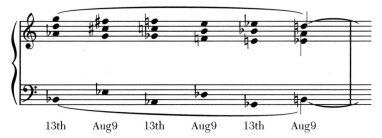

13th Aug9 13th Aug9 13th Aug9

Warm die Lüfte, es sprießt Gras auf sonnigen Wiesen, Horch! Horch, es flötet die Nachtigall. Ich will singen: Droben hoch im düstern Bergforst, es schmilzt und glitzert kalter Schnee, ein Mädchen in grauem Kleide lehnt an feuchtem Eichstamm, krank sind ihre zarten Wangen, die grauen Augen fiebern durch Düsterriesenstämme. "Er kommt noch nicht. Er lässt mich warten . . . " Stirb! Der Eine stirbt, daneben der Andre lebt: Das macht die Welt so tiefschön.	Warm are the breezes, grass flourishes on sunny meadows. Hark! Hark! the nightingale is warbling. I want to sing: High up in the gloomy mountain forest, Cold snow melts and glitters, A girl dressed in gray leans on a damp oak trunk Sickly are her tender cheeks; Her gray eyes burn from between the great dark trunks. "He still hasn't come. He leaves me waiting . . . " Die! The one dies while the other lives: That is what makes the world so deeply beautiful.

As the bass moves upward by perfect 4ths (mm. 20–22), the (TT–P4)'s progress downward by half steps. This passage sounds remarkably contemporary, the resulting harmonies representing an alternation of two chords standard in modern jazz: an Aug9th chord and an altered thirteenth chord (Example 7b). The final sonority of the progression, an Aug9th built on B♮, is prolonged to the end of the song. This allusion to a kind of B tonality may refer to the concluding "Liebestod" ("Love-death") or Transfiguration from Wagner's *Tristan und Isolde,* which ends in the same key. Can you think of another reason why Berg might have picked this chord to end the cycle?

There is much more to be discovered in these pieces. In this analysis we have focused on the waning of traditional tonality within an already atonal environment. Indeed, the tonal relationships within Berg's *Four Songs* are often obscured by the surrounding linear texture and sound quite tenuous. In his next work (the String Quartet, Op. 3) Berg would finally abandon any remnants of tonality and begin writing in a purely atonal idiom, an idiom being simultaneously adopted by his compatriots Arnold Schoenberg and Anton Webern. We can only muse over the prophetic words that Schoenberg set in the added soprano line within the finale of his Second String Quartet (1908): "I sense the air of other planets."

Terms and Concepts for Review

atonality   trichord

Some Fundamentals of Acoustics

In this appendix we will summarize four basic properties of a musical tone: (1) its frequency or pitch, (2) its intensity or loudness, (3) its vibration pattern, which produces its particular sound quality or timbre, and (4) its duration or length. We will distinguish between a musical tone's physical properties and the subjective manner in which we perceive it. You may find information on related acoustical topics (tuning systems, room acoustics, the acoustical characteristics of musical instruments, sound reproduction, and so forth) in the standard texts in this field.[1]

FREQUENCY AND PITCH

Sound originates in the vibration of elastic or flexible objects. Included in this family of vibrating objects are strings, reeds, lips, drum heads, and even the molecules of air in a wind instrument. A regular or periodic vibration produces a musical *tone.* You can see the graphic representation of a tone on the screen of an *oscilloscope,* an electronic instrument used to view and evaluate wave-form patterns. Three of these patterns are illustrated in Figure 1.

1. Two recommended texts are John Backus, *The Acoustical Foundations of Music,* 2nd ed. (New York: W. W. Norton, 1977) and D. W. Campbell and Clive Greated, *The Musicians Guide to Acoustics* (New York: Schirmer Books, 1987). Neither requires an extensive background in mathematics.

A.   B.   C.

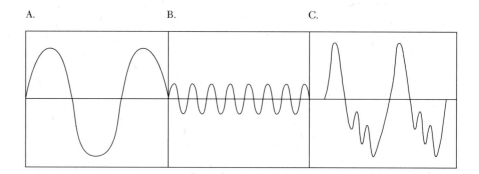

Figure 1

One complete to-and-fro motion, or vibration, of an elastic body is called a *cycle*. The *frequency* of a tone is the speed of the vibrations, which is measured by the number of complete cycles per second (cps), or *Hertz* (Hz). For instance, A^4, which vibrates 440 times per second, has a frequency of 440 Hz. We perceive frequency as *pitch,* the "highness" or "lowness" of a tone; the greater the frequency (that is, the faster the vibration), the higher the pitch. Frequency or pitch is indicated on the horizontal axis of the oscilloscope screen. The frequency of the tone in the second pattern of Figure 1 is greater (or higher) than that in the first, since the distance between the successive vibration peaks is less. Doubling the frequency of a given pitch produces a pitch an octave higher; conversely, halving the frequency of a given pitch produces a pitch an octave lower. That is, the *interval ratio* between successive octaves is 1:2, where 1 represents the original note and 2 the higher octave; thus, frequencies of 220, 440, and 880 represent the pitches A^3, A^4, and A^5, respectively. Since each additional octave doubles or halves this ratio, we perceive pitch according to a logarithmic scale, or by powers of 2: 2^2, 2^3, 2^4, 2^5, etc.[2]

The frequency distribution of fixed pitches within an octave (on a keyboard instrument, for example) is called a *tuning* or *temperament system. Equal temperament* has been employed as the basic tuning system in Western music since about 1800. In this system, each of the twelve half steps in the octave is of equal size. This equality permits the use of enharmonic notation, since F♯ and G♭, for example, will represent the same pitch. An equal-tempered half step may be expressed mathematically as $12\sqrt{2}$, or

2. A logarithm of a number is the power to which 10 must be raised to obtain that number. Thus, if $10^2 = 100$, then log 100 = 2; if $10^1 = 10$, then log 10 = 1; and so on. As a number doubles or increases by a power of 2, its logarithm also doubles; for example, log 2 = .301, and log 4 = .602. A logarithmic scale consists of the logarithms of each number in a given series: for instance, the logarithmic scale from 1 (10^0) to 10 (10^1) would consist of a series of numbers from 0 to 1.

1.0595, and occurs on a continuum where 1 is the lower note and 2 is the note an octave higher. Therefore, if we increase the length of tubing in a woodwind or brass instrument, or the length of a string on a string instrument, by 5.95 percent (or from 1 to 1.0595), we lower the pitch by one tempered semitone.

INTENSITY AND LOUDNESS

The energy or *amplitude* created by the displacement of vibrating objects is carried through the air to reach our ears. Amplitude is expressed as a measurement of *intensity* (compared to absolute silence) and is represented on the vertical axis of the oscilloscope screen. The intensity of the first pattern in Figure 1 is greater than the second, since the extremities of its vibrations are higher and lower on the vertical axis. In order to avoid extremely large or small ratios, intensity is measured on a logarithmic scale of *decibels* (dB). Intensity may range from the background noise of a quiet room (about 30 dB) to the threshold of aural pain (about 120 dB). Since each additional increment of 10 dB represents a tenfold rise in intensity, this decibel range involves an increase of about 10^9, or one billion times.

Our ear is more sensitive to the frequencies of the top notes of the piano (about 4000 Hz) than to those of the lowest octaves of the piano (below 100 Hz). Therefore, in softer passages the bass must be boosted (either electronically or acoustically) to achieve a better balance.

Another unit used by acousticians to measure relative loudness is called a *sone;* each sone is equivalent to an increase of 10 dBs at the frequency of 1000 Hz. Based on an average of numerous individual responses, two sones sound "twice as loud" as one sone, four sones sound twice as loud as two sones, and so on. Assuming that each violinist plays the note B^5 (approximately 1000 Hz) with the same intensity, it takes ten violins to sound "twice as loud" as one instrument. Why is this true?

Because musical dynamics are so subjective, we employ the very approximate Italian terms *piano* and *forte* and the prefix *mezzo-* and suffix *-issimo* to distinguish relative loudness in music. Thus, *mezzo-piano* indicates "moderately soft," while *pianissimo* indicates "very soft." *Crescendo* and *diminuendo* respectively denote a gradual rise and fall in loudness.

VIBRATION FORM AND TIMBRE

The tone quality or *timbre* of a musical tone is dependent on its physical *vibration form,* or characteristic wave shape. A pure or *sine tone* consists of only a simple wave form, which sounds quite uninteresting to our ears. (The sound used by doctors to check a patient's hearing is a sine tone.) Its characteristic wave pattern is shown in the first two diagrams of Figure 1. Pure tones are rare in most musical situations; however, we may hear them in the tones of a tuning fork, the low range of a flute, or the highest notes sung by a soprano. Most instruments produce *complex tones,* whose wave forms are more complicated; a typical example is given in the final diagram of Figure 1. The diverse patterns of complex tones result from the interaction of a series of simultaneously sounding pitches, only the lowest of which we actually perceive. This pitch, called the *fundamental,* is overlaid by a series of *overtones* or *harmonics,* which we do not hear as distinct tones but which serve to "color" the sound of the fundamental. The relative strengths or intensities of the various harmonics add a distinctive sound or timbre to the fundamental tone. For instance, the particular combination of differing harmonic strengths in a tone such as A^4 produced on an oboe, violin, or trumpet allows us to distinguish one instrument from another. If we turn the treble knob on a stereo amplifier to the left, the upper harmonics of each tone in the music being played are gradually attenuated and finally eliminated by means of a filtering system, changing their timbres by causing them to lose their "brightness."

This blending of natural overtones on acoustical instruments (except for some percussion instruments) is caused by the predictability of a series of numbers that form the harmonic relations, numbers that theoretically extend to infinity. The successive interval ratios of these numbers are arithmetic: 1:2:3:4:5:6:7:8, and so forth. That is, the interval ratio between the first two harmonics is 1:2 and that between the next two harmonics is 2:3.[3] If we take C^2 as the fundamental or first harmonic, this *harmonic series* produces the pitches shown in Example 1. (Only the first sixteen harmonics are shown.)

Example 1

3. The interval ratios may be calculated by dividing the frequency of a higher note by the frequency of a lower note. For instance, A^4 = 440 divided by A^3 = 220 equals the interval ratio 2:1 (or an octave).

Thus the ratio of a perfect 5th (C^3–G^3) is 2:3, and that of a major 6th (G^3–E^4) is 3:5.

The harmonic series not only affects the sound of each musical tone but also lies at the basis of our Western theoretical and tuning systems. For instance, if we consider the ratio of each harmonic to the fundamental, or the ratio of one harmonic to another, we can identify most of the diatonic intervals that are familiar to us: 1:2 = an octave, 2:3 = a perfect 5th, 3:4 = a perfect 4th, 4:5 = a major 3rd, 5:6 = a minor 3rd, 3:5 = a major 6th, and so on. Each of these ratios represents a *pure* harmonic musical interval, expressed in its simplest possible relation.[4] We can produce the harmonic series' separate tones on certain musical instruments, such as the flute, trombone, violin, and organ; how can they be demonstrated on a piano?

Attempts to produce a workable musical scale using the natural tones of the harmonic series have proven unsuccessful, since the intervals within the harmonic series produce two different sizes of melodic major 2nds: 8:9 (C–D) and 9:10 (D–E). As a result, Western musicians devised the system of equal temperament, where the distance or ratios between major 2nds and all the other intervals remain constant. The tones that are indicated with black noteheads in Figure 1 seem severely out of tune in relation to our equal-tempered system. Now have some of your fellow students demonstrate the harmonic series on their instruments. Which tones sound in tune and which out of tune?

DURATION

The duration of tones used in music is fairly short; even a whole note in slow tempo will rarely last longer than four seconds. There is, however, an aural limit to a tone's brevity. If tones occur at a rate faster than twenty per second, the human ear can no longer keep them distinct. The notes will instead fuse together, giving us the sensation of a single sustained tone or a sliding *glissando* between two tones.

On an oscilloscope, most musical tones exhibit a characteristic shape made up of intensity or loudness and duration called an *envelope*. A sound normally consists of an initial *attack* followed by a *steady state* or sustained sound, and concludes with its eventual *decay* or release. The envelopes of a typical piano and clarinet tone, given in Figure 2, show that a sound sharply

---

4. Music theorists of the medieval and Renaissance periods based their distinction between perfect and imperfect consonances on these numeric ratios. The ratios for the perfect octave and perfect 5th are based on the indivisible and therefore simpler numbers 1:2:3. The ratios for the imperfect intervals incorporated the more complex, mostly divisible numbers 4:5:6:8.

expands in intensity just after the initial attack and usually takes much longer to decay. What accounts for the basic difference between these two envelopes?

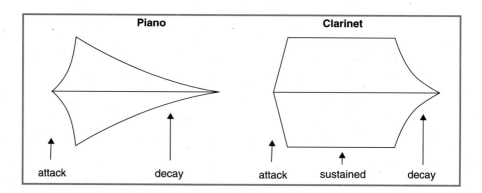

Figure 2

The Diatonic Modes and Other Scales

In this appendix we will briefly examine the diatonic Church modes as well as several other scales that occasionally appear in the music of the common-practice period.

THE CHURCH MODES

Within each octave span of a diatonic white-key scale, there are five whole steps and two half steps. These intervals are indicated in Example 1, using the symbols ⌣ for whole steps and ⌢ for half steps.

Example 1

The whole steps are grouped into patterns of 3 + 2 (F–G–A–B and C–D–E), which are separated by half steps (E–F and B–C). Any stepwise seven-tone scale that traverses an octave will exhibit the same number of tones and semitones; you might wish to confirm this by experimenting on a keyboard.

Within the white-key diatonic collection (A–B–C–D–E–F–G), we may assign the role of tonic to each of the seven tones in turn and then build a scale above each of them. The resulting seven scales are related by their common 3 + 2 whole-step construction, as shown by the numbers below the staff in Example 1. These are the scales that form the basis of the *diatonic* or *Church modes*. The diatonic modes were known and employed by musicians of great antiquity. The early Babylonians and Greeks derived some of their names for them from various geographical areas in the ancient world: Lydia, Phrygia, Ionia, and so forth. Despite some confusion in terminology, these modes formed the pitch basis of most early Western monophony, such as liturgical chant, and went on to form the basis of polyphonic music well into the Renaissance period.

Example 2 illustrates the seven *authentic modes,* each of which begins with its *finalis,* the note that carries a tonic-like function.

Example 2

The first column in Example 2 shows the scale of each mode, beginning with its *finalis*. The brackets on the left indicate three pairs of inversionally related modes; that is, the succession of whole and half steps between the

Lydian and Locrian, the Ionian and Phrygian, and the Mixolydian and Aeolian modes is exactly reversed. They form a symmetrical grouping around the central Dorian, which is a mirror form of itself. The Locrian mode was never accorded equal status with the other modes, because of the difficulty of establishing a sense of tonic. Why was this so difficult?

The modes may be transposed to other pitch levels. They normally employ the empty key signature of C major (C Ionian). Thus, to transpose any mode up a 4th, for example, simply write the key signature of F major (F Ionian) and build the modal scales on the same successive scale degrees: Dorian on $\hat{2}$ (G), Phrygian on $\hat{3}$ (A), Lydian on $\hat{4}$ (B♭), Mixolydian on $\hat{5}$ (C), and Aeolian on $\hat{6}$ (D).

Another method of comparing modes is illustrated in the second column of Example 2. Here each mode is compared to the familiar major or natural minor scale; a common tonic of G is retained throughout. The first three modes are basically major modes, since they contain a major 3rd above their tonic. Two of them differ from major by one *characteristic tone* or altered scale degree: for Lydian it is ♯$\hat{4}$, for Mixolydian ♭$\hat{7}$. The remaining modes have a minor 3rd above their tonic but differ slightly from the natural minor scale: Dorian's characteristic tone is ♯$\hat{6}$, Phrygian's ♭$\hat{2}$, and the ambiguous Locrian has two, ♭$\hat{2}$ and ♭$\hat{5}$. Recognizing the characteristic tones of each mode is especially helpful in aurally identifying modal melodies.

The best examples of modal compositions that have a strong sense of tonic are found in the folk music of certain countries—particularly England, but also the Balkan and Slavic nations. Liturgical chant, by contrast, may sound odd to the modern ear; because of the construction of the chant melodies, the last tone, or *finalis,* does not always convey the impression of a tonic.

Interest in the modes has occasionally resurfaced in later years—during the Impressionist period in the music of Debussy and Ravel, for example, and even today in many jazz and rock pieces. Some instances of pure modal melodies appear in Example 3.

Example 3

A. MUSORGSKY: *A NIGHT ON BALD MOUNTAIN* — PHRYGIAN ON A

B.   "ORIENTIS PARTIBUS" (MEDIEVAL CONDUCTUS) — MIXOLYDIAN ON G

C.   "SCARBOROUGH FAIR" (ENGLISH FOLK SONG) — DORIAN ON D

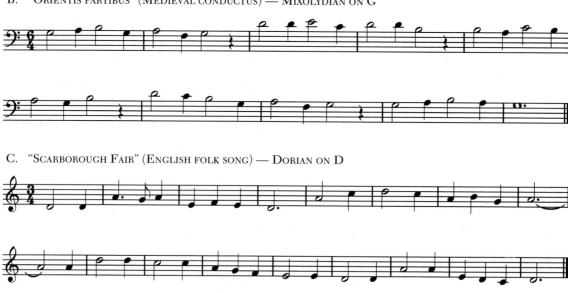

OTHER SCALES

Pentatonic Scale

Another scale sometimes used in music of the common-practice period is the familiar *pentatonic* or five-tone scale, shown in Example 4 using the notes A–C–D–E–G. Pentatonic scales that employ only natural pitch-classes may also be constructed with the notes F–G–A–C–D and G–A–B–D–E.

Example 4

The pentatonic scale may be considered a five-note subset of the diatonic seven-tone scale. Perhaps humanity's most primal tonal scale, it can be found in civilizations throughout the world. Its absence of tonal tension is not surprising, since it lacks both a tritone and a minor 2nd, two intervals that call out for resolution. The pentatonic scale has five possible modes, which are labeled in Example 4 with the numeric designations used by most authorities on folk music.

This ancient scale recurs throughout the entire span of music history. Two excerpts employing different pentatonic modes are shown in Example 5.

Example 5

A. "A<small>ULD</small> L<small>ANG</small> S<small>YNE</small>" (<small>TRADITIONAL</small> S<small>COTTISH</small> <small>TUNE</small>)

B. "S<small>ATAN</small> G<small>ONNA</small> T<small>EAR</small> Y<small>OUR</small> K<small>INGDOM</small> D<small>OWN</small>" (A<small>FRICAN</small>-A<small>MERICAN</small> <small>CHURCH</small> <small>SONG</small>)

Gypsy Minor Scale

Other scales tend to appear within a given passage of tonal music rather than provide the basis for an entire composition. The so-called *Gypsy minor scale* is one such scale, characterized by the substitution of ♯$\hat{4}$ for $\hat{4}$ in the harmonic minor scale and thus containing a conspicuous pair of augmented 2nds (♭$\hat{3}$–♯$\hat{4}$ and ♭$\hat{6}$–♯$\hat{7}$). It most commonly occurs in the folk music of Israel, Moorish Spain, and the Balkan countries. Liszt employed this scale in several of his Hungarian Rhapsodies, probably intending to imitate Gypsy music rather than authentic Hungarian folk songs.

Example 6   L<small>ISZT</small>: H<small>UNGARIAN</small> R<small>HAPSODY</small> N<small>O</small>. 13 <small>IN</small> A <small>MINOR</small>

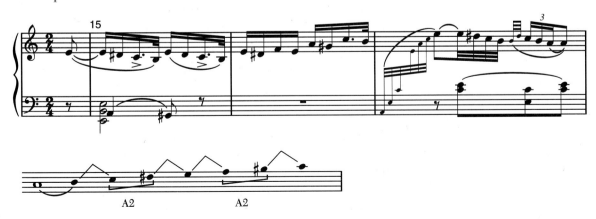

Whole-tone Scale

The two scales shown in Examples 7 and 9 occur commonly in twentieth-century music and may also be occasionally encountered in the music of the late Romantic period. Both are symmetrical collections that divide the octave into a number of equal segments. The first, the *whole-tone scale,* consists exclusively of whole steps, thereby dividing the octave into six major 2nds. Why do you think this scale is tonally ambiguous?

Example 7

There are two whole-tone scales, one based on C and the other on D♭; whole-tone scales based on any other notes will consist of notes identical to those of the C or D♭ scale. Mozart employs this scale in his satirical *Musical Joke* to parody a violinist who has "lost his way" in the higher positions during a cadenza (Example 8a). The Debussy passage in Example 8b centers around an altered dominant seventh chord, which resolves to the tonic of F♯ minor.

Example 8

A. MOZART: *A MUSICAL JOKE,* K.522, III

B. DEBUSSY: "EVENING IN GRANADA" FROM *ESTAMPES*

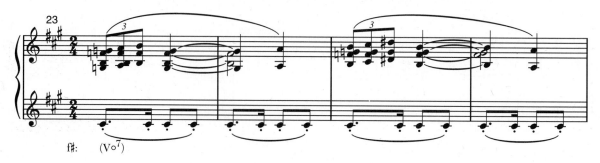

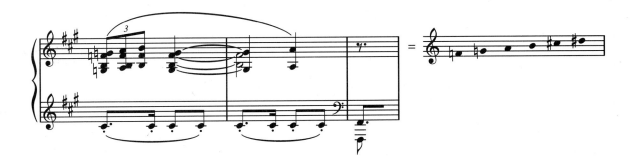

Octatonic Scale

The *octatonic scale* alternates half steps with whole steps. This synthetic scale results from the division of the octave into two different successions of minor 3rds, one starting on C, the other on D in Example 9.

Example 9

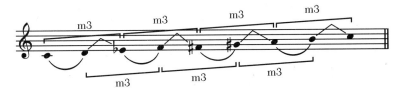

How many times can you transpose this scale up or down by semitone before it will duplicate its original pitch-classes?[1] What type of chords support the scalar upper voice in the Rimsky-Korsakov excerpt?

Example 10   RIMSKY-KORSAKOV: *SADKO*, ACT II

1. The whole-tone and octatonic scales are examples of a larger group of symmetrical scales called *modes of limited transposition.*

An Introduction to Species Counterpoint

The art of *counterpoint* involves the combination of independent melodic lines. While the study of harmony focuses on the vertical or chordal aspects of music, the study of counterpoint directs our attention to the interaction of different melodic lines. The contrapuntal duet between soprano and bass in the voice-leading reductions and melody harmonizations of this text are but two instances of its use. Although contrapuntal writing was optional in the basically homophonic music of the Classical and Romantic periods, it was the prevailing texture during the fifteenth and sixteenth centuries (the Renaissance) and in the late seventeenth and early eighteenth centuries (the mid- to late Baroque).

Examples of two-voice counterpoint, especially first-species or note-against-note style, may appear very abstract, and you may well ask "What does all this have to do with real music?" Throughout this text we have emphasized the importance of good melodic writing in the soprano and bass voices and how their lines interact. The surface elaborations of these outer parts often tend to disguise their underlying voice leading, which we can uncover through successive reductive analyses. As the layers of elaboration are stripped away from these parts, the passage's underlying contrapuntal foundation is revealed. We will see that these foundations follow many of the principles of species counterpoint.

In this brief appendix, we will commence with the note-against-note framework of the soprano and bass and successively elaborate this frame-work, ultimately producing a texture that resembles the actual surface of a piece of music. We will achieve this goal by means of the so-called *species technique,* a didactic method perfected by the composer and theorist Johann Joseph Fux. His treatise *Gradus ad Parnassum* (1725) attempted to systematize the teaching of counterpoint.[1] Although based on the musical practice of Palestrina, who lived nearly 150 years earlier, Fux's treatise formed the foundation for contrapuntal instruction during the Classical period and continues to be used today.[2]

Fux began his *Gradus* by adding a melodic line or *counterpoint* to a preexisting melody consisting of pitches of equal duration, called the *cantus firmus* (abbreviated CF in the following musical examples). He devised five *species,* each of which represents a different rhythmic model and handling of consonance and dissonance for the counterpointing voice or voices. Since Fux's method simulated the modal counterpoint of the late Renaissance, we will incorporate the following adjustments in order to bring it in line with our study of tonal music in the common-practice period:

1. In place of the Church modes of the Renaissance, we will use only the standard major and minor modes.
2. All of the examples will begin and end in the same key (either C major or C minor) and conclude with an authentic cadence. Other cadences, such as the half, deceptive, and Phrygian, though theoretically possible, are seldom encountered in species writing.
3. In place of the whole-note notation of the cantus firmus typical of the Renaissance, we will use the more familiar meter signature of $\frac{2}{4}$ (and occasionally $\frac{6}{8}$) and notate the cantus firmus in quarter notes, each of which receives one beat.
4. We will regard the harmonic intervals between the two voices as representing triads in root position or first inversion. In many instances the succession of intervals will suggest functional chord progressions. The handling of rhythm and consonance and dissonance will adhere to Fux's principles.

MELODIC CHARACTERISTICS

Before beginning our study of two-part contrapuntal writing, we will first examine some characteristics of good melodic writing, as exemplified in the counterpointing voice.

1. A translation of the two-voice portion of *Gradus* may be found in Fux's *The Study of Counterpoint,* revised edition, translated by Alfred Mann (New York: W. W. Norton, 1965), 27–67.
2. For instance, see Knud Jeppesen's *Counterpoint* (New York: Prentice-Hall, 1939; repr. ed. New York: Dover, 1992).

1. The counterpoint should exhibit a definite sense of melodic direction, a feeling of "going somewhere," rather than appearing static or leaping about aimlessly with no apparent destination. The range of this voice should lie approximately within the span of an octave.

2. Stepwise motion should prevail. Melodic leaps of 3rds, perfect 4ths and 5ths, and ascending 6ths are also common, but descending 6ths, 7ths of any kind, and augmented and diminished intervals (including the tritone) are never used. Passages in which the counterpoint highlights an augmented 4th in its melodic contour (for instance, G–F–G–A–B–A) are also avoided. Melodic lines usually employ only the diatonic tones of C major or C minor; chromatic motion is never used.

3. After a leap of a 4th or more, the melody usually changes its direction. Two consecutive leaps that outline a major or minor triad may be used.

FIRST SPECIES

First species employs a 1:1 rhythmic ratio between the cantus firmus and its accompanying counterpoint. It is also referred to as *note-against-note style.* In fact, the term *counterpoint* derives from the Latin expression *punctus contra punctum,* the "punctus" being a type of note in the medieval period.

The following comments characterize the use of harmonic intervals in first species:

1. Only consonant intervals are allowed: unisons, octaves, perfect 5ths, and diatonic 3rds and 6ths, plus their compound equivalents. Consequently, all dissonant intervals are forbidden: 2nds, 7ths, perfect 4ths, and any augmented or diminished intervals (including the tritone).

2. Each phrase may begin with a unison, octave, perfect 5th, or rarely a 3rd, any of which will imply a "tonic triad." The final interval of the cadence must be either an octave or unison on the tonic note. These possible opening and closing intervals are shown in Example 1.

Example 1

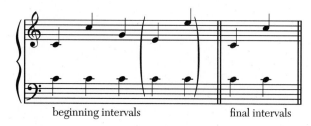

beginning intervals   final intervals

3. Perfect intervals (especially unisons and octaves) are generally reserved for the opening or cadence of the phrase. Imperfect consonances (3rds and 6ths) are characteristically employed *within* the phrase.

4. The distance between the two voices (which represent the soprano and bass) rarely exceeds a 12th. On occasion the parts may temporarily cross each other.

The last set of observations pertains to the intervallic motion between the voices:

1. A good mixture of *contrary motion* (where the voices move in opposite directions), *oblique motion* (where one part holds while the other moves), and *similar motion* (where both move in the same direction) ensures melodic independence between the parts. Similar stepwise motion should not exceed three stepwise intervals.

2. Parallel motion between perfect consonances (the unison, octave, and perfect 5th) is avoided, as is similar (or direct) motion into a perfect consonance; see Example 2. Direct motion from a 5th to an octave is allowed at the cadence, however.

Example 2

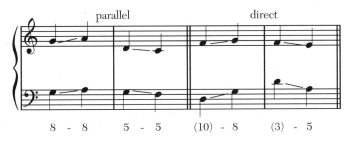

3. While all types of motion between 3rds and 6ths are permissible, both voices normally do not leap in the same direction to one of these intervals.

All the cadences in this appendix conclude on the tonic note, with either a harmonic octave or unison. If the cantus firmus is in the *upper* voice (usually proceeding $\hat{2}$–$\hat{1}$ or $\hat{7}$–$\hat{8}$), the bass will normally leap from $\hat{5}$ to $\hat{1}$, implying a perfect authentic cadence (V–I), as shown in Example 3a. If the cantus firmus is in the *lower* voice ($\hat{2}$–$\hat{1}$ or $\hat{7}$–$\hat{8}$), the soprano must still move stepwise to the tonic, as shown in Example 3b. This stepwise bass motion implies an imperfect cadence of either vii°⁶–I or V⁶–I.

Example 3

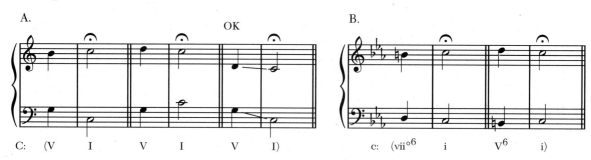

A.

C: (V I V I V I)

B.

c: (vii°6 i V6 i)

Three passages of first-species counterpoint appear in Example 4. Examine the consonant harmonic intervals, the positioning of perfect and imperfect consonances in the phrase, the individual melodic characteristics of each part, and the intervallic motion between the voices. An interval analysis is provided below each example, and abbreviations are used for contrary (*C*), oblique (*O*), and similar (*S*) motion. The interval of the octave in the second measure of Example 4c represents a passing motion in a voice exchange; it is approached and left by contrary motion and occurs on a weak beat.

Example 4

A.

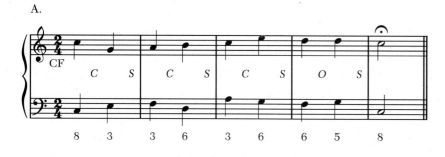

CF

C S C S C S O S

8 3 3 6 3 6 6 5 8

B.

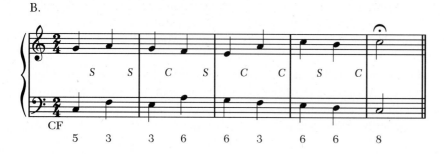

S S C S C C S C

CF

5 3 3 6 6 3 6 6 8

C.

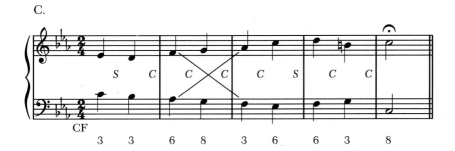

SECOND SPECIES

The four remaining species may be considered as melodic and rhythmic elaborations (or "diminutions") of the underlying note-against-note style. *Second species* employs a rhythmic motion of two equal eighth notes in the counterpoint for each quarter note in the cantus firmus, resulting in a 2:1 relation. The rules for first species remain in effect but with the following exception: dissonant passing tones on offbeat eighth notes are now permissible (Example 5a). It is not always possible to incorporate continuous passing motion—whether consonant or dissonant—in the counterpointing voice. In such cases, a 5–6 or 6–5 motion (Example 5b) or leap to a consonant tone (Example 5c) may be used to maintain the flow of eighth notes; in these cases no dissonant passing tones are employed. The added eighth notes in the counterpoint should not produce parallel perfect 5ths or octaves with the cantus firmus (Example 5d).

Example 5

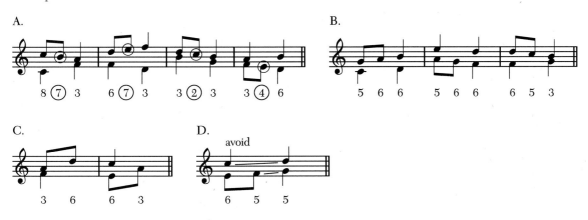

Study the two passages of second-species writing in Example 6, where the passing tones are circled. In each phrase the soprano and bass notes on the first of each beat continue to provide an underlying first-species basis.

Example 6

A.

B.

THIRD SPECIES

In *third species,* the counterpoint either employs a 4:1 rhythmic relation to the cantus, where four sixteenth notes are set against each quarter note (as in $\frac{2}{4}$ meter), or a 3:1 rhythmic relation, where three eighth notes are set against each dotted quarter note of the cantus firmus (as in $\frac{6}{8}$ meter). In addition to unaccented passing tones, dissonant neighboring tones may now occur. In 4:1 settings these dissonances appear on the second and fourth sixteenth notes of each beat; in 3:1 settings they occur on the second eighth note. Thus, the first and third eighths in both meters are always consonant. Leaps to consonant tones are found in third species just as in second species. Examine the passages of third-species writing in Example 7; these may be considered as further elaborations of second species.

Example 7

A.

B.

Other dissonant melodic figures may occur in third species. These idioms include the descending accented passing tone (AP), which can occur only on the third sixteenth note of each beat, and the changing tone (or double incomplete neighbor); the latter figure contains four notes (Example 8).

Example 8

FOURTH SPECIES

In *fourth species,* eighth notes are tied over from the offbeat to the beat, producing a continuous stream of rhythmic syncopations. The featured dissonances are suspensions, which are prepared by a consonant interval, occur on the beat, and resolve downward by step on the following offbeat. In doing so they delay the consonance of a 6th, 3rd, or 10th. The rhythm in the counterpointing voice is ♪♪. Where it is not possible to continue these tied-over figures throughout the entire phrase, one usually resorts to second species.

When the counterpointing voice is above the cantus firmus, both 7–6 and 4–3 suspensions are possible (Examples 9a and 9b). The 9–8 suspension is avoided, since in two-voice writing it resolves into an empty octave (Example 9c). In the 4–3 suspension, the perfect 4th is usually preferred to an augmented 4th (Example 9d).

Example 9

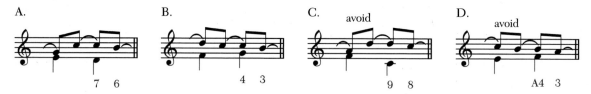

If the counterpointing voice is below the cantus firmus, it can utilize only one possible suspension: the 2–3 or 9–10 (Example 10a). As a result, some second-species writing is usually necessary to link the suspensions. Tied figures with 6–5 or 5–6 are also possible (Example 10b).

Example 10

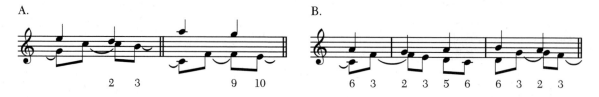

Some additional examples of fourth-species writing may be found in Example 11.

Example 11

A.

B.

FIFTH SPECIES

The rhythmic restrictions of the first four species are removed in *fifth species,* where the counterpointing voice may employ all the melodic and rhythmic figurations of the previous species in various combinations. In addition, ornamented suspensions using pairs of thirty-second notes or consonant anticipations (in sixteenth notes) can occur, as shown in Example 12.

Example 12

A phrase from a hymn tune serves as the cantus firmus in the two passages in Example 13. At the end of the first measure of Example 13b, the F♯ in the bass produces a harmonic tritone with the C in the soprano. This can be rationalized as a V^6_5.

Example 13

A. "EIN' FESTE BURG," LAST PHRASE

B. LOUIS BOURGEOIS: "OLD ONE HUNDRED," LAST PHRASE

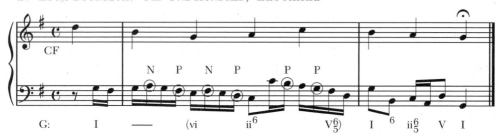

Species technique may involve more than two voices; the counterpointing voices may employ a single species or a combination of various species. Example 14 illustrates a three-voice passage that combines third and fourth species; the cantus firmus is in the middle voice.

Example 14

UNDERLYING SPECIES TECHNIQUE IN TWO-VOICE PASSAGES

Reducing the surface elaborations in most two-voice passages from the common-practice period reveals an underlying voice leading that can be related directly back to species counterpoint. The reduction on the bottom staves of Example 15 resembles a mixture of first and second species.

Example 15   BEETHOVEN: PIANO SONATA IN F MINOR, OP. 2, NO. 1, TRIO

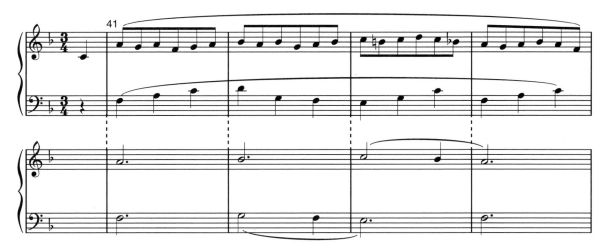

Instances of cantus firmus technique, where a preexisting melody serves as the foundational voice, occur frequently in cantus-firmus (or tenor) Masses of the Renaissance era and chorale preludes of the Baroque period.

Chord Symbols for Jazz and Commercial Music

Jazz and commercial music is often notated on a score called a *leadsheet,* which simply gives the melody and a shorthand notation that symbolizes the chordal harmony. These symbols, usually written directly above the melody notes, provide a quick and convenient way of identifying the root and chord types of the harmonies that should be played. Commercial symbols, however, do not indicate anything about the chords' harmonic functions.

The commercial symbols for triads, seventh chords, extended tertian (ninth and eleventh) chords, and added-note chords are given below. For the sake of comparison, all the chords use a common root of E.

TRIADS

1. A major triad uses only a capital letter for the root (E = E major, or E G♯ B).
2. A minor triad uses a capital letter for the root, followed by a lower-case *m* (Em = E minor, or E G B). A minus sign is sometimes substituted for the small m (E⁻ = Em).
3. A diminished triad uses a capital letter for the root, followed by the superscript ° (E° = E diminished, or E G B♭).
4. An augmented triad uses a capital letter for the root, followed by the superscript ⁺ (E⁺ = E augmented, or E G♯ B♯).

Root position is always assumed. If a first or second inversion is required, the note to be played in the bass is indicated after a slash: thus, G/B indicates the first inversion of a G-major triad, and F♯m/C♯ indicates the second inversion of an F♯-minor triad. A 4–3 suspension is often written in the form D^{sus4}.

Example 1

SEVENTH CHORDS

The standard symbols for the five basic types of seventh chords are the following:

1. Major seventh chord (M^7) = E^{MAJ7} (E G♯ B D♯)
2. Major-minor seventh chord (Mm^7) = E^7 (E G♯ B D)
3. Minor seventh chord (m^7) = Em^7 (E G B D)
4. Half-diminished seventh chord (^{ø7}) = (E G B♭ D)
5. Fully diminished seventh chord (^{o7}) = E^{o7} (E G B♭ D♭)

Inversions of seventh chords are also symbolized by a slash followed by the note to be played in the bass: Em^7/G, E^7/B, E^{ø7}/D, and so on. In some cases, the seventh chord may occur over a bass note that does not belong to the harmony: for example, Em^7/A, E^7/A.

Example 2

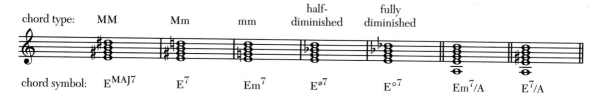

NINTH AND ELEVENTH CHORDS

There are only four common types of ninth chords. The tritones in the first two chords listed below give them a particularly dominant sound. Chords 3 and 4 contain no tritones. The capital and lowercase M's in the various chord names represent the major or minor qualities of (in order) the chord's basic triad, 7th, and 9th.

1. MmM9th chord = E^9 (E G♯ B D F♯)
2. Mmm9th chord = E^{-9} (E G♯ B D F)
3. MMM9th chord = $E^{9\,(MAJ7)}$ (E G♯ B D♯ F♯)
4. mmM9th chord = Em^9 (E G B D F♯)

The augmented-ninth chord actually contains a *split third*—that is, both a major and minor 3rd above the root:

5. MmA9th chord = E^{+9} (E G♯ B D F𝄪 [or G♮]).

Example 3

chord type: MmM   Mmm   MMM   mmM   MmA

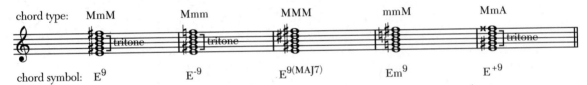

chord symbol: E^9 E^{-9} $E^{9(MAJ7)}$ Em^9 E^{+9}

The 11th of extended tertian chords may either be perfect or augmented. In the first two chords listed in Example 4, the underlying sonority is some form of dominant ninth chord: either a V^9 (usually with the 3rd omitted) or a V^{-9} chord. The augmented 11th is usually added to the V^9 chord. In the following chord names, P stands for "perfect."

1. MmMP11th chord = E^{11} (E B D F♯ A); the 3rd is omitted.
2. MmmP11th chord = $E^{11(-9)}$ (E B D F A); the 3rd is omitted.
3. MmMA11th chord = E^{+11} (E G♯ B D F♯ A♯).

A nondominant eleventh chord is usually built on a mmM9th chord:

4. mmMP11th chord = Em^{11} (E G B D F♯ A).

Example 4

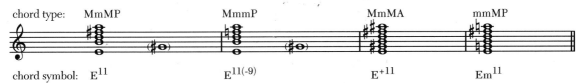

chord type: MmMP   MmmP   MmMA   mmMP

chord symbol: E^{11} $E^{11(-9)}$ E^{+11} Em^{11}

Thirteenth chords do not have any standard shorthand notation, though they are widely used in the jazz and popular-music repertories.

ADDED-NOTE CHORDS

Notes that are added to tertian chords in commercial music and jazz are indicated in the following way:

1. $E^{(add6)}$ = E G♯ B C♯
2. $E^{(add6 \text{ and } 9)}$ = E G♯ B C♯ F♯

Example 5

$E^{(add6)}$ $E^{(add6 \text{ and } 9)}$

Conducting Patterns

Most conductors keep the beat by tracing certain standardized patterns with their right hand. These patterns indicate the number of beats in a measure as well as exactly when each beat must be played. The conducting pattern used for a particular piece is dependent on the interpretation of the meter signature, a topic that we discuss in Chapter 2. Music students should become familiar with these various patterns so that conducting them becomes an unconscious reflex. One way of achieving this facility is to practice them while focusing on other academic pursuits, such as reading one's literature assignments.

A downward motion indicates the downbeat (or first beat) of a measure, while an upward motion indicates the upbeat (or last beat). The *ictus,* the point where each beat occurs, must be apparent in each pattern. One way of marking each ictus is to think of an invisible surface, such as a table, off of which each beat motion rebounds. Thus the point of the beat always occurs along an imaginary horizontal line at the bottom of the pattern, as shown by the dotted lines in the first three meter patterns that are illustrated below.

DUPLE METER

Each measure of duple meter consists of a basic downward–upward motion, corresponding to the two beats of the measure. Notice that each larger motion contains two smaller curved movements, each of which rebounds off of our hypothetical "surface" to mark the ictus of each beat. Contrast the correct duple-meter pattern with a simple mechanical down–up motion (Figure 1).

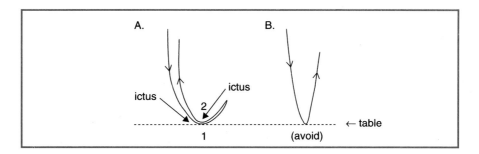

Figure 1

TRIPLE METER

In a triple meter, after the downbeat motion, the second beat is indicated by a sideways motion to the right, and the third beat (the upbeat) by an upward motion. Notice that the ictus of each beat remains at the bottom of the pattern (Figure 2).

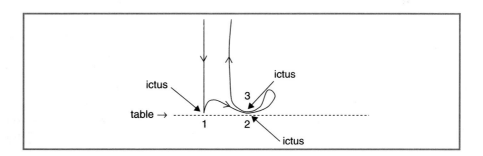

Figure 2

QUADRUPLE METER

In quadruple meter, the second beat is marked on the left, and the third beat by a corresponding motion to the right (Figure 3).

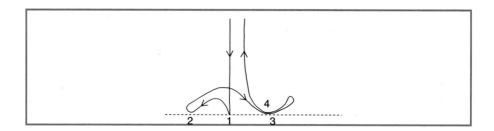

Figure 3

SINGLE METER

Since there is only one beat to a measure of single meter, the conducting pattern consists of a single quick downward motion with a very rapid rebound (Figure 4).

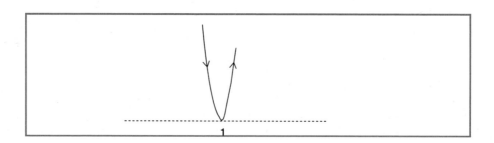

Figure 4

QUINTUPLE METER

Each measure of five beats may be divided into groupings of 2 + 3 or 3 + 2, depending on the music. An additional motion on the left or right side will indicate the extra beat (Figure 5).

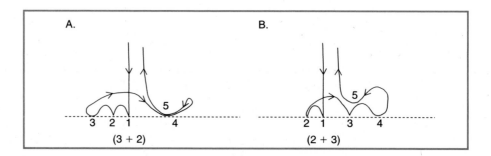

Figure 5

Sextuple Meter: Divided Beat

In a very slow $\frac{6}{8}$ the beat is divided. The conducting pattern begins with three beats at the center and left followed by three on the right, producing a 3 + 3 grouping (Figure 6a). In a very slow $\frac{3}{4}$, where the beat is divided, each of the three main beats of triple meter is in turn divided into two smaller motions, producing a 2 + 2 + 2 grouping (Figure 6b).

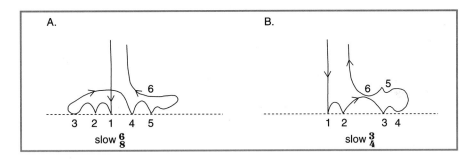

Figure 6

This principle is extended to other meters with divided beats, such as a very slow $\frac{4}{4}$ (2 + 2 + 2 + 2), $\frac{9}{8}$ (3 + 3 + 3), or $\frac{12}{8}$ (3 + 3 + 3 + 3).

Complex Meters

In a fast $\frac{5}{8}$ the conducting pattern indicates two basic beats (duple meter), but one of the beats must be prolonged slightly. If the basic grouping is 3 + 2 (long–short), the first beat is prolonged; if it is 2 + 3 (short–long), the second beat is prolonged (Figure 7).

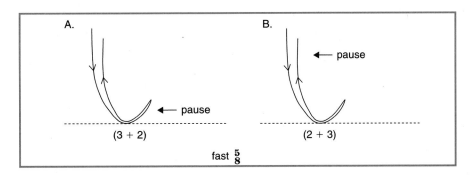

Figure 7

Other complex meters will employ this same principle; for instance, $\frac{7}{8}$ may be conducted as three basic beats: 3 + 3 + 2, 3 + 2 + 3, or 2 + 3 + 3.

GLOSSARY

The terms in this glossary appear in tempo, dynamic, and expression markings and directions that are commonly given in Italian, French, and German in music scores. Terms in italic within a definition are cross-referenced in this glossary.

accelerando (accel.) (*It.*)   Gradually quickening the tempo.

accent   Emphasis on a specific tone, beat, or chord; usually through dynamic (accent mark >) or quantitative stress (agogic or durational accent).

adagio (*It.*)   Slow; faster than *lento* but slower than *andante*.

affettuoso (*It.*)   With affection.

agitato (*It.*)   In an agitated manner.

agréments (*Fr.*)   Ornaments, embellishments.

allargando (*It.*)   Becoming gradually slower.

allegretto (*It.*)   Slightly slower than *allegro*.

allegro (*It.*)   Fast, but slower than *presto*.

allmählich (*Ger.*)   Gradually.

andante (*It.*)   Moderately slow (literally, "walking").

andantino (*It.*)   Slightly faster than *andante*.

Anfang (*Ger.*)   The beginning.

animato (*It.*)   In an animated style.

arco (*It.*)   Using the bow (on a stringed instrument).

arpeggio (*It.*)   The playing of a chord in broken fashion, usually from the bottom note up.

attacca (*It.*)   Begin ("attack") immediately.

battuta (*It.*)   Beat (as in **a battuta,** "beat in strict tempo").

breve   A double whole note.

calma (*It.*)   Calm.

cantabile (*It.*)   In a singing or lyrical manner.

cédez (*Fr.*)   Slightly decreasing the tempo.

coda (*It.*)   An additional appendage (or "tailpiece") to a composition following the main tonic cadence.

654

con brio (*It.*)   With spirit.

corda (*It.*)   String (on a stringed instrument).

crescendo (cresc.) (*It.*)   Gradually increasing in loudness.

da capo (D.C.) (*It.*)   Return to the beginning (literally, "from the head").

Da capo al segno (*It.*)   Return to the beginning and play until the sign (literally, "from the head to the sign").

decrescendo (*It.*)   Decreasing in loudness.

détaché (*Fr.*)   With long separate bow-strokes, not slurred.

deux (*Fr.*)   Two.

diminuendo (dim.) (*It.*)   Gradually decreasing in loudness.

divisi (*It.*)   Divided (indicates the temporary division of an orchestral string section into two or more parts).

dolore (*It.*)   In a sorrowful style.

doppel (*Ger.*)   Double.

drängend (*Ger.*)   Slightly hurrying.

drei (*Ger.*)   Three.

due (*It.*)   Two (as in **a due,** "both instruments play the same part").

dur (*Ger.*)   Major.

également (*Fr.*)   Play equally or evenly.

ein (*Ger.*)   One.

etwas (*Ger.*)   Some, somewhat.

expressif (*Fr.*)   Expressively.

facile (*Fr.*)   In a light or "easy" style.

fermata (*It.*)   Hold; "bird's eye" symbol (⌒) over a note signifying that it should be held indefinitely.

fine (*It.*)   End.

flüchtig (*Ger.*)   In a fleeting manner.

fois (*Fr.*)   Time (as in **première fois,** "the first time").

forte (f) (*It.*)   Loud.

fortissimo (ff) (*It.*)   Very loud.

forzando (fz) (*It.*)   Sharply marked or emphasized.

frei (*Ger.*)   Freely, with license.

für (*Ger.*)   For.

ganz (*Ger.*)   The whole, all.

gegen (*Ger.*)   Against, contrasted with.

giocoso (*It.*)   Playfully, merrily.

giusto (*It.*)   Strict, exact (as in **tempo giusto,** "strict time").

gleich (*Ger.*)   Equal to, alike.

gran (*It.*)   Great.

grave (*It.*)   As slow as possible.

gross (*Ger.*)   Large, great.

halb (*Ger.*)   Half.

Haupt (*Ger.*)   Head, principal (as in **Hauptstimme,** "principal voice or part").

haut (*Fr.*)   High, shrill.

jouer de (*Fr.*)   To play on (an instrument).

Klang (*Ger.*)   Sound; ringing.

Klavier (*Ger.*)   Keyboard (instrument).

klein (*Ger.*)   Little, small.

langsam (*Ger.*)   Slowly.

largando (*It.*)   Broadening.

larghetto (*It.*)   A little faster than *largo.*

largo (*It.*)   Slow; usually slower than *lento.*

legato (*It.*)   In a smooth, connected style.

leicht (*Ger.*)   Light, easy.

lent (*Fr.*)   Slow.

lento (*It.*)   Slow; usually between *andante* and *largo.*

librement (*Fr.*)   Freely.

loco (*It.*)   Return to normal octave or position (literally, "place").

lontano (*It.*)   Distant.

louré (*Fr.*)   In a smooth, legato style.

lustig (*Ger.*)   Merry, cheerful.

mano (*It.*)   Hand.

mässig (*Ger.*)   Moderate.

mehr (*Ger.*)   More.

meno (*It.*)   Less (as in **meno mosso,** "slightly slower").

mezzo (*It.*)   Medium (as in *mezzo forte* (**mf**), "medium loud").

moderato (*It.*)   Moderate in tempo.

moll (*Ger.*)   Minor.

molto (*It.*)   Much, very.

mosso (*It.*)   In a rapid manner (literally, "moved").

moto (*It.*)   Motion (as in **con moto,** "with motion").

nach (*Ger.*)   After.

neu (*Ger.*)   New.

noch (*Ger.*)   Still; yet.

non (*It.*)   No, not (as in **non legato,** "not smooth").

obbligato (*It.*)   An optional part; a counter-melody.

peu (*Fr.*)   A little (as in **peu à peu,** "little by little").

pianissimo (pp) (*It.*)   Very softly.

piano (p) (*It.*)   Softly.

poco (*It.*)   A little (as in **poco a poco,** "little by little").

portando (*It.*)   Sliding from one note to the next (literally, "carrying").

pour (*Fr.*)   For, in order to.

premier, première (*Fr.*)   First (as in **à première vue,** to sight-read).

pressez (*Fr.*)   Accelerate.

prestissimo (*It.*)   As fast as possible.

presto (*It.*)   Very fast.

primo tempo (*It.*)   Play the first tempo indicated.

quasi (*It.*)   Like or similar to (as in **quasi recitativo,** "like a recitative").

reprise (*It.*)   To repeat or recur.

ritard, ritardando (rit.) (*It.*)   Get slower gradually.

rubato (*It.*)   A gradual fluctuation of the tempo, usually in slow movements (literally, "robbed").

ruhig (*Ger.*)   Calm, restful.

sans (*Fr.*)   Without (as in **sans sordine,** "without mute").

Satz (*Ger.*)   Theme; section; movement.

schnell (*Ger.*)   Quick.

sec (*Fr.*)   Dry, short.

segno (*It.*)   Sign (as in **dal segno,** "repeat from the sign").

segue (*It.*)   "Now follows"; continue in the same manner.

sehr (*Ger.*)   Very.

semplice (*It.*)   Simply.

sempre (*It.*)   Always; throughout.

senza (*It.*)   Without (as in **senza vibrato,** "without vibrato").

sforzando (sf, sfz) (*It.*)   Accented (literally, "forcing").

sordino (*It.*)   A mute.

sotto (*It.*)   Below, under (as in **sotto voce,** "in an undertone, very softly").

spielen (*Ger.*)   To play.

spirito (*It.*)   Spirit.

staccato (*Ir.*)   Detached, short.

Stimme (*Ger.*)   Voice, part.

stringendo (*It.*)   Accelerating.

subito (*It.*)   Suddenly (as in **volta subito,** "turn the page quickly").

sul (*It.*)   On or near (as in **sul tasto,** "on the fingerboard").

süss (*Ger.*)   Sweetly.

tacet (*Lat.*)   Omit, do not play.

tactus (*Lat.*)   The beat or single motion of the hand in a conducting pattern.

Takt (*Ger.*)   Time; beat; measure.

tasto (*It.*)   Touch; keyboard; fingerboard.

tempo (*It.*)   Rate of speed.

tout (*Fr.*)   All.

très (*Fr.*)   Very.

trois (*Fr.*)   Three.

troppo (*It.*)   Too much (as in **ma non troppo,** "but not too much").

tutti (*It.*)   The entire ensemble (literally, "all").

über (*Ger.*)   Above, over.

unter (*Ger.*)   Below, under.

valeur (*Fr.*)   Value or duration (of a note).

vibrato (*It.*)   Varying the pitch slightly and rapidly (literally, "shaken").

vif (*Fr.*)   Quick, lively.

vivace (*It.*)   Fast (literally, "lively"), usually faster than *allegro*.

voce (*It.*)   Voice (as in **mezzo voce,** "in a medium voice").

voll (*Ger.*)   Full.

volta (*It.*)   Time (as in **prima volta,** "the first time").

wieder (*Ger.*)   Again.

Zeitmass (*Ger.*)   tempo.

zwei (*Ger.*)   Two.

zwischen (*Ger.*)   Between.

INDEX OF MUSIC EXAMPLES

Arlen, "Over the Rainbow" (p. 61): © 1938 (Renewed) Metro-Goldwyn-Mayer Inc. © 1939 (Renewed) EMI Feist Catalog Inc., All Rights Reserved. Used by Permission. WARNER BROS. PUBLICATIONS U.S. INC., Miami, FL 33014.

Bartók, *Mikrokosmos*, Vol. 1, No. 7 (p. 147): © Copyright 1940 by Hawkes & Son (London) Ltd; Copyright Renewed. Used by permission of Boosey & Hawkes, Inc.

Berg, *Four Songs*, Op. 2 (pp. 607–608, 610, 611, 613, 614–15, 618, 619): © 1928 by Robert Lienau Edition (Germany). Copyright renewed. All rights reserved. Reprinted by Permission.

Ellington, "Sophisticated Lady" (p. 564): Words and Music by Duke Ellington, Irving Mills and Mitchell Parish. Copyright © 1933 (Renewed 1960) and Assigned to EMI Mills Music, Inc., Famous Music Corp. & Everbright Music, in U.S.A. Rights for the world outside the U.S.A. Controlled by EMI Mills Music Inc. and Warner Bros. Publications Inc. International Copyright Secured. All Rights Reserved. Used by Permission.

Harrison, "Something" (p. 398): Words and Music by George Harrison. © 1969 HARRISONGS LTD. International Copyright Secured. All Rights Reserved.

Kern, "All the Things You Are" (p. 314): Lyrics by Oscar Hammerstein II. Music by Jerome Kern. Copyright © 1939 PolyGram International Publishing, Inc. Copyright Renewed. International Copyright Secured. All Rights Reserved.

Lennon/McCartney, "You Never Give Me Your Money" (p. 399): © Copyright 1969 Northern Songs. Used by permission of Music Sales Limited. All Rights Reserved. International Copyright Secured. Distributed in the U.S. by the Hal Leonard Corporation.

Porter, "Every Time We Say Goodbye" (p. 497): Words and Music by Cole Porter. copyright © 1944 by Chappell & Co. copyright Renewed, Assigned to John F. Wharton, Trustee of the Cole Porter Musical and Literary Property Trusts. Chappell & Co. owner of publication and allied rights throughout the world. International Copyright Secured. All Rights Reserved.

Porter, "I Get a Kick out of You" (p. 228): © 1934 (Renewed) Warner Bros. Inc. All Rights Reserved. Used by Permission. WARNER BROS. PUBLICATIONS U.S. INC., Miami, FL 33014.

Purcell, "Passing By" (p. 360): © 1930, 1934 (Copyrights Renewed) Summy-Birchard Music, a division of Summy-Birchard Inc. All Rights Reserved. Used by Permission. WARNER BROS. PUBLICATIONS U.S. INC., Miami, FL 33014.

Rachmaninoff, *Isle of the Dead* (p. 117): Used by permission of Boosey & Hawkes, Inc.

Rachmaninoff, *Vocalise* (p. 251): Used by permission of Boosey & Hawkes, Inc.

Ravel, "Rigaudon" from *Tombeau de Couperin* (p. 484): © 1916 Durand S.A. Editions Musicales. Editions A.R.I.M.A. & Durand S.A. Editions Musicales. Joint Publication. Used By Permission Of The Publisher.

Rodgers, "Bali Ha'i" (p. 495): Lyrics by Oscar Hammerstein II. Music by Richard Rodgers. Copyright © 1944 by Chappell & Co. Copyright Renewed. Assigned to John F. Wharton, Trustee of the Cole Porter Musical and Literary Property Trusts. Chappell & Co. owner of publication and allied rights throughout the world. International Copyright Secured. All Rights Reserved.

Schoenberg, *Chamber Symphony* (p. 435): Used by permission of Belmont Music Publishers, Pacific Palisades, CA 90272.

Strauss, *Also Sprach Zarathustra* (pp. 122, 181): By permission of C. F. Peters Corporation, New York.

Strauss, *Death and Transfiguration* (p. 188): By permission of C. F. Peters Corporation, New York.

Strauss, *Don Quixote* (p. 153): By permission of C. F. Peters Corporation, New York.

Strauss, *Der Rosenkavalier* (p. 464): © Copyright 1910, 1911 by Adolph Fürstner; Copyright Renewed. Copyright assigned to Hawkes & Son (London) Ltd. for the world excluding Germany, Italy, Portugal and the former territories of the USSR (excluding Estonia, Latvia, and Lithuania). Used by permission of Boosey & Hawkes, Inc.

Strauss, *Till Eulenspiegel's Merry Pranks* (pp. 124, 435, 494): By permission of C. F. Peters Corporation, New York.

Stravinsky, *Petrushka*, 1st Tableau (p. 122): © Copyright 1912, revised edition © Copyright 1947 by Hawkes & Son (London) Ltd; Copyright Renewed. Used by permission of Boosey & Hawkes, Inc.

Strayhorn, "Take the A Train"(p. 436): © 1941 (Renewed) by Tempo Music Inc./Music Sales Corp. All Rights Administered by Music Sales Corp. (ASCAP). Reprinted by Permission.

Youmans, "Tea for Two" (p. 523): © 1924 (Renewed) Warner Bros. Inc. Rights for Extended Renewal Term in U.S. controlled by WB Music Corp. and Irving Caesar Music Corp. All Rights o/b/o Irving Caesar Music Corp. administered by WB Music Corp. Canadian Rights controlled by Warner Bros. Inc. All Rights Reserved. Used by Permission. WARNER BROS. PUBLICATIONS U.S. INC., Miami, FL 33014.

Young, "Stella by Starlight" (p. 484): Words by Ned Washington. Music by Victor Young. Copyright © 1946 (Renewed 1973, 1974) by Famous Music Corporation. International Copyright Secured. All Rights Reserved.

665

I N D E X

In this index, a **boldface** number indicates the primary discussion or definition of the entry word. The compositions listed here are mentioned in the text without a music example. Please see the Index of Music Examples for compositions accompanied by examples.

A

absolute meaning, 461
accented incomplete neighbors, **83–84**
accented neighbors, **81.** *See also under* neighboring tones
accented passing tones, **81.** *See also under* passing tones
accidentals, **10**
acoustics, 621–26
added 9ths, **486–87,** 649
added 6ths, **485–87,** 618, 649
Aeolian mode, 31, 628–29
"Alberti bass," 75
alla breve, 22
allemande, 271
altered dominant seventh chords, **492–95,** 546, 632
altered harmony. *See* chromatic harmony
altered mediant triad, 402–403, 406–407
altered tonic, 612
ambiguity, **475,** 546, 553, 590
"America," 18, 169
"America the Beautiful," 19

"American" sixth chord, 434
amplitude, 623
analytical symbols
    usage guidelines, 40, 106, 108, 128, 133, 160, 378–79, 489, 501
answer, **455**
antecedent phrase, **142**
anticipation, **78–79,** 86, 188
applied dominants, **358–59.** *See also* secondary dominants
appoggiatura, **84,** 186, 188
Arban, Joseph
    "The Carnival of Venice," 279
arpeggiation, **100,** 104–106, 109, 136, 480, 587
    bass, 132, 139, 160–61, 220–21
atonality, **605–606,** 618
attack, 625
augmentation, **151,** 455, **456**
augmented eleventh chord, 483
augmented ninth chord, 480, 609, 619
augmented prime, 352–53, 355

C

**Library and Learning
Resources Center
Bergen Community College**
400 Paramus Road
Paramus, N.J. 07652-1595

Return Postage Guaranteed